Black France / France Noire

Black France / France Noire

The History and Politics of Blackness

TRICA DANIELLE KEATON,

T. DENEAN SHARPLEY-WHITING,

AND TYLER STOVALL,

EDITORS

Duke University Press

DURHAM & LONDON

2012

© 2012 Duke University Press
All rights reserved.
Printed in the United States of America
on acid-free paper ∞
Designed by C. H. Westmoreland
Typeset in Arno Pro by Keystone Typesetting, Inc.
Library of Congress Cataloging-in-Publication Data
appear on the last printed page of this book.

For Dorothy J. Holman,
with all love and appreciation

In memoriam:
Aimé Césaire, Michel Fabre, Ousmane Sembène,
Édouard Glissant

Contents

Foreword

Black . . . A Color? A Kaleidoscope!

CHRISTIANE TAUBIRA, MEMBER OF THE FRENCH NATIONAL
ASSEMBLY, DEPUTY FROM GUIANA

What must we remind the world?

That we are its majority.

That we resemble those who populate every continent.

That with a joyous deceit, we know how to take on the guise—even to the extent of averting our eyes—of those who could be born anywhere in the world. This extraordinary gift terrorized the inventors of the infamous one-drop rule.

However, it was and still is nothing more than a demonstration that we, Black women, are alchemists, forever possessing the secret of the unexpected, capable of transforming the sordid sap of rape into beauty and grace. Purifying improbable love. Ennobling the fleeting or subterranean passions resisted by the plantation slaveowner. Offering thus to the world a diversity that men could never have imagined. And, in so doing, fleeing the madness of this world of indescribable violence.

What is left to say to the world?

That we are not dupes. Neither are we naive. Nor are we stupefied by the absurdities of a religious indoctrination embroidered with docility, submission, resignation; absolving servitude; forgiving of subordination; promising heaven as recompense. That we know what was the vicious circle of the collusion of the sword, the Church, the scale, and the scourge, at the service of the most common and widespread of cupidities.

That if we have resorted to rancor, resentment, revenge, retribution, it is neither through candor nor holiness, neither with joy, nor without rage. We only do so in order not to burden ourselves with despair nor bitterness, not to transport nor transmit them to our loved ones, not to evade our present nor miss out on our future.

And, nevertheless, not to forget. With the exception of what we choose to remove, to retrench in the dormant space of our memories, for our own good.

What do we want to shout to the world?

That its order is disorder. That it will remain so as long as a tiny financial elite is able to speculate on the common good of all life on this Earth; as long as the great mass of the disinherited has the power to envy or condemn this ill-gotten opulence; as long as human relations go from domination to domination; that even the most contemptible, the most despised, the most excluded man who can dominate a woman yields a paradoxical effect such that by crushing someone perceived weaker than he—the woman whom he has oppressed—he will be accepted into the society of men.

Disorder will remain as long as the world pretends to delude itself by an act of "race," inventing an illusory purity and sinking into a barren, rampant, sermonizing nostalgia, obscuring its endogamous violence, laying a cumbersome foot and a heavy hand on the world. This disorder manifests for us, the wretched of the earth who represent many colors including white, its material violence. Worse still, its symbolic violence.

Precisely. All my brothers are not Black and all Blacks are not my brothers. Our common misery has never prevented an uneven commitment to common causes, inglorious self-interest, lazy accommodations, shameless capitulations. Indeed, already during those times of denied humanity, we had divided our hearts between those who were necessary to protect and save, and those to be distrusted. The culture of fugitive slaves is a culture of silence, secrecy, mistrust. The underground railway imposed silence or defeat, suppressing those too talkative as would be excised a mutilated or gangrenous organ to protect the body. Inflexible ideals were necessary to survive and act at such a price! It appears that there are no more ideologies, that the torrent that swept all before it also drowned ideals.

How to set the world straight?

To see clearly is not the end of ideals. Without a doubt, ideologies, as they were conceived of in the nineteenth century, have collapsed completely, shipwrecked by the excesses of those who, taking themselves for God, wanted to create man's collective happiness by refusing the individual man's right to tinker with his own vision of happiness, the privilege of being imperfect. But the doctrines remain, even devastated, even dilapidated. If ideologies have perished body and soul, this sad fate impedes neither the cynical desecration of their graves nor the theft of their doctrines. When the powerful financiers announce their wish to moralize their system that has gone mad, when ethical funds invade the trading floor and take over portfolios, when the proponents of the "clash of civilizations" defeat their laws to accommodate the funding of Islamic *sukuks* (bonds), when the fiercest defenders of the free market invoke great minds to justify the regulation of extravagant bonuses, the accommodation of abuses and the excesses of top-up pensions and golden parachutes, when fail-safe false prophets hold up the revolutionary and progressive pantheon to disguise the brutality of their acts—hostile to the most vulnerable—the ruse is everywhere, and even if it is enormous, it still abuses. Simply put, everything must change so that nothing changes. So preached *Il Gattopardo de Lampedusa* (*The Leopard*).

As for ideals, we rightly continue to water them. And we sow utopias. For we must not surrender.

How to teach the world?

There is no "Black question." Neither in France nor elsewhere.

There is the issue of stratagems invented by the status quo to forge, if not its legitimacy, at least its supremacy.

There is the issue of representations that produce economic systems and their roots in the mental world of those who, through their conscious or accidental acceptance, become the guardians of social hierarchies, even if those hierarchies work to their own detriment.

There is the question of otherness. For the most deadly ignorance is the one that ignores the original diversity of the world.

There is a white issue with regard to difference.

There is the question of the creative capacities of humanity that weaken or destroy exclusions, domination, corruption, preconceptions. And there are the contradictions of the societies of the North, preying on the goods and the cultural knowledge of the South, who are passionate about the supposed "primitive" or "first" arts while taking life from them by uprooting them from their places, ridding them of their authors, and desecrating their magical virtues integral to the communities from which they originate.

"The whole world is creolizing," warns Édouard Glissant. All societies in the world are indeed plural, but, in particular, the contact, the mixing, the syncretism, the multiple affiliations produce unpredictability. And this world in the making, like previous worlds, escapes official diagrams and legal categories because life is effervescence, and if legislation is needed to make society whole, it is not in order to control everything in the lives of others but rather to provide a framework for the development of an elusive humanity.

Segalen, already in the nineteenth century: "Variety shrinks, such is the threat."

But what does the world reveal?

The French Republic is the largest manufacturer of communitarianism. It was built on a delightful and wonderful fiction: egalitarianism. It ostentatiously adorns itself in order to face with dignity challenges to its flagrant violations of this fiction when manufacturing communities of elites, believers, relegated people, Jewish representatives, Muslim spokesmen, Black delegates, correspondents from the *banlieue*. It acts coy when it is caught red-handed in reinforcing the transgression of airtight seraglios from which it draws these yes-men for public enterprises, banks, Theodule commissions, promoting apprentices toward the narrowing of identities, favoring intermediaries of all sorts of causes defined in haste. Still working with the management methods of colonial populations, this republic, which disregards gender, origin, creed, color, disability, sexual preferences, claims to treat all equally, blindly, stubbornly neutral, and impartial. So blind and so stubborn that it no longer sees biases and inhibitions.

But ah! Let's be specific. The Republic is not the culprit. Its first community, the Government, is. And in its continuity, the Executive branch, hermetically sealed from differences, disparities, and variations that are precisely defined one at a time, does not understand that it is faced by its citizens. Instead it sees believers, even among those convinced that heaven is uninhabited at times by "foreigners."

And it is within this egalitarianist republic, which, in order to keep its positive image, proclaims itself democratic, social, and secular, that

difference is organized not only by laws but by mediating mechanisms, practices, and discriminatory procedures.

How does one demand equality and not merely content oneself
with formal statements, contradicted by a merciless reality of persistent and often renewed inequalities? The trap, and that which
causes us grief, is that this ambiguity, instituted because it resists the
claim of equality on the grounds that it is egalitarian, allows funda-
mentalist Republicans to verbalize their selfish assumptions similar to
the generous ideals formulated by those who refuse to accept these
ambiguities. Worse, they express this by citing countries that have
officially implemented laws of segregation and discrimination. More
subtly, the egalitarianist republic does not make assumptions. But this
would be a very tragic irony if all these countries, whose apartheid is
more or less abjectly pronounced, should lead the way faster and more
decisively to equal rights, less formally stated but more realized in
voluntary public policies.

This would be the final defeat of the republican idea itself.

What do we desire from the world?

To improve it? This is the concern of clergy and charitable activists.
To change it? A stimulating chimera! To fight against injustices of all
kinds is a priority of the insomniac. To reduce social injustice remains
a startling urgency when, rather than having differential treatments to
correct inequalities of birth, nature, fortune, and luck, they dig them
into a deeper hole, all the while chirping at the peril of the poorest.

Do we allow selfishness and fear to rule the world?

We come from peoples who have vanquished fear, from the dark
depths of the ship's hold to the whips and the mastiffs. And we understand the illusions of individualism, for we had to be numerous, across
all ages, all colors, from all continents, joined together with the same
indomitable fighting spirit, in order to strangle slavery, to destroy the
colonial regime!

Indeed, as we seize the helm of public Power to ease our immediate
condition, we must invent the future in all its finery. And in so doing,
the most elegant and most fruitful of insanities for some consist in
entrusting this century to the minds and hands of these blossoming
youth—held by some to be barbarians, yet who are our most promis-

ing heirs—each accompanied by one lesson, a single lesson from Frantz Fanon: "There is my life, roped in by existence. There is my liberty, which brings me back to myself. No, I'm not allowed to be Black. . . . The destiny of mankind is to be set free."

Acknowledgments

Collections of this nature that are the result of conference proceedings result always and in all ways from the collective support and labor of a range of individuals. We begin by thanking everyone who made possible the "France Noire—Black France: The History, Poetics, and Politics of Blackness" conference that took place in Paris on June 6–7, 2008. In particular, we must thank and acknowledge our co-organizer of this event, Marcus Bruce, whose unfailing encouragements to persevere, particularly at those precise moments when spirits and resources were in very low supply, are beyond measure. Trica would like to additionally express her highest appreciation to Tyler Stovall for his inspiration and kindness throughout this journey, indeed adventure, and who epitomized the essence of being a scholar. Tracy and Tyler are both very grateful to Trica Keaton whose boundless energy and exacting standards of scholarship have made this book a wonderful reality. While interest in this conference was exceptionally high, insufficient funding constantly plagued our efforts, nearly to the brink of this event's demise. It is for this reason that we are especially indebted to Tracy Sharpley-Whiting, without whose financial support, generously offered at a critical time of need, this conference simply would not have happened. We were additionally elated by Tracy's acceptance of our invitation to be a co-editor of this volume when Marcus was unable to assume that role. We extend our thanks to Fred Constant for his marvelous tenacity and support in securing the esteemed Member of the French Parliament and Députée de la Guyane Christiane Taubira as our keynote speaker, who delivered what was simply a brilliant address. And, we would be remiss in failing to thank Dominic Thomas for his kindhearted cyber-sharing of his time and social capital in the early stages of this event. Allow us to acknowledge as well Danielle Haase-Dubosc, then executive director of Reid Hall and Columbia University's Institute for Scholars, and Marcus Bruce, who was a fellow of the institute at the time, for providing the intellectual space for this international gathering of distinguished and distinctive panelists. Their tremendous contributions and sheer stamina to endure the travails of "warrior conferencing," with our schedule, not only made the "France Noire" conference a success, but also drew exceptional voices to a burgeoning and important field of study. We express our appreciation to our esteemed panelists: Rémy Bazenguissa-Ganga, Allison Blakely, Jennifer Boittin, Elisabeth Elisabeth Mudimbe-Boyi, Marcus Bruce, Barbara-Chase Riboud, James Cohen, Fred Constant, Denis-Constant Martin, Mamadou Diouf, Brent Edwards, Geneviève Fabre, Eric Fassin, Arlette Frund, Michel Giraud, Veronique Helenon, Abiola Irele, Bennetta Jules-Rosette, Jake Lamar, Patrick Lozès, Alain Mabanckou, Daniel Maximin, Simon Njami, Jean-Paul Rocchi, Tracy Sharpley-Whiting, Hortense Spillers, Tyler Stovall, Christiane Taubira, Dominic Thomas, Fatimata Wane-Sagna, Gary Wilder, and Michelle Wright. We additionally express our gratitude to our sponsors: African American and Diaspora Studies, the Center for Ethics, the Robert Penn Warren Center for the Humanities, and the "Black Europe" Seminar at Vanderbilt University; the Office of the Senior Vice President for System Academic Administration and the Office of the Vice President and Vice Provost for Equity and Diversity at the University of Minnesota, Twin Cities; the Office of the Dean of Faculty, African American Studies, and American Cultural Studies at Bates College; Dr. Irma McClaurin and the Ford Foundation; and last but certainly not least Henry Louis Gates Jr. and the W. E. B. Du Bois Institute for African and African American Research at Harvard University. Permit us as well to thank our exceptional interpreter, Eve Boutilié, who channeled Madame Taubira before our very eyes! We also thank everyone who provided administrative, technical, and other forms of support, including Brunhilde Biebuyck, Naby Avcioglu, Mihaela Bacou, and Joelle Theubet at Reid Hall in addition to the doctoral candidates Maya Smith at the University of California, Berkeley, and Annette Quarcoopome at Vanderbilt University, as well as Tara Williams, who has been the wind beneath our wings in African American and diaspora studies at Vanderbilt University. We also greatly appreciate the patient and thoughtful readers and editors at Duke University Press, including Valerie Millholland, Gisela Fosado, Fred Kameny, and Nancy Hoagland.

Introduction

Black Matters, Blackness Made to Matter

Pour une fois, je me suis mis à travailler comme un nègre. Je ne sais pas si les nègres ont toujours tellement travaillé, mais enfin. (And for once, I started working like a *nègre*. I don't know if a *nègre* ever worked that hard.)—PERFUMER JEAN-PAUL GUERLAIN of the Maison Guerlain, October 15, 2010

Eh bien le nègre, il t'emmerde! (Well, you know what this *nègre* says, F . . . you!)—AIMÉ CÉSAIRE, 1961 / Audre Pulvar to Guerlain, October 18, 2010

In recent years, France has seen an extraordinary flourishing of interest in blackness, anti-blackness, and Black identity, coupled with trenchant debates about the significance of race as a socio-political question. Past and recent collectives continue to organize around these issues alongside matters of diversity, the memory of slavery, colonization, empire, and what it generally means to be French, Black, *indigènes* and a citizen within the French Republic.[1] The Conseil Représentatif des Associations Noires (CRAN),[2] the Comité pour la mémoire et l'histoire de l'esclavage,[3] and [the] Alliance Noire Citoyenne[4] are indicative of such groups that have formed around these questions amid a number of existing (and often disconnected) anti-discrimination and anti-racism associations in France. The CRAN—a prominent "Black" lobby that emerged in response to the revolts in 2005 in the nation's poorest and racialized suburbs—is particularly interesting both for attempting to document the specificity of anti-blackness statistically, in the first survey of that nature in France (where ethnoracial statistics are banned under French law), and for strategically and intentionally deploying the taboo-ridden nomenclature "Noir" to self-represent, in direct defiance of social prohibition specific to the term. These coalitions are positioned, then, against and within the prevailing discourse of colorblind indivisibility, designating nonetheless an unmarked normative whiteness intrinsic to a powerful republican ideology expressed in the narratives, symbols, and representations of French national identity.

And yet, the prevailing difficulty and anxieties about speaking of race and blackness outside highly restricted spaces (such as certain elite French academies that are not themselves immune) illustrate just how deeply inured the taboos around these formations are. Even as new waves of scholarship and anti-racism associations focused specifically on "les Noirs" in France continue to emerge,[5] the co-existence of the in/visibility of blackness as a conspicuous body antithetical to a universal norm *and* as something simply unreadable as universal in dynamics of race and racism is far from a full excavation specific to "Afro/Black Europeans" in France and Europe.[6] In localized politics of blackness, Paris in particular has long been a critical site of Black internationalism, well illustrated by Négritude, the Harlem-in-Paris Renaissance, the invention of "Negrophilia,"[7] and persistent "negrophobias" that permeate France.[8]

In reconceptualizing the socio-historical discourses, narratives, and formations underpinning the commonsense-making in France specific to its distinctively configured Black populations (self-declared and perceived), the engaging and discerning chapters in this book lay bare a rather potent conundrum residing at the heart of French society. On the one hand, there is an evident constitutional and legal discourse of colorblindness in various spheres of French life whereby race has been rejected as a meaningful category, having been discredited as biology and rightly so. Thus, there are, in effect, no French "racial minorities," only French people; nor is there an officially recognized identity discourse as there is, for instance, in the United States or the United Kingdom, where one finds terms such as "Black Americans," African Americans," and "Black British" to express such differentiation. On the other hand, the lived experience of race—more saliently, anti-blackness—belies the colorblind principle enshrined in the universalist-humanist thought upon which the Republic was forged.

In seeking to make sense of this conundrum, this book contends that blackness does indeed exist as a social, cultural, and political formation in France, but with a distinctively French cast. In particular, the existence of distinct and very different communities of African and Afro-Caribbean descent means that to be "Black" politically and self-reflexively or "black" in ascriptive racialized discourse in France does not imply the same kind of cultural and historical homogeneity that has traditionally characterized Black life in the United States. Rather, Black identities exist in dialogue with each other and with the universalist principles of the French Republic. As several of the authors in this book argue, blackness in France is primarily a response to and rejection of anti-black racism. To be Black is, above all, to be targeted by such racism and to develop strategies to resist it.

In keeping with this central argument, nowhere is this more evident than with regard to self-declared "French Blacks" who have reached a critical and visible mass in metropolitan France and who trouble neat notions of belonging in this site. Indeed, the very emergence of the term "visible minorities" and the confrontational use of the nomenclature "Noir" instead of the once pervasive English word "Black" by individuals and groups politically mobilizing in France represent a critical shift in French political culture on the terrains of race, identity, and other categories of recognition in the public space.[9] A very real stake in these debates includes the opening up of the Republican library of political and social categorization toward their ultimate revision and remaking. Further complicating matters is the impact of a Black American presence for over two centuries on the French socio-cultural landscape, that is, a small yet no less consequential community whose positive reception in France—real, perceived, and utilitarian—has amplified intergroup tensions and unmasked presumptions of solidarity already questioned within Black populations and communities. Racism in the United States would not only engender the chain expatriation and ultimately migration of Blacks from the United States to France, it would also provide a racially symbolic community seemingly tailor-made to buttress France's colorblind and race-free ideals, even at the height of French colonialism. Both the African American community in Paris, and the considerable influence of African American politics and culture more generally, have helped to shape and cross-pollinated with discussions about race and blackness in French society.

These and a variety of timely and pertinent questions are thoroughly examined in this book. The chapters in this book derive from the "France Noire—Black France: History, Politics, and Poetics" conference, held at Columbia University's Reid Hall in Paris on June 6–7, 2008. In many ways, this event was indebted to and followed in the tradition of the diaspora dialogues and debates that preceded it, ranging from the first Pan-African Congress in 1919 at Versailles, organized by W. E. B. Du Bois and Blaise Diagne (the first Black African elected to the French National Assembly), to the Clamart Salon organized by Jane and Paulette Nardal in the 1930s, to the Festival Mondial des Arts Nègres organized by Présence Africaine and Léopold Sédar Senghor in 1956, to the International Congress of Black Writers and Artists in 1956 spearheaded by Alioune Diop and the commemoration of this milestone in Black empowerment fifty years later, led by Présence Africaine in conjunction with the W. E. B. Du Bois Institute for African and African American Research in 2006.

Similarly, the Reid Hall gathering, comprising distinguished and luminary panelists representative of the African diaspora in its purest sense, sought not only to engage what Aimé Césaire would describe as a radical Black humanism and counter-narrative to Western interpretations of life, but also, and more directly, to interrogate preexisting, unfinished questions of race, blackness, representations, intergroup relations, and identity politics that abide in France. The depth and breadth of these ideas were captured by the eminent member of the French National Assembly and deputy from Guiana Christiane Taubira,[10] who proposed and defended before the National Assembly the legislation that recognizes slavery and the slave trade as crimes against humanity, legislation synonymous with her name. Introduced in 1998 amid considerable governmental and public opposition, the Taubira Law was not adopted until 2001, and it was not until 2006 that the article specifying the observance of a national day of commemoration was applied. As one of the most powerful and influential Black political figures in metropolitan France, Taubira, in her keynote address, set a decisive tone for the stimulating series of discussions that took place, and this speech now serves as a brilliant, penetrating foreword to this book.[11]

As African American editors of this book, we approach the topic of race in France, and anywhere outside the United States, cautiously, well aware that the mere mention of the word, one so freighted with a history of violence in Europe, readily invites the charge not only of imposing a U.S. construct of the United States on French social realities, but also of supposedly promulgating or promoting communitarian ideas through an assertion of "blackness" in a French Republic, where, again, race does not officially reside, even as racism and discrimination are long-term residents.[12] While we understand the reasons for such suspicions, we reject this charge, arguing that questions of race and blackness abound in French life and are not simply imported from the United States. Rather, they are very much rooted in European and French histories. The remarks casually advanced by the prominent perfumer Jean-Paul Guerlain of the Maison Guerlain and televised in October 2010 (quoted in the epigraph) are a stark reminder of the limits of race- and colorblindness in contemporary France. The same can be said of the French-Martinican journalist Audrey Pulvar's channeling of Aimé Césaire's riposte—Pulvar who in 2004 was the first recognized Black television news anchor in metropolitan France.

It should not be overlooked that Céaire's re-signifying of the epithet "nègre" (the "French N Word") both emerges from and reflects a history of race-making in France, inseparable from slavery and colonialism.[13] Certainly, this point has been evinced by Aimé Césaire and a range of Black French intellectuals and scholar-activists in France (including those in this book) across generations, such as Suzanne Césaire, Léon Gontran Damas, Rokhaya Diallo, Édouard Glissant, Frantz Fanon, Dieudonné Gnammankou, Léopold Senghor, Maryse Condé, Euzhan Palcy, Alexis Peskine, Françoise Vergès, François Durpaire, Romuald Fonkoua, Pap Ndiaye, Jean-Paul Rocchi, Maboula Soumahoro, Kadya Tall, Lilian Thuram, Mahamet Timera, and Louis-Georges Tin, among others, in their sundry writings, films, and activism related to Négritude, Creolité, Black subjectivities, and antiracism in France. The "Pulvarization" of Guerlain, as Audrey Pulvar's rejoinder has been characterized, takes on a different hue at this moment in French society when anti-other sentiments are state-driven to divert attention from real social problems that the Republic has created and has failed to address. This would include President Nicolas Sarkozy's advocacy of legislation designed to strip of their citizenship naturalized French nationals (namely, disaffected, socially aggressed outer-city youth, indiscriminately categorized as aggressors of the police) and of the deportation of the Roma from France, a political posturing that is frighteningly evocative of Vichy's persecution and deportation of Jews.

While we ultimately reject the colorblind model and argue for the importance of recognizing the social reality of race, and in particular anti-blackness, in French life, we also acknowledge the importance of analyzing how and why these social formations—race and anti-blackness as well as the tensions and uneasiness evoked by these terms —have been constituted, deployed, evaded, and renamed in France to designate human existence and grotesquely define life chances. The ideas of race and blackness in France can differ significantly from those in the United States and elsewhere, and yet, what these thought-provoking chapters effectively demonstrate is that these entities constitute an integral part of France's national *patrimoine*, even when misrecognized or concealed.

This is not just an issue in France. A concept of race has appeared from the shadows of culture and ethnicity in many European countries where "culture" has long served as a proxy. Moreover, for well over the past decade, there has been a great deal of discussion among European Union members about the spread of racism in Europe, and increasingly anti-black racism, as eyes in France turn toward and away from the United States for both models and counter models to address these growing concerns. This book offers a rich opportunity for comparative analysis of these questions, while providing a framework for theorizing and retheorizing race, anti-blackness, and belonging in France and Europe in relation to those who trace their actual and symbolic origins to the continent of Africa, and expressly those who self-identify and are identified as "Noir" in French society.

There are many aspects of racialization and blackness common to the United States that appear across France: for instance, the role of race in the political domain (e.g., immigration and struggles for representation); racial profiling, law enforcement, and violence and hostility to immigrants (and those perceived as such); the concentration of Blacks in lower sectors of employment, in the worst housing and schools, and disproportionately in prisons; underrepresentation in universities; and representations in the media linked with entertainment, sports, or crime. This provides fertile grounds for systemic comparisons.

And yet, France and other European nations reveal fundamental differences compared to the United States on issues of race and blackness historically and at present. For example, plantation slavery was not focused on home territories, as was the case in the United States. Many European countries have no long-standing Black population descended from enslaved Africans in Europe. The absence of both legalized racial apartheid and a civil rights movement and the relatively smaller urban concentrations of Blacks compared to the United States are all important differences, even as there is now a critical mass of Black citizens in metropolitan France who have been there for generations. Such differences have distinctly and respectively shaped conceptions of blackness and being, as well as national identities in these sites.

As a range of theorists persuasively argue and lived reality keenly illustrates, a meaningful definition of "France" must go well beyond the boundaries of the Hexagon to trouble neat notions of geography and belonging. The controversial national identity debate launched by President Nicolas Sarkozy at the onset of regional elections in 2010, a debate examined in this book, failed to address what constitutes French identity at this moment and in the future.[14] More to the point, what the debate on national identity and the well-crafted and illuminating chapters in this book document in myriad ways is that issues of race, discrimination, racism, and religious intolerance continue to occupy center stage in French society.

Explicitly naming and interrogating the taboo and contested issue of race and its idiom, this book represents an important and distinct contribution to the critical scholarship on these issues in relation to the African diaspora and France. With its complex and dynamic portraits of Black experiences, it sits in the eye of this storm, and ultimately offers new perspectives at this critical juncture when France is confronted by an unanticipated and, for some, an unwanted plural society that must indeed ask itself: "What does it means to be French *now*?"

This book is divided into three parts that connect and juxtapose critical themes undertaken by our contributors and illustrates the fundamental and historical role of race in both subtle and explicit dimensions of Black life in French society. It takes an interdisciplinary and multidisciplinary approach to the subject of Black France, offering analyses of key issues from different perspectives and disciplines. Black French studies is a relatively new field of inquiry, one that owes much, like many new bodies of scholarship, to the interaction of contrasting disciplinary approaches. As with African diaspora studies in the United States, Britain, and other parts of the world, it features analyses from historians, literary scholars, and social scientists. Consequently, we have felt it crucial to feature these different approaches, and moreover to place them in dialogue with each other. Each part therefore features a central theme analyzed by scholars from different disciplines.

Part 1, "Theorizing and Narrating Blackness and Belonging," examines how blackness and race are imagined and bound up with empire and the prospects of a formation of belonging that has become naturalized in hegemonic power relations. It contrasts wide-ranging theoretical perspectives on the relationship between blackness and Frenchness with more localized and personal considerations of what it means to be Black in France. Elisabeth Mudimbe-Boyi goes straight to the heart of the issue in her interrogation of the significance of the term "black" in relation to an idiom of blackness, both political and self-referential. Mamadou Diouf explores how the wounds left by colonialism continue to shape debates on cultural pluralism in postcolonial France. Gary Wilder also considers France's relationship, past and present, with Black Africa, critiquing President Nicolas Sarkozy's infamous address at the Université Cheikh Anta Diop in Dakar, Senegal, relative to Léopold Sédar Senghor's notion of "Eurafrique" and its broader implications. Finally, the personal narratives of the award-winning writers Alain Mabanckou and Jake Lamar illustrate both the challenges and rewards of Black life and Black identity in contemporary France.

Part 2, "The Politics of Blackness—Politicizing Blackness," investigates how anti-blackness in French society, born of slavery, colonization, and immigration, politically galvanizes groups whose subjectivity (or rejection thereof) as "Blacks" defines neither a community nor a group perspective, but rather the limits of solidarity. In representing various ways of being and not being "Black" that operate, nonetheless, within the Republican model, these chapters also illustrate the real prospects for political mobilization in France. To this end, Patrick Lozès examines the presence, radicalization, and incipient populism of the "Blacks of France" through the prism of the organization of which he was until recently the president, the CRAN. In his essay Dominic Thomas explores the hot-button issue of immigration and national identity relative to ethno-racial diversity and discrimination at present in France that would give emergence to the CRAN and other anti-racism associations, such as les Indigènes de la Republique. Using the national identity debate of 2009 as a lens to understand divergent perspectives of blackness among French Blacks, Fred Constant argues they are divided on their views of race and French national identity, and offers an insightful critique of the assumption of a monolithic "Black perspective" in France. Rémy Bazenguissa-Ganga's critique of the very meaning of "Black" for Africans and African-descended people in contemporary France takes as its point of departure the 1990s, when, as he argues, many Africans and Afro-Caribbeans increasingly referred to themselves as "Noir" in popular discourse. Lastly, Michel Giraud considers the "question of blackness" in relation to Afro-Caribbean identity in France and debates about the memory of slavery.

Part 3, "Black Paris—Black France," considers the centrality of Paris to the Black American migration experience and France symbolically to this narrative in addition to France as a global nexus of Black culture. Ever since the First World War, the French capital has been the site of Black diaspora interactions in music, literature, and politics, a role it continues to play in the contemporary era. These essays examine how that role also became important for the creation of a sense of blackness that is also French. Marcus Bruce's chapter is the perfect opening for this part, since it focuses on the American Negro Exhibit at the Paris Exposition of 1900. Jennifer Boittin's chapter takes us to the interwar years to compare Black anti-imperialist activism and life in a tale of two French cities: Paris and Marseilles. Bennetta Jules-Rosette examines the socio-historical significance of Black Americans in Paris through a reconsideration of the life of Josephine Baker, emphasizing the history of the Rainbow Tribe and her utopian dream of universal solidarity. Arlette Frund concludes this part with a chapter that explores the meaning of Black France by examining a series of commemorative projects in the French capital aimed at negotiating and constructing acceptable Black identities.

Allison Blakely's chapter serves as a fitting coda to this volume. Blakely compares the French debates over black identity to similar considerations in other European countries, illustrating the transnational significance of the study of Black France.

Conclusion: The Silences That Blind Us

Inevitably, with such a rich topic, one can easily think of other themes worthy of exploration that emerge and are submerged in a multiperspective examination of the Black presence in France, topics that point to both the need for and significance of "Afro/Black French Studies" *in France* and trained scholars in this field. Gender, everyday racism, feminist thought, film studies, intersectionality, and legal studies specific to Blacks are among other areas ripe for further exploration, since they pertain to historical and present Black experiences in France.[15] Issues of performativity, especially with regard to music and to athletics, have played a major role in the "French Black" experience. From jazz to hip hop and Afro-pop, music has not only frequently defined blackness in France, but also provided spaces for Blacks in French society. Sport has also emerged as a key locus of blackness and anti-blackness, especially with regard to football at both the local and national levels. In fact, as reported by the European Commission against Racism and Intolerance (ECRI), the Council of Europe's independent human rights monitoring body, "anti-black racism persists in member States, often taking extreme forms, such as organized attacks against individuals and communities. Colour-related insults are widespread during sports activities."[16] Certainly the football quota scandal in 2011 reinforces this point while illustrating how racism and anti-black racism coalesce, as exemplified by the French Football Federation's (FFF) attempt to limit the number of Black and Arab players on the national team.

Questions of sexuality are another field of inquiry well worth developing. The rise of Black queer theory in Britain and the United States also sets a rich agenda for studies of Black France that challenge us to consider how ideas of normative sexuality have interacted with the marginalization of racialized Others in French society and culture. In addition, the issue of uncompensated and exploitative labor, so repugnantly expressed in Paul Guerlain's remarks, merit further study. Both slavery and immigration, two key reference points of the "Black condition" in France, are above all systems for extracting labor power. Many of the most powerful images of Blacks in France, from the African immigrants sweeping the streets of Paris with twig brooms to the Black American musicians performing in nightclubs, are about people not simply working for a living, but most certainly working for a life.[17]

All of these issues, and more, will hopefully receive greater scholarly analysis in years to come, and future studies will no doubt bring new insights and scholarship on these subjects specific not only to France but also Europe writ large. We hope that this book will help further ongoing analyses and the debates that arise from them. As they said in May 1968, "Ce n'est qu'un début!"

Notes

1. The politics of national identity in France have given rise to contemporary voices of African origin (North and sub-Saharan) who are precisely calling into question what constitutes indigenity in France amid great consternation. See "L'Appel des indigènes de la république: nous sommes les indigènes de la république!" web site of *Les indigènes de la république*, January 20, 2005.

2. Well in advance of the CRAN, a number of groups engaged in what could be characterized as "Black activism" and incipient Black populism in France. As the sociologist Abdoulaye Gueye argues, "The emergence of the CRAN is neither an isolated nor a unique event in France; it is part of a continuity in a politically-informed dynamic amongst people of African descent. The CRAN is probably the most visible, the most influential, and the most generalist organization of African-descended people. . . . Prior to the emergence of the CRAN, associations such as the Collectif Égalité, founded in 1998; Africagora, created in 1999; Cercle d'Action pour la Promotion de la Diversité, founded in 2004; and the Diaspora Africaine, formed in 1985, were all committed to shaping a Black identity in France and to defending the interests and rights of people of African descent regardless of their territorial extraction, place of birth, social class, or administrative status." A. Gueye, "Breaking the Silence: the Emergence of a Black Collective Voice in France," *Du Bois Review: Social Science Research on Race* 7, no. 1 (2010): 82.

3. See the compelling work on slavery and the recentering of the enslaved at the heart of modernity by the political scientist Françoise Vergès, who is also the president of the Comité pour la Mémoire et l'Histoire de l'Esclavage: Vergès, *L'homme prédateur* (Paris: Albin Michel, 2011).

4. Alliance Noire Citoyenne emerged about five years ago and became more visible through its organized boycott of the Guerlain boutique on the Champs-Élysées and the upscale department store Galeries Lafayette. Internal to the group is a collective known as La Brigade Anti-négrophobie, which was violently expelled from the commemoration of the abolition of slavery event on May 10, 2011. The members' wearing of their group's t-shirt to the ceremony in the Luxembourg Gardens triggered a swift police reaction that was caught on film and went viral in France and beyond.

5. The intense interest in the role of blackness in French life has also produced a flood tide of writing that explores this question from a variety of

perspectives that are in many ways a prolongation of colonial and postcolonial work specific to the African diaspora in France. Especially since 2005, a number of works have emerged on these topics that include Moïse Udino, *Corps noirs, têtes républicaines: le paradoxe antillais* (Paris: Présence Africaine, 2011), François Durpaire, *France blanche, colère noire* (Paris: Odile Jacob, 2006); Rama Yade-Zimet, *Noirs de France* (Paris: Calmann-Lévy, 2007); Patrick Lozès, *Nous les noirs de France* (Paris: Danger Public, 2007); Jean-Louis Sagot-Duvauroux, *On ne naît pas noir, on le devient* (Paris: Albin Michel, 2004); Jean-Baptiste Onana, *Sois nègre et tais-toi!* (Nantes: Éditions du Temps, 2007); and Pap Ndiaye, *La condition noire: essai sur une minorité française* (Paris: Calmann Lévy, 2008), a major study in France that treats the history and conceptualization of the nation's Blacks. For other historical studies, see P. H. Boulle, *Race et esclavage dans la France de l'Ancien Régime* (Paris: Perrin, 2007); M. Cottias, *La question noire: Histoire d'une construction coloniale* (Paris: Bayard, 2007); Y. Chotard, *Les ports et la traite négrière: France* (Nantes: Anneaux de la mémoire, 2007); J. A. Boittin, *Colonial Metropolis: The Urban Grounds of Anti-imperialism and Feminism in Interwar Paris* (Lincoln: University of Nebraska Press, 2010); V. Hélénon, *French Caribbeans in Africa: Diasporic Connections and Colonial Administration, 1880–1939* (New York: Palgrave Macmillan, 2011); P. Blanchard, É. Deroo, and S. Chalaye, *La France Noire: trois siècles de présences des Afriques, des Caraïbes, de l'océan indien et d'Océanie* (Paris: La Découverte, 2011). Also recommended are existing and forthcoming writings by Claude Ribbe and the award-winning historian Dieudonné Gnammankou on Alexandre Dumas, which explore and document the African ancestry and blackness of this celebrated French writer. Additionally see Gnammankou's work on the Russian poet Alexander Puskin's great-grandfather, Abraham Hannibal, in *Abraham Hanibal, l'aïeul noir de Pouchkine* (Paris: Présence Africaine, 1996). See also "La pensée noire: les textes fondamentaux," in a special issue of *Le Point*, April–May 2009.

6. For an illuminating analysis of the notion of "in/visible universal bodies," see N. Puwar, *Space Invaders: Race, Gender and Bodies Out of Place* (New York: Berg, 2004).

7. "Negrophilia" here refers to the formation most noted during the 1920s and 1930s to identify a "white" bourgeois escapist and primitivist gaze, indeed obsession, with all things "Negro," in particular art, music, and sports. See, e.g., J. Clifford, "Negrophilia," in *A New History of French Literature* (Cambridge: Harvard University Press, 1989), 901–8; and P. Archer-Straw, *Negrophilia: Avant-Garde Paris and Black Culture in the 1920s* (New York: Thames and Hudson, 2000).

8. See, e.g., B. Diop, O. Tobner, and F. Verschave, *Négrophobie* (Paris: Arènes, 2005).

9. The anti-racism association Les Indivisibles effectively deploys humor to critique this very point concerning the anxieties around the use of the word "noir" in public discourse in France, which is well illustrated in their short film *N'ayez pas peur du noir . . .*, recognized at the "France Noire / Black France" film festival in 2010 in Paris, organized by Arlette Frund, Trica Danielle Keaton, Tracy Sharpley-Whiting, and Maboula Soumahoro. See the web site of Les Indivisibles for this film.

10. In this context, it bears noting additionally that the politician, writer, and scholar Christiane Taubira is one of very few women and faces of color in the French Parliament and that in 2002 she was a noteworthy presidential candidate in France.

11. For more on Christiane Taubira's position on the law that bears her name and her political positions, see Taubira, *Égalité pour les exclus* (Paris: Temps Présent, 2009), among her other publications.

12. "Communitarian" in France is apprehended as a divisive and rejected multiculturalism based on race that is equated primarily with the United States and the United Kingdom, and is held to be indicative of identity politics and solidarity formations predicated on intrinsic racial essentialisms.

13. In addition to the magnum opus of the promethean poet, intellectual, and politician Aimé Césaire, see his revealing views on this and other issues pertaining to slavery, colonization, and discrimination in one of his last interviews: F. Vergès, *Aimé Césaire, nègre je suis, nègre je resterai: entretiens avec F. Vergès* (Paris: Albin Michel, 2005). See also the award-winning filmmaker and writer Euzhan Palcy's documentary *Aimé Césaire: A Voice for History*, released in 1994.

14. The national debate in 2010 on French identity was viewed skeptically and criticized heavily as yet another attempt by Nicholas Sarkozy to court ultra-conservative anti-immigrant votes, shore up bona fides in regions dominated by the National Front, and reinvigorate his controversial Ministry of Immigration, Integration, National Identity, and Cooperative Development. This gamble, in the end, did not benefit Sarkozy: the Left won twenty-one of the twenty-two regions.

15. In this regard, important comparative work with theorists who have already extensively written on these topics, such as Philomena Essed, Kimberlé Crenshaw, Patricia Hill-Collins, and Hortense Spillers, among others, would be intellectually fascinating and instructive.

16. European Commission against Racism and Intolerance, Annual Report, 2009, p. 9, on the web site of the Council of Europe.

17. Studies addressing these themes include J. Jackson, *Making Jazz French: Music and Modern Life in Interwar Paris* (Durham: Duke University Press, 2003); J. Winders, *Paris Africain: Rhythms of the African Diaspora* (New York: Palgrave Macmillan, 2006); J. Timothée, *Champions noirs, racisme blanc? La*

métropole et les sportifs noirs en contexte colonial, 1901–1944 (Grenoble: Presses Universitaires de Grenoble, 2006); L. Dubois, *Soccer Empire: The World Cup and the Future of France* (Berkeley: University of California Press, 2011); P. Benson, *Battling Siki: A Tale of Ring Fixes, Race, and Murder in the 1920s* (Fayetteville: University of Arkansas Press, 2006); H. J. Elam and K. Jackson, eds., *Black Cultural Traffic: Crossroads in Global Performance and Popular Culture* (Ann Arbor: University of Michigan Press, 2005); K. Mercer, *Welcome to the Jungle: New Positions in Black Cultural Studies* (New York: Routledge, 1994); M. Warner, ed., *Fear of a Queer Planet: Queer Politics and Social Theory* (Minneapolis: University of Minnesota Press, 1993); J.-P. Rocchi, "Littérature et métapsychanalyse de la race," *Tumultes* 31 (2008); M. Samuel, *Le prolétariat africain noir en France: témoignages* (Paris: Maspero, 1978); J. Adélaide-Merlande, *Les origines du mouvement ouvrier en Martinique, 1870–1900* (Paris: Karthala, 2000).

PART I

Theorizing and Narrating Blackness and Belonging

Black France: Myth or Reality?

Problems of Identity and Identification

ELISABETH MUDIMBE-BOYI

The session of the conference "Black France," in which I presented a short version of this text, was entitled "Black Ontology in Formation." For me, the two components in the title, "ontology" and "in formation," reflect the general concepts that constitute ontology: essence and existence. "Black ontology" thus can be read as an interrogation of the Black being-in-the-world: a question that concerns identity and identification, but one that is also relational whereby the Black subject evolves, asserting both belonging and difference, that is, being-for-self and being-for-others, located both here and elsewhere.

The foundation of a Black ontology is thus necessarily "in formation"; it is both dialectical and an always-unfinished process, thus a project, in a Sartrean sense. "Black ontology in formation," echoes Jean-Paul Sartre's philosophy of the subject, in which he inverts the order of succession by making existence precede essence: "l'existence précède l'essence." If such is the condition, the Black as a subject is neither predefined nor a given for all. On the contrary, he is constantly in flux, a dynamic subject, able to create and transform the self by one's own will or actions. Existence preceding essence, as Sartre advocates, allows the subject to face down stereotypes as well as entrapment in rigid representations, preconceptions, and reductive images created by the self or by others.[1] This commentary in the form of an introduction echoes "Black Orpheus," Sartre's well-known preface to Senghor's anthology of African and Malagasy literature.[2]

"Black France" too could be taken as a fixed semantic utterance, as a generic image of the Black, or as a clearly defined identity and an obvious identification with a distinct and homogeneous group constituted by Blacks in France. In the following pages, I would like to first parse the problematic character of the term "Black" as well as its limitations and complexity. I will then seek to show, quickly perhaps, that in spite of this trend, the affirmation of a Black identity has served as a common reference for identification with a specific community in France. Even if it is not the only factor, this identification has been productive; it has, throughout the twentieth century, allowed for, among Black intellectuals in France, a cultural awakening that has led to a political awareness, a common social consciousness, and a sentiment of common belonging across time and space. If, in spite of the problematic nature of the term "Black," one can nowadays speak of a "Black France," it is because this group represents an "imagined community" based more on other factors than on race or skin color.[3] Therefore, if existence precedes essence, and existence is a becoming, then a Black ontology—the Black both which he is and who he is—can only be conceived as a project. The reflection presented here in fact seeks to mine the signifiers "Black" and "Black France," as an identity and as a group with which one identifies in the name of that identity.

A glance at the history of language and the history of mentalities reveals changes in representations of the Black as well as semantic fluctuations of the word "black."[4] Over the course of centuries, meanings and images have been modified according to attitudes and ways of thinking, but also according to the political, economic, and religious interests of those in positions of power. When ancient writers in Greco-Roman antiquity such as Herodotus and Pliny depicted Blacks as strange creatures with strange morays, as Frank Snowden argues they did, the color black was generally perceived as a mark of difference or as an object of artistic attention, and not according to the racialism of later epochs.[5] In the Middle Ages the Greek antiquity's *aithiops* (man with burnt skin) is replaced by the Moor, found, for example, in medieval French epics such as *chansons de geste*.[6] The Renaissance and the Age of Discoveries bring the Black to Western Europe where he will serve as a domestic and an exotic object.[7] By the early modern period, the Black can be found in the works of the great masters of Western European painting such as Rembrandt, Velasquez, and Rubens.[8] In the Enlightenment, despite notions of progress and an open-mindedness imputed to the *philosophes*, the Age of Reason is yoked to slavery and the slave trade, which in turn influenced their attitudes. In addition, the discourse about Blacks during the Enlightenment is inscribed in an intertextual relationship that reproduces stereotypes about Blacks.[9]

The classification of humanity proposed by the racialist theories of the nineteenth century characterizes the "Black race" in these terms: "À propos de la race 'nègre': ses lèvres sont proéminentes, son front bas, ses dents en saillies, ses cheveux laineux, à demi-frisés, sa barbe rare, son nez large et épaté, son menton en retrait, ses yeux ronds, lui donnent un aspect spécial parmi tout le reste des races humaines" (With respect to the "Negro" race: his thick lips, low forehead, protruding teeth, partially woolly and frizzy hair, sparse beard, broad and flat nose, receding chin, and round eyes give him a peculiar look amongst all other human races).[10] Such definitions based solely on external features are reductive and globalizing. If one considers the entire so-called Black population of the world, these external characteristics are not necessarily found among all Blacks, nor are they visible among everyone classified as such. At the end of the nineteenth century and during the twentieth, the Black swings completely into savagery, excluded even from the category of the "noble savage" that nurtured the West's nostalgia for a Golden Age.[11] Literature, in turn, serves as a vehicle of representation informed by ethnocentric sensibilities drawn from prejudices and stereotyped images of the Black, which have been propagated and crystallized in the collective Western imaginary.[12]

This brief synopsis reveals the lexical uncertainty between the terms "Africans" and "Blacks," with the "black" becoming more directly linked to Africa, savagery, and slavery. "Black" becomes further confused with "African," followed at times by a lexical fusion that makes the two words interchangeable. The semantic and representational transformations of the word "black" cannot escape, after all, preconceived ideas and negative images associated with Black people, because they are all rooted in the ideology of their time and are part of the various discourses that have justified and legitimized slavery, colonial conquest, and the missionary enterprise.[13] Marked by negative connotations, the word "black" is oftentimes banished from the language and replaced by "African" for reasons of political correctness. My contention is that by abolishing the term "black" rather than restoring its neutral value through regular use, political correctness has not only contributed to its derogation but installed a *political incorrect-*

ness that defies the logic that all Black people are not African, and all Africans are not "black."

On the other hand, over time, colonization, slavery, and migratory phenomena have, alongside cultural hybridity, produced biological hybridity, which, whether one cares to admit it or not, renders relative the definition of "black" as a fixed racial category and destabilizes group identification. The skin color of all who have been racialized "black"—the *aithiops*, the Pharaohs of Egypt, the Moors, those of Africa or of the Americas—spreads across a chromatic spectrum, varying from the very black to the almost white. One might be reminded here that many African Americans and West Indians can trace their lineage back to a white or, to a lesser extent, Native American ancestor. There is also the phenomenon of "passing," which in the Americas typically refers to a Black person passing for white, if one's complexion is especially fair and one's features are not marked phenotypically as "black."[14] The "one-drop rule" in the United States in effect racially codifies anyone as "black" who has a hint of "black blood."[15] One could add to this racial litany the kinds of intraracial distinctions that have existed in Afro-American and Afro-Caribbean societies along color and class lines. Among Afro-Caribbeans, color and class often combine and evolve into the desire for what has been called *lactification*: light skin is considered ideal, and those possessing lighter skin are frequently situated on a higher socio-economic level.[16] All of this brings to mind the question, albeit pointless, of whether the President of the United States, Barack Obama, son of a Black African father and white American mother, is "really" Black: some find him "too Black," still others feel he is "not Black enough." The long arc of history reveals indeed that the contours of what or who is considered Black/ black is not fixed, is uncertain and susceptible to vicissitudes.[17] Therefore, in our contemporary moment, can one speak of a "Black France"?

"Black" can be a generic term that designates multiple and diverse subjects originating from various continents and parts of the globe with completely different trajectories and historical paths: Africa, the Americas, Asia, and now Europe.[18] Linguistically, it does not seem certain that in English "Black France," the title of a recent book, necessarily covers all that is signified in the words "France noire."[19] While "Black France" may be transparent in the same way that "Black America" is, "France noire" by contrast proves to be polysemic. The first meaning is devoid of any racial reference: it trivially refers to an underground France, parallel, clandestine, and invisible. In the second sense "France Noire" is amenable to politics and history, and embodies the French imperialist vision. It designates, in effect, Blacks outside France, but from a territory in France's possession and under French political dominance, as is the case with the African colonies and the French overseas departments and territories. Book titles such as AOF AEF *La France noire: ses peuples, son histoire, ses richesses* illustrate this significance, which compartmentalizes the Black as a colonized subject and a subaltern.[20] The third meaning of "France noire," a contemporary one, concerns the Blacks within Metropolitan France. It implicitly raises the questions of belonging and non-belonging while simultaneously acting as an intervention, affirming the Self as a being and as a subject.[21] It thus relates to the signification of "Black France," which is the topic of Dominic Thomas's book. In their semantic similarity, "Black France" and "France noire" go well beyond a simple physical Black presence in France. In the signified, they carry a subtext: a claim for the right to speak, the contestation of dominance, marginalization, and invisibility within French society where these exclusionary practices contradict republican ideals.

A France noire situates the Black in a double liminal position: French *but* Black, or Black *but* part of France. Speaking of the West Indies, the Guyanese writer Léon Damas, with his usual humor and irony, summarizes this liminality with a pun: "pas Français à part entière mais entièrement à part" (not fully French, but French fully apart). These multiple levels of meaning equally establish France noire as both a semantic and political subversion: the colonial partitioning of the voiceless and the assimilated is substituted by the desire to break the colonial mold and to escape marginalization by speaking out.

Who then is this France noire? They are the Blacks both from and in France: Black French, French Blacks, Blacks and French, Franco-Africans, the Franco-Afro-Americans. One could add Franco-Caribbean, a label that would be in principle tautological since Antillians are officially French. These terms, in their variation, sufficiently show the fluidity and the semantic indeterminacy of the word "black," as well as the open and non-exhaustive character of what constitutes a France noire. The appellation seems transparent, but in reality is diverse and complex: multinational, multicultural, transcontinental, and even multicolor.

Black Metropolitan France is not established as a homogenous block but instead represents an assemblage of micro societies. Today, it brings together individuals of multiple and distinct geographic origins. Born and raised in France or elsewhere, they are of mixed and non-mixed unions; they have come from Africa or the Americas, at different times and for various reasons: to fight for France, to study, to seek political freedom, or to find better economic opportunities. Their ideological orientations follow distinctive paths: involvement in the promotion of Black culture, union involvement, or participation in entertainment or sports.[22] Generally, the majority of these Blacks, despite their diversity, find themselves similarly positioned in this global orbit with respect to their origins, France, colonization, political domination, cultural assimilation, and even social marginalization and invisibility. They belong, however, to a diversified local milieu, other and different. The history of the Black Americas diverged from that of Africa with the slave trade, which in turn, inaugurated a new history, created new cultural forms, new identities, and new identifications, even as those Black and African origins are not necessarily disavowed but reclaimed.[23] This was the case in the first quarter of the twentieth century with the Indigenist Movement in Haiti and the Harlem Renaissance in the United States. Within these multiple cleavages, one could add that in the case of union militancy, the workers' solidarity is also a class solidarity and not just racial. In his novels, Ousmane Sembène shows, for example, how these different categories are related.[24] The relationship with the place of origin comes with ambiguity: despite their desire for identification with Africa, Black Americas' gaze on Africa is one of an outsider. The French Caribbean writer René Maran's novels, for example, offer a benevolent gaze from an outsider's position, not from within.[25] The Africa of the Harlem Renaissance is an appealing Africa, but one that is equally trapped in a vision from the outside that exoticizes her: as attractive and mysterious as she appears in various, though certainly not the vast majority of, Western European representations.[26] It is this mysterious Africa that Countee Cullen, a poet from the Harlem Renaissance, questions in his poem "Heritage":

What is Africa to me:
Copper sun or scarlet sea,
Jungle star or jungle track,

Strong bronzed men, or regal black
Women from whose loins I sprang
When the birds of Eden sang?
One three centuries removed
From the scenes his fathers loved,
Spicy grove, cinnamon tree,
What is Africa to me.[27]

Another example, taken from Claude McKay's *Banjo*, illustrates the distance that sometimes exists between Blacks of different origins, such as that expressed in the following dialogue between Ray, who is in search of and nostalgic for Africa, and a student from Martinique, who refuses to identify with the "Black race" or with Africa:

> Non, mais elle [l'impératrice Joséphine] était créole et, à la Martinique, nous sommes plutôt des Créoles que des Noirs. . . . Ils étaient dans un café de la Cannebière. Ce soir-là, Ray avait rendez-vous avec un autre étudiant, un Africain de la Côte d'Ivoire. Il demanda au Martiniquais de l'accompagner, voulant leur faire connaissance. L'autre refusa disant qu'il ne tenait pas à fréquenter les Sénégalais et que leur bar africain était d'ailleurs un bar des *bas-fonds*. Il crut devoir mettre Ray en garde contre les Sénégalais.
>
> "Ils ne sont pas comme nous," lui dit-il. "Les Blancs se conduiraient mieux avec les Noirs, si les Sénégalais n'étaient pas là."

> No, but she [the Empress Josephine] was Creole, and in Martinique we are rather more Creole than Negro. . . . They were in a café on the Cannebière. That evening Ray had a rendezvous at the African Bar with another student, an African from the Ivory Coast; he asked the Martiniquan to go with him to be introduced. He refused, saying that he did not want to mix with the Senegalese and that the African Bar was in the seedy part of town. He warned Ray about mixing with the Senegalese.
>
> "They are not like us," he said. "The whites would treat Blacks better in this town if it were not for the Senegalese."[28]

To these examples, one might add the Négritude movement, whose founding fathers were Black intellectuals from Africa (Léopold Sédar Senghor from Sénégal) and the Caribbean (Aimé Césaire from Martinique, Léon Gontran-Damas from French Guiana). Césaire and Damas reclaimed their identity as Black subjects and wanted to be reconnected with Africa as the place of origin, although it was unknown to them. Senghor (see his poem "Joal," for example), or Camara Laye with his *L'Enfant noir*, both also express nostalgia and entertain a romantic vision of Africa as the *royaume d'enfance* (childhood kingdom) that they had known and lived in. This form of auto-exotization that might have reproduced or reinforced the exotic vision of Africa by the West embodies a lost paradise for sure. Yet, it functions not as an Otherness inscribed in the Western discourse. In the context of the time, it rather constituted a will to assert difference and cultural identity and, at the same time, the expression of a desire to rehabilitate Africa in regard to the negative stereotypes embedded in the discourse of the West.

While the Caribbean proponents of Négritude, Césaire and Damas, fully identified with the Black continent, subsequent movements such as Antillanité, Créolité, and Relation, as put forward by Edouard Glissant in his book *Poétique de la Relation*, renounce a Black identity or *identité racine unique* (one root identity) and embrace an *identité rhizomatique* (rhizomatic identity) that embodies the multiplicity and the ethnic diversity of the Caribbean people's origins and identities. A younger generation of Caribbean intellectuals Jean Bernabé, Patrick Chamoiseau, and Rafaël Confiant open their manifesto *Éloge de la créolité* with these striking and forceful words: "Ni Européens, ni Africains, ni Asiatiques, nous nous proclamons Créoles" (Neither Europeans, nor Africans, nor Asians, we proclaim ourselves Creoles).

My questions on the subject of Black identity and identification with a Black community arise from a genealogical perspective that reveals simplistic and homogenizing images, attitudes, and behaviors as well as semantic uncertainties and changes in which the political (the *polis* "relative to the life of an organized society") and the ideological (system of representations which serve the economic or political interests of a particular social group) intervene. Between the two components, France and noire, there is a relationship of similitude and difference, inclusion and mutual exclusion, and thus, at the same time, of belonging and non-belonging.

The expression "France noire" itself is inscribed in an ambiguity that fractures the republican ideals of *liberté, égalité, fraternité* and establishes a discrepancy between these ideals and everyday reality. Slavery and colonization have created the conditions for the possibility of a France noire, which has been formed both in a context of political domination and through contact between cultures from Africa, Europe, and the Americas. On the other hand, the affirmations of the contemporary discourse concerning the category of "race" would seem to deny the reality of lived experiences in which "race" has generated negative representations, exclusion, discrimination, and non-belonging. In a political world where the Black finds him- or herself in a subaltern position, and in the context of a colonizing France, subalterneity is a consequence of the political and the cultural. How then can one be located in the political and the cultural without a reference to that other component, which is racial or pertaining to skin color?[29]

Several recent works view Blacks in France from different perspectives.[30] These publications do not only remedy a long occultation of the Black's presence in France, they highlight, as well, their multiple faces and diverse voices. They confront, each in their own way, the relationship between the political and the cultural, the social and the racial, re-actualizing some elements of the debate that was formerly present in the first mediums of Black expression in France, such as the journals *Légitime Défense*, *La Revue du Monde Noir*, *L'Étudiant noir*, and *Présence Africaine*. In the context of that time, the debate engendered by the relationship between politics and culture could not have been sterile, as Gary Wilder seems to suggest in an essay-response to a review of his excellent book *The French Imperial Nation-State: Negritude and Colonial Humanism between the Two World Wars*,[31] but importantly crucial insofar as it alleviated the reductive racial essentialism associated with Négritude, even as Négritude's critics neglect to consider the political and cultural context in which that movement emerged. One could, in effect, read in this debate a desire to be part of a dimension that would go beyond the racial, and that would mean existing, asserting oneself, and being recognized as a subject. In this France and in the Paris where it was conceived, Négritude constitutes a founding moment that made possible a reflection on the Black's being-in-the-world. During this colonial era, the affirmation of a racial identity and identification served as weapons for combat.

Négritude, despite its limits, permitted, albeit temporarily, the erasure of geographic differences or nuances in skin color. If the works that I mentioned here emphasize being Black, they do so on a level different from the initial debate during the time of the Negritude movement: they introduce a reflection on the current social experiences of the Black and his or her place in the Republic. In his analysis in *La condition noire: essai sur une minorité ethnique française*, Pap Ndiaye rejects the notion of a Black identity as a biological fact or as an essence, choosing to focus on the social relation. It is by virtue of this relation that, according to him, the "Black" identity emerges: a prescribed rather than chosen identity. Instead of an *identité épaisse* (thick identity) grounded in origins and in culture, Ndiaye advocates an *identité fine* (thin identity) that defines Blacks on the basis of a common historical and shared destiny through common experiences of domination and enclosure in stereotypical representations.[32] If the authors of these publications invoke a seemingly Black category, it is not as much for the affirmation of a racial identity or for the promotion of race discourse, but rather to stigmatize the perpetuation of social erasure, of discrimination, and of invisibility lived by Blacks within a society to which they belong, that holds fast to republican values while steadfastly denying them a place within the Republic. The question is not to promote what Amin Maalouf calls *identités meurtrières* (killer identities),[33] nor to lock oneself in *communautarisme*, but rather to take into consideration the objective contexts of everyday life as factors and conditions that abet the possibility of a Black France. Black France, like Black identity, becomes ambiguous when one considers what Ndiaye calls *le paradoxe minoritaire* (the minority paradox): that is, questioning and rejecting discrimination to erase the differences based on skin color, but at the same time demanding recognition or acceptance of their alterity as well as visibility.

This "minority paradox" could reflect a tension between the problematic character of a Black identity or of identification with a group made up of a diversity of Blacks, and the existence of a "Black France" as an expression of an *identité fine* prescribed at first, but then appropriated. One could perhaps then conclude that France noire represents an example of the "imagined communities" that Benedict Anderson describes. In imagined communities, as Anderson notes, there are no defined contours, the members do not know all the other members, and in fact have never even heard of each other; yet they maintain a form of solidarity due to some common experiences.[34] Their affirmation as a group proves necessary for a recognition of their presence as well as for political and social recognition.

The influx of other populations and the demographic changes

within the space of the Hexagon have given rise to an anxious questioning of what forms or defines French national identity today. Would a "Black France" constitute a threat to that identity? Is a "Black France" a given, a self-enclosed entity, a formed body, or a body in formation? Does "Black France" represent only a provisional moment in a transitional process? Should a "Black France" be erased and deracialized, defined no longer in terms of color and race, but simply as an ethnic French minority, as Ndiaye advocates? In other words, should a "Black France" be similarly engaged in the dialectic process proposed decades before by Sartre in *Orphée noir* in relation to Négritude?

The theme of the "France Noire" conference, from which this chapter originates, was posed as an affirmation. I would recapture it as a continuous interrogation that might perhaps in the end find an answer in a sea change of mentalities and sensibilities as well as in the political will to end all forms of discrimination based on racial phenotypes or complexion. A "Black France" as a way of self-assertion would perhaps cease to be the day a new France emerges that is at once global and inclusive and practices in everyday and public life the ideals and universalist principles of the Republic: *liberté, égalité, fraternité*. However, the question remains: will this day ever come?

Notes

My thanks to the translators and editors of this chapter.

1. M. Rosello, *Declining the Stereotypes: Ethnicity and Representation in French Cultures* (Hanover, N.H.: University Press of New England, 1998).

2. J.-P. Sartre, "Orphée Noir," preface to L. S. Senghor, *Anthologie de la nouvelle poésie nègre et malgache de langue française* (Paris: Presses Universitaires de France, 1948), ix–xliv.

3. I borrow the title from B. Anderson, *Imagined Communities: Reflections on the Origin and Spread of Nationalism* (London: Verso, 1983).

4. See, among others, S. Delesalle and L. Valensi, "Le Mot 'nègre' dans les dictionnaires d'Ancien Régime, histoire et lexicographie," *Langue française* 15 (1972); S. Daget, "Les Mots 'esclave,' 'nègre,' 'noir' et les jugements de valeur sur la traite négrière dans la littérature abolitionniste française de 1770 à 1845," *Revue française d'histoire d'outre-mer* 221, no. 4 (1973).

5. F. M. Snowden, *Blacks in Antiquity: Ethiopians in the Greco-Roman Experience* (Cambridge, Mass.: Belknap, 1970); *Before Color Prejudice: The Ancient View of Blacks* (Cambridge: Harvard University Press, 1983). See also A. N.

Sherwin-White, *Racial Prejudice in Imperial Rome* (Cambridge: Cambridge University Press, 1970); D. Droixhe and K. Kiefer, eds., *Images de l'africain de l'antiquité au XXème siècle* (New York: Peter Lang, 2004); B. H. Isaac, *The Invention of Racism in Classical Antiquity* (Princeton: Princeton University Press, 2004); A. Bourgeois, *La Grèce antique devant la négritude* (Paris: Présence Africaine, 1971); G. H. Beardsley, *The Negro in Greek and Roman Civilization: A Study of the Ethiopian Type* (Baltimore: Johns Hopkins University Press, 1929). For the relationship between Ancient Greece and Black Africa, see E. Mveng, *Les Sources grecques de l'histoire négro-africaine depuis Homère jusqu'à Strabon* (Paris: Présence Africaine, 1972).

6. See M. McIntosh, "The Moor in the Text: Modern Colonialism in Medieval Christian Spain," *Journal of Romance Studies* 6, no. 3 (2006): 61–70.

7. See, e.g., the heroine in the novel by Claire de Durfort Duras, *Ourika* (New York: Modern Language Association of America, 1994).

8. In the domain of art, one should consult the immense collection of works in four volumes under the auspices of the Menil Foundation, *The Image of the Black in Western Art* (Cambridge: Harvard University Press, 1983).

9. See E. C. Eze, ed., *Race and the Enlightenment: A Reader* (Cambridge, Mass.: Blackwell, 1997); D. Droixhe and J. P. Gossiaux, eds., *L'homme des lumières et la découverte de l'autre* (Brussels: Éditions de l'Université de Bruxelles, 1985); "The Philosophers and Africa," in *The French Encounters with Africans: White Response to Blacks, 1530–1880*, ed. W. Cohen (Bloomington: Indiana University Press, 1980), 60–99; C. Gallouët, D. Diop, M. Bocquillon, and G. Lahouati, eds., *L'Afrique du siècle des lumières: savoirs et représentations* (Oxford: Voltaire Foundation, 2009).

10. L. Figuier, *Les races humaines* (Paris: Hachette, 1885). Translated by the editors.

11. See E. Mudimbe-Boyi, *Essais sur les cultures en contacts: Afrique, Amériques, Europe* (Paris: Karthala, 2006), 49–85.

12. For general representations, see P. Blanchard, E. Deroo, and G. Manceron, *Le Paris noir* (Paris: Hazan, 2001); for theatre, see the excellent work by S. Chalaye, *Du noir au nègre: l'image du noir au théâtre de Marguerite de Navarre à Jean Genet, 1550–1960* (Paris: L'Harmattan, 1998); for literature, see L.-F. Hoffmann, *Le nègre romantique, personnage littéraire et obsession collective* (Paris: Payot, 1973); L. Fanoudh-Ziefer, *Le mythe du nègre et de l'Afrique noire dans la littérature française de 1800 à la deuxième guerre mondiale* (Dakar: Nouvelles Éditions Africaines, 1968); C. Laurette, *L'image du noir dans l'oeuvre de Jacques-Henri Bernardin de Saint Pierre: essai de caractérisation des stéréotypes et des images novatrices* (Villeneuve d'Ascq: Presses Universitaires du Septentrion, 2000); "Images du Noir dans la littérature occidentale: du Moyen Age à la conquête coloniale," special issue, *Notre Librairie* 90 (October–

December 1987); "Images du Noir dans la littérature occidentale: de la conquête coloniale à nos jours," special issue, *Notre Librairie* 91 (January–February 1988); for advertising, see R. Bachollet et al., *Négripub: l'image des noirs
dans la publicité* (Paris: Somogy, 1992); for art, see *The Image of the Black in
Western Art*; for popular culture, see N. J. Pieterse, *White on Black: Images of
Africa and Blacks in Western Popular Culture* (New Haven: Yale University
Press, 1992); N. Bancel, P. Blanchard, and L. Gervereau, *Images et colonies:
iconographie et propagande coloniale sur l'Afrique française de 1880 à 1962*
(Paris: Bibliothèque de Documentation Nationale, 1993).

13. See E. Mudimbe-Boyi, *Essais sur les cultures en contacts*, 17–47.

14. This theme of "passing" is represented in several African American
literary works: see, among others, J. W. Johnson, *The Autobiography of an Ex-
Colored Man* (New York: Vintage, 1927); J. R. Fauset, *Plum Bun: A Novel
without a Moral* (New York: Stokes, 1929); N. Larsen, *Passing* (New York:
Arno, 1969). However, to have a Black ancestor in a white family was considered a curse and a hidden secret; this is the subject of the book by B. Broyard,
One Drop: My Father's Hidden Life: A Story of Race and Family Secrets (New
York: Little, Brown, 2007). It is only after the death of her father that she
discovers that he was part Black.

15. An abundant literature exists on these subjects: see, e.g., T. F. Gossett,
Race: The History of an Idea in America, new ed. (New York: Oxford University Press, 1997); F. J. Davis, *Who Is Black? One Nation's Definition* (University
Park: Pennsylvania State University Press, 1991). For a new racial nomenclature concerning subjects on mixed marriages, see J. M. Spencer, *The New
Colored People: The Mixed-Race Movement in America* (New York: New York
University Press, 1987); F. Sweet, "The Invention of the One-Drop Rule in
the 1830s North: Essays on the Color Line and the One-Drop Rule," working
paper, Backintyme Publishing, January 1, 2005.

16. In the novels of Mayotte Capécia lies the literary example of the desire
of "lactification": Capécia, *Je suis martiniquaise* (Paris: Corrêa, 1948); *La
négresse blanche* (Paris: Corréa, 1950). See also M. Giraud, *Races et classes à la
Martinique* (Paris: Anthropos, 1979).

17. Racial belonging or identification can sometimes be uncertain. Thus in
the United States, correctly or not, people of nonvisible black phenotypes
could have been accused of "racial fraud" by claiming to be black, or they
could have been challenged on their claim to a Black identity, and required to
go to court in order to be recognized as Black. See F. W. Sweet, *Legal History
of the Color Line: The Rise and Triumph of the One-Drop Rule* (Palm Coast,
Fla.: Backintyme, 2005).

18. That was precisely the challenge of the First Festival of Black Arts in
Algiers in 1969: to gather and present the arts and the Blacks from every
continent.

19. D. Thomas, *Black France: Colonialism, Immigration, and Transnationalism* (Bloomington: Indiana University Press, 2007).

20. L. Abensour and R. Thévenin, *La France noire: A.O.F., A.E.F.: La France noire: ses peuples, son histoire, ses richesses* (Paris: Société Parisienne d'Édition, 1931).

21. When it refers to this political sense, I put "Black France" in quotation marks, and without quotation marks when the appellation is used to simply denote the Black group in France.

22. As an example, for Négritude and its cultural engagement, Union's militantism represented in Ousmane Sembène's first novel, *Le Docker noir* (Paris: Présence Africaine, 1973); and for the world of show business, Josephine Baker and the jazz musicians. For the Black presence in France, see, among others, S. Peabody and T. Stovall, eds., *The Color of Liberty: Histories of Race in France* (Durham: Duke University Press, 2003); H. Raphael-Hernandez, ed., *Blackening Europe: The African American Presence* (New York: Routledge, 2004); S. McCloy, *The Negro in France* (Louisville: University of Kentucky Press, 1961); T. Stovall, *Paris Noir: African Americans in the City of Light* (Boston: Houghton Mifflin, 1996); T. Stovall and G. Van Den Abbeele, eds., *French Civilization and Its Discontents: Nationalism, Colonialism, Race* (Lanham, Md.: Lexington Books, 2003); B. Jules-Rosette, *Black Paris: The African Writers' Landscape* (Urbana: University of Illinois Press, 1998).

23. See, e.g., the succession of identity movements in the French Caribbean: from Négritude to Antillanité, Créolité, and Tout-Monde.

24. Sembène, *Le Docker noir*. See also the relationship between class and race in *Le docker noir* and *Les bouts de bois de Dieu* (Paris: Le Livre Contemporain, 1960).

25. See the novels of R. Maran, *Batouala, véritable roman nègre* (Paris: Albin Michel, 1921); *Bacouya, le cynocéphale* (Paris: Albin Michel, 1953); *Le livre de la brousse* (Paris: Moulin de Pen-Mur, 1946); *Djouma, chien de brousse* (Paris: Albin Michel, 1927).

26. See E. Mudimbe-Boyi, "Harlem Renaissance and Africa: An Ambiguous Adventure," in *The Surreptitious Speech: "Présence Africaine" and the Politics of Otherness, 1947–1987*, ed. V. Y. Mudimbe (Chicago: University of Chicago Press, 1992), 155–64.

27. Cited in H. Baker, *Black Literature in America* (New York: McGraw-Hill, 1971), 154.

28. C. McKay, *Banjo: A Story without a Plot* (1929; New York: Harcourt Brace Jovanovich, 1957), cited in French, "L'étudiant antillais vu par un noir américain," *Légitime défense* (1932; Paris: Jean-Michel Place, 1978), 13.

29. Let us recall here Aimé Césaire's resounding letter of resignation to the secretary general of the French Communist Party after the invasion of Buda-

pest. He used the occasion to show his disagreement with the party's line, which focused on the category of class, not race. Contrary to other proletariat comrades, the Black was subjected to other forms of domination because of the color of his skin. See A. Césaire, *Lettre à Maurice Thorez*, 3rd ed. (Paris: Présence Africaine, 1956).

30. See, e.g., R. Yade-Zimet, *Noirs de France* (Paris: Calmann-Lévy, 2007); P. Lozès, *Nous les noirs de France* (Paris: Danger Public, 2007); J.-L. Sagot-Duvauroux, *On ne naît pas noir, on le devient* (Paris: Points, 2008); J.-R. Zika, *Réflexions sur la question noire: réponse à Gaston Kelman* (Paris: L'Harmattan, 2008); G. Kelman, *Au-delà du noir et du blanc* (Paris: Livres de Poche, 2007); C. Ribbe, *Les nègres de la république* (Monaco: Alphée, 2007); G. Faes, *Noir et français* (Paris: Panama, 2006); P. Ndiaye, *La condition noire: essai sur une minorité ethnique française* (Paris: Calmann-Lévy, 2008); F. Durpaire, *France blanche, colère noire* (Paris: Odile Jacob, 2006).

31. G. Wilder, *The French Imperial Nation-State: Negritude and Colonial Humanism between the Two World Wars* (Chicago: University of Chicago Press, 2005).

32. See Ndiaye, *La condition noire*, 36, 71.

33. A. Maalouf, *Les identités meurtrière* (Paris: Grasset, 1998).

34. Anderson, *Imagined Communities*. His definition of "imagined community" applies to the nation. I transfer its usage here to a micro level to characterize a Black France.

The Lost Territories of the Republic

Historical Narratives and the Recomposition of French Citizenship

MAMADOU DIOUF

The objectives attempted in this chapter are twofold. On the one hand, it seeks to present an account of the wounds left by the colonial French Empire, wounds evident in current debates on cultural pluralism with respect to the long-term existence of culturally plural citizenship and belonging—so often questioned and called into question—not only in contemporary France, but also historically in its former colonies. The case of the *originaires* of the Four Communes of Senegal exemplify this point in that they were French citizens but resisted French cultural assimilation to maintain their own cultures and religious values within colonial public space.[1] Consequently, this chapter is interested in a specific moment in a protracted history, one punctuated by relatively successful attempts by the Western colonizer/ civilizer[2] to (re)imagine and discursively (re)invent the so-called *native/indigène*.[3] This recomposition occurred through devices such as the "civilizing mission" and the "colonial library"[4] (with its inventory of African traditions)[5] used to legitimize policies whose aim was to contain and de-territorialize, while making and unmaking as "citizens," France's so-called Other.

This chapter, on the other hand, seeks to explore the sound and the fury unleashed in France's "lost territories," its *banlieues* (metropolitan suburbs), in relation to these issues.[6] These blighted spaces of questioned and qualified belonging emerge as extensions of France's colonial mission (indeed, the failure of this mission) in its compromises and revisions, its violence and paternalism, and its selective and limited economy of knowledge where absence legitimates the smooth and fluid narrative of the Republic's fraternal universalism, its nation-hood, its citizenship, and its moral and socio-cultural codes. These two different situations—the location of the colonial subject in the political economy of the French empire and the postcolonial moment, and the exclusion of African immigrants and "second generation" French citizens of African origin situated in the French nation and Republic—ultimately converge as much in public opinion and percep-tions as in the discourse of political propaganda. Through its capacity to prescribe, this discourse both targets and seeks to disinherit, in ways historically familiar, that "second generation" who now occupies the French suburban landscape. By dint of their very presence in such space, they are rendered an anathema to their country, France.

The perpetuation not only of the qualification but also the quality of the *native/indigène* fits squarely within this context, one marked by French identity politics and struggles, which have become a veritable bombshell, at once ironic and destructive, hurled forcefully at the feet of the French Republic by those whose rightful membership in this nation continues to go unrecognized. The moment of this (re)discov-ery and litmus test of the language and concepts of colonial knowl-edge opened multiple sites for examining the representations of France and the role of immigration and cultural diversity in the tur-bulent identity discourses disrupting the French political and demo-graphic landscape. These issues find expression in, for example, three decades of xenophobic and racist ranting by Jean-Marie Le Pen's Na-tional Front that succeeded in contaminating the political discourse of the French Right. This becomes evident less, for example, in the election of Nicolas Sarkozy to the heights of the French Republic, and more in relation to his speeches in Dakar and Tunis as the new French head of state. Sarkozy's recycling of racist, pathological, and infantiliz-ing ethnological discourses about Africa and African societies glar-ingly ignored past suffering and was ignorant of Africa's progress and its long-standing civilizations. Further, the creation of the Ministry of Immigration and National Identity attests not only to the trivializa-tion of everyday xenophobia, but most certainly to the return of the colonial ideology inherent in the ongoing "civilizing mission" in the French banlieue. Here, I am referring to the ambiguities and ambiva-lences of this ideology and mission, its nationalist and racist fervor, its missionary and pedagogic ambitions, its violence, and even its roman-tic lyricism, all designed to transform the "noble savage" into an image that the Republic has fashioned of such beings and against which this same Republic has defined its national identity.

This moment is commonly characterized in public discourse by its *malaise* (unease) or by *un mal français* to illustrate two situations. On the one hand, there are the various and changing ways in which the French public and political leadership constitute their anguish and fears about the meaning of French identity when confronted by different forms of violence generated, for instance, by globalization, (neo)liberalism, or European economic consolidation and France's socio-economic and cultural "exceptionalism."[7] Then, there is the violence born of, for example, the return to religious fundamentalism, the narratives, politics, and practices of which target disaffected immigrants and their descendants, who are seen by the public as incarnating the ideas of this fundamentalism. Their body (the color of their skin) as much as their religious, culinary, and intellectual traditions, their sexual mores, and their ways of dressing distance them from the core constituents of French national identity, structured by Enlightenment philosophy and translated into French universalist republican citizenship. In other words, they are fundamentally nothing more than "black,"[8] Arab, or Asian, and their existence and presence in the world is strictly, if not exclusively, constructed from a racialized Western perspective and discourse.[9]

This mal français has also emerged with the rise of so-called communitarian claims, a flash point of which was the publication of the manifesto "Indigènes de la République." This mal français surfaced with the parliamentary vote on February 23, 2005, which insisted that educators highlight the "positive aspects of French colonization," and clearly it was present during the revolts in 2005 that shook up the suburbs of major French cities, to which France responded by resorting to a law from 1955 designed for a state of emergency. This law sanctions repressive containment measures to suppress civil disobedience. The very racialized colonial context in which this law was deployed, one that necessitated digging deep into the "colonial library," compels, if not commands, us to interrogate its redeployment in 2005 as an ongoing colonial device used to administer the French banlieues.

These methods of social control, indicative of the powerful arsenal and arbitrary violence of the colonial system, hark back to the tactics carried out during the last colonial period, in Thiaroye (Senegal,

1944), in Madagascar (1945), or in Setif (Algeria, 1947), to cite only a few examples of the sequence of events that followed the end of Second World War.[10] Writing on the clumsiness of resorting to a law dating from the Algerian War to quell the unrest in the banlieues, the politician Jean-Pierre Chevènement's interview in *Jeune Afrique l'Intelligent* is symptomatic of the blindness that dominates the French political landscape:[11] "This law, in effect, dates back to 1955, but clearly a law must have historical origin!"[12] The Socialist former defense minister (under François Mitterrand) and interior minister (under Lionel Jospin) is vigorously stating that he is bothered neither by the colonial origin of the law and its repressive nature, nor by what it and its deployment conjures in relation to French colonial memory. He is, however, extremely disturbed by its limited execution of only three months.

Today, forgetful of this genealogy and shrouded in fear, the native / indigene, now placed in opposition to an aging Hexagon, is ordered to conform to the rules of French modernity through integration and assimilation. In one fell swoop, they are denied the material, emotional, and political benefits of the grand victories of the very modernity to which they have to submit, all the while being made the manifestation of a dysfunction and disorder that threaten the survival of French society. Migrants, new generations of French citizens of color, and in particular those of Islamic confession are perceived, indeed *constituted* simultaneously, as a demographic, health, cultural, and religious threat that multiplies like vermin, at a vertiginous speed. In French society, they become those who are the carriers of all maladies—HIV, an eradicated tuberculosis, SARS, H1N1—and whose conditions of poverty, all too readily equated with a promiscuity, become the conduit for all manner of pandemics likely to wipe humanity off the face of the earth. In the courts of politicized public opinion, their cultural and religious practices are blamed for surreptitiously introducing cruel and barbaric traditions into a sanitized French society beyond reproach, practices such as female circumcision, domestic violence, patriarchal domination, and polygamy, the principal victims of which are women and children. Their dysfunctions, somehow excised from the greater society, are attributed to educational failure, delinquency, trafficking of all kinds, and the loss of parental authority, if not a rejection of authority writ large.

The word *malediction*, it seems to me, captures all the paradoxes of this "French dilemma,"[13] spanning the history of a nation that refuses to make space for diverse populations to join the French community. The acquisition of the status of citizen or the granting of a precious work permit or identity card is predicated on an unattainable integration, conditioned by the erasure of historical memory, an erasure of the past. As the price of admission, they are to exist without their memory and accept the very real prospect of not even being offered a place in the present and future of the French nation to which they belong. Because no one truly engages this question of diversity, a will to violence and rioting becomes a viable alternative for one side, while repression, regulations, and disciplinary methods (including intellectual and in particular historical production) become the response from the other.

The construction of history that drives, for example, Jean Pierre Chevènement's interpretation relies upon two blind spots to ensure its legitimacy. The first blind spot entails returning to a French history that is either amputated by its colonial dimension or subject to the forces of revisionism that leave the colonial moment unrecognizable. The "riots" in 2005 are precisely a testimony to the salience of colonial references to French culture, both administratively and in relation to law enforcement. The second blind spot very powerfully reflects the refusal to take part in multicultural debates spearheaded by migrant communities and second-generation citizens whose visible presence and impact cannot be ignored in contemporary European societies. In the first case of an unrecognizable history, mainly overlooked are the administrative operations to which France had recourse by dint of its civil code, republican ideology, and principles geared toward ensuring the economic and political success of the colonial venture. Significant among them were laws establishing France's legal and moral authority to secure public order. Those operations that privileged an administrative rather than the legal treatment of numerous social transactions and negotiations can be identified, for example, in the history of the Four Communes of Senegal (Saint Louis, Gorée, Rufisque, and Dakar).[14] Here, the legal and administrative discourses, as much as the forms they take on, emerge precisely in response to certain circumstances that are perceived by the actors in conflict or competition as moments of crisis. For illustrations, one can refer to several episodes in the history of the colony of Senegal and of French West Africa more broadly.

Historical Detours

The key historical events that situate the question of preexisting cultural pluralism relative to the inclusion of ethnic diversity in France take on a theatrical quality, a staging of French colonialism as a series of surreal acts. The first act unfolds during the Revolutionary War of 1789 and the Napoleonic wars when the originaires of Saint Louis, as part of the colony of Senegal, succeeded in obtaining citizenship rights—in particular the right to vote—without being subjected to the French civil code.[15] These rights were gradually extended to the populations of Gorée, Rufisque, and Dakar between the French Revolution and 1887. The suspension of the civil code testifies to the recognition of cultural pluralism within the French empire, since it was an essential mechanism to ensure the loyalty of the indigenous peoples to the French cause (and against the competition) in order to claim and occupy colonial possessions. During Louis Faidherbe's first tenure as governor of Senegal (1854–61), Muslim institutions were incorporated into the colonial governance structure and public space, even as the civil affairs of the originaires were outside the reach of the legal and administrative colonial systems.[16] This critical dimension has been overlooked in the metropolitan republican narrative of citizenship and demonstrates the uncompromising vocation of the French nation to conceal its history of plural citizenship-making with respect to its colonial subjects. More administrative than legal, this approach maintains the fiction of a successful and seamless assimilation policy, which winds up erasing the reciprocal exchanges that configured public colonial space economically, politically, and socio-culturally.

The second act is played out during the First World War: Blaise Diagne was elected the first Black deputy to the French National Assembly by the originaires of the Four Communes. In the context of war, he aimed to establish the citizenship status of the originaires on a solid legal ground. Taking advantage of the French army's need for African soldiers, Diagne ushered in the law of 1915 that allowed for the conscription of adult males from Senegalese urban centers for military purposes. And the following year, he initiated another law that recognized the full citizenship status of the inhabitants of the Four Communes, hitherto excised from the territories outlined in the civil code. The most significant advancement of pluralism since the nomination of Faidherbe as the head of the colony of Senegal in 1854 was marked by the laws of 1915–16 that sanctioned the legal recognition of cultural pluralism in the empire and in the Republic. In fact, Faidherbe's colonial administration's interpretation of citizenship prevailed against the one advocated by the colonial magistrates, which stressed the centrality of the civil code.

The third act stages the discussions for the first French constitutional assembly of 1946, which failed to mention anywhere the impact of cultural diversity on the attribution of citizenship to these colonial subjects of the empire. In addition, the Lamine Gueye law of 1946, which extended French citizenship to these subjects, survived the rejection of the first proposed constitution following the mobilization of the colonial party. The fourth act takes shape around Charles de Gaulle's return to power and the referendum that created the French Union in 1958. While the Union sanctioned the recognition of each colony as an autonomous political unit, it also established a federal union with France. For the majority of leaders who had chosen to vote positively for the Union—Guinea being the sole exception[17]—there was more than just a new federation of assembled entities comprising France and its "colonies," there was also the maintenance of a common political, economic, and educational space that structurally connected them. As the historian Fred Cooper observes: "The French Commonwealth that they imagined made it possible for them to build a federation of African states that shared a common colonial experience and language, a political unity, both territorially and demographically significant, to be an actual player on the world stage of inequalities, which is more an expression of African nationality than a colonial fiction of singular territories. An African federation could be on equal footing with metropolitan France in a French supranational confederation." As Senegalese politician, Mamadou Dia understood it: "It is essential, in the final analysis that the imperialist conception of the nation-state ultimately yields to the modern conception of the multinational state."[18] In the four cases cited, there is, whether deliberate or not, a strict disjunction between cultures and rights, in addition to the administrative, legal, and institutional recognition of a cultural pluralism that combined or juxtaposed French, Wolof, and Muslim resources. In other words, the orginaires of the Four Communes were French citizens, but not culturally French.

The last act, which opens in the middle of the 1970s, is played out against the backdrop of those blighted suburbs "invaded" by objects, bodies, smells, languages, and music, in short, the perceived customs and habits of migrants and their often unemployed French offspring, whose rates of unemployment have reached (and at times have even surpassed) 40 percent. The population of the French suburbs, estimated at five or six million French citizens, or roughly 8 percent of the French population, have become receptacles for nonimmigrant and immigrant populations (though the former are often presumed to be the latter).[19] Their harsh conditions have been translated into highly negative representations of the inhabitants of the French banlieue, who are both tarred and defined by all social and moral maladies imaginable, including delinquency, insecurity, irresponsibility, poverty, disorder, and communitarian tendencies. The social, religious, and cultural practices that insidiously insert France within an ethnic logic also divert it from a republican, secular, and democratic identity.[20]

It is no longer a question of accommodating their material cultures and social practices for the economic and military needs of the empire (as in 1789 or 1916), or its labor needs (as after the Second World War), or of sustaining the prestige and grandeur of France in the context of the Cold War (as in 1958). Rather, it becomes a question of minimizing their presence and imposing on them republican rule to counter a communitarian consciousness in formation and, in many instances, already in force. The economic and political motivations that once ensured the triumph of imperial logic over racial reasoning—the strict implementation of the rule of difference—have widely opened the doors of the metropolis to migrants of the colonial empire and to the creation of the French "pré-carré" (i.e., the African neo-colonies of France) that have been progressively yielding to the forces of French integration into the European Union.[21] Those developments have led to the definitive settlement of migrants, the formation of a second generation, and the rise of European right-wing nationalist movements and ideologies.

The era of immigrants and their controversial presence in the French public space ushered in a revision of French colonial history measured by the yardstick of republican, secular, and democratic ideology. Such a revision expresses itself in the implementation of projects of inclusion and exclusion, predicated on the rejection of cultural pluralism—previously recognized historically—and on a dogged refusal to consider other options. The rejection of pluralism and of multicultural options precisely constitutes the second blind spot in the construction of a history that caters to present interests. The most dramatic example of this is the speech by the archbishop of Canterbury, Rowan Williams, in February 2008 and the violent reactions it provoked. When considering the weight of the Muslim and Jewish communities in the British population, Williams wondered whether the legal system of Great Britain might permit "non-Christian courts" to decide certain questions about family law. Carefully choosing his words and establishing preconditions, such as a preliminary agreement for the parties concerned and the recognition and the protection of equal rights for women, he suggested that establishing courts for Muslims and Orthodox Jews to address questions related to marriage and divorce was not a bad idea. The outrage generated by Williams's speech was shared across the political and public spectrum, despite the Archbishop's carefully chosen words. According to the professor of law Noah Feldman: "Then all hell broke loose. From politicians across the spectrum to senior church figures and the ubiquitous British tabloids came calls for the leader of the world's second largest Christian denomination to issue a retraction or even resign. Williams has spent the last couple of years trying to hold together the global Anglican Communion in the face of continuing controversies about ordaining gay priests and recognizing same-sex marriages. Yet little in that contentious battle subjected him to the kind of outcry that his reference to religious courts unleashed. Needless to say, the outrage was not occasioned by Williams's mention of Orthodox Jewish law. For the purposes of public discussion, it was the word 'Shariah' that was the radioactive referent."[22] In actuality, the referent and object of the Archbishop of Canterbury's remarks were communities of men and women identified with 'Shariah' who are deemed radioactive to the public.

The practice of memory particularly serves at this juncture to produce narratives that fashion new identifications, either to break with the community to which the individuals do not feel they belong or to demand a revision and a renegotiation of the signs and resources of membership. The new citizens and members of the community are attempting to expand, at times reformulate, the master narrative of historical, genealogical, and geographic references by introducing within it their own singular narratives and references that have been denied, effaced, and ignored.[23] In seeking to be incorporated into the historical past of the nation, on their terms and with their historical resources, they are staking a claim in the future of the national community. This can only be accomplished by rewriting the place that they occupy in the past. Though decidedly political, this rewriting of history is not simply an intellectual or cultural exercise, it is most certainly the object of recriminations, conflicts, and violence. France experienced this in October through November of 2005.

Suburban Ethnographies

The ethnographic exploration of the French suburb that is examined in this chapter involves a digression that deliberately appropriates the proposition of an "Americanization of the French banlieue," a corollary of which is a novel republican ethnicity. "Americanization" refers to, on the one hand, the everyday despair in these disadvantaged neighborhoods and the brutal surge of violence that expands social, ethnic, cultural, educational, and religious cleavages that accentuate a logic of segregation and ghettoization. And, on the other, it applies to a retreat into religious and cultural identities and a (re)turn to cultural and ideological resources in opposition to the republican model. This digression draws from the sociologist Loïc Wacquant, namely his discussion of the category of "ghetto"[24] and his comparative analysis of "ghetto," "banlieue," and "*favela*."[25] Wacquant defines the ghetto as a space in which pariah populations, defined by it, are contained and controlled. He continues, "a ghetto is a social-organizational device composed of four elements (stigma, constraint, spatial confinement, and institutional encasement) that employs space to reconcile the two antinomic purposes of economic exploitation and social ostracization."[26]

This approach stresses the sociological factors that contribute to the formation of the ghetto and its precise role as a "symbolic incubator" in the production of a "deviant identity" attributed to groups, both dispossessed and dishonored, who are comparable to populations on reservations, in refugee camps, and in prison.[27] Wacquant's observations saliently lay out the geographical contours of this site while highlighting its physical constraints, infrastructures, and social function as a space of containment, management, and control. And while he vehemently rejects what he sees as a hasty amalgamation of the "ghetto" in the United States with the French banlieue because of their differing historical conditions of emergence and social logics, what he identifies, nonetheless, as distinctive to the case of the United States are existing realities in those socializing spaces on the fringes of French society.[28] In other words, the critical components of the African American ghetto are locatable in the French banlieue. It is, therefore, the similarities between ghettos in the United States and French banlieues that are of interest to me and on which I wish to place the accent rather than the differences insisted upon by Wacquant.

Its inhabitants, as a subject people, are thus the product of ideological, political, and sociological formations and lived reality that converge and diverge depending on the actors and the objects on which their interventions are focused and against which they battle. Their lived-reality includes ostracism, racism, discrimination, a functional existence as a reserve labor force, and deleterious representations generalized to entire peoples. Such representations also point to their supposed exclusive dependence on social services from the state or charitable organizations, ascriptions of cultural pathology bordering on parasitism, their laziness and total absence of a work ethic, and a perceived lack of social and moral responsibility. It is a territory where good, decent, and redeemable people are held simply not to exist. Even if social segregation is not as rigid in the French suburbs or as monoracial, they share with American ghettos the same social ills—unemployment, educational failure, criminality, drugs, alcoholism, delinquency, a high number of unwed teenage mothers—issues closely aligned with stigmatized zones highly marked by economic and social marginalization. These factors render them more similar than different. The illustration of their decline is evident in the overpopulation of apartments, excessive loitering, the criminalization and deterioration of public places—of building lobbies, plazas, and public parks—the deterioration of infrastructures, and generalized poverty. These populations, in particular the youngest segment, re-create in all its sound, fury, and violence a marginal space, a marginalized "zone," captured by its overall physicality in its buildings and circuits, its squares, its loudness, its surfaces and spaces of social gathering, in short, an experience lived as both home and hell for its inhabitants.[29]

The philosopher François Lyotard draws out the tragic simplicity of these zones of men and women, young and old alike, who live "nowhere, neither outside, neither in."[30] Bad boys, lost girls, rebels, living outside the rule of law, they roam the margins of society, penetrating it occasionally to dance, fight, or cut loose, or to offer and enjoy the only commodity at their disposal, their bodies. Lyotard's powerful description of disillusionment offers some illuminating insights for those who seek to grasp the new lines of convergences and divergences in French urban societies, particularly among the youngest groups in those sites. Neither variations in France's integration policies, nor targeted social and educational interventions, nor religious and charitable organizations, nor multiple versions of urban policies from the Right and the Left—from Valéry Giscard d'Estaing to François Mitterrand and Jacques Chirac—are able to propose solutions to the despair and utter frustration that characterize life in the French suburbs. This reflection points to a generation left by the side of the road, a road that goes nowhere, with "the zone" as its only horizon. Left to fend for itself by the state and the national community, French society is confronted by the following question: how does society tackle the challenges of precariousness and engage the indeterminate struggles in this "zone," this site of passage, of life between city and country, between two extremities and two worlds? If, as continues Lyotard, "the *Urbs* become the *Orbs* and if the zone becomes the whole of the city, then the megalopolis has no outside. And consequently no inside. Nature is under cosmological, geological, meteorological, touristic, and ecological control. Tightly supervised, stashed away, gated. One no longer enters the megalopolis. It is no longer a city that needs to begin again. The former 'external' provinces—Africa and Asia—inhere in it, coalesced with native Westerners in a variety of ways. Everything and nothing is foreign."[31]

It is precisely the spatial and cultural indetermination, the social and moral uncertainties associated with economic and intellectual misery, that perform two types of labor, not only containment and control, but also integration and protection. As Wacquant notes, "enforced isolation from outside leads to the intensification of exchange and cultural sharing and identity on the inside."[32] Again, such is evident in the French banlieue. But, unlike the African American ghettos, again born of a different racial history, the French suburbs have been less successful in establishing their own social, cultural, and religious institutions, their own journals, and their own political, civil, and cultural associations, owing to the French republican ideology of citizenship, secularism, and democracy. All such practices have been conveniently relegated to the realm of "communitarian" practices, at times with the consent of the banlieu-ized of the republic to whom this discourse refers.[33]

This statist response has radicalized them in unanticipated ways, forcing them to seize a Black identity and subjectivity and, at times, to become fiercely anti-establishment against institutions of socialization, even though they are its products, all the while challenging the "republican fiction" of "colorblindness."[34] It has opened up a public space and alternative civic formations, capable of bearing, at once, economic, social, religious, and musical propositions, as well as memories, a history, and demands for inclusion in France's national narrative. Such inclusion is accomplished by adding indigenous cultures to metropolitan cultures to build a co-authored "colonial library,"[35] not one erected by the authoritarian and violent imposition of French republicanism's citizenship theories and histories, the ideology and practices of which sought to permanently adjust colonial circumstances and demands.

As in colonial situations, residents of the suburbs are not only acted upon, but act. Individually and collectively, persons question, divert, dissolve, widen, and scorn the discourse and prescriptions of the triple heritage that envelops them: familial, colonial, and metropolitan. In this generative tension, they seize a territory (their banlieue) and vest it with social, cultural, and religious practices. In so doing, they forge a community that self-identifies by race, culture, religion, and, of course, membership in the French nation, itself a self-declared community.

An area is designated—the suburbs—where they reinvent French identity, reintroducing cultural pluralism and reopening the debate on citizenship, race, and culture. They do so under circumstances marked by the ethnic diversification of the French population, poverty, racism, immigration, unemployment, a shrinking job market, reduction of social programs, a daily and massive police presence, and so forth. What becomes interesting is that this new historical sequence of cultural pluralism is no longer defined as an administrative will to put African "mores and customs" in the service of colonial governance, as was the case with British indirect rule or French ethnology, where the native/indigène was deemed incapable of participating in the same modernity as those singularly and racially defined as "French."[36] On the contrary, he is a product of the mixing of urban cultures and a bricolage that rejects any essentialist approach, that is, one that "respects the inherited cultural borders and serves to incorporate the individuals in one of the socio-ethnic groups to be protected and preserved."[37] Thus, the suburb becomes a vested space, a territory in permanent construction in which protest ultimately serves to loosen the republican narrative so that other histories, other traditions, and other languages are welcome.

The meaningful recognition of France's racial and cultural diversity hinges upon a meaningful recognition (and comprehension of the social impact) of the cultural transactions, social networks, and large consumer groups who have used the cultural products of their diverse heritages to resist, subvert, manipulate, and engage relations of power. The most salient illustrations of the art of citizenship and identity formation processes are the hip hop, rap music, lyrics, painting, and sculpture that define the banlieue aesthetic, already incorporated into mainstream metropolitan space, even if its cultural producers—banlieue youth—are not.[38] These formations, strongly influenced by instable and changing familial and community cultures, merge multiple sources and resources. The voices, rhythms, and sounds that accompany those trajectories and processes adopt neither the intonation nor the colors of the so-called master or subject. Instead, voices, rhythms, sounds, dances, clothes target a national audience. As a counterpoint to the narrow conceptions of republican culture, they constitute, in their instability and changing structures and functions, the powerful referential and re-creative operations of both the native/indigène and the citizen of the republic in all their socio-historical plurality. This citizen, an indispensable economic agent who operates according to his own formulas and practices, yet one in search of his own subjectivity, is freed from the pitfalls of the republican library and its supposedly unique and exclusive modernity. The "native" announces the end of a republic and the rise of new sociabilities whose foundations are a pluralism and diversity both apprehended and assumed by them.

Native/Indigène of the Republic in the Process of Dissolution

A colonial and postcolonial frame seems quite appropriate for exploring the cultures of French suburban youth, cultures whose very presence challenges the fiction of citizenship and undifferenciated belonging in Hexagonal society. Their example can serve to advance our understanding of the call to consciousness by the "Native / Indigène of the Republic," or at least to understand this call less rigidly.[39] In paying careful attention not to disjunctions and ruptures, but to the dialogue constantly fostered by the settlers and the "natives," one can radically interrogate the notion of integration so dear to French political rhetoric, which begs the following question: Is it possible to integrate oneself into a collective to which one already belongs without artificially refusing to recognize one's existence or by concealing one's presence ideologically, and without becoming mentally and emotionally locked into a form of isolation, imprisonment, or distance? For those who hail from the former colonies and their offspring, always seen as migrants without rights but always in a posture of anticipated recognition, their production of new forms of French identity cuts against the very core principles of the Republic and its myth of assimilation: "Today, we talk of integration, but I am French like you. . . . We are neither immigrants, or emigrants, or migrants."[40] What we saw in the revolts of 2005 was the demand for that recognition.

To understand the confluence of these demands born of the crisis in the French suburbs, demands voiced by the "Natives / Indigène of the Republic," I would like to examine in the rest of this chapter two questions that seem of the utmost importance to me: (1) the question of historiography, in particular the writing of colonial history in a multicultural French society, and (2) the dramatic quest for the inclusion of "indigenous" memory in the *lieux de mémoire* (sites of memory) of the French Republic.[41] The stakes of writing history for a recognized and archived presence in the nation's past cannot be reduced to a mere mention in textbooks or to the superficial and vacuous pedagogy that passes for the teaching of the history of a given people. Nor can historiography be mandated by revisionist politicians who conjure up revisionist history, as in the case of law of February 23, 2005, article 4, emphasizing "in particular the positive role of the French presence overseas." Rather, the fundamental problem has to do with the brutal fact that a community rendered absent from, or simplistic in, a nation's past is also rendered incapable of claiming a role and demanding recognition of its rights in the present and future of that nation. As such, marginal or marginalized communities have no other choice than to write their own histories and construct their own narratives to make their voices heard, ensuring their legitimate recognition and claims to political rights and citizenship.[42] This constraint is precisely the reason for the retreat to victimization and speeches focused on exclusion and oppression that emphasize the moral obligation to redress the wrongs done to non-European and nonwhite European humanity. Such recourse echoes the concern of historians about distinguishing historical work from activism and raises the following critical questions: Who writes history and how? Who authorizes the public versions of the past? Is it possible to breach the national narratives through dissonant histories, alternative and complementary histories, monuments, and multiple commemorations for the "communities" that evolve from being made fragments of the nation where multiple national imaginings and tensions remain?

The case of Great Britain, by no means perfect, is nonetheless instructive in this context. Since 1989, Great Britain was shaken by the same controversies concerning the theme of colonization and its insertion in textbooks. The then all-powerful Prime Minister Margaret Thatcher offered the following contribution to the debate: "The history of the ways in which Europe has explored, colonized, and— without any excuses—civilized much of the world [is] a saga of talent, expertise, and courage."[43] In contrast, the historian Raphael Samuel's remarks about the debate on the content of school curricula invites particular attention to the elements of national culture and to the processes by which they are reconstituted and fractured over the long duration.[44] British historians' recognition of the process of reconstitution and fragmentation of the national experience and narrative resulted not only in revisiting the whole of the historical narrative, along with British national imaginings, but also in a rethinking of colonization that opened spaces for inscribing other histories, commemorations, cuisines, leisure activities, styles of dress, perfumes, and so forth in relation to its ethnic diversity and communities. In opposition to the traditional French Republican model that resists unpacking citizenship, one finds in these reconstitutions a strategic use of positivist essentialism in which authenticity becomes a weapon wielded by different groups, including the nationalists, the feminists, the indigenous, and marginalized groups.[45] Such an option offers resources to resist the attempts at ethnic annihilation, while opening paths to liberation and emancipation. What is in question is the right to self-representation and the production of one's own "ethos" and "ethnos" in defiance of the temptation of a universalism realized always at the expense of the "native" and the settler.[46] Indeed, the specific language

of remembrance and commemoration is at once a language of reclamation, revendication, and the quest for recognition as well as resource redistribution and reparations.[47]

The work of the historian Pierre Nora, who maintains an arguable
relationship with postcolonialism, gives the appearance of offering
interesting insights into the reconstitution of sites of memory and
French identities.[48] It is possible to interpret his endeavor as an attempt to loosen the French national identity from its old nation-state
obsessions. Nora also appears to depoliticize the national question in
order to substitute for the national consensus of the old Jacobin republican tradition a subtle and fragmented cultural and political
blending of a variety of resources (i.e., metropolitan, empire, and
global) without necessarily erasing the ethno-eurocentric nature of
the undertaking. Does this refocusing to which Nora's work leads,
even as it accommodates certain social categories in contemporary
French society, allow for the presence of Africans (North and sub-
Saharan), of Islam, and of immigrants? Can it be authorized (is it
authorized) to include their history, their memory in the new mosaic
of the national past?[49] Ultimately, Nora's revisionism only provides an
oblique and incomplete response to the "Black, Blanc, Beur" (Black,
White, and second generation North African) nation that racially
adapted Italian, Polish, Portuguese, and Spanish immigrants into the
white of the flag, that is, into a racialized national identity synonymous with "whiteness." Further, despite his ranting and raving and the
sticks and stones that accompanied it, Nicolas Sarkozy attempts to
conform to the imperatives of globalization by supposedly privileging
skills and productivity (over nationality and ethnicity) and his project
of selective immigration reinforces this point. Yet, Sarkozy also appears to have no problem privileging bloodlines over skills and merit
in his decision-making schemes, as the attempt to maneuver his
twenty-three-year-old son Jean into the head position at La Défense,
Europe's largest business district, well illustrates. Will this move only
occur within a framework of selective immigration or will it spread to
the "native" populations, resulting in a renewed policy of affirmative
action?[50]

Ultimately, has it become impossible to fathom the nature of the
French nation absent colonial and postcolonial experiences? The historian Jacques Marseille attributes the delay of French economic modernization to the preponderance of colonial interests in French eco-

nomic and financial structures in addition to political weight and activities spearheaded by lobbies operating in the French empire and in the French public space.[51] Indeed, France's multiple financial scandals, its widening disconnect between its socio-economic policies and practices with (and within) its overseas territories, and its budgetary and cultural crises are collectively indicative of the profound dysfunction of the nation and are well illustrated by the election of the extreme right candidate Jean-Marie Le Pen to second place in the first round of the presidential election in 2002. European cities, Paris in particular, are not African villages, according to the historian Hélène Carrère d'Encausse's insulting and outrageous remarks[52] that were reminiscent of Jacques Chirac's infamous phrase about the "stench" of Africans,[53] and Sarkozy's ridiculous Hegelian speeches in Dakar and Tunis. What they are, however, are African suburbs, if not Africa's suburbs, thanks to Europe's imperial past so evident still in this present moment. Indeed, it is in the metropolis where the colonial and postcolonial converge in the making and remaking not only of the French national narrative and identity but also of the native/indigène who is, in turn, (re)making France.

Notes

1. "*Originaires*" is the self-definition adopted by the African inhabitants of the Four Communes. It could be translated as "natives," meaning the original population of the land. This term situates persons both in relation and distinction to the other groups of French citizens living in the communes, such as the French traders and colonial administrators who were considered "settlers."

2. According to Partha Chatterjee, such operations put into practice one of the key elements of colonial domination, "the rule of difference." P. Chatterjee, *The Nation and Its Fragments* (Princeton: Princeton University Press, 2000), 16.

3. By using "*native/indigène*" (native/indigenous), I seek to draw light to the current reappropriation of stigmatizing colonial categories that were originally constituted as "primitive" in the colonial empire and later reformulated as "immigrant" or a "second generation" French citizen in the métropole. In resignifying these understandings, one sees precisely why the formation and deployment of "*Indigènes de la République*" by those who have assumed this representation is so arresting, even if one does not agree with their political stances.

4. V. Y. Mudimbe, *The Invention of Africa* (Bloomington: Indiana University Press, 1988).

5. T. Ranger, "The Invention of Tradition in Colonial Africa," in *The Invention of Tradition*, ed. E. Hobsbawm and T. Ranger (Cambridge: Cambridge University Press, 1992), 221–62.

6. The *banlieues* have been described as "lost territories of the Republic" by the former French secretary of state for urban affairs, Fadela Amara, in reference to the zones inhabited by the second generation "who do not feel like citizens" in these spaces dominated by unemployment, limited cultural options and mobility, economic precariousness, crisis states in education and security, as well as ongoing and powerful police interventions. S. Erlanger, "A Daughter of France's 'Lost Territories' Fights for Them," *New York Times*, June 18, 2008. It is interesting to note that in this interview with an American journalist, Fadela Amara clarifies that the movement she founded in 2003, "Ni putes, ni soumises" (Neither sluts, nor slaves), battles to protect women from violence, from ideology, and from patriarchal prescriptions inherited from colonization and traditional societies now found in the territories of the banlieues. She asserts further in that same piece that "life belongs to great principles" and to the values of the Republic "all over our country, especially in sensitive neighborhoods." It is worth noting that Amara, handpicked by President Sarkozy as part of his project to bring visible ethnic diversity to his cabinet, was dismissed in November 2010 along with the minister of sports, Rama Yade (another handpicked Sarkozy appointee), in what observers call an end to his policies of French-style affirmative action and openness to racial diversity.

7. "France's exceptionalism" refers to the invention of French identity and the nation as a bounded community configured by the core Republican traditions of *liberté, égalité, et fraternité* (for all citizens), and *laïcité*, which emerged from the French Revolution. It insists on a singular unitary vision and ideology of the French Republic. See, e.g., F. Braudel, *L'identité de la France*, 3 vols. (Paris: Arthaud-Flammarion, 1986); H. Lebovics, *True France: The Wars over Cultural Identity* (Ithaca: Cornell University Press, 1992); T. Shepard, *The Invention of Decolonization: The Algerian War and the Remaking of France* (Ithaca: Cornell University Press, 2006).

8. The use of "black" here in lower case denotes a nonpolitical imposed racialized identification.

9. E. Said, *Orientalism* (New York: Random House, 1978); D. Chakrabarty, *Provincializing Europe: Postcolonial Thought and Historical Difference* (Princeton: Princeton University Press, 2000); *Habitations of Modernity: Essays on the Wake of Subaltern Studies* (Chicago: University of Chicago Press, 2002); G. Prakash, *Another Reason: Science and the Imagination of Modern India* (Princeton: Princeton University Press, 1999).

10. On this subject, see the theoretical and activist interventions of Sartre: "Colonialism Is a System," *Interventions International Journal of Postcolonial Studies* 3, no. 1 (2001): 127–240; preface to F. Fanon, *The Wretched of the Earth* (New York: Grove, 1963). See also the psychological interventions of O. Mannoni, *Prospéro et caliban: psychologie de la colonisation* (Paris: Éditions Universitaires, 1949); A. Memmi, *Portrait du colonisé*, prefaced by *le portrait du colonisateur* (Paris: Buchet/Chatel, 1991), published in English as *The Colonizer and the Colonized*, trans. H. Greenfield (Boston: Beacon, 1991).

11. This political class also includes "second-generation" immigrant actors. Again, the Sarkozy appointee Fadela Amara provides a perfect illustration of French Republicanism when she declares publicly that "our principles defend equality, condemn cultural relativism, and combat archaic traditions.... This is why I reclaim the heritage of the French Revolution. . . . I am a universalist. I strongly believe in the values of the Republic—liberty, equality, fraternity—and in secularism." Erlanger, "A Daughter of France's 'Lost Territories' Fights for Them."

12. *Jeune Afrique L'intelligent*, November 2005, 20–26, 29.

13. For an instructive ethnography of this "French dilemma" in a Parisian banlieue, see T. D. Keaton, *Muslim Girls and the Other France: Race, Identity Politics, and Social Exclusion* (Bloomington: Indiana University Press, 2006).

14. G. W. Johnson, *The Emergence of Black Politics in Senegal* (Stanford: Stanford University Press, 1971).

15. As early as the French Revolution, the Wars of the Revolution, and the First Empire, the "originaires," the inhabitants of Saint Louis and Gorée (since the French Revolution), Rufisque (since 1880), and Dakar (since 1887) have been granted the right to elect representatives to different French colonial assemblies, including city councils and mayors as well as a parliamentary representative to the French National Assembly in Paris, the latter starting in 1848. In addition, their rights included access to the French justice system as well as the capacity to adjudicate their civil affairs in Muslim courts established by the colonial administration in 1857. They retained their customary civil status. Their recognized status and the legal and cultural infrastructures that supported it are an indication that *they were treated as a community of French citizens*, not as abstract individuals or groups who were excluded from territories governed under the civil code. Their claims to and practices of citizenship have always been contested by the French magistrates. Some segments of the colonial administration denounced the legal dualism in the Four Communes as a violation of French political, cultural, and national identity, as defined by the principles of the French Revolution, principles that proclaim a unitary nation-state based on a common civil law and culture. The "originaires" resisted such a unitary definition and fought to retain their Wolof, Muslim, and colonial cultures. On these issues, see L.

Gueye, *De la situation politique des sénégalais originaires des quatre communes* (Paris: Éditions de la Vie Universitaire, 1921); G. W. Johnson, *The Emergence of Black Politics in Senegal,* esp. 178–91); S. Searing, "Accommodation and Resistance: Chiefs, Muslim Leaders and Politicians in Colonial Senegal, 1890–1934" (Ph.D diss., Princeton, 1985), esp. 452–543; M. Diouf, "The French Colonial Policy of Assimilation and the Civility of the Originaires of the Four Communes (Sénégal): A Nineteenth Century Globalization Project," in *Globalization and Identity: Dialectics of Flows and Closure,* ed. B. Meyer and P. Geshiere (London: Blackwell, 1999), 71–96.

16. Here I am referring to institutions such as tribunals, Qadis (Muslim judges whose decisions are guided by Islamic law or Shari'ah), administrative committees that assisted Muslim "originaires" to attend the pilgrimage at Mecca, and Arab-French schools, among others.

17. Concerning the exception of Guinea, see E. Schmidt, *Cold War and Decolonization in Guinea, 1946–1958* (Athens: Ohio University Press, 2007), esp. chap. 6.

18. F. Cooper, "Possibility and Constraint: African Independence in Historical Perspective," *Journal of African History* 49 (2008): 167–96.

19. Erlanger, "A Daughter of France's 'Lost Territories' Fights for Them."

20. Braudel, *L'identité de la France.*

21. "Pré-carré" refers to the name given to the group of independent French African territories that remained under strict French military, economic, political, and diplomatic control.

22. N. Feldman, "Why Shariah? Millions of Muslims Think Shariah Means the Rule of Law. Could They Be Right?" *New York Times Magazine,* March 16, 2008, 47.

23. This history, which belongs exclusively to a community, evokes the most traumatic moments and always distills a historic inventory of these experiences of pain and suffering.

24. L. Wacquant, "Ghetto," in *International Encyclopedia of the Social and Behavioral Sciences,* rev. ed., ed. N. J. Smelser and P. B. Baltes (London: Pergamon, 2004), 129–47. See also L. Wacquant and W. J. Wilson, "The Cost of Racial and Class Exclusion in the Inner City," *Annals of the American Academy of Political and Social Science* 501 (1989): 8–25; L. Wacquant, "The Rise of Advanced Marginality: Notes on Its Nature and Implications," *Acta sociologica* 39 (1996): 121–39; cf. T. Stovall, "From Red Belt to Black Belt: Race, Class, and Urban Marginality in Twentieth-Century Paris," in *The Color of Liberty: Histories of Race in France,* ed. S. Peabody and T. Stovall (Durham: Duke University Press, 2003).

25. L. Wacquant, "Ghetto, *Banlieue, Favela,* et caetera: Tools for Rethinking Urban Marginality," in *Urban Outcasts: A Comparative Sociology of Advanced Marginality* (Cambridge: Polity, 2008); "Urban Outcasts: Stigma and Divi-

sion in the Black American Ghetto and the French Urban Periphery," in *Urban Sociology Reader*, ed. J. Lin and C. Mele (London: Routledge, 2005), 144–51.

26. Wacquant, "Ghetto, *Banlieue, Favela*, et caetera," 129.

27. Ibid.

28. In his comparative analysis of ghettos in the United States and the French banlieue, in particular La Courneuve, a public housing complex once known for its four thousand apartments, he notes the large concentration of ethnic minorities, unemployment, and the like, and observes: "This analysis reveals that the declining urban periphery of France and the African-American ghetto constitute *two disparate sociospatial formations*, produced by different institutional logics of segregation and aggregation, which result in sharply higher levels of blight, isolation and hardship in America's dark ghetto. Social closure and spatial regulation operate on the basis of race first and foremost, modulated by class position after the break of the 1960s, and both are anchored and aggravated by public policies of urban triage and neglect. It is just about the reverse in the Red Belt, where marginalization is primarily the product of a class logic, in part redoubled by ethnonational origin and in part accentuated by state action." Wacquant, "Ghetto, *Banlieue, Favela*, et caetera," 5. Wacquant additionally avers that the "strong stigmas" attached to and "coping strategies" employed by both of these isolated spaces of the socially and economically marginalized might explain why one sees amalgamations of these two sites.

29. J.-M. Besse and A. Lhomme. "Le philosophe dans la cité," *Cahiers de philosophie* 17 (1993–94): 9.

30. J.-F. Lyotard, "Zone," *Cahiers de philosophie* 17 (1993–94): 15–24.

31. Ibid., 17.

32. Wacquant, "Ghetto, *Banlieue, Favela*, et caetera."

33. In the French context, the term "communitarianism" seems to cover any claims of membership to a community based on race, religion, and ethnicity, with entities seen as contradicting the only meaningful community in France, the *national community*, which is defined by republican citizenship.

34. The emergence of groups such as the Conseil Représentatif des Associations Noires (CRAN) that willfully and strategically deploy a "Black identity" illustrates this point. See, e.g., P. Lozès, *Nous les noirs de France* (Paris: Broché, 2007); P. Ndiaye, *La condition noire: essai sur une minorité française* (Paris: Calmann-Lévy, 2008); T. Shelby, *We Who Are Dark: The Philosophical Foundations of Black Solidarity* (Cambridge: Harvard University Press, 2005); T. D. Keaton, "The Politics of Race-Blindness, (Anti)blackness and Category-Blindness in Contemporary France," *Du Bois Review: Social Science Research on Race* 7, no. 1 (2010): 1–29.

35. Mudimbe, *The Invention of Africa*.

36. Chinua Achebe captures nicely the disposition of the colonizers relative to the colonial subject when he writes: "to the colonialist mind it was always the utmost importance to be able to say: *I know my natives*, a claim which implied two things at once: (a) that the native was really quite simple and (b) that understanding him and controlling him went hand in hand— understanding being a precondition for control and control constituting adequate proof of understanding." C. Achebe, *Morning Yet on Creation Day: Essays* (Garden City, N.Y.: Anchor, 1975), 5.

37. Certain authors—such as D. Hollinger, *Postethnic America: Beyond Multiculturalism* (New York: Basic, 1995, 3)—oppose a cosmopolitism that favors multiple identities and highlights the dynamic and changing character of communities along with the production of multiple cultural formations, though pluralism is considered essentialist.

38. Also consider the exhibit "Né dans la rue Graffiti" shown in 2009 at the prestigious Fondation Cartier pour l'Art Contemporain in Paris; and for an insightful comparison with the United States, see T. Sharpley-Whiting, *Pimps Up, Ho's Down: Hip Hop's Hold on Young Black Women* (New York: New York University Press, 2007).

39. L'Appel des indigènes de la république: "Nous sommes les indigènes de la république!" January 20, 2005, web site of Les indigènes de la république (http://indegenes-republique.org).

40. Much has been written about this topic. See G. Courtois, "Les blessures de la colonisation," *Le Monde*, January 26, 2006; L. Van Eeckhout, "Lycéens, petits-fils de l'empire," *Le Monde*, January 26, 2006. These serve as telling examples of how these debates during this period attempted to draw connections between systematized exclusion and colonization. In fact, all those interviewed expressed similar sentiments in revolting against the fact that they are always perceived as not being from France, sentiments that persist to this day. Additionally, I chose this phrase, taken from a young person of Tunisian origin, to illustrate how the quest for recognition, both collective (community) and individual, is being articulated in order to point to the difficulty in dissociating or opposing the two.

41. P. Nora, *Les lieux de mémoire* (Paris: Gallimard, 1992).

42. W. Kymlicka, ed., *The Rights of Minority Cultures* (Oxford: Oxford University Press, 1995).

43. The citation is from the work of D. Morley and K. Robins, *Spaces of Identity: Global Media, Electronic Landscapes and Cultural Boundaries* (New York: Routledge, 1995), 50.

44. Raphael. Samuel, "Grand Narratives," *History Workshop Journal* 29 (1990): 120–33 [special issue: *History, the Nation, and the Schools*].

45. Gayatri C. Spivak writes "that elements of their text would warrant reading of the project to retrieve the subaltern consciousness as the attempt

to undo as massive historiographic metalepsis and 'situate' the effect of the subject as a subaltern. I would read it, then, as a *strategic* use of positivist essentialism in a scrupulously visible political interest. This would put them in line with the Marx who locates fetichization, the ideological determination of the 'concrete,' and spins the narrative of the development of money-form; with the Nietzsche who offers us genealogy in place of historiography, the Foucault who plots the construction of a 'counter-memory,' the Barthes of semiotropy and the Derrida of 'affirmative deconstruction.' This would allow them to use the critical force of anti-humanism, in other words, even as they shate its constitutive paradox: that the essentializing moment, the object of their criticism, is irreducible." G. C. Spivak, "Subaltern Studies: Deconstructing Historiography," in *Subaltern Studies*, vol. 4, *Writing on South Asian History and Society*, ed. R. Guja (Delphi: Oxford University Press, 1985), 341–42.

46. G. Viswanathan, *Power, Politics and Culture. Interviews with Edward W. Said*, edited and with an Introduction by G. Viswanathan (New York, Vintage, 2002), 341–42.

47. W. Kymlicka, *Multicultural Citizenship* (Oxford: Oxford University Press, 1995), and C. Taylor, *Multiculturalism: Examining the Politics of Recognition* (Princeton: Princeton University Press, 1994). And for a discussion on multicultural citizenship, see K. A. Appiah, *The Ethics of Identity* (Princeton: Princeton University Press, 2005).

48. Geoff Eley elaborates quite a convincing argument related to this connection. See G. Eley, *A Crooked Line: From Cultural History to the History of Society* (Ann Arbor: University of Michigan Press, 2005), 149, which takes an interest in how the locale becomes one of the sites of political struggle. See also F. Jameson, *Postmodernism, or, the Cultural Logic of Late Capitalism* (Durham: Duke University Press, 1991), esp. 150, 279–96; P. Carrier, "Places, Politics and the Archiving of Contemporary Memory," in *Memory and Methodology*, ed. S. Radstone (Oxford: Berg, 2000), 37–57.

49. See Eley, *A Crooked Line*, 150; Carrier, "Places, Politics and the Archiving of Contemporary Memory."

50. Shepard, *The Invention of Decolonization*, has documented very meticulously the policy of affirmative action implemented by the Fourth and the Fifth Republics in France pertaining to "Algériens musulmans" after the Second World War. For more texts, see D. Sabbagh, *Equality and Transparency: A Strategic Perspective on Affirmative Action in American* (New York: Palgrave Macmillan, 2007); A. Begag, *Ethnicity and Equality: France in the Balance*, trans. and with an introduction by Alec G. Hargreaves (Lincoln: University of Nebraska Press, 2007).

51. J. Marseille, *Empire colonial et capitalisme français: histoire d'un divorce* (Paris: Albin Michel, 1984).

52. Hélène Carrère d'Encausse is a Russian historian and the permanent secretary of the Académie Française, the official arbiter of French language and literature since the reign of Louis XIV. D'Encausse also serves on commissions of the European Union and French government. In attempting to explain the causes of the revolts in 2005 to the Russian press, she was quoted in *Libération* on November 2005 as having said: "These people come directly from their African villages [of course, never urban cities, then]. . . . Why are the African children in the street and not at school? Why can't their parents buy a flat? The reason is obvious: many of these Africans are polygamous. In one flat there are three or four wives and twenty-five children. They are so crammed that they're no longer apartments, but God knows what! You can understand why these children are running about in the street."

53. It is worth reproducing Chirac's words. In 1991, before he became president of the Republic, he described Africans as having "three or four wives and twenty some-odd children, who receive 50,000 francs in public assistance without, of course, working. . . . If you add to that the noise and stench, the French worker living on the same floor becomes crazy." *Le Monde*, October 1, 2009.

Eurafrique as the Future Past of "Black France"

Sarkozy's Temporal Confusion and Senghor's Postwar Vision

GARY WILDER

On July 26, 2007, President Nicolas Sarkozy of France delivered his instantly infamous address at the Université Cheikh Anta Diop in Dakar, Senegal. Remarkable in its display of ignorance and arrogance, this moralizing lecture chastised a primitive and stagnant Africa for choosing stubbornly to remain outside the stream of modern history. After blaming the continent's current problems on cultural backwardness, Sarkozy concluded with an invitation for a new partnership with a reformed Africa. Critics immediately denounced the speech's unreconstructed racial stereotypes and outmoded colonial discourse. And they understandably dismissed his promise of renewed Franco-African cooperation as a facile endorsement of *la françafrique*—the French state's persistent support for authoritarian rulers of neocolonial client regimes in postcolonial Africa.

But rather than only dismiss this speech as racist—which it was and which we should—we may *also* recognize that it unwittingly conjured up an obscured moment in the history of decolonization that warrants our attention. The instant that Sarkozy cynically invoked the name of Léopold Sédar Senghor and referred to *Eurafrique*, he, to use Walter Benjamin's language, allowed a fleeting image of the past to flash up in an instant of recognizability.[1] In the spirit of Ernst Bloch and Reinhart Kosellek, we might say that Senghor's "Eurafrique" may be understood as a "future past" of "Black France": a past vision of a not-yet realized possible future of plural democracy.[2] The "Black France" implied by Senghor's postwar interventions is neither simply one in which overseas Africa is integrated into the existing Republic nor one in which African immigrants are extended equal rights in metropolitan France. This was not a call for the departmentalization of Africa or the assimilation of Africans.[3] Rather it was a vision of multiplicity, reciprocity, and *métissage* whereby France itself, through formal partnership with Francophone Africa, would be transformed into a postnational republic.

Recognizing Senghor's unrealized future past, as well as its relation to the unfolding present, requires us to attend to the untimely character of Sarkozy's speech and to the postwar moment that it cynically but also unwittingly conjured. This chapter will thus be divided into two parts. The first is a close reading of Sarkozy's Dakar discourse about relations between France and Africa as well as critical reactions to it by African intellectuals. The second is a historical discussion of Senghor's postwar vision of Eurafrique as enabling and enabled by a different kind of decolonization whereby colonial emancipation would entail the remaking of France—a form of revolutionary integration, rather than autarchic separation, that would reconstitute its relationship with Black territories, communities, and cultures.

Sarkozy's Allocution

Addressed specifically to "the elite youth of Africa," Sarkozy's moralizing "allocution" about historical responsibility and intergenerational inheritance proffers a series of anachronistic assertions about Africa's inability to embrace the modern world.[4] Sarkozy begins by announcing that although slavery was a crime against humanity and colonialism the source of immense suffering, he has no intention of apologizing for France's past participation in these institutions. However misguided their belief in assimilation may have been, he explains, sincere French colonizers had also introduced Africa to modern civilization.[5] And Africans, he insists, also "bore responsibility for their own unhappiness" by having participated in the slave trade. Claiming to speak frankly, he explains, "I did not come to erase this past because the past cannot be erased. . . . But nobody could ask the generation of today to atone for [*expier*] this crime. . . . Youth of Africa, I did not come to speak to you of repentance."

Sarkozy thus seems to plead for the past to be allowed to pass so that the dead can bury the dead. He also purports to challenge those who would politicize history by freighting facts with moral condemnation. But Sarkozy himself subordinates historical reality to political ideology and attempts to seize the moral high ground by shifting responsibility to Africans themselves for their past and present misfortunes. Their culpability, he argues, derives from the mythical and childlike understanding of time that, in his view, characterizes African culture. In this account, colonialism was regrettable not because of crimes perpetrated but because French "errors" led Africans to return to a regressive worldview and retreat from the modern world: "The drama of Africa is that *l'homme africain* has not sufficiently entered into history. The *paysan africain* . . . only knows the eternal cycle of time according to the rhythm of . . . endless repetition . . . where . . . there is no place for the human adventure, nor for the idea of progress. . . . This man never throws himself toward the future. . . . The challenge for Africa is to stop always repeating, always dwelling, to liberate itself from the myth of eternal return, to realize that the golden age that it never stops missing will never return because it never existed." Sarkozy thus relates African stagnation to a cultural inability to escape a mystical "time of the eternal present" and refusal to enter modern history. At the same time, he blames Africans' supposed failure to progress on their pathological investment in ancient injuries caused by slavery and colonialism. He calls on them to stop dwelling on past suffering and start working for a new future.

Sarkozy thus criticizes what he sees as an African refusal to be historical even as he exhorts Africans to overcome their history. Africans here are guilty of both ignoring history and dwelling on it. According to Sarkozy, they cannot forget (a mythic past) and must forget (a painful past). This dual failure to be properly historical, he suggests, is the source of the violence, poverty, scarcity, and overpopulation that currently afflicts the continent. Here African malaise is figured as a function of primordial culture, melancholy attachments, and mythical thinking. Conversely, Sarkozy calls for an "African Renaissance" that will require Africans to wake up, grow up, and catch up. Doing so will entail a simple attitude adjustment: "The challenge of Africa is to learn to feel itself an heir to all that is universal in all human civilizations." This inheritance, he explains, was the gift of French colonialism which introduced Africans to "world civilization" and "opened African hearts and mentalities to the universal and to history" through a process of cultural "métissage" which "however painful" was a source of "strength" and "luck" for Africa. Identifying with the European cultural heritage that they already possess, according to Sarkozy, will allow for a new Franco-African partnership founded upon "our common [shared] history" (3). He declares, "What France wants to create [make] with Africa is codevelopment. . . . France wants to . . . prepare the arrival [*l'avènement*] of *Eurafrique*, this great common destiny that awaits Europe and Africa . . . the first step in the greater dream of peace and prosperity that Europeans and Africans are capable of conceiving together."[6]

Sounding neither like a formal economic nor political arrangement, the proposed Franco-African partnership seems only to offer moral rather than material support. Sarkozy asserts that "Africa does not want charity, . . . aid, . . . favors. What Africa wants . . . is solidarity, understanding, and respect, . . . cooperation, association, . . . partnership between two nations with equal rights and duties. African youth, you want democracy, you want liberty, you want justice, you want Law? It is up to you to decide. France will not decide for you. But if you choose democracy, liberty, justice, and Law, then France will associate with you to construct them." Yet even these minimal gestures are immediately held in reserve as Sarkozy preemptively scolds Africans for the possibility that they might not be ready to assume full responsibility for their present misfortune and future prospects. If, alternatively, they choose finally to "to look reality in the face," he promises that France and Africa could pursue jointly their common interest in constructing an "other globalization, with more humanity, more justice, more rules." We can imagine that the association proposed under the sign of Eurafrique would resemble Sarkozy's plan for a Mediterranean Union that would function as a neoliberal trading bloc.[7] Or it might simply signal a relationship in which French rulers pretend to arrive from the metropolitan future to deliver precisely this kind of paternalist allocution about African self-help that *itself* denies history, refuses responsibility, and disavows any ongoing financial or ethical responsibilities toward former colonial subjects.

Temporal Confusion

Although Sarkozy's remarks hinge upon the idea that their culture placed Africans outside of historical time, his own discourse is remarkable as a performance of temporal confusion. By repeating ana-chronistic racial stereotypes, colonial discourse, and modernization theory, Sarkozy acts as if France were still a colonial power. With remarkable economy, whether unconsciously or strategically, his dis-course conjures and condenses distinct periods and logics of empire, including nineteenth-century evolutionism, belle époque assimila-tionism, interwar welfarism, developmentalism from after the Second World War, postindependence neocolonialism, and post-Fordist neo-liberalism.

This temporally confused discourse smoothly performs a number of reversals and displacements. What first appears like France ac-knowledging responsibility for its imperial past is in fact a demand that Africa assume full responsibility for its present misfortunes. The French state's refusal to repent for colonial history and its insistence that Africans take charge of their future allows it to disregard France's implication in the existing political and economic arrangements apart from which Africa's current constraints cannot be adequately under-stood. Sarkozy's call to construct an "other globalization" obscures the global processes and pressures that are producing the very problems that the proposal is meant to combat. The speech instructs Africans to confront present realities yet erases the actual conditions that might account for them. It calls for an alternative future yet outlines a neo-colonial partnership that would mark a return to the very colonial past that it instructs Africans to overcome. Sarkozy's gesture of support reveals itself to be a moralizing tautology: the key obstacle to African development is lack of African development; France will help you after you have already succeeded.

African critics, including the Senegalese historian Ibrahima Thioub, the Senegalese writer Boubacar Boris Diop, and the Cameroonian political theorist Achille Mbembe, responded quickly and forcefully to the unreconstructed racial assumptions and imperial assertions guiding Sarkozy's remarks.[8] They all challenged what we might call the untimely character of the Dakar speech, which was delivered as if from another epoch. Contending that the speech "revealed . . . [that] the intellectual armature which subtends France's Africa policy dates literally from the end of the nineteenth century . . . [and] depends on an obsolete intellectual heritage," Mbembe called Sarkozy an "ethno-philosopher president."[9] Diop noted that "perhaps [the president] does not know that his Dakar discourse is much older then he is."[10]

Thioub remarked that Sarkozy's appearance in Senegal specifically recalls de Gaulle's highly publicized visit there in 1958 when he sought (successfully) to mobilize support for the referendum in which Africans would decide whether or not to join La Communauté Française which the new constitution of the Fifth Republic would establish to replace the French Union.[11]

These critics condemn Sarkozy's primitivist speech for distorting history. It erases the well-documented ways in which African societies self-consciously participated in the unfolding of modern world history. It displaces the effects of actual colonial violence onto a childlike African culture. And it fails to appreciate the profound and persistent wounds still felt by African peoples for whom this painful past remains powerfully present. The distortion of history, in other words, is inseparable from a refusal of responsibility and a desecration of memory.[12] Diop, for example, invokes France's own collaboration with the Nazis and condemns Sarkozy's attempt to displace responsibility for the slave trade onto Africans as "an insult to the memory of the victims and a shameful [infâme] relativization of the fundamental violence of the triangular trade."[13]

For these African intellectuals, Sarkozy's shocking insensitivity was not only a function of arrogance but also ignorance. They identify his disavowal of history, displacement of responsibility, and disrespect for memory with a broader political sensibility in France today that also subtends state racism, xenophobic nationalism, and overseas neocolonialism. Mbembe contends that Sarkozy's speech was in fact strategically addressed to right-wing voters in metropolitan France, whose racist assumptions are confirmed, and authoritarian client rulers in postcolonial Africa, who are reassured that the old arrangements will remain in place.[14]

From this perspective, the Dakar speech shared the same political logic as the program initiated by Sarkozy, when minister of the interior, to militantly police the banlieues, including his infamous references to "racaille" and "Kärcher" following the "uprising" there in 2005;[15] his sponsorship of the law of February 23, 2005, requiring public schools to teach French students about the positive aspects of French colonialism;[16] and his incendiary UMP party speech in Agen on June 25, 2006, in which he linked self-help neoliberalism, anti-immigrant nationalism, and the insistence that France owes neither apologies nor debts for its colonial past.[17] Given Sarkozy's direct participation in and identification with these metropolitan racial confrontations and given the incendiary response by young people in the banlieue to his policies and prescriptions, we may wonder to whom Sarkozy is really directing his paternalistic injunctions—to the French-speaking youth of Africa or to the youth of metropolitan France descended from Africa? Sarkozy's temporal confusion seems to have been compounded by a spatial displacement.

According to these African critics, the Dakar speech is consistent with a resurgence of imperial nostalgia, historical revisionism, and refusal of repentance in France today that recasts colonial history as benevolent and African injuries as self-inflicted. It figures so-called immigrant communities as ungrateful and treats sovereign African nations as fields for imperial adventurism.[18] Diop understands Sarkozy's insistence on African culpability as an attempt to divert attention from France's support for perpetrators in Rwanda, Côte d'Ivoire, and Togo.[19] More provocatively, he interprets France's refusal to repent as symptomatic of a "quasi-obsessional relationship with its colonial past" that pathologically inverts the proper ethics of forgiveness.[20] He writes: "if one does not have the strength to repent, one should at least have the decency to keep quiet.... It is the privilege of the victim and not of the torturer [bourreau] to decide if such abominable crimes should or should not be invoked. The constant reaffirmation by [the perpetrator] of his refusal to repent is the sign of a veritable sickness of the soul. A society whose leaders and so many citizens only have this compulsive and contorted [grimaçant] relation of denegation with their past reveals ... the malaise that grips it [le tenaille] and deserves, truthfully, more compassion than hatred."[21] What then would it mean for Africans to stake their future prospects, as Sarkozy asks them to, on a partnership with a society so obsessed and haunted by an un-worked-through history that it is compelled to reenact repeatedly?[22]

These intellectuals are indeed strongly critical of Sarkozy's promise of a new Franco-African association. Thioub questions whether there can be any "rupture" in France's Africa policy as long as the current mistreatment of immigrants and protection of dictators continues. Mbembe dismisses Sarkozy's proposed alliance as "a chimerical Eurafrique" which can only be understood as a barely concealed commitment to the old neocolonial system of la françafrique.[23] He identifies Sarkozy as a "negrophile lesson-giver" whose "will to misunderstand"

and penchant for "invective, . . . exhortation, . . . imprecations, . . . and delcarations" forecloses the kind of dialogue upon which any genuine partnership would have to be founded.[24] "The long Dakar mono-logue," he explains, "does not address us in a face-to-face relation in which we count as interlocutors. . . . When he pretends to dialogue with us, it is not in the framework of a relation of moral equality and, as a result, justice. It is in the register of the will to power."[25]

Mbembe reads the Dakar discourse as a symptom of France's bad faith and growing irrelevance toward Africa: "Today, the intellectual and cultural prism through which the new ruling French elites regard, judge, and administer lessons to Africa is not only obsolete. It allows no room for the relations of friendship that would be a sign of liberty . . . coextensive with relations of justice and respect. For the moment, regarding Africa, France is simply lacking the moral credit that would allow it to speak with certitude and authority."[26] He warns that "if France persists in its autism, that is to say, [a] refusal to understand the world . . . we will no longer listen to it."[27] This lack of moral credibility leads Mbembe to conclude that the Dakar speech was not a genuine "invitation to build a human society, a common language, let alone a common world . . . not an invitation to create together an ex-perience of liberty [*faire ensemble l'expérience de la liberté*]."[28] Mbembe declares that "a half-century after formal decolonization, the younger generations learned not to expect great things from France. . . . Afri-cans will save themselves or they will perish."[29]

Against what he sees as Sarkozy's hollow solicitation of postcolonial partnership, Mbembe counterposes a tradition of "Black thought" that includes W. E. B. Du Bois, C. L. R. James, Frantz Fanon, and Fabien Éboussi Boulaga, which elaborated a "dream of a new human-ism, a world-wide renaissance beyond race, a universal polis in which everyone is granted the right to inherit the entire world in its totality. The Africa for which they call is a living multiplicity which . . . is linked, in its origins, to the future of the universal."[30] Similarly, Thioub conjures a history of African hospitality by provocatively figuring French colonialism as a history of unregulated and uninvited migra-tion between the North and South. He writes, "from Europe migrants arrived in Africa."[31] "Reciprocity," he explains, requires contemporary France to now treat African immigrants to Europe with the same respect "that Africans once treated French colonial migrants.[32] "Mr. President," he writes, "we find it difficult to understand that French

identity, constructed on the dynamism of perpetual métissage—
Saint-Louis du Senegal, the old French city, is the best example—
makes of Francophone immigration its negative."[33] Thioub here
points to the contradiction of a contemporary France supposedly
committed to the project of Francophonie that also demonizes and
dehumanizes Francophone immigrants in France. Such attitudes, he
argues, denies the long historical legacy and reciprocal "migration"
that links France to Africa in profound and persistent ways. French
immigration policy, he thereby suggests, negates precisely the shared
conditions and mutual implication that can serve as the basis for the
partnership that Sarkozy proposed in Dakar. Thioub observes that
"348 years ago France disembarked [here] without asking authoriza-
tion of the indigenous inhabitants. . . . It is not ready to leave. Nor do
we wish for them to leave. On the contrary, we want them to stay but
otherwise than they came and lived until now."[34]

In short, Thioub and Mbembe trace the links between shared colonial history, France's historical responsibility toward Africans, and the
prospect of a transformative partnership between the two peoples and
places. Their visions of an alternative future echo a remarkably prescient statement published in Le Monde on February 13, 2007, before
Sarkozy's election, by representatives of hundreds of organizations
from twenty-one African countries: "Seizing the occasion of the twenty-
fourth Sommet France Afrique, we, organizations of African civil society, launch a solemn appeal to all the candidates in the French presidential election to seize this 'historic opportunity' to construct, on a
basis of truth, justice, legality, and liberty, a new contrat de générations
between France and Africa."[35] It expresses their wish that Chirac's departure will mark the end of the cronyism associated with la françafrique
and help Africa finally recover from "centuries of exploitation."[36]

Refusing to dwell on the past, and unconcerned with either repentance or restitution, this public appeal directs attention to the existing
French policies and practices that contribute to Africa's present economic and political malaise. It denounces France's policy of supporting corrupt and authoritarian "heads of state lacking any legitimacy or
prospective vision," which "has ruined the stock of hope of our populations and confined our peoples in a situation of unprecedented
destitution."[37] Those Africans lucky enough to reach Europe, it explains, "meet with a policy of humiliation: police harassment, intern-
ment zones, deportation flights, . . . dehumanizing living conditions."[38]

The authors of this statement insist that a renewed and "fruitful relation with France is possible" only if it "assumes responsibility for its
past in Africa," ceases to interfere in sovereign African affairs, and
revises its "repressive and selective immigration policies."[39] The appeal then outlines a series of concrete proposals through which France
could aid Africans seeking to take charge of their own development.[40]
This is an appeal for France to overcome its own stasis and immobil-
ity, to wake up and confront its own history, and to take concrete steps
toward constructing a new future in alliance with Africans already
committed to helping themselves.[41] This programmatic intervention
may thus be read as a proleptic response to Sarkozy's imperial mono-
logue, which it anticipates uncannily. Insfoar as it responds to a challenge that had not yet been launched, this ghostly intervention is
another instance of the untimeliness of Sarkozy's allocution.

I have suggested that the Dakar discourse conjures numerous ghosts,
including colonial commandants, ethnophilosophers, Presidents de
Gaulle and Chirac, banlieue youth, metropolitan xenophobes, African
dictators, and even French collaborators during the Occupation.
Among such seemingly absent but powerfully present figures, none
was more spectral than Léopold Sédar Senghor, former president of
Senegal and longtime legislator in the French National Assembly during the Fourth and Fifth Republics. In support of his spurious arguments about colonial history and African culture, Sarkozy cynically
invokes "President Senghor who sought his entire life to reconcile the
heritages and cultures at the crossroads of which the accidents and
tragedies of history had placed Africa." He then cited Senghor on
Africans as "culturally *métis*" and on French as "a language of universal
vocation" that provided Africans with "the gift of its abstract words."[42]

By transforming Senghor into a Francophile apologist for empire
and selectively appropriating rhetoric that had been produced in relation to the promise and perils of decolonization, Sarkozy commits
another act of acute temporal confusion. His speech conjures the
spirit of Senghor for a public performance that he would never have
sanctioned. These African intellectuals were understandably disturbed by this instrumentalization of the Senegalese poet-president.
Thioub reminds us of a more critical Senghor whose poem on the infamous massacre of Senegalese soldiers at Thiaroye he cites regarding
France's refusal to recognize Africans' contribution to the nation's
history: "Is France therefore no longer France?"[43] Diop recuperates a

sensitive and combative Senghor who recognized that the slave trade "continued to weigh both on the present and future [*destin*] of Africa." Indirectly criticizing the current president, Abdoulaye Wade, who had served as Sarkozy's host in Dakar, Diop writes, "whatever one might think about Senghor, it is not certain that he would have allowed a guest of Senegal to say such enormities . . . without delivering [*porter*] one response or another."[44]

Mbembe does not share these qualified endorsements of Senghor. Instead, he offers a critique of Senghorian Négritude as consistent with Sarkozy's portrait of timeless and childlike Africans. Mbembe identifies the "inestimable debt" that in his "concept of Négritude [and] . . . notions of culture, civilization and even cultural blending the Senegalese poet owes [to] the most racist, most essentialist and most biologizing theories of his time."[45] Such ideas, he explains, have been definitively refuted by African critics. Also challenging what he regards as Senghor's neocolonial complicity, Mbembe observes that "Senghor was content, throughout his career, to pursue French policies in Africa [*de faire la politique de la France en Afrique*]."[46] He contends that Senghor's ideas about "the Black soul" and "African authenticity" have served as, "above all, means for corrupt regimes and their political and intellectual elites to valorize difference in the hopes of legitimizing their brutality and their venality."[47] Mbembe proposes "the concept of 'Afropolitanisme' as an antidote to Négritude nativism."[48]

Mbembe rightly recognizes aspects of Senghorian discourse in certain of Sarkozy's primitivist generalizations about African culture.[49] But the spirit of Senghor is also present in the French president's remarks about civilizational métissage, historical reconciliation, and the imperative for a "Eurafrican" partnership. Mbembe certainly has reason to suspect the motives behind Sarkozy's proposal to create a new Eurafrique as well as France's capacity to realize such a plan honestly and equitably. But Senghor's postwar vision of an alternative Franco-African future also anticipates Mbembe's own calls for Black humanism and Afropolitanisme as well as Thioub's calls for reciprocity and hospitality.

If Sarkozy's unacceptable imperial address appropriated Senghorian language, our African critics also condemned it in language that was itself inherited from Senghor's postwar writings. Sarkozy's invocation of Eurafrique was an act of temporal confusion. However unwittingly,

he conjured the ghosts of decolonization by calling forth past struggles whose not-yet realized possibilities for "Black France" are con-
densed in that long-discredited idea of which Thioub and Mbembe
are also unwitting heirs.

The Specter of "Black France"

"Black France" here is a polysemic term. On one level, it refers to the
(history of) relations between continental France and overseas territories and populations in Africa and the Antilles. On another, it refers
to the presence of peoples of African descent within French society,
whether as migrant laborers, colonial students, imperial citizens, expatriates, or foreign immigrants (from French colonies, non-French
colonies, or the United States). In both of these cases "Black France"
implies the specter of empire, the long-term imperial history that
shaped relations between France and various Black communities and
that accounts for their promiscuous presence within and profound
influence on the French nation. "Black France" thus also indexes histories of imperial hybridity and processes of cultural métissage.

From this line of thought, an imperial optic allows us to recognize
yet a deeper and more radical meaning of "Black France"—not only a
home for Blacks, but a Black homeland; not only a nation influenced
by Black populations and cultures, but, in some real way, an irreducibly Black nation; not simply a national state that possessed African
and Antillean colonies, but an imperial nation-state constituted in part
by African and Antillean components. If we take empire as our analytic
and historical starting point, France itself is irreducibly Afro-French,
Franco-African, Eurafrican. From this perspective, Eurafrique is not
only either an artifact of a superseded colonial era or a cynical ideological fiction meant to mask the crude reality of ongoing neocolonialism.
It is also a spectral figure that discloses a deeper and occluded truth
about (the future past of) imperial France and (the past present of)
France as postcolony. If "Black France" implies the specter of empire,
the fact of empire also implies the specter of "Black France."

It is not difficult to understand why Sarkozy would want to appropriate Senghor's postwar rhetoric about Eurafrican partnership. Nor is
it surprising that in France today this anachronistic invocation of late-
colonial debates about postimperial reconciliation would confirm, or

even fuel, currents of colonial nostalgia and the attendant refusal to repent for colonial crimes. It therefore makes perfect sense that African and French critics of Sarkozy's ongoing commitment to neocolonialism abroad (in the form of la françafrique) and anti-immigrant xenophobia at home would reject as empty or even insidious his rhetoric about African Renaissance, Franco-African partnership, and Eurafrican interdependence. But should we allow Sarkozy's cynical resurrection of Eurafrique to override and subsume Senghor's past vision of an alternative Franco-African future?

Rather than use Sarkozy to dismiss Senghor, we can treat the spectral return of Eurafrique as an opportunity to revisit Senghor and ask new questions about what was opened and foreclosed in the postwar period. Such a task warrants the attention of all of us concerned with the actual and possible contours of "Black France," whether we want to untangle the political unconscious of postcolonial discourse there today, to understand adequately the postwar history that Sarkozy is attempting to instrumentalize, or to explore how Senghor's untimely vision of decolonization without state sovereignty might speak directly to any number of political and philosophical challenges that haunt our postnational present, especially in France. If we are interested in the radical implications of an idea of "Black France" as signaling some deeper truth about France itself (as imperial, plural, multicultural), we need to listen closely to someone like Senghor rather than, as Sarkozy has done, instrumentalize his past statements to make political points today. Senghor, after all, hoped to fashion a postcolonial *and* postnational democracy founded on the long-term history of interpenetration and interdependence that has been the cause and consequence of "Black France." The task of tacking back and forth between the late colonial past and the postcolonial present is especially challenging precisely because of how incredibly fine the line is that separates Eurafrique from la françafrique, partnership from empire, interdependence from domination, emancipatory from reactionary programs for Eurafrica.

Eurafrique

The discourse of Eurafrique that circulated throughout imperial France in the early 1950s emerged in relation to debates over the

creation of a new European economic community.[50] Among the proponents of a European "third force" that could counterbalance the
international power of the Soviets and the United States were those in
France who insisted that any European community would have to
include the whole French Union. They argued that France could only
enter a new European federation if it was treated as an entity that
encompassed its overseas territories. Eurafrique was one name given
to this entity. Proponents of this new formation thus included defenders of a now-threatened French Empire, whether representatives
of commercial and settler interests or liberal reformists who believed
that the imperial project could be salvaged.[51]

But advocates of Eurafrique also included the African deputies associated with the Indépendents d'Outre Mer (IOM) bloc in the National Assembly. This coalition of independent overseas legislators,
engaged in constitutional struggles to democratize the French Union,
was anxious about the future economic consequences for Africans of
a European community from which their territories would be excluded.[52] Playing on metropolitan fears about national decline in an
era of decolonization, these African deputies developed a realist argument that Franco-African geopolitical and socio-economic solidarity
would ensure French supremacy in a European Union. But they insisted that Africans would only consent to such an arrangement if the
Union could guarantee democracy and development overseas. As a
deputy from Senegal in the National Assembly, Senghor served as
president of the IOM group and became an eloquent spokesperson for
Eurafrique. He seized the concept from metropolitan imperialists and
incorporated it into a critique of the actually existing French Union.
He also elevated the concept above where it began, as the idea among
IOM deputies of a purely defensive and pragmatic arrangement between vulnerable Africans and a declining France.[53]

In the legislative debate following the Schuman Declaration of 1950,
Senghor, speaking on behalf of the IOM group, announced to metropolitan legislators that overseas deputies would support France joining a European community as long as it did so in the form of a "[Eura-
frique] founded upon the association and equal development of two
complementary continents."[54] Senghor reiterated this concern following the Treaty Establishing the European Coal and Steel Community.
Addressing the Assembly in January 1952, he pointed out that a "Eurafrican France with eighty-eight million inhabitants will play its role

as guide and leader [*animatrice*] of the European Union."[55] And, he warned, this "Eurafrique cannot be created without the consent of Africans," who "will not lend their support to a union in which the overseas countries are a means and not an ends, where political and social democracy would have as its border the Mediterranean."[56]

For Senghor this was not a matter of respectful consultation, but one of legal obligation. He reminded his colleagues that under the constitution of the Fourth Republic, "France" legally included the overseas territories. This meant, he explained, that "by "Europe" we understand, generally, the states of the West and their African possessions." In this provocative and expansive formulation, based on constitutional law, Senghor invited his fellow parliamentarians to understand the European Union as a medium through which "to realize Eurafrique" and Eurafrique as a medium through which the European Union could be realized.[57] And such a realization, we can see, presupposes and produces a radically different "France," one that links overseas and metropolitan peoples within a nonimperial democracy. This new entity, he contended, would not only guarantee Africans "the democratic management of [their] affairs" but would also extend to them the benefit of "national solidarity" in "the social and economic domain."[58] This proposed deal—French supremacy in a new Europe in exchange for democracy and development in French Africa—did not only outline a pragmatic alliance. As envisioned by Senghor, it also indexed a new social contract, political compact, and cultural configuration through which metropolitan and overseas territories would be integrated within a novel postcolonial state on the bases of equality *and* autonomy, shared development and cultural complementarity. This was a vision of France as constitutionally (in the legal and cultural senses) "Black."

Senghor elaborated on these ideas more fully in an important essay published in 1955, "Europe and Africa: Two Complementary Worlds," where his earlier cultural concerns of the 1930s join his postwar interest in imagining political forms that might correspond to a new world order after empire.[59] Here too we find precisely the kind of Senghorian images and ideas that, in a very different epoch, Sarkozy will appropriate. In it, Senghor contends that "Eurafrique . . . can only be a marriage in which each of the partners contributes its share and its qualities—a transaction, to put it crudely. . . . [T]here is no privileged continent. Each has its grandeur and its misery, each developed a singular trait of the human condition." No longer referring either to an instrumental alliance or to an integrated juridical and political entity, Senghor expansively identifies Eurafrique as a "cultural force prepared for peace" that would exist "between the two antagonistic [Cold War] blocs, who only believe in violence."[60]

This transcendent potential, for Senghor, derives from Eurafrique's ability to unite complementary cultural orientations, each of which he attempts to specify. He explains that "the spirit of Negro-African civilization" has long endowed Africans with the "gift" of "wisdom, which is the art of living."[61] This existential joy in being flows from a "civilization of unity in which everything is linked to everything and to oneself" such that the human person lives in a state of "harmonious plenitude" and the collectivity forms a life-affirming democratic community organized around public deliberation and popular consent. In Senghor's mythic account, this communal and democratic "wisdom" subtends African religion, epistemology, and aesthetics, all of which are interconnected within a holistical vision (and experience) of human existence. Here Senghor implies that Black-African civilization is integrated and reconciled while modern Europe has been deformed by processes of alienation associated with modern capitalism, individualism, and scientific and technical rationality: "If the goal of politics is indeed to make it so that the greatest number of people, if not all people, are happy, because living a life of harmonious plenitude, it seems, first of all, that Africa has nothing to ask of Europe."[62] On the contrary, Senghor explains, Africa must defend itself against Europe's destructive economic and cultural impact. "By propagating . . . its rationalist, scientistic, materialist, and atheist civilization, its capitalist civilization, Europe disorganized . . . Negro-African civilization by drying up [its] very sources."[63] Senghor calls, therefore, for a return to the vital sources of African culture in order to reanimate values and capacities through which a disalienated form of modern life and a politics of human plenitude could be pursued.

This is the perspective from which we need to understand Senghor's discussion of ostensible differences between what he identifies, on the one hand, as Europe's rational, progressive, and development-oriented outlook and, on the other, as African stagnation, repugnance to progress, and indifference to change.[64] We might well judge as misguided his decision to borrow language from the primitivist discourse of midcentury colonial ethnology and administration. But we need also to appreciate the broader critical strategy in the service of which he does so.

On a practical level, these invidious distinctions allow Senghor to argue that metropolitan France must pursue a forward-looking socio-economic development policy overseas to raise peoples' standards of living. More generally, these negative evaluations of traditional Africa serve a deeper critique of European colonialism and civilization which, Senghor argues, had reduced human imagination to automatism, collective organization to statism, and life to routine.[65] The "most spectacular" inventions of European "discursive reason," he explains, are, "today, in the process of destroying the very existence of men. . . . [F]ar from combating our true problems [maux], which are the egoisms of class, nation, race, or continent, European reason has made itself their docile servant. If it helped Europe to transform the world and . . . its material life, it has not transformed its true life [sa vie véritable], that is to say, its moral life. This, rather, depends [ressortit] not on formal reason, on rational reason, but on analogic reason, which is sympathetic intuition."[66] He therefore asks Europeans to no longer "impose their religious faith" on Africa, by which he means not Christianity but an atheism, a "faith which rests on progress and money."[67] Senghor calls for a return to the vital sources of African culture not to travel back in time or to avoid history, but to reanimate values and capacities through which a less alienated and more human form of modern life could be fashioned.

On the basis of such criticism, Senghor is then able to reframe and revalue the supposed distinctions between European and African civilization as a contrast between, on the one hand, a "centripetal" instrumental reason that serves material power by distancing and "dismantling" the object of knowledge and, on the other, a "centrifugal" intuitive reason that equates knowledge with the plenitude of being through a loving and aesthetic identification with an object that it approaches. What may at first seem to be a distinction between rational Europe and irrational Africa reveals itself as a distinction between two types or aspects of reason—as a distinction within reason itself.[68]

Senghor's decision to criticize modern instrumental reason from the standpoint of a quasi-ontological Africanity may be analytically and politically problematic. But we should also appreciate that Senghor's argument is more nuanced than it may have first appeared to be. Rather than simply contrasting African stasis and backwardness to European historicity and progress, he establishes a link between European modernization and modern social misery. Rather than contrasting an emancipatory European rationalism to an oppressive African superstition, he identifies an underlying relation between European technical and scientific rationality, on the one hand, and modern systems of oppression, on the other. Rather than contrast African poverty with European comfort, he contrasts superficial material well-being to a more profound sense of human fulfillment. Rather than contrasting "Europeans as rational" to "Africans as emotional," he makes a distinction between two types or aspects of reason: the superficial, degraded, and instrumental discursive or analytic reason most fully developed in Europe and a vital, holistic, and empathetic intuitive or analogical reason developed in Africa—both of which are legitimate means of confronting, apprehending, and knowing the world.

Senghor, in short, implies that the antinomies around which modern life in *both* Europe *and* Africa are organized and impoverished will only be transcended through a holistic vision of the human being that combines *instrumental* (analytic, discursive, technical) reason with *intuitive* (analogical, sympathetic, aesthetic) reason. He contends that when "reunited in the same person, [these complementary civilizations allow] for the realization of the whole human condition."[69]

Senghor accords special status to aesthetics in this process of cultural integration and reconciliation, a status that anticipates and conjures a historical epoch that does not yet exist. He writes: "the art object, by its very reality, creates a new world, that of tomorrow. It is thus that a new Africa is being created in the heart and spirit of our writers who, because rooted in the reality of the present, already project its roots, full of sap, into the air of the future. This world will no longer be wholly African, nor will it be only Europe; it will be a *métis* world" that "reunites complementary virtues in a dynamic symbiosis."[70] Senghor regards Eurafrique as both the source and product of this dialectic of métissage and aesthetic transcendence. He writes: "What Africa expects from Europe is . . . to illuminate its intuition by the light of reason, to guide the impulses of its heart, to realize its projects. But, to be effective, this European action requires total disinterestedness, the repudiation of economic colonialism and cultural imperialism. It also requires a certain humility on the part of Europe. It must understand that if it has a lot to give, it has no less to receive.

Only thus will this Eurafrique be realized which we call for . . . and which must be the cornerstone of civilization."

Eurafrique thus indexes a process of reciprocal exchange through which, on the one hand, European and African civilizations could each more fully realize their singularity and, on the other hand, an entirely new Franco-African civilization could be created. Each case would also contribute to the formation of what Senghor would later call "the civilization of the universal."[71] Through a process of perpetual borrowing, internalization, and adjustment, Africans and Europeans could be reconciled and redeemed in the service of the overarching aim of human self-realization on a planetary scale.

For Senghor in the mid-1950s, Eurafrique signaled cultural reciprocity, socio-economic interdependence, and political partnership—as *both* a reality *and* a possibility. On one level, the concept functioned as a description of the shared imperial history that already had bound France and Africa together within an integrated entity (the imperial nation-state). At the same time, Eurafrique also referred to a prospective vision of what imperial France might one day create and become.

For Senghor, Eurafrique never simply figured a pragmatic partnership between (a vulnerable) Africa and (a declining) France. Rather, it transfigured "France" itself into something legally plural, multicultural, and supranational. Through this concept, Senghor challenged the reification of Africa and France as entities supposedly standing in an external relation to one another. His task was to fashion a political form that could build upon this history of imperial interdependence *and* end colonialism, without retreating into what he regarded as the territorialist trap of "national autarchy," which he argued was an outmoded and inadequate framework for postcolonial democracy and development.[72]

Federalism and the "Black France" That Might Have Been

Senghor's vision of Eurafrique was the cultural counterpart of his constitutional project during the postwar period to transform imperial France into a postcolonial federation that would include overseas territories as freely consenting member states. Under such an arrangement, formerly colonized peoples would enjoy political autonomy, legal equality with metropolitan France, full citizenship in the federal republic, and the material benefits of socio-economic solidarity with the Fordist welfare state (including unfettered mobility to the métropole, the right to work there, social protections and entitlements, investment funds, and development initiatives). Eurafrique signaled the socio-cultural substrate upon which this postcolonial federation could be built as well as the novel socio-cultural entity that could emerge from such a federalist framework.

Between 1946 and 1958, Senghor waged a constitutional struggle to reconstitute France as a decentralized federal democracy characterized by disaggregated sovereignty, legal pluralism, and cultural multiplicity. This attempt to overcome colonialism *and* transcend the unitary republic was based on a cosmopolitan commitment to decolonization without national independence. Through an immanent critique of the actually existing French Union, he insisted that late imperialism had created the political conditions and institutional infrastructure for a radically different postcolonial republic through which Africans could pursue political emancipation while evading what he called the "poison gift" of formal independence. To use Marxian language, Senghor recognized empire as federation in a still alienated form. His project was at once concrete and utopian, instrumental and ethical, gradualist and revolutionary, realist and visionary, timely and untimely. It linked gestures to emancipate futures past not yet realized with attempts to anticipate futures yet to come.

It is beyond the scope of this chapter to elaborate Senghor's federalist program in detail, but it is inextricable from his formulation of Eurafrique, both of which were elements of a nonnational approach to the postwar "problem of freedom" that confronted colonized peoples on the eve of decolonization, the emancipatory possibilities of which were partly foreclosed precisely by the territorialist form of decolonization that was actually instituted.[73] My point here is that Sarkozy's cynical attempt to present paternalism as partnership by instrumentally invoking Senghor must be examined in relation to that postwar context in a way that also grasps the transformative possibilities that were crystallized in Senghor's utopian vision of Eurafrique.

Despite the idea's entanglement with instrumental calculations regarding the (nascent) European Union and ideological justifications for the (imperial) French Union, the Eurafrique that might have been should not be conflated with la françafrique that came to be, however infinitesimal the distance between them might appear to us now. But that crucial gap will remain obscure as long as we continue to regard Senghor's postwar political initiatives from the standpoint of an entrenched logic of decolonization that presumptively equates colonial emancipation with national liberation. Senghor in the 1950s did not settle for an alternative *to* decolonization (as scholars often argue); he pursued an alternative form *of* decolonization.

I am not suggesting that there is anything to recuperate in Sarkozy's Dakar discourse, nor that Senghor's postwar vision for postcolonial federation could be mechanically resurrected in our own historical epoch. The point, rather, is to indicate that the history of what might have been—a legally grounded, politically constituted, and culturally plural "Black France"—could ground a critical history of the present that may also provide a glimpse of a possible future.

Senghor hoped to avoid the pitfalls of what he called "nominal independence"—which he rightly believed would entail a painful process of expropriation and denationalization—by inventing a legal framework that would protect overseas peoples' material, political, and moral claims on a French society and state that they themselves helped to create and that they were already an integral part of.[74] He therefore envisioned a political form that could reconcile republican universality and cultural multiplicity, as well as popular sovereignty and legal plurality. Such an arrangement would also help to mediate local autonomy and transnational solidarity, democratic self-determination and planetary reconciliation. Imagine a postcolonial France and global order in which African migrant laborers in Europe were no longer foreigners but citizens whose rights of mobility, family reunification, participation in national politics, and social security were constitutionally protected, an order in which Africans would not have to appeal as outsiders for economic aid from a foreign French state, one in which West African nations were already founding members of an expanded European Union, and one in which violations of Africans' human rights could be adjudicated in a federal justice system.

Senghor anticipated the predicament that the African denizens of postcolonial France now experience. He also foresaw the postnational constellation (to use Habermas's term) that we now inhabit. We too live at a world-historical turning point. The limitations of national autarchy for postcolonial states have become manifest. The challenge of converting formal liberty into substantive freedom for their peoples is imperative. Yet the options for a partnership between North and

South seem to be restricted either to the neocolonial patron-client relation of la françafrique or to the neoliberal market imperialism of regional free trade zones.

But, as in the 1940s, innovative responses to the kinds of challenges posed by immigrants rights, French Islam, and European Union membership have, in various ways, attempted to move beyond unitary republicanism, whether through attempts to unbundle and redistribute the traditional package of citizenship rights, to dissociate citizenship from nationality and ethnicity, or to create constitutional orders that might accommodate cultural pluralism, regional autonomy, and rights of hospitality. Proposals for postnational democracy and transnational citizenship seek to envision political forms located between an outmoded national state and an implausible global state, forms through which the perennial "democracy deficit" of globalization could be confronted, and through which the persistent antinomy between national rights and human rights could be overcome. The hope is to find a constitutional framework that could link the kind of democratic participation and socio-economic solidarity enabled by citizenship in a determinate political community with planetary commitments to a world constitution, cosmopolitan democracy, and a global public sphere. Traversing such proposals (among scholars, activists, and international lawyers) is the spirit of federalism, which reappears sixty years after it flashed up in that postwar opening between, as Hannah Arendt might say, the "no-longer" of late colonialism and the "not-yet" of the Cold War order.

Now that territorial sovereignty no longer presents itself as the necessary telos of human freedom, the radical, cosmopolitan, and utopian dimensions of Senghor's program for decolonization without national independence may become newly legible to us. His refusal to reduce self-determination to national independence reminds us that political emancipation requires not merely the mechanical implementation of territorial sovereignty but an experimental program that links immanent critique, concrete acts, and political imagination. His insights and interventions—as a legislator, party leader, public intellectual, philosopher, and poet—demonstrate that we cannot know a priori the political framework through which a given people might best pursue human emancipation.

As we seek today to invent new forms of postnational democracy or plural republicanism that would correspond adequately to the realities of "la France Noire," Senghor's strategic utopian legacy remains available now to us here. His untimely visions of Eurafrique and postcolonial federalism can inform our task of crafting the future present in ways that would explode precisely the kind of racial paternalism and autarchic nationalism expressed in Sarkozy's provincial and outmoded assumptions that France may continue to act as if it were an imperial state and dominant world power, as if it could be interested, without being implicated, in African affairs. (For all his talk about common history and intimate association, Sarkozy insists on the kind of external relationship between metropolitan France and Francophone West Africa that Senghor consistently refused, and that his formulations of federalism, Eurafrique, and universal civilization were meant to contest.) But an outmoded and discredited vision like Senghor's can only inform our historical present if we are able to recognize the image of that evanescent future past of "la France Noire" when it flashes before us, however unexpectedly, as during that untimely performance of temporal confusion in Dakar in 2007.

Notes

1. W. Benjamin, *The Arcades Project*, ed. Rolf Tiedemann, trans. H. Eiland and K. McLaughlin (Cambridge, Mass.: Belknap, 1999), 462–63; W. Benjamin, "Theses on the Philosophy of History, in *Illuminations* (New York: Schocken, 1969), 261, 262, 264.

2. E. Bloch, *The Principle of Hope* (Oxford: Basil Blackwell, 1986); R. Kosellek, *Futures Past: On the Semantics of Historical Time* (New York: Columbia University Press, 2004). For more recent work, see D. Scott, *Conscripts of Modernity: The Tragedy of Colonial Enlightenment* (Durham: Duke University Press, 2004); G. Wilder, "Untimely Vision: Aimé Césaire, Decolonization, Utopia," *Public Culture* 21, no. 1 (2009): 101–40.

3. On the "strategic utopian" resonances between Senghor's transformative vision of Eurafrique and Césaire's untimely vision of departmentalization as a form of nonnational colonial emancipation, see Wilder, "Untimely Vision," as well as N. Nesbitt, "Decolonization and the Logic of Departmentalization," *L'esprit créateur* 47, no. 1 (2007): 32–43.

4. "Allocution de M. Nicolas Sarkozy, Président de la République, prononcée à l'Université de Dakar" (www.elysee.fr), which is available on the

president's official government web site (http://www.elysee.fr/president/accueil.1.html). The speech was actually composed by Sarkozy's aide Henri Guiano, a former Chirac speechwriter. In the following discussion, however, I will refer to Sarkozy as if he were the author.

5. Sarkozy sponsored the law of February 23, 2005, one article of which required public schools to teach students about the positive aspects of French colonialism overseas: Loi n° 2005-158 du 23 février 2005 portant reconnaissance de la Nation et contribution nationale en faveur des Français rapatriés (http://www.assemblee-nationale.fr/12/projets/pl1499.asp). The text of the law is available on the web site of the Assemblée nationale (http://www.assemblee-nationale.fr).

6. "Allocution de M. Nicolas Sarkozy," 13, 9–10, 3, 18–19.

7. On Sarkozy's initiative to create a Mediterranean Union trading bloc, see "Comment construire l'Union méditerranéenne?," Renaud Muselier, Jean-Claude Guibal, Assemblée nationale, Commission des affaires étrangères, Documents d'information de l'Assemblée nationale n° 449, Assemblée nationale: 5 décembre 2007; Déclaration commune du sommet de Paris pour la Méditerranée, Paris, 13 juillet 2008, Conseil de l'Union Européenne, Bruxelles, le 15 juillet 2008 11887/08 (Presse 213).

8. Ibrahima Thioub, "À Monsieur Nicolas Sarkozy, Président de la République française," August 9, 2007, http://www.africultures.com/php; Boubacar Boris Diop, "Le discours inacceptable de Nicolas Sarkozy," August 13, 2007, http://www.rewmi.com; Achille Mbembe, "L'Afrique de Nicolas Sarkozy," Le Messager, August 1, 2007; Mbembe, "France-Afrique: ces sottises qui divisent," Le Messager, August 10, 2007. See also M. Gassama, ed., L'Afrique répond à Sarkozy: contre le discours de Dakar (Paris: Philippe Rey, 2008).

9. Mbembe, "L'Afrique de Nicolas Sarkozy." This is a reference to a tradition of primitivist scholarship on Africa that Mbembe identifies with Hegel, Lucien Lévy-Bruhl, Léo Frobenius, Placide Tempels, Pierre Teilhard de Chardin, Maurice Delafosse, and Robert Delavignette. On this tradition of colonial ethnology, see E. Sibeud, "La naissance de l'ethnographie africaniste en France avant 1914," Cahiers d'études africaines 34, no 136: 639–58; G. Wilder, The French Imperial Nation-State: Negritude and Colonial Humanism between the Two World Wars (Chicago: University of Chicago Press, 2005).

10. Diop, "Le discours inacceptable de Nicolas Sarkozy," 2. Diop suggested the "degrading popular, folkloric welcome" granted to Sarkozy created "an atmosphere recalling that of the [colonial] commandants" during which "he pronounced a sort of State of the Union . . . for France without our even being able to remind him that he was mistaken about the epoch [de s'être trompé d'époque]" (1, 2).

11. De Gaulle's visit in 1958 was itself marked by spatio-temporal confusion

insofar as his appeal to Africans to join the new French community must be understood in relation to, as refracted through, and as a displacement of his failure to persuade Algerians fighting for national liberation that their future interests would best be served in a French-led Eurafrique.

12. For a further critique of Sarkozy's attempt to shift responsibility for the slave trade onto African collaborators, see also J. L. Rharimanana, Boris Boubacar Diop, Abderrahman Beggar, Patrice Nganang, Koulsy Lamko, Kangni Alem, and Jutta Hepke, "Lettre Ouverte à Nicolas Sarkozy," August 19, 2007, http://kinoks.org, which Diop signed. This open letter challenges Sarkozy's claim that Africans have not entered world history by reminding him that Africa was at the center of world-historical developments, such as slavery and colonialism as well as acts and movements to resist slavery and colonialism that shaped the course of modern history. The letter also challenges Sarkozy's claim to be ready to support Africans seeking liberty, justice, and law by mentioning that he left Dakar to meet with Omar Bongo, one of France's most corrupt client-leaders in Africa.

13. Diop, "Le discours inacceptable de Nicolas Sarkozy," 2. Diop wonders "how we have arrived at a situation in which a European leader could allow himself to publicly make such remarks about the slave trade at the very scene of the crime." Criticizing Sarkozy's revisionist attempt to distinguish between good and bad colonizers, Diop asks, "Would he allow a German to apply the same grid to the reading of his country's history? . . . We await the day when, instead of reflecting on a system of foreign domination that, by its very nature is violent and illegitimate, someone will have the audacity to separate the Nazis of good will from the others." And Thioub provocatively asks the reader to "imagine the unimaginable for every French person: the Bundestag votes for a law requiring German historians to conduct research on the positive aspects of the occupation of France by the Nazi regime. . . . Can we understand that the African memory of the Atlantic slave trade and of colonization is, for Africa . . . of the same order as the memory of the occupation is for France?" Thioub, "À Monsieur Nicolas Sarkozy."

14. "It pretends to address the African elite. In reality, it continually winks at the most dubious [obscuritantiste] fringe of the French electorate—the extreme-right, les colo-nostaligiques, those who, suffering from postcolonial melancholy, think that four or five million immigrants and French citizens of Black and Arab origin in a country of more than fifty-five million souls threatens French identity." Mbembe, "France-Afrique: ces sottises qui divisent." "Of course [certes], le cartel des satrapes [from Omar Bongo, Paul Biya, and Sassou Nguesso to Idris Debay, Eyadema fils, and the others] congratulate themselves on what clearly appears to be a decision to continue in the management of 'Françafrique'—the system of reciprocal corruption

that, since the end of the colonial occupation, links France to its African *affidés*." Mbembe, "L'Afrique de Nicolas Sarkozy," See also F.-X.Verschave, *La Françafrique: le plus long scandale de la république* (Paris: Stock, 1998).

15. "Racaille" (scum) is the term Sarkozy famously used to refer to the young urban rioters in the housing projects in November 2005. "Kärcher" is the name of the German company that makes high-pressure water hoses used for street cleaning. Sarkozy promised to clean up the streets "Kärcher-style." Both remarks were understood as racial epithets, part of a xenophobic anti-immigrant discourse that revealed his contempt for racialized populations in France whom he consistently attempted to transform into unwanted and unwelcome foreigners and immigrants. On the riots in 2005, see P. Silverstein and C. Tetreault, "Urban Violence in France," *Middle East Report Online*, 2005, http://www.merip.org/mero/interventions/silverstein_tetreault_interv.htm; A. Mbembe, "La France peut-elle réinventer son identité?," *Le Messager*, November 15, 2005; E. Balibar, "Uprisings in the Banlieue," *Constellations* 14, no. 1 (2007): 47–71; and the essays collected at the web site of the Social Science Research Council (http://riotsfrance.ssrc.org).

16. Thioub, "L'Afrique de Nicolas Sarkozy."

17. Diop, "Le discours inacceptable de Nicolas Sarkozy," 4. For the full speech, see "Discours: réunion publique Agen, 22 juin 2006," Nicolas Sarkozy, Président de l'Union pour un Mouvement Populaire, website of Un Mouvement Populaire (http://www.u-m-p.org). Diop quotes the following crucial passage from Sarkozy's Agen speech: "those who have deliberately chosen to live off the labor of others, those who think that everything is due to them without them owing anything to anyone, those who want everything right away without doing anything, those who, instead of struggling to earn a living [*se donner du mal pour gagner leur vie*], prefer to leak in the folds of history for an imaginary debt that France would have contracted with them and that, in their eyes, it has not yet settled, those who prefer to inflame the one-upmanship [*surenchère*] of memories, to demand [*exiger*] a compensation that nobody could give them, rather than seek to integrate themselves through effort and work, those who do not love France, those who demand everything from it without wanting to give it anything, I tell them that they are not obligated to remain on the national territory." Quoted in Diop, "Le discours inacceptable de Nicolas Sarkozy."

18. Mbembe denounces the rise of conservative "colo-nostalgiques" in France (in "France-Afrique: ces sottises qui divisent") and relates this repugnant revisionism to a broader "refusal of repentance" and "politics of unlimited irresponsibility" regarding France's colonial history and Africa's current maladies. Mbembe, "L'Afrique de Nicolas Sarkozy." Mbembe cites Pascal Bruckner, Alain Finkielkraut, and Daniel Lefeuvre as emblematic of this revisionist impulse. Diop condemns an "ambient negrophobia."

19. Diop, "Le discours inacceptable de Nicolas Sarkozy," 2, 3. On colonial revisionism, see also B. B. Diop, F.-X. Verschave, and O. Tobner-Biyidi, *Négrophobie* (Paris: Arènes, 2005), which was a critical response to S. Smith, *Négrologie: pourquoi l'Afrique meurt* (Paris: Calmann-Levy, 2003). Thioub writes, "No one could in good faith contest that a number of these regimes that followed independence were made and unmade, whether secretly by French secret services or overtly by military interventions bringing à bout de bras authoritarian regimes or crushing states whose great error was to have wanted a little bit more dignity for Africa and Africans." Thioub, "À Monsieur Nicolas Sarkozy." Diop argues that Sarkozy's refusal to address the singularity of the Rwandan genocide, his attempt to "seed confusion about this painful subject," was meant precisely to divert attention from France's recent implication in and responsibility for tragic African violence and to keep anyone from "opening Pandora's box of the bloody adventures [*dérives*] of la françafrique." As Diop notes, "curiously more concerned with evoking our most distant past than the present, the orator protected himself from the slightest allusion to la françafrique," even though Sarkozy was surely perfectly aware that since "the facade of independence" in the 1960s, "Paris has continued, between coups d'État, support for dictatorial regimes, and total control of economic levers and ruling personnel, to make the law in its former colonies." Beginning with de Gaulle, and his successors on the right and left, this "pillage of the continent" has operated through clandestine networks and secret services, military interventions, targeted assassinations of political figures, the Elf oil company, and powerful financial groups. Diop contends that despite "the putrefaction" of the Françafrique relation, its powerful supporters have prevented Sarkozy from lucidly facing contemporary realities and trying to reform the system. "His notable silence on la françafrique clearly shows that he does not intend to perform a rupture" with France's illegitimate clients in Africa, including Idriss Deby (Chad), Sassou Nguesso (Republic of the Congo), and Omar Bongo (Gabon). Diop, "Le discours inacceptable de Nicolas Sarkozy," 2–3. Diop reflects at greater length on France and Rwanda in B. B. Diop, *L'Afrique au-delà du miroir* (Paris: Philippe Rey, 2007). On France's implication in the genocide, see F.-X. Verschave, *Complicité de génocide? La politique de la France au Rwanda* (Paris: La Découverte, 1994); J.-P. Gouteux, *Un génocide secret d'état: la France et le Rwanda, 1990–1997* (Paris: Éditions Sociales, 1998); A. Wallis, *Silent Accomplice: The Untold Story of France's Role in the Rwandan Genocide* (London: I. B. Tauris, 2006); and D. Kroslak, *France's Role in the Rwandan Genocide* (London: Hurst, 2007).

20. Diop, "Le discours inacceptable de Nicolas Sarkozy," 3. In acts like the "negationist laws" of 2005 concerning the positive aspects of colonialism, he argues, France's political classes have made "repentance a state affair of exceptional importance."

21. Diop, "Le discours inacceptable de Nicolas Sarkozy," 3. Cf. Emanuel Levinas and Jacques Derrida on the ethics of forgiveness.

22. This obsessive relationship to a past that will not pass is similar and likely related to the "Vichy Syndrome," which also operates through instances of temporal refraction whereby people act as if they are in a different historical epoch. See H. Rousso, *The Vichy Syndrome: History and Memory in France Since 1944* (Cambridge: Harvard University Press, 1987); *The Haunting Past: History, Memory, and Justice in Contemporary France* (Philadelphia: University of Pennsylvania Press, 2002). On acting out and working through in relation to trauma, see S. Freud, *Standard Edition of the Complete Psychological Works of Sigmund Freud*, vol. 14, *Mourning and Melancholia* (London: Hogarth, 1957); D. LaCapra, *Writing History, Writing Trauma* (Baltimore: Johns Hopkins University Press, 2001).

23. Mbembe, "L'Afrique de Nicolas Sarkozy."

24. Mbembe, "Afrique-France."

25. Mbembe, "L'Afrique de Nicolas Sarkozy."

26. Ibid.

27. Mbembe, "France-Afrique."

28. Ibid.

29. Mbembe, "L'Afrique de Nicolas Sarkozy."

30. Mbembe, "France-Afrique." This current of criticism, which Mbembe traces forward through the work of Paul Gilroy, Édouard Glissant, Maryse Condé, Francoise Vergès, and Raphael Confiant, insists that "fixed identity is a source of cultural death . . . the present and future will necessarily be hybrid."

31. Thioub, "À Monsieur Nicolas Sarkozy."

32. Ibid. His concrete proposals concern the free circulation of academic researchers (between Europe and Africa) and genuine cooperation and collaboration between African and European colleagues and institutions. He argues that a scientifically grounded understanding of the historical record could only be produced through the cooperation of African and European researchers which, in turn, will require "a veritable politics of rupture in several domains" "extending to sacralized freedom of circulation of capital, . . . to the free circulation of academics from all countries," and to funding "mixed research teams in all domains of knowledge [*savoir*]."

33. Thioub, "À Monsieur Nicolas Sarkozy."

34. Ibid.

35. "Pour une autre relation de la France avec l'Afrique," *Le Monde*, February 13, 2007.

36. Ibid.

37. Ibid.

38. Ibid.

39. Ibid.

40. These include promoting democratization, the rule of law, and respect for human rights as well as instituting transparent international economic rules that might benefit African populations, such as ending the European Union's imposition of commercial liberalization on unwilling African societies, regulating extractive industries, requiring French companies to respect social and environmental laws, publicizing records of the funds that they provide to African states, and forgiving state debts.

41. "Pour une autre relation de la France avec l'Afrique."

42. "Allocution de M. Nicolas Sarkozy," 11.

43. Thioub, "À Monsieur Nicolas Sarkozy."

44. Diop, "Le discours inacceptable de Nicolas Sarkozy," 3. This of course is also a criticism of Senegal's current President Abdoulaye Wade, who was also Sarkozy's host.

45. Mbembe, "L'Afrique de Nicolas Sarkozy."

46. Mbembe, "France-Afrique."

47. Ibid.

48. Ibid. See A. Mbembe, "Afropolitanism," *Africultures* 66 (2006): 9–15.

49. For an analysis of Senghor that does not reduce him to a nativist thinker, see Wilder, *The French Imperial Nation-State*.

50. See the Schuman Declaration in 1950, the European Coal and Steel Community in 1952, and the Rome Treaty in 1957. On the emergent European community, see R. Schuman, "Declaration of May 9, 1950: The Schuman Plan for European Integration," in D. Karmis and W. Norman, eds., *Theories of Federalism: A Reader* (New York: Palgrave Macmillan, 2005).

51. For an imperial vision of Eurafrique as a realpolitik attempt to prevent African secession and preserve French international stature with respect to the United States and the Soviet Union, see P. Nord, *L'Eurafrique, notre dernière chance* (Paris: Librairie Arthème Fayard, 1995). For useful historical discussions of the early debates around Eurafrique in relation to the European Economic Community, see J. K. Gosnell, "France, Empire, Europe: Out of Africa?" *Comparative Studies of South Asia, Africa and the Middle East* 26, no. 2 (2006): 203–12; L. Sicking, "A Colonial Echo: France and the Colonial Dimension of the European Economic Community," *French Colonial History* 5 (2004): 207–28. For a history of the concept, see M. Liniger-Goumaz, *L'Eurafrique, utopie ou réalité? Les métamorphoses d'une idée* (Yaoundé: Éditions Clé, 1972). The concept of Eurafrique was also seized upon by French imperial apologists at the height of the Algerian War who used it as either an argument to defend "French Algeria" at all costs or an argument to reform France's sub-Saharan Africa policy along more cooperative lines, since the loss of colonial Algerica was imminent. Eurafrique as a utopian vision of cultural symbiosis and postnational federation persisted into the 1970s. See

the first publication of the Fraternité Eurafricaine: *Vers une nouvelle civilisation de l'être* (Paris: Michel Touroude, 1974).

52. On constitutional struggles around the definition and reformation of the French Union between 1946 and 1958, as well as the IOM, see D. B. Marshall, *The French Colonial Myth and Constitution Making in the Fourth Republic* (New Haven: Yale University Press, 1973); R. S. Morgenthau, *Political Parties in French Speaking West Africa* (Oxford: Oxford University Press, 1964).

53. Although the position on Eurafrique developed by Senghor and the IOM was not purely instrumental, these deputies allied on this issue with their "realist" colleagues in the MRP, RPF, and Radical parties who also argued that without Africa, Europe would not be economically viable. Senghor participated in these debates about a new European community not only as a deputy in the National Assembly but as a delegate to the European Consultative Assembly. See the brief firsthand memories of this moment by Senghor's close colleague Émile-Derlin Zinzou, then a senator, vice-president of the Assembly of the French Union, and secretary general of the IOM group: Zinzou, "Il aura honoré l'Homme . . ." in *Léopold Sédar Senghor: la pensée et l'action politique* (Proceedings of a Conference on Senghor on June 26, 2006, published in Paris in 2007 by the French Parliament), 68–69. With respect to Senghor's commitment to federalism and warnings about "balkanization," Zinzou writes, "One can always hold forth about that which would have become of a given project [*construction*] without being able to affirm that the fruits would have realized the promise of the flowers. However, I myself, in the depth of my heart, of my reflections, am convinced that the future [*destin*] of France and of francophone Africa could have taken a somewhat different path at certain crucial and decisive moments, if France had not given itself, as Senghor happily said, to 'des gouvernements immobiles' " (69).

54. Léopold Sédar Senghor, Assemblée Nationale, 30 juin 1950, reprinted in *Liberté* 2 (Paris: Le Seuil, 1971), 79. He demanded that any agreement include explicit "safeguards for the future of Africa and the French Union, clauses that allow for the creation of an economic infrastructure and, especially [*singulièrement*] the development of industry for the processing of raw materials." Senghor thus anticipates more recent arguments from historians that French decolonization is motivated by a deliberate economic turn toward the European market and away from Africa. See J. Marseille, *Empire colonial et capitalisme français: histoire d'un divorce* (Paris: Albin Michel, 1984); F. Cooper, *Decolonization and African Society: The Labor Question in French and British Africa* (Cambridge: Cambridge University Press, 1996).

55. Senghor, Assemblée Nationale, 17 janvier 1952, reprinted in *Liberté* 2 (Paris: Le Seuil, 1971), 91. Senghor also suggests that "Eurafrique" would serve as a counterweight to the "Eurasian" Soviet bloc.

56. Ibid., 91.

57. Ibid., 90.

58. Ibid., 93. Senghor asks rhetorically: "This Eurafrique, is it a Eurafrique à la française, in the sense of respect and real equality, or is it a German-style Eurafrika, that of *pot de fer* and of *pot de terre?*"

59. See, e.g., Senghor, "Ce que l'homme noir apporte"; Wilder, *The French Imperial Nation-State*.

60. Léopold Sédar Senghor, "L'Afrique et l'Europe: deux mondes complémentaires," *Liberté* 2:148.

61. Ibid.

62. Ibid., 149.

63. Ibid., 150.

64. Ibid., 150–51.

65. Ibid., 154.

66. Ibid.

67. Ibid., 155.

68. Although Senghor here associates one form of reason primarily with Europe and the other primarily with Africa, these are historical rather than primordial designations. For Senghor also identifies currents of modernist European thought and art that seek to explore and exploit the intuitive reason that he associates primarily with Africa. On Senghor's engagement with currents of European modernist, vitalist, and phenemonlogical thinking, see Senghor, "The Revolution of 1889 and Leo Frobenius," trans. Richard Bjornson, *Africa and the West: The Legacies of Empire*, ed. Isaac James Mowoe and Richard Bjornson (New York: Greenwood, 1986); Wilder, *The French Imperial Nation-State*.

69. Senghor, "L'Afrique et l'Europe," 155.

70. Ibid., 157.

71. See, e.g., Senghor, *Liberté* 3, *Négritude et civilisation de l'universel*; *Liberté* 5, *Le dialogue des cultures*.

72. See the speeches and essays collected in Senghor, *Liberté 2, Nation et voie africaine du socialisme*.

73. I am developing this argument in a book provisionally titled "Freedom Time: Negritude, Decolonization, Utopia." See Thomas C. Holt, *The Problem of Freedom: Race, Labor, and Politics in Jamaica and Britain, 1832–1938* (Baltimore: Johns Hopkins University Press, 1991). See also Wilder, "Untimely Vision."

74. On decolonization as separation and denationalism, see F. Cooper, *Decolonization and African Society*; T. Shepard, *The Invention of Decolonization: The Algerian War and the Remaking of France* (Ithaca: Cornell University Press, 2006).

Letter to France

ALAIN MABANCKOU

From now on I watch France from afar. It is an attitude that was imposed on me by the course of events. I am not a disillusioned lover, far from it. I am instead a thwarted lover. I write these lines, dictated by my Congolese roots which over time wound up settling in French soil before branching out to America where I live and work. I had chosen France in my soul and conscience, but it was America that chose me one day while I was wandering in the desert in search of an oasis. I have said nothing to America about my troubles, my worries, my disappointments, and yet I would like to tell France everything. This is the land of reason, of the mind. Does she still know this or does she most often forget?

I am not an angry man—this feeling has never resided in me. I wonder, however, because it is the only attitude to be observed when surrounded by cynicism, indifference, and contempt, qualities that remind me of how I am nothing more than the damaged product of a society that is no longer mine.

So why do I write these words? Well, because my hope never fades. Because I believe that France could be seen differently. Because one can lose battles and still win the war. Because while I am certainly on my knees, I am not sprawled out on the ground. Because I would like to stand up, look at the horizon, and breathe a new breath of air—this pure air that has long been polluted by the ideology of universalist thought and by the emptiness of principles that supposedly put me in the heart of this nation until one day I had to be content with my placement at the margins where French society leaves a man of color. Because he is first a color, and secondly a man.

I write because silence is often perceived as a sign of approval—and, indirectly, as guilt by abstention. When there is a vote, the silent are subject to the laws of the majority. Silence implies consent, as the saying goes. The majority, as we know, can become the democracy of fools. Quantity does not necessarily assure reason and clarity. The main thing is to know where the majority lies. And yet, I do not see myself in the principles that the majority is supposed to enact for my well-being.

I lived in France, and France is my adoptive country. That should have been enough to shelter me from the eternal question, "Where are you from?" and even from "I know you are French but where did your parents come from?" As it turns out, my parents, born before the African Independence movements, were French citizens of the former French Empire. It so happens that Brazzaville, the main city of the Congo, was the capital of unoccupied France during the Occupation, which means that the French were all Congolese while Europe was at war and Germany was madly bent on conquering the planet. What remains from this period, when France was exported to Brazzaville, is the Case de Gaulle downtown, which looks toward the other Congo, the former Belgian Congo. I am French like the majority of those French who had chosen my native land as a place of refuge, a place to preserve France's grandeur. The Congolese did not expel these "brothers." In fact, they were honored.

Someone once told me that I was "French-something." Did he want to erase my Congolese heritage or did this mean that France never looked me straight in the eyes, as if I were Ralph Ellison's "Invisible Man," or that France never learned how to define what I really was?

I know that presently it is up to me to define myself. Before starting these lines, I looked at a map of France for a while. No place seemed foreign. Yet, I did not like the map. It seemed strange, distant. I turned my back to it and even sulked. But I knew deep down that this was not the France that had filled me with wonder. I was dreaming of a France, the France that I always wait for with all my heart. I think that it is in the process of being conceived. I fear that it will be stillborn.

The map of France in front of me has resisted alterations, especially considering the abundance of those colors that the average Joe notices when walking down the street, when lingering at La Chapelle market or at the Château Rouge, Barbès Rochechouart, or Château d'Eau metro stations. This map is the image that has been surreptitiously sold for decades. It represents a uniform society, unchanging even though we progress in an era of multiplicity. The uniformity of France was supposed to appease the conscience and reassure those who invested their energy in a *certain* idea of this country. This *certain* idea proclaims that the decline of the nation is the doing of the Other, he who does not resemble the "real French" and who would have invaded Gaul in due time because of the allegiance of certain humanists on the Left, ready to cede land to the highest bidder. The Other has been established as the public enemy of society. The Other is inevitably a delinquent, a parasite. He takes the bread out of the mouths of the true-blooded French. Moreover, when he is seen on the six o'clock news, it is because of a transgression of social norms or during a report about the squalor of these people packed like sardines into dilapidated buildings. Africa must have moved into the heart of the Republic. If the West is now agonized and infected by the poverty of the South, it is because of the Other.

What should be done? Don't make a mountain out of a mole hill: this Other, it was enough to hunt him down, to push him across the border, not to mention to take him back *manu militari* to his land of famine, drought, dictatorship, civil wars, and the last genocide of the twentieth century, where these barbarians used machetes to disembowel each other. And yet, they were handed a beautiful civilization, the best version that could exist at this time, and they messed it all up. They wanted independence, they got it. But they have since acted like wild animals. Therefore, it's not Europe's place to welcome them. Forget the fact that the wrongs of their continent, those confrontations since the Jurassic Era, those plagues of every type, have had an inseparable connection with Europe. These people only had to contain their misery, their barbarity far far away, in the heart of darkness. And, if necessary, they only had to eat like their ancestors: feast on human flesh or the serpents that abound in their regions, which are infested with mosquitoes and tsetse flies. What did Europe do to deserve such a massive invasion by these people? Doesn't a paradise exist somewhere other than the North?

Yes, Europe did not need them. Or rather, she *no longer* needed them. Don't dare remind her of "the glory of great deeds" of these people from afar. They fought for Europe. So what? That's the past, now is the future. France must protect her greatness. Ages ago, she had the help of those "people." Now she can do it on her own, for she is strong, she glows, she inevitably attracts. But she cannot "bear all the misery in the world," and these words are from a leftist, Michel

Rocard. It is true that he qualified his remarks in his commentary in *Le Monde*, clarifying: "I have often said, and I want to write it explicitly here, that we cannot advocate all or nothing in terms of immigration. The fact that we, alone, cannot possibly take on all the world's misery does not excuse us from doing something to ease it." France should thus ease "a share" of the world's misery. For the rest—undoubtedly the most painful part—other remedies must be found. In short, France is not the only world power.

And we are at the heart of ambiguity. One of the principles of compensation under French law requires that he who inflicts injury on another is obligated to give reparations. It all depends on how one defines injury. Colonization—to return to this—is it an injury? In reading Aimé Césaire's *Discours sur le colonialisme*, we would say yes. In reading certain texts written by the French who condemn the "repentance" of the West or "the sobbing of the white man," we would say no. There is a wide gap between the proponents of the legitimacy of colonization and the diehard opponents. But we will no longer veil our face. Césaire adds: no one colonizes with impunity. All colonization is inevitably a "rape of the imagination"—to borrow the words of Aminata Traoré. To colonize means to decide to impose your rhythm, your time, your vision on others. This implies the death of gods, the corruption of thought. But, it is not China or America that embarked on the conquest of the Black continent and installed a backyard, a *françafrique*, and therefore a safety belt for various African dictators. These dictators are putative sons of France. They look to be. They eat the same food and drink from the same spring as if they were. France naturally protects them because they are natural offspring. They are intermediaries, puppets—and one can measure the strength of the ties between France and these dictatorships by the promptness with which France recognizes an African head of state as soon as he gains power through a coup.

In the eyes of the proponents of French uniformity, multiplicity— some would say *diversity*—is an octopus that swallows up the substance that their Gallic ancestors left them, those who had "the whitish blue eyes, the narrow skull, and the awkwardness in combat," as Rimbaud would say. It is therefore no coincidence that nowadays the debates are oriented toward the question of blood and soil, the main sources of nationality, if one excludes other sources such as marriage, adoption, and the like. Blood—though red on all continents—is the favorite argument of the most obscurantist nations. If we are wary of the idea of the preeminence of soil, it is because it embodies *openness* and *mobility*—therefore, annihilation and obliteration, the detractors will say. Blood, by itself, is not a specificity on which humankind is based. After all, we do not have a monopoly on this red liquid; animals would compete for it without passing through a man-made tribunal, and they would win the lawsuit hands down. Animals do not know what an oath is—certainly because they are the only ones to understand that all words lead to corruption, to a montage destined to ruin the clarity of the majority in order to impose the dictate of a minority hung up on the antiquated idea of nation, or even of *identity*, this last word meaning nothing since it has been insidiously appropriated by the supporters of birthright. It is also blood that summons the idea of 100 percent purebred stock. What is "stock," or rather, how would the first dictionary you come across define it: as the base of a tree trunk (or a large shrub) extended by its *roots*? It is the part that is pulled up or that remains in the ground after the tree is chopped down. It is also the set of individuals from a common ancestor. Who, in France today, could claim such a lineage? What would this purebred French person look like?

What really matters is taking into account the efforts of those who maintain the tree, and also understanding that the tree does not stop with the trunk. Imagine it without leaves and without sap and we would have a vegetable, a victim of drought. Many have risked their lives for the survival of that tree while the "trunk" burrows into the depths of the soil, far from the sky where war planes fire. The trunk feeds on what comes from outside. We are the rain; we are the air.

Consequently, to define a man as a trunk (i.e., by blood) is to privilege an origin by *destination* and to eliminate that which makes us human: free will. Yes, the free will that Sartre dissects in *L'existential-isme est un humanisme*, the free will that leads to subjectivism: man makes himself. By our actions, the French philosopher essentially explains, we create the man we want to be, and what we want to be inevitably creates the image that is made of man.

If I attack this "origin by destination," it is because I conceive of belonging to a nation as a dynamic, positive act, which needs to start with the individual. There are two categories of French: those that have done nothing to become French and have gained their nationality by blood; and those who have undertaken the burden of Hercules to be recognized as belonging to that nation. The former believe they are French *naturally*. For the latter, their status is in permanent discussion, and it happens that the laws leave them in a situation of statelessness. On paper they may be French, but it is the constant look that questions their origin. Perhaps if everyone were French by blood, then discrimination would be done through blood group!

We Are Not There

The tragedy of our era is that an image of man is imposed on us, and we gravitate toward it in the hope that one day we will blend in with the prototype declared as the norm. These are the stakes of these principles, which are well crafted and well protected and difficult to improve without a clash, a showdown. Therefore, all social conflict becomes a redefinition of man, his place and his status. And the state, called upon to be above injustices and discrimination, implements rules, the famous general principles etched in the Constitution, with which the judge's duty is to ensure that they are applied without making allowances for origin, race, religion, and so on. On paper we are all equal before the law, and we have the same duties to the nation. Always on paper. The goal of these principles is to instill impartiality and fairness under the law. The role of Parliament is not to explain the application of a law—this is the judge's job. But how many of these principles have received the satisfaction of the population? Is it the destiny of these great principles to proclaim humanism without understanding mankind in all his variety? Everyone has heard of liberty, equality, fraternity in France. This trinity of words has long resounded in our most optimistic dreams. This trinity of words will lift France for a long time above the majority of Western nations—and we others have studied these words with special attention from our most remote countries, the former territories of the Empire, in the hope that we become used to them, and transmit them to future generations as a legacy of our time on Earth. While we did not understand these words then, we thought that in the depths of our souls they rang true and they rhymed well, and that the most beautiful sound could never be corrupted by the cackle of off-the-wall folk. The poet Louis Aragon wrote on every wall the word "liberty." And most of all, the nation has promised unending fraternity as long as you devote yourself to the nation and put her above all else—which many Africans did to defend the French Empire.

Yes, we believed it, until the current social divide—a divide so deep that the politicians, to wash their hands of it, constantly place the blame on each other. The Left. The Right. The Center, that is no longer the Center, like de Gaulle's. The Left and the Right are going toward extremes, as if to follow what's in fashion. In Europe, from time to time the parties on the extreme triumph. And we cry scandal—the last gasp that reminds us that we have a conscience. A presidential election presents the French population with a dilemma: vote for the Right with Chirac or the far Right with Jean-Marie Le Pen. There was nothing in between. The people on the Left had the impression that they were choosing between the plague and cholera. But since it was necessary to choose, they rushed en masse toward Jacques Chirac, the same one who some years earlier worried about the smells in the stairwells of immigrants, an argument that Le Pen would have claimed without astonishing anyone. Jacques Chirac and Le Pen found themselves in the final, the famous, second round of the presidential elections in 2002. France swept this image under the rug, acting as if this situation was not what she wanted. Except that these are not extraterrestrials going to the polls. These are humans made of flesh and blood. These are the French who went to the polls and who decided to display this original picture to the world. Certainly Le Pen didn't win the presidential election, but the far Right showed that it was not a minuscule group, ringing in at 7 or 8 percent, if not more. However, they could have been a real alternative, a visible display of French politics, and the whole world would have simply said: France voted for the Far Right.

Lawyers have promised always to apply the law with the most absolute equality without taking into account our status, powerful or weak. When the rights of man are brought up, we applaud. At the end of the applause a question springs up: what man, exactly? Man in the abstract sense, that which is born from subjectivity, the subjectivity of a world that would have imagined these rights and would have perceived man according to their definition, their civilization, that which they would have tried to impose on other peoples, I mean the backward peoples that did not know how to tell beef from human flesh. The response to such a question leads immediately to exceptions to the decreed principles. Of course an abstract man! We have waited a long time to reap the fruits of all the promises sown. The harvest was guaranteed to be exceptional, however, and good intentions were not lacking, and the sowers competed in plotting the earth. We will be told that each decade a more humane policy has been implemented, that France has never failed in its duty as a welcoming country. There was no need for her to feel guilty for her course—the other great powers have not excelled either. We have therefore heard the voices that demanded France to not be ashamed of her civilizing action in the former colonies. Basically, where would these far off people be if colonization had not reached them? Would these people, moreover, be able to talk to their former colonizer by using the colonizer's language, sometimes even better than the colonizers use it themselves, as André Breton highlighted in his preface to Aimé Césaire's *Cahier d'un retour au pays natal*?

It's not Black France that is worrisome; it is France's entrance into a fragmented world that freezes over the conservative part of de Gaulle's country. Because, of all the countries of Europe, France is unquestionably the state that still thinks of its territory with images of an antiquated history. There is on one side the purebred French and on the other side the French-something. A kind of apartheid that dares not speak its name.

French Impressionism

JAKE LAMAR

I'll never forget the first time I missed the last métro. It was October 1993, and I'd been living in Paris for only a few weeks. I'm from New York, where the subway runs twenty-four hours a day. In Paris, underground rail service shuts down at 1 a.m. At around 2 a.m. I was standing on a corner in the center of town, trying to hail a taxi to take me to my inconveniently located sublet. Me, a six-foot-tall, thirty-two-year-old Black man, wearing a baseball cap and high-top sneakers. No white cab driver in New York would have stopped for me at 2 in the afternoon let alone 2 in the morning.

But a white cabbie did pull up to me on the Rue de Rivoli. At that moment, an elegantly dressed white French couple approached the taxi. The driver rolled down his window and asked where I was going. I told him. Then he turned to the couple and asked where they were going. I felt a sudden rush of anger, certain the driver would pick up the white couple and leave me standing on the sidewalk. "I'm sorry," the driver said. "This is my last run of the night, and he's going in my direction." I hopped into the car, and we drove off. I felt as if I had stepped through a socio-cultural looking glass. In New York, the color of my skin would have been the dominant factor in a cab driver's decision *not* to pick me up. In Paris, in this instance, race wasn't even part of the equation. The only thing that mattered was the direction in which the driver was headed. Here was colorblindness at its most pure and pristine.

Fast forward to February 1, 1994, what would have been Langston Hughes's ninety-second birthday. Back in those days, Ted Joans, the great Black Beat Generation poet, used to arrange an annual reading to celebrate the Hughes legacy at Shakespeare and Company, the ramshackle Left Bank bookshop and cultural landmark. Ted had invited me to join him and the poets James Emanuel and Hart Leroy Bibbs in reading selections from Hughes's work and our own. There must have been about forty people crammed into the musty upstairs reading room that night. One of them was a gregarious American brother about my age who had lived in Europe for some time. I'll call him Maurice. He was trying to make a name for himself in the film business. And he seemed to be quite the connoisseur of Paris nightlife. After the reading, Maurice took me to a couple of jazz clubs, where he seemed to know everybody. No cover charge; drinks on the house. All night Maurice talked about how much he loved France, about how open-minded and colorblind the French were.

At about 3 that morning, Maurice and I were walking down an otherwise deserted street. I was going to get a taxi home. At that moment, an unmarked car pulled up to the curb. Two plainclothes cops jumped out, flashed their police IDs, and gruffly ordered us up against the wall. With the grainy videotaped images of the Rodney King beating swirling in my head, I calmly assumed the position—palms pressed against the side of the building, legs spread. One of the cops frisked me and started going through my knapsack. Maurice, meanwhile, was fighting the other cop. He was kicking and flailing as the cop, a much larger man, struggled to get a grip on him. Maurice screamed in French: "I respect France, you must respect me!"

By now, the cop was twisting Maurice's right arm behind his back and had him pressed against the wall. The other cop had found a copy of my first book, *Bourgeois Blues*, in my knapsack. In those days, I could only speak French in the present tense. "I am writer," I told the cop. "Tonight I give reading. I meet him. We go to club. We walk in the street. We are innocent." I repeated these words over and over again, emphasizing the last sentence. The cop asked to see my passport. Not knowing that I was supposed to carry it with me at all times, I had left it at home out of fear of losing it. A blue, white, and red police van pulled up and five uniformed officers hopped out. Maurice was handcuffed; I was not. I was detained at the station until 5 a.m. Maurice was released some time later.

Why had we been stopped in the first place? I was at fault for not carrying my passport, but the police could not have known that when they pulled up to us. And Maurice's violent reaction was, I think, because he could not believe this was actually happening to him here, in enlightened France. Our only offense, after all, was being two Black men walking down the street at 3 a.m.

Sixteen years after I first arrived here, multicultural France is a bundle of racial contradictions. Take my early encounter with the colorblind cab driver. I've found myself in a thousand similar situations in this country. The snubs, the slights, the suspicions—all the weirdness of white folks that a Black person in America just gets used to—are often absent in comparable situations here. Walking the streets of most Paris neighborhoods, one is struck by the number of cross-cultural couples, by the mixed groups of friends sitting and talking in cafés: Asians with Europeans, Europeans with Africans, Africans with Asians. Yet despite the general live-and-let-live attitude, police have stopped me several times since that memorable incident on Langston Hughes's birthday. On those occasions, the cops simply asked for my papers. Naturally, I had learned from experience always to carry my passport and, later, my residence card. When the cops found out I was American, they sent me on my way. But had I been, say, Senegalese and been caught without my papers that night in 1994, it's doubtful that I would have been released from police custody after a mere two hours.

I live on the border of Barbès, a rambling African and Arab neighborhood. It is one of the few areas within the Paris city limits where one can walk for blocks and blocks and not see a single white person—unless it's a cop. There is always a heavy police presence in Barbès, and there are frequent crackdowns on immigrants whose papers might not be in order. Some of my African friends have told me I was crazy to leave America. An Ethiopian woman who attended an elite Paris university believed that institutional racism was far more widespread and socially accepted here. An ambitious Nigerian acquaintance told me he was eager to go to the United States because it was "the only country in the world where a Black man can get really rich."

Racism in France is more ambiguous than a simple matter of black and white. It is more a question of national history and cultural baggage. If most African Americans I have known in France feel freer and more respected here than in the States, it is because most French people seem to have a genuine appreciation of African American history and culture. Just as the worst victims of American racism tend to be the descendants of African slaves, the worst victims of bigotry here are the descendants of France's former colonial subjects in Africa, the Caribbean, and the Arab and Muslim worlds. They are victims of France's tortured history with their ancestral homelands.

Unlike a lot of the Black American expatriates of days gone by—from Josephine Baker to Richard Wright—I have never felt exiled from the United States. I came to Paris thinking I would stay for a year and ended up falling in love with the place, with the beauty and the beat of the city. And, yes, I love the open-mindedness of most of the folks I've met here. First impressions can be lasting. I often reflect on my experience with the taxi driver in 1993. What if it had been the white couple who was going in his direction on his last run of the night? What if he had taken them and instead had left me standing on the sidewalk? Would I still be living in Paris today?

PART II

The Politics of Blackness—Politicizing Blackness

The Invention of Blacks in France

PATRICK LOZÈS

The word "Black" has long been taboo in the French political vocabulary, perhaps because it referred to a reality that no one wanted to face. In a country that considers itself the "land of human rights," in a republic whose motto is "Liberty, Equality, Fraternity," it is difficult, even shameful, to admit that millions of citizens suffer massive discrimination on a daily basis, limiting their access to housing, employment, education, credit, creating businesses, and leisure activities.

This denial of the existence of discrimination is rooted in French history. In the late nineteenth century, teachers, who had been baptized the "Black Hussars of the Republic" because of the color of their coats and the central mission conferred on education in the building of the new regime, banned local languages and forced each left-handed pupil to write with his right hand by tying the other hand behind his back. The Republic wanted to be of only one mind. The mission of the young Republic was to eliminate the idiosyncrasies and the castes of the Old Regime in order to unify the country under the banner of education and in order to impose a single language and a single law for all citizens, regardless of their status.

From this radicalism, considered necessary in the early history of the Republic, we have conserved a certain number of Republican "traditions," including an intolerance of the public expression of minority identities. As incredible as this may seem from abroad, in France before the creation of the Conseil Représentatif des Associations Noires (CRAN), when Blacks expressed themselves as Black in public to demand an end to discrimination, this expression was resented by a large number of intellectuals, and oddly by intellectuals on the Left, as a threat to the Republic. The fact that a "Black community" does not exist in France and that Blacks themselves overwhelmingly reject any notion of community, having had the same republican education as other French people, was not enough to curb this prejudice during the early stages of CRAN's existence.

It is necessary to understand that the relationship of French political culture to religious or cultural minorities is marked by two major ruptures. On the one hand, there is the historic and difficult rupture between the State and religious communities, which was transcribed into French law in 1905 with the separation of church and state. This first event led to one of the major pillars of French political thought, the fight for secularism. On the other hand, there is the debacle of 1940 and the establishment of the Vichy state, which rested on the right of "corporations" and on the segregation of Jews, Gypsies, homosexuals, Blacks, and North Africans, all minorities that, for one reason or another, would wind up in Nazi camps, escorted by French police.

These ruptures explain in part why what was true at the beginning of the Republic, when the memory of the Old Regime was still alive, remains true today, in a profoundly changed context. All "categorization" of the population, other than in terms of social status, is problematic. Certain French intellectuals such as Pierre-André Taguieff have theorized this position, not hesitating to declare that any affirmation of difference in the public sphere would constitute a step toward "differentialism," an ideology that would serve the interests of the Far Right. In other words, because the Far Right champions the idea of "genetic differences" between social groups to better affirm social hierarchies with the goal of installing a type of apartheid, the Republic must impede, by any means necessary, differences from being expressed within the Republic to avoid the establishment of this apartheid. This prohibition is sometimes formulated in a more positive manner, as a "right" of minorities to "indifference." It must be understood that this paradoxical attitude, which prevents entire sections of the population from expressing themselves, in the name of their own well-being and of that of the Republic, is one of the components of the debate over minorities in France.

All peoples who fought for equal rights within the French Republic, not only in theory but also in practice, needed to go through a difficult struggle for the recognition of their right to speak, collectively, in the public sphere: women, gays, lesbians, the transgendered, Jews, the disabled, and now Blacks. This recognition has yet to be realized.

The CRAN prefers the word "diversity" instead of "difference" or its corollary "indifference." This choice is anything but rhetorical. The use of the words "difference" or "indifference" supposes, in effect, the implicit existence of a "norm," against which all others are measured, and which excludes visible minorities. Clearly, "the right to indifference" like the "right to difference" is another way of saying that the norm in France is to be white, male, heterosexual, able-bodied, and so on. If one is different, it is indeed in relation to someone or something. The word "diversity" affirms, *a contrario*, an egalitarian situation, where no social group serves as the reference point, not even implied, in the public debate. No group dominates the others. In addition, one ceases to define the public debate with regards to the Far Right, as do the intellectuals who denounce "differentialism." On the contrary, the victims of racism and discrimination, who are recognized as French, are placed in the center of the debate, and are compensated, by appropriate means, for the social inequalities that they suffer because of the color of their skin. The use of the word "diversity" constitutes, in itself, a major paradigm shift.

However, the road ahead of us is still long. For as the media and French intellectuals are increasingly employing the concept of "diversity," the notion of "ethnicity" has emerged to denote in recent years all "nonwhite" groups of citizens. The notion of "ethnicity" conveys a colonial "kitsch" in the literal sense of the word. It recalls the prerepublican vision. It has no scientific validity in contemporary France. But it is, nevertheless, widely used. This is yet another way—one might almost speak of "unconscious discursive strategies"—of situating visible minorities outside of public debate, and thus not recognizing them as equal.

The CRAN, for its part, contends that apart from the use of the word "diversity" there are categories based on *a shared experience of discrimination*. The CRAN has black, white, brown, and yellow members, and unites "Blacks" because "Blacks" share a common, *specific* experience of discrimination. Women do not suffer from the same type of discrimination. Neither do North Africans, Jews, or disabled persons. In the public sphere, each group acts in its own interest, which in no way threatens the Republic. On the contrary, it is the lack of a means of expression for these groups in the public sphere that frequently leads to situations of tension, or even riots (as in 2005), at a considerable cost to the community. The CRAN was founded following the riots in

2005 precisely to facilitate democratic and nonviolent ways of challenging discriminatory practices in France.

To create a space for debate on the social experience of Blacks in France, it was necessary to invent the term "Noirs de France." That was the audacity of the CRAN. The CRAN was founded on the conviction that the question of discrimination, and notably indirect discrimination (known as the "glass ceiling"), which is the most important and most serious type of discrimination, could not be tackled without the existence of visible minorities in the public sphere.

And, in fact, as amazing as it seems when viewed from abroad, the fight against discrimination was largely absent from French political debate before the creation of the CRAN.

The CRAN in France is a federation of associations founded on November 26, 2005. It includes nearly 150 Black associations and is active throughout the national territory. This federation's main objective is the fight against discrimination. While the CRAN fights against this discrimination, the fight against discrimination is not a fight against racism. Racism is a reprehensible ideology. Discrimination constitutes concrete situations that must be remedied. The fight against racism is a moral combat. Its priority is to reform individuals so that they stop being racist. The objective of the fight against discrimination is completely different. It seeks tangibly to ameliorate the living conditions of people experiencing discrimination. The fight against racism unfolds over an extremely long period of time. Mentalities are not reformed in a day. The fight against discrimination is more urgent. Every new instance of discrimination is a failure for the Republic. The fight against discrimination rests upon a collective rather than individual approach to the problem. It shows the global rather than fragmented reality of discrimination. Ultimately, it focuses attention on the people confronted with discrimination who are in need of public support.

In this framework, categories do not constitute an option. They are indispensable. Therefore, it is very necessary that the category "Black" exist to measure the discrimination practiced against "Blacks." Origin, place of residence, nationality, or surname is not enough to explain, for example, why a Black French woman named Marie Dupont whose family has been French for centuries was refused work because, as is still heard all too often in France, "the clients prefer not to be served by a Black woman." (Marie Dupont is a hypothetical name to denote any Black French woman.) You cannot turn a blind eye to this reality in order to stress a hypothetical "French model of the fight against discrimination," which would, like Roquefort cheese, be unique in the world.

Ultimately, the paradoxical invisibility of visible minorities in the public sphere is a cover, concealing problems and suffering. It becomes an injustice. It becomes even criminal, in regards to millions of children whose fate is ruined at birth because of being born Black or Arab or female or disabled in France, where all are stigmatized, if not understood as a mistake. In 2003, early in our thinking which led to the creation of the CRAN, we asked ourselves if studies concerning the situation of Blacks in France existed in sociology, anthropology, history, or demography. It soon became clear that this type of study had never been realized. Works exist on "African families," "African students," civil servants from the DOM/TOM, "migrants," "immigrants" from sub-Saharan Africa, and "illegal immigrants," but, astonishingly, no study had been done on French Blacks. As the political scientist Fred Constant explained in 2005, in reality several invisibilities exist that reinforce each other: "historical invisibility," "scientific invisibility," "economic invisibility," "cultural invisibility," "invisibility in the media," and "political invisibility." This "multiple invisibility" impedes the full participation of Blacks in the political community in France. They are not, strictly speaking, part of French history. They do not count statistically. As the philosophers Avishai Margalit and Axel Honneth noted, to be *invisible* in the eyes of others—whether it be one person or a group of people—constitutes one of the most profound experiences of humiliation and contempt. Those not taken into account literally do not count. The invisibility which afflicts the Black populations of France is itself rendered invisible, that is, not analyzed factually or statistically. From this perspective, the discrimination that strikes the Blacks of France is the *perfect crime*. It is not counted by statistics, its consequences cannot be evaluated, and the victims themselves do not exist.

In reality, visible minorities, including Black populations, are still perceived as foreign to French society. They are most often identified through the reductive prism of "immigration" and "integration." It is skin color that turns a French person into a foreigner and asks him "to integrate" throughout his life. This is what led to the creation of the Ministry of Immigration, National Identity, Integration, and Co-development in 2007, an event accompanied by increasing restrictions on the granting of citizenship and the multiplication of administrative obstacles to the renewal of the French identity card.

A French soldier, Ounoussou Guissé, saw his nationality contested before a tribunal because his father of Senegalese origin, who lived in France in 1960 at the moment of Senegalese independence, had opted, as the law authorized, for French nationality. His right to transmit this nationality was disputed, while all other French people have the right through *jus sanguinis*. The novelist Tatiana de Rosnay was refused the renewal of her identity card on the grounds that "according to the new laws," which are not retroactive in France, "any person born in France to French parents who were born abroad must prove his nationality." In other words, *jus soli* was insufficient. Far from being isolated, these cases have become commonplace.

Nationality can be obtained three ways in France: jus sanguinis, jus soli, or naturalization. These three methods are currently the subject of unprecedented challenge. One quickly sees the nature of the problem that is posed for people whose color is read as an indication of foreignness. All their actions and gestures are interpreted according to this model. Their crimes, if they commit them, are not just crimes but attacks on the national community. To summarize, if a white person boos during the "Marseillaise" at a match, one would say that he is unpatriotic or is challenging authority. Meanwhile, if a French person of North African origin boos during the "Marseillaise," one would say, and it has actually happened, that he does not like France and should leave. At the heart of the matter, the situation of visible minorities is similar to that of Captain Dreyfus, who was suspected of leaking intelligence to the enemy because as a Jew in the early twentieth century, he was not really considered French.

In the expression "Noirs de France" that the CRAN chose, each word is important, as a way both to put an end to the invisibility of these populations in the public sphere and to bring them back to the political community to which these populations belong, which is the French community. Many in France have celebrated the rise of Barack Obama, who symbolizes the "American dream." But one should wonder where the "French dream" is, this dream born during the French Revolution of 1789 and completed with the abolition of slavery in

1848. The United States managed in less than half a century to end legal segregation and to acquire enough political maturity to make possible the election of a Black man to the head of the country. In France, however, 160 years after the abolition of slavery, we have only one Black deputy representing Metropolitan France in the National Assembly, no Black ministers (there is only one Black secretary of state, a position that in France corresponds to a lower rank than that of minister), no Black generals, no Black chiefs of staff, no Black ambassadors, no Black CEOs of any large companies, and of course no Black president.

Aware that time is not on our side and that if concrete actions are not promptly taken, this situation will persist and even worsen, the CRAN wants:

> —To know how many Black French are discriminated against in our country, and the specific forms such discrimination takes. For this to happen, there need to be statistics on diversity;
> —To create the conditions necessary for the development of a Black middle class and a Black elite so that Blacks can themselves participate in politics, economics, and the media. For this, we need a committed policy of affirmative action à la française.

The objective of the CRAN is to make the values of France truly universal, in other words, to ensure that they apply to Black French people and, more generally, to all visible minorities. We do not want to "essentialize" the notion of "Black," but neither do we want this notion forgotten. The objective is for the Blacks of France to pass from a *negative invisibility* to a *positive invisibility*. The day when Black children can have the same dreams as white children is the day that France can speak of "colorblindness."

Immigration and National Identity in France

DOMINIC THOMAS

He spoke in public several times a day, and on each occasion puffed out his breast like a pigeon and engaged in peculiar contortions to liven up his pronouncements, the substance of which was of less importance than the form itself, which in any case varied depending on his audience. . . . [I]n spite of his limited attractiveness, he was able to negotiate and build alliances like no other. This Hungarian aspired to unify the French and the Visigoths in Gaul against a declining Roman Empire, and to recreate it to his advantage.—PATRICK RAMBAUD, *Chronique du règne de Nicolas Ier*, 2008

The temptation to build walls is certainly not a new one. Whenever a culture or civilization has failed in thinking the Other, in thinking self and Other together, and thinking the Other in the self, stiff and impenetrable preservations of stone, iron, barbed wire, electric fences, or closed-minded ideologies have been erected, collapsed, only to return with newfound stridency.—EDOUARD GLISSANT AND PATRICK CHAMOISEAU, *Quand les murs tombent: l'identité nationale hors-la-loi*, 2007

Whether or not one agrees with the effectiveness of such mechanisms as affirmative action in the United States or the Race Relations Act in the United Kingdom, these devices represent at the very least recognition that race constitutes a category for discrimination. Ethnic or diversity monitoring has been extensively debated in recent years in France, a country in which all citizens are considered equal and indistinguishable before the law. Yet, racial invisibility has complicated a constructive discourse on difference, which is compounded by the fact that there is now general consensus with regards to the ineffectiveness of assimilation, insertion, and integration policies. More recently, the question of political underrepresentation—only one minority representative was elected from mainland metropolitan France in the legislative elections of June 2007—has been at the forefront of claims articulated by activist organizations endeavoring to displace the status quo. Having said this, the multidimensionality of the ethnic minority question in France makes its analysis at once compelling and intriguing, and inquiries into the specific domain of Black France inevitably entail a consideration of a broad set of political and social factors with roots in the history of slavery, colonialism, immigration, and, naturally, the postcolonial.

The findings of multiple research groups have indicated the prevalence of negative sentiments concerning visible minorities in France. Efforts at applying qualitative and quantitative sociological data to the immigrant experience—insisting, for example, on France's long history of immigration, or providing statistics on job and school performance and information on access to health care and housing—have often proved futile precisely because politicians have successfully capitalized upon the electoral appeal and capital such negative characterizations offer. Not surprisingly, statistics relating to the presidential elections in 2007 revealed that 77 percent of practicing Catholics voted for Nicolas Sarkozy and 80 percent of Muslims supported the Socialist candidate, Segolène Royal, with 64 percent of Sarkozy supporters believing there are "too many immigrants in France." During the 1980s and 1990s, debates on immigration, a term which refers simultaneously in French to the physical act of migrating *and* to race relations,[1] were almost exclusively on what Etienne Balibar has described as "the insurmountability of cultural differences, a racism which, at first sight, does not postulate the superiority of certain groups or peoples in relation to others but 'only' the harmfulness of abolishing frontiers, the incompatibility of lifestyles and traditions."[2] Yet, the social uprisings that occurred during the fall of 2005 in several French housing projects located in the urban peripheries known as the *banlieues* served to highlight exclusionary realities based on both class and racial structures.[3]

These social uprisings are often referred to as the French "Katrina" in an attempt to establish parallels between the socio-economic circumstances of disadvantaged populations in Louisiana that exposed them to the devastating impact of Hurricane Katrina and the profound inequities in French society, including the existence of a "global South" within metropolitan France, which were brought to public attention in fall 2005 by the uprising and served to accord a key role once again to issues of immigration during the electoral campaign in 2007. On June 20, 2005, Nicolas Sarkozy, then minister of the interior, visited the Cité des 4000 housing project outside Paris (in La Courneuve), claiming that he would "clean it out with a high-pressure hose." Later, during a visit to the Argenteuil banlieue on October 25, 2005, he promised one resident he would rid the project of its "scum." These irresponsible comments further exacerbated tensions between banlieue residents and the authorities, such that when on October 27, 2005, a fifteen-year-old boy named Bouna and seventeen-year-old Zyed (both ethnic minorities) were electrocuted at Clichy-sous-Bois in a power plant as they ran from police officers, riots ensued.[4] The authorities were quick to deflect responsibility, attributing blame instead to cultural and religious practices at odds with Republican ideals and values (such as Islam, polygamy, and the like), even declaring on November 8 a state of emergency, which was justified by an existing law (the decree of April 3, 1955) previously adopted to prevent French citizens from organizing against the war in Algeria. These measures underscored the nature of transcolonial alignments, introducing disturbing echoes of a colonial past, updated and in the guise of repressive mechanisms that included arbitrary raids, racial profiling, and confinement in tower blocks. Many argued that these events signaled the failure of economic integration. But one could also argue that social protest of this nature—albeit one that lacked organizational cohesiveness and failed to articulate specific claims for social and economic reparation—inscribes itself in a long French tradition of fighting against injustice, pointing instead to an appropriation of Republican ideals in order to highlight inconsistent applications of justice to an identifiable spectrum of the French community.

No matter what interpretation of these events finally prevails or proves satisfactory, the fact nevertheless remains that they forever altered the configuration of ethnic minority discourse in France. The new French administration has been eager to instrumentalize these social problems, and, for President Sarkozy, immigration concerns both the *external* component (migration flows, border control, and so on) and the *internal* dynamics of race relations. The stated mission of the Ministry of Immigration, National Identity, Integration, and Co-development created in 2007 is to "cover the full journey of the migrant," that is, from the point of origin all the way to integration.[5] This ministry essentially completes a project Sarkozy started as minister of the interior (which he served as from 2005 to 2007): in that capacity he had already made the fight against illegal immigration a priority, resulting in dramatic increases in expulsions. Initially under the leadership of his close friend and political ally, Brice Hortefeux (subsequently promoted to minister of the interior in June 2009), the new ministry endeavoured to capitalize upon the widespread belief that national identity had eroded. The key principle guiding the operations of this ministry concerns "the right to choose who can or cannot settle on French territory,"[6] and four main pillars define its operational objectives: chosen or selected immigration based on particular skill sets, co-development policies to assist sending countries, the implementation of integration policies and requirements (comprising language proficiency tests and contracts certifying a commitment to respect Republican values and ideals), and "the promotion of our identity as a way of countering communitarian (ethnic factionalism) practices and in order to preserve the equilibrium of our Nation. Immigration and national identity are complementary. They are in fact intimately connected."[7]

These measures have fostered a results-driven mentality, what Gérard Noiriel has aptly described as an "increase in arrest quotas,"[8] where the personal accountability of officials is symbiotically linked to the imperative to demonstrate the effectiveness of policies and the various measures adopted. Statements made by Brice Hortefeux are indicative of this: "The number of people deported from France increased from just over 10,000 in 2002 to 24,000 by the end of 2006."[9] Thus, not only are quotas effectively implemented, but perpetual action and vigilance are now required to reach targets and thereby respond to "migratory pressures at the borders."[10] As we shall see, recourse to this type of methodology "has its origins in a security-based logic aimed at defending national identity against the 'threat' posed by those external and internal enemies."[11] The obsession with the alleged threat posed by foreigners and illegal and undocumented workers, along with domestic communitarianism, has its roots in Sarkozy's presidential campaign.

Indeed, Noiriel has provided a lucid analysis of the organizing principles of this politics of fear: "The objective is always to achieve a definition of national identity by denouncing its opposite, through a classical logic that juxtaposes the 'them' with the us. . . . One must also point out that unlike the National Front, Nicolas Sarkozy does not name the group he has in mind . . . but rather, through allusions, leaves it up to his commentators and electoral supporters to fill in the gaps."[12] Sarkozy's discourse is deliberately vague in the language used, though he often is understood to be referring to something precise, for "each of the examples he provides to designate what corresponds to the anti-France [polygamy, excision, and so on] has been the subject of media stories in recent years, and all of them conjure up immigration from North Africa and sub-Saharan Africa."[13] Effectively, "all of these references to immigration serve as symbols of the decadence and crisis of values in France today" and therefore rationalize the necessity for monitoring threats to Republican ideals and values.[14] On the one hand, the logic, according to which the figure of the *clandestin* emerges as "an individual who neither speaks nor writes the national language, who does not respect the law or Republican values, and who makes no effort to integrate,"[15] is readily substituted as the "antithesis of the French person";[16] whereas on the other hand, the "communitarian" materializes as the "antithesis of republican values."[17] In *Chronique du règne de Nicolas Ier*, a brilliant satire of Sarkozy's presidency, Patrick Rambaud has been able to illustrate the discursive potential and adaptability of such representations, foregrounding a dynamic, which, for Olivier Le Cour Grandmaison, epitomizes "state-sanctioned xenophobia and a politics of fear" which is thought to "protect the cohesion of our national community."[18] As the French philosopher Alain Badiou has argued, these forms of French insecurity on the new global landscape are increasingly expressed in a vocabulary of "fear," one that includes a "fear of foreigners, workers, of the people, banlieues youth, Muslims, blacks from Africa."[19]

The interchangeability and mutability of the words applied to minority populations have been studied by Azouz Begag, the author, sociologist, and former minister for equal opportunities (2005–7). In his book *Ethnicity and Equality: France in the Balance*, Begag provides a list of the different appellations that are used to describe these populations, such as "second generation," "of North African descent," and "Muslim," which define them according to "territorial, ethnic, religious, and temporal criteria."[20] With this list, he emphasizes what Balibar has shown as the figure of the "foreigner," a part of which, the "immigrant," functions as signifier for a broad range of cultural, political, and social issues, which shows that, as Balibar says, "the less the social problems of the 'immigrants,' or the social problems which massively affect immigrants, are specific, the more their existence is made responsible for them."[21] In other words, more attention is commonly granted to the *problems* associated with social integration than to the *obstacles* to that objective. How, after all, can one be born an immigrant? Antecedents are to be found in the United Kingdom, where Enoch Powell spoke during the 1970s of "invading hordes" of immigrants "lacking inherent cultural qualities and the desire to integrate with indigenous society and polity" in his famous "Rivers of Blood" speech.[22]

In France too, former president of France Jacques Chirac had, as mayor of Paris in 1991, alluded to the noise and the smell of immigrants, carefully outlining how "*they* come over here with there three to four wives and twenty or so children. . . . [T]hink about the poor French worker. . . . [H]e has to deal with the noise and smell."[23] Sarkozy promised a *rupture* and new models for dealing with these questions, yet statements such as the one that follows have become only too familiar: "One needs to respect France's rules, which means that you don't practice polygamy, excision on girls, that you don't slaughter sheep in your apartment, and that you respect Republican rules."[24]

In fact, during his campaign for the presidency, Sarkozy repeatedly instrumentalized these paradigms, insisting on the interpretation of French history as glorious. Not surprisingly, a report commissioned for the creation of a French history museum by the Ministry of Defense and the Ministry of Culture and Communication and completed April 16, 2008, underscored the importance of France's "long historiographic tradition," one that "calls for *historical culture* to occupy a central place in the national identity and in the national sentiment of French people."[25] The problem with this attempt to restrict the conceptualization of identity to a long history is that immigration from the more recent colonial and the postcolonial era cannot exceed the role of complex supplements to a falsely structured, preexisting, monolithic France. Olivier Le Cour Grandmaison has illustrated how this functions: "The nation is Great because it can conjure up a long list of ancestors who, endowed with exceptional qualities, have both forged and perpetuated it.... Confronted with this reality, newcomers to the history of nation-states . . . are unable to get others to forget their relative youth or their recent entry to the ranks of sovereign and independent national entities; they are forever marked in this way, and any comparison with France always works against them, given that the latter enjoys precedence that cannot be matched."[26]

Ultimately, the more central question concerns, of course, the matter of who belongs and who does not belong in and to France. The creation of a new Ministry for Immigration, National Identity, Integration, and Co-development in 2007 indicates the degree to which this is a concern. In a speech delivered in Toulon in 2007, Sarkozy emphasized France's one-dimensional history: "To be French is to be the proud heir of a single and shared history for which we have every reason to be proud."[27] However, as Patrick Weil has convincingly shown in his book *How to Be French: Nationality in the Making Since 1789*, access to French nationality has been far from a straightforward process.[28] The practice of "invoking a monumental past makes it possible to believe in a return to grandeur and power while also restoring the belief and confidence in a glorious future, since what has been can surely be achieved again."[29] In a similar fashion, the proposal and attempt by the new ministry to introduce DNA testing as a scientific way for foreign families—who are thereby defined differently from their French counterparts—to prove their ties to France has instead served to support prevalent assumptions that *visible* minorities and immigrants belong to a distinct social configuration outside the dominant order of things,[30] while also relegating all other individual and human attributes in order to "arrive at a supposedly irrefutable truth located somewhere in the genes or bones."[31]

The multiple registers employed in the media and in political debates have, for the most part, blurred the distinction between immigrants and ethnic minorities, while necessarily associating these categories with urban violence and delinquency. As Begag has argued: "The republican idea of the city has been gravely weakened by social exclusion and the desocialization of young ethnics. The violence associated with these neighborhoods is constantly present in the media. . . . Without any doubt media treatment of 'urban violence' involving young ethnics has impeded the social integration of so-called Arabs, on whom urban disorders are blamed. Racism on one side, counter-

hatred on the other, and fear everywhere. Social exclusion first concealed these young ethnics, then manufactured them, and finally pro-
pelled them onto the public scene."[32] A crucial component has been
evacuated from this discourse, namely, those claims made by activist
organizations that have mobilized both to humanize the experience of
migration and to accord a voice to those populations who have been
traditionally unheard or at the very least silenced by the prevalence of
disparaging depiction.[33] To this end, domestic policy and foreign policy can no longer be decoupled, since they unambiguously concern
both facets of immigration, namely, the dynamics of internal race
relations *and* policies aimed at controlling the entry of migrants into
France.

Closer scrutiny of this discourse reveals the extent to which colonial
and postcolonial rhetoric pertaining to Africa and Africans continues
to be expounded by contemporary leaders. In a much commented on
and critiqued speech delivered in Dakar, Senegal, on July 26, 2007,
Sarkozy stated that "the problem with Africans is that they continue to
live in symbiosis with nature. . . . The problem with Africa is that it
continues to hold on to a lost paradise."[34] "The real difference therefore," as Jean-Loup Amselle has explained, "concerns that which juxtaposes France, or more broadly speaking Europe, with sub-Saharan
Africa since the latter, albeit the cradle of humanity and therefore
the bearer of all the world's wisdom, is nevertheless hindered because of its attachment to a tradition from fully engaging in modernity
and globalization."[35] Broadly speaking, Sarkozy updates paradigms
that started "under the colonial gaze," in which "Africa [finds] itself
stripped of all historicity to better justify domination by the European
powers as the only bearers or carriers of progress," as Laurence de
Cock has shown.[36] Today, de Cock continues, "all these stereotypes
infused with racist and archaic overtones reveal an ethnocentric and
paternalistic posture that allows the president to update the civilizing
mission of an ancient metropole."[37] Naturally, such negative representations continue both to influence and structure policy making
and to guide principles and inform strategies adopted to address the
claims, issues, and problems of concern to visible minorities in France.
What remains obfuscated in these constructs are the African contributions to that *long history* (among others), the constitutive nature
of the relations between France and Africa, and, of course, the ficti-
tious nature of demographic singularity.[38] As Catherine Coquery-

Vidrovitch has suggested, there is an urgent need to "relocate that historical object that is 'France' according to its . . . complexity, plurality."[39]

Analogies to race relations in the American context with established historical trajectories[40] continue to enjoy currency in France, and have been more frequent since the American election in 2008.[41] Whereas significant advances have been made in the United States for minority rights, the question remains very much in its embryonic stages in France. A French-style model of positive discrimination has been discussed, and both the support and opposition to such an approach have been in evidence on all sides of the political spectrum. Two government reports were commissioned in 2008: *Comité de réflexion sur le préambule de la Constitution: rapport au Président de la République* and *La diversité: rapport à la ministre de l'enseignement supérieur et de la recherche*.[42] The former was written by a committee chaired by Simone Veil, the latter a committee chaired by Michel Wieviorka. Each explored the question of diversity in contemporary France, acknowledged the degree to which this was an important question, and made several recommendations. But for the most part, they concurred that existing constitutional mechanisms provided adequate structures to implement new measures. Subsequently, President Sarkozy appointed as high commissioner for diversity Yazid Sabeg, who established an expert Comité pour la Mesure et l'Évaluation des Discriminations (COMEDD). At the same time, another group made up of eminent scholars challenged the usage of ethnic statistics in France, the Commission Alternative de Réflexion sur les "Statistiques Ethniques" et les "Discriminations" (CARSED).[43] These dissenting approaches have also been reflected in several publications. Alain Foix has recommended prudence in applying the American example to France, and has challenged people instead to identify "other forms of combat on the political, economic, social, and cultural terrain specific to the nation in question,"[44] while the elected representative from French Guiana Christiane Taubira has applied to the French Republic Barack Obama's notion of an *ultimately unfinished* political and racial project, which, though "sumptuous in its original conception, has not quite fulfilled its promise of equal rights."[45]

For Sarkozy's government, the solutions to all these questions have been anchored in shortsighted policies under the aegis of his new ministry, where a "dangerous liaison" has been established between "immigration" and "national identity."[46] As Noiriel has stressed, the government has set itself "the task of selecting today's immigrants according to criteria relating to 'republican values,' while affirming at the same time that one is protecting French identity in the future."[47] Yet these measures, public declarations, and speeches reveal deep-seated subconscious patterns that reinforce global dissymmetries. Sarkozy argues for the need for France to *globalize* while also advocating the crucial importance of protecting French identity against *globalization* and *communitarianism*. If ethnic mobilization during the 1980s served to underscore the deficiency of assimilation, insertion, and integration policies, then the uprisings of 2005 must surely be understood as the glaring failure of decolonization *and* the survival of transcolonial structures of inequity in the métropole. Not surprisingly, organizations such as the Conseil Représentatif des Associations Noires and Les Indigènes de la République are passionately combating policies that draw upon racist principles as a way of enlisting support. Once elected, President Sarkozy endeavored to capitalize upon the renewed attention accorded to race, and accordingly made three high-profile (visible?) appointments to his first cabinet: Rachida Dati as minister of justice (now a representative at the European Parliament), Fadela Amara as junior minister for urban affairs, and Rama Yade as secretary of state for foreign affairs and human rights (then secretary of state for sports). (The first two are of North African origin, the third Senegalese-born.) Once again, the question emerged as to whether or not such choices represented mere gestures or instead significant steps toward transforming the French political landscape were met with considerable debate, more so now since the removal of these women from those very positions. When one contrasts these appointments with the racist overtones of speeches made during the electoral campaign and after, and when one considers the repressive nature of subsequent policies that either proposed or implemented targeting ethnic minorities and immigrants, these disquieting realities undermine any tangible signs of progress. Indeed, reflection on the lack of minority representation in French politics today, especially when contrasted with the important role played by various representatives of the French Empire in the French Parliament and French government during the 1940s, such as Félix Eboué, Félix Houphouët-Boigny, and Jean-Félix Tchicaya, suggests rather social and political regression.

Notes

1. A. Hargreaves, *Multi-ethnic France: Immigration, Politics, Culture and Society* (New York: Routledge, 2007), 2.

2. E. Balibar, "Is There a 'Neo-Racism,'" in *Race, Nation, Class: Ambiguous Identities*, ed. E. Balibar and I. Wallerstein (London: Verso, 1991), 21.

3. See, e.g., D. Fassin and E. Fassin, eds., *De la question sociale à la question raciale: représenter la société française* (Paris: La Découverte, 2006).

4. T. D. Keaton, " 'Black (American) Paris' and the 'Other France:' The Race Question and Questioning Solidarity" in *Black Europe and the African Diaspora*, ed. D. C. Hine, T. D. Keaton, and S. Small (Urbana: University of Illinois Press, 2009), 183–213.

5. B. Hortefeux, preface to *Les orientations de la politique de l'immigration* (Paris: La Documentation Française, 2011), 7.

6. Ibid., 8–9.

7. Retrieved from www.immigration.gouv.fr.

8. G. Noiriel, *À quoi sert "l'identité nationale"* (Marseille: Agone, 2007), 146.

9. Hortefeux, preface, 7.

10. *Les orientations de la politique de l'immigration* (Paris: La Documentation Française, 2007), 133.

11. Noiriel, *À quoi sert "l'identité nationale,"* 142.

12. Ibid., 95–96.

13. Ibid., 95.

14. Ibid., 97.

15. Ibid., 93–94.

16. Ibid., 93.

17. Ibid., 94.

18. O. Le Cour Grandmaison, "Xénophobie d'état et politique de la peur," *Lignes* 26 (May 2008): 24.

19. A. Badiou, *De quoi Sarkozy est-il le nom?* (Paris: Nouvelles Éditions Lignes, 2007), 9.

20. A. Begag, *Ethnicity and Equality: France in the Balance*, trans. Alec G. Hargreaves (Lincoln: University of Nebraska Press, 2007), 19.

21. É. Balibar, "Racism and Crisis" in Balibar and Wallerstein, *Race, Nation, Class*, 220.

22. T. Abbas, "Recent Developments to British Multicultural Theory, Policy and Practice: The Case of British Muslims," *Citizenship Studies* 9, no. 2 (May 2005): 154.

23. The video is available on YouTube.

24. A. Begag, *Un mouton dans la baignoire* (Paris: Fayard, 2007), 9.

25. H. Lemoine, "La maison de l'histoire de France," *Pour la création d'un centre de recherche et de collections permanentes dédié à l'histoire civile et militaire de la France* (Paris: La Documentation Française, 2008), 16.

26. O. Le Cour Grandmaison, *La République impériale: politique et racisme d'état* (Paris: La Découverte, 2009), 369.

27. Ibid., 362.

28. P. Weil, *How to Be French: Nationality in the Making Since 1789*, trans. Catherine Porter (Durham: Duke University Press, 2009), 29.

29. O. Le Cour Grandmaison, *La république impériale*, 372.

30. See D. Thomas, "Sarkozy's Law: The Institutionalization of Xenophobia in the New Europe," *Radical Philosophy* 153 (January–February 2009): 7–12.

31. "La technologie du soupçon: tests osseux, tests de pilosité, tests ADN," in *Cette France-là*, vol. 1 (Paris: La Découverte, 2009), 159.

32. Begag, *Ethnicity and Equality*, 38.

33. See J. Dakhlia, "La France dedans dehors," *Lignes* 25 (March 2008): 160–76.

34. "Allocution de M. Nicolas Sarkozy, président de la république, prononcée à l'Université de Dakar," available on the president's official government web site (http://www.elysee.fr).

35. J.-L. Amselle, "Nicolas Sarkozy, Ségolène Royal et le post colonialisme," *Raison présente*, 2010.

36. L. de Cock, "Afrique," in *Comment Nicolas Sarkozy écrit l'histoire de France*, ed. L. de Cock, F. Madeline, N. Offenstadt, and S. Wahnich (Marseille: Agone, 2008), 30–31.

37. Ibid., 32.

38. See D. Thomas, *Black France: Colonialism, Immigration, and Transnationalism* (Bloomington: Indiana University Press, 2007).

39. C. Coquery-Vidrovitch, *Enjeux politiques de l'histoire coloniale* (Marseille: Agone, 2009), 168.

40. See T. Stovall, *Paris Noir: African Americans in the City of Lights* (New York: Houghton Mifflin, 1996).

41. See T. D. Sharpley-Whiting, ed., *The Speech: Race and Barack Obama's "A More Perfect" Union"* (New York: Bloomsbury, 2009).

42. S. Veil, *Comité de réflexion sur le préambule de la Constitution: rapport au Président de la République* (Paris: La Documentation Française, 2009); Michel Wieviorka, *La diversité: rapport à la ministre de l'enseignement supérieur et de la recherche* (Paris: Robert Laffont, 2009).

43. CARSED, *Le retour de la race: contre les "statistiques ethniques"* (La Tour d'Aigues: Éditions de l'Aube, 2009).

44. A. Foix, *Noir de Toussaint Louverture à Barack Obama* (Paris: Galaade, 2009), 81.

45. C. Taubira, *Égalité pour les exclus: la politique face à l'histoire et à la mémoire coloniale* (Paris: Temps Présent, 2009), 80–81.

46. A. Maillot, *Identité nationale et immigration: la liaison dangereuse* (Paris: Les Carnets de l'Info, 2008).

47. Noiriel, *À quoi sert "l'identité nationale,"* 99.

"Black France" and the National Identity Debate

How Best to Be Black and French?

FRED CONSTANT

France is once again engaged in a rather bizarre and deeply political debate, initiated by President Nicholas Sarkozy, over its national identity. Interestingly, this is not the first time that Sarkozy has launched such a top-down public discussion as part of his campaign promises.[1] While his popularity has plummeted halfway through his five-year term (lasting from 2007 to 2012),[2] the undisputed leader of the conservative party, Union for a Popular Movement (UMP), has decided to return to his political roots—crime, immigration, and national identity—particularly before crucial and pivotal regional elections in March 2010 when polls projected 8 percent of the votes going to the extreme Right party, the National Front.[3] In attempting both to appease disgruntled members of the UMP who feared losing key regions during the elections and attract votes from the National Front, Sarkozy sought to deploy a highly politicized gimmick, disguised as an intellectual national discussion. This Internet "debate" arguably posed a loaded question—"What does it mean to be French *today*?"—that is, during this period of existing, often violent, exchanges about "race," "ethnicity," "diversity," and ongoing anti-immigrant sentiments in French society.[4]

This chapter discusses the impact of this nation-wide debate on the Black segment of France's population, whose views on these and other critical issues are both underdiscussed and underprobed largely because "race" and "ethnicity" supposedly do not exist in a French society that rejects anything resembling an ethno-racial community within the republican model.[5] Relying on data generated from an ongoing research project,[6] I will explore a set of intertwined issues—

racial prejudice,[7] *la discrimination positive* (i.e., a biased translation of affirmative action),[8] and racial statistics[9]—that appear to divide Black French along conflicting and competing visions of "Frenchness" and "blackness." Far from being mutually exclusive, these contrasting views represent rather critical currents in French historical thought and practices in relation to the formation of the national identity. As has been increasingly documented, French national identity has been race-coded from its early definition both in theory and practice.[10] Strikingly, Black French views of Frenchness seem to be replicating the traditional opposition between the "old France" (an absolutist and ethnocentric form of republican universalism) and the "other France" (a multicultural vision of a country still in the making, one that encompasses every single aspect of its religious and ethnic components).[11] Accordingly, "French Black" or "Black French" views of "blackness" seem to be reflecting the classical antinomy between an official version of a Republican, race-neutral, liberal country (perceived as the "good" France) and an unofficial version of a race-coded, xenophobic, conservative society (defined as the "bad" France). It is not only important to examine the two extremes of these views (i.e., "old France" versus "other France"), but also instructive to exteriorize their internal complexity in terms of the overlapping or blurring of views and visions that tend to shift according to situation or context.[12] Thus, my objectives are threefold and entail identifying the cleavages within "Black France,"[13] examining the social variables that impact public opinion within this population, and accounting for the underlying causes of prima facie conflicting and competing views of "Frenchness" and "blackness," as they relate to the broader discussion of it what may (or may not) mean to be French in the twenty-first century.

The Debate on National Identity in Context

Eric Besson, a former Socialist Party member and currently the minister of Sarkozy's controversial Ministry of Immigration, National Identity, Integration, and Co-development, launched the three-month national debate at a press conference held on November 25, 2009. Besson's ministry carries the stigma of being associated with Sarkozy's administration and policies that are widely held to be anti-immigrant among both scholars and immigrant advocacy associations. For instance, during the presidential campaign in France in 2007, Sarkozy criticized immigrants and their offspring, insisting that they resist the French model of integration, which presumes equal opportunity to achieve this end and implies that acceptance within the society is its natural or guaranteed outcome. He later went on to say that it was unacceptable to want to live in France without respecting and loving the country or learning French. Then, on March 8, 2007, during a televised speech, he declared that, if elected, he would create the ministry that Besson now heads.

After this announcement, a serious national controversy erupted in France. Sarkozy was accused in creating such a ministry of harking back to the darkest period in modern French history: the collaborationist Vichy government during the Nazi occupation.[14] In fact, Simone Veil, a beloved former minister and Holocaust survivor, found herself denouncing Sarkozy's idea shortly after she endorsed him for the presidency. Unsurprisingly, Ségolène Royal, the left-wing leader and then serious contender for the presidency, also rejected Sarkozy's proposal and suggested that his project was disingenuous, or worse, racialized, since foreign workers had never threatened French identity in the past. More generally, opponents of Sarkozy accused him of pandering to Far Right anti-immigrant electors to whom such a ministry and debate would carry great appeal.

Sarkozy's supporters who subscribe to the idea that immigrants must assume the national identity—however ambiguous or (mis)understood—militated fiercely for restricted immigration policies that particularly targeted Muslims, whom they saw as willfully not conforming to secular French customs. Even supposedly "educated" people and top-ranked officials appeared to share this phobia of Islam. Of the many examples, consider this salient one: as the controversy concerning the national identity debate increasingly fomented discord, Pascal Clément, former minister of justice and member of Parliament, declared during a meeting of UMP's elected representatives in December 2009, that "the day when there are as many minarets as cathedrals, France will no longer be France."[15] Despite the strong opposition that this statement generated across the political spectrum, two related issues were presented as priorities by the Sarkozy administration: developing ways to halt the influx of undocumented immigrants, already characterized publicly as a drain on the country's economy and social services, and developing zero tolerance laws, including those banning practices such as polygamy and the wearing of head scarves by Muslim girls and women in schools and universities, laws ostensibly directed at French citizens of immigration and immigrants, in particular the youth, who are often associated with delinquency and criminality.

Accordingly, Minister Besson explicitly denied any connection between immigration and the debate on national identity that his ministry was expected to lead. Rather, Besson asserted that there was a necessity to collect the opinions of the French people about "Frenchness," and stated that this debate was vital for France to foster a more united nation. He also rejected any preconceived definition of "Frenchness" and invited everyone, irrespective of their opinions or social status, to post a statement on the ministry's official web site, although those appointed to oversee e-mail responses were instructed to toss out statements deemed "racists" or "xenophobic."[16] There is, nonetheless, an implicit message in this debate that relies on preconceived notions of "Frenchness," a message that says "France for the French," because "Frenchness" signifies European ancestry, in short, "whiteness." Among a spectrum of others, the sociologist Michel Wierviorka strongly opposed the debate, its political framing of "Frenchness," and the clumsy way it had been handled by this Ministry of Immigration, National Identity, Integration, and Co-development, the first ministry of this kind in the history of Republican France. "As a researcher and director of a research institute," Wierviorka stated, "I am in contact with academic circles around the world. I can tell you that [this national identity debate] is an intellectual and political catastrophe for France's international image."[17] This implicit message—"France for the French" or "old stock" French (*français de souche*)—performs not only a political function during an electoral period, but also seeks to reassure jittery voters that France will remain an important power even as its prominence shrinks within a larger European Union and a globalized world. This France is also struggling with disaffected Muslims and African populations that it has no idea how to address. By raising in this debate issues such as the Islamic veil, secularism, citizenship, the importance of singing the national anthem in schools, cultural inclusion (*assimilation*), tradition, and patriotism, there is obviously a strong political will to oppose two conflicting representations of France.

There are, on the one hand, France's national mottos (i.e., *Liberté,*

Égalité, Fraternité and *Laïcité*), which incarnate the official national representation so celebrated and trumpeted on every public occasion, and which vividly illustrate Republican France's self-image. Here, the construction of French national identity is premised on cultural and political unity. It reflects the very ideal of the French Revolution in 1789, the centrality of *La déclaration des droits de l'homme et du citoyen,* the "colorblind" republican model, and its universal pretence. It gives saliency to the principle of French secularism (*la laïcité*) as the freedom of belief and neutrality of the state toward religious matters, and to the primacy of *jus soli* which allows anyone virtually born in France to attain French nationality above and beyond *jus sanguis,* or bloodlines. Moreover, a strong emphasis on a universalistic definition of citizenship (leading to a common acceptance of cultural and ethnic pluralism) within a putatively indivisible France is supposedly enshrined in the national identity. On the other hand, there is an unofficial representation of France, generally marginalized since at least the French Revolution, except of course during the catastrophic Vichy era. This vernacular version of "Frenchness" that surfaces from time to time celebrates "traditional France" (i.e., the supposedly true France), its alleged Christian roots, its very telling myriad of local parishes (more than 36,000), and its specific, though rarely explicitly asserted, Caucasian ethnic background.[18] Here, primacy is given to jus sanguis over jus soli such that bloodlines, genealogy, language, and indeed the implicit idea of "race" prevail over the idea of a community of equal citizens.

Having contextualized the debate on national identity, I now turn to how this top-down discussion is echoed, partially or entirely, within the Black French population. By analyzing a set of public opinion polls, I attempt not only to document the range of views pertaining to a number of critical issues, particularly racial prejudice, affirmative action, and racial statistics, but also to relate these issues to the polarized national identity debate. Again, this polarization occurs between the idea of France as a dynamic, democratic, inclusive, and multicultural Republican France and the idea of France as an old, conservative, exclusive, and xenophobic one, represented by Minister Besson's discourse and office. Although the lack of ethno-racial statistical information about the Black segment of the French population limits considerably this type of research, it is my aim to draw light to views on these issues held by France's Black public in an attempt to disrupt an often homogenized and undifferentiated perception and representation of it.

Exploring "Black France": Public Opinion Polls and Interviews

Contrary to commonly held views that obtain in France, the Black segment of the French population is as divided as the rest of French society on issues of "race," as the studies that have been done on public opinions specifically within the French Black population illustrate.[19] It is instructive to discuss the internal differentiations within this population, the diversity of which extends well beyond the typical one-dimensional view of Blacks in France as an "oppressed category."[20] Socioeconomic differences are one critical distinction internal to the French Black population, but that status does not necessarily translate into greater protection for elite or middle class Blacks or lessen the need for anti-discrimination laws and policies. As is the case elsewhere, differing conceptions of "blackness" as well as disparate views about and reactions to anti-blackness prevail within the Black segment of the French population, which is evidenced in public opinion polls and interview data derived from my fieldwork.[21]

Public Opinion Polls

To gain insight into the views held by the French public about discrimination, particularly racial discrimination in France, several public opinion polls were conducted by private agencies and sponsored by major French newspapers, such as *Le Monde, Le Parisien, La Croix,* and nongovernmental organizations, such as SOS Racisme, the Conseil représentatif des associations noires (CRAN), and l'Union des Étudiants Juifs de France (UEJF). The main findings of these surveys were widely published in these newspapers. Some were also commented on during television news broadcasts, in particular *France 2, TF1,* and *FR3.*

These polls were generated by a few different organizations: the Conseils-Sondages-Analyses (CSA) produced one in 2006, Taylor Nelson/Institut d'Études Marketing et d'Opinion International

(TNS/SOFRES) in 2007, Institut Français d'Opinion Publique (IFOP) in 2008, and the CSA again in 2009. Each poll attempted to respond to differing aspects of the discrimination question. For instance, the TNS/SOFRES poll survey sought to evaluate the perception of racial discrimination among a sample of 581 persons who self-identified as "Black" or "*Métis*" (i.e., mixed ethno-racial heritage). The CSA poll survey attempted to address directly the issue of *discriminations positives*, or French affirmative action, among a sample of 497 Black French persons born in France's overseas departments as well as among residents in mainland France. Finally, drawing from a sample of 1,050 persons from the general public both overseas and in mainland French, a second CSA survey targeted the public's opinion about racial statistics and the efficiency of such data to combat racism and racial discrimination.

The most telling evidence pertaining to racial prejudice from the TNS/SOFRES poll in 2007 emerged in response to the question: "In your daily life, would you say that you are, personally, discriminated against racially?" An overwhelming majority of those polled (i.e., 67 percent) indicated having experienced racial discrimination.[22] However, under greater scrutiny, data show that there was important and insightful variance or differences of degrees among pollsters. That is, out of that 67 percent, only 16 percent indicated having experienced racial discrimination "often," and 23 percent indicated "from time to time," while 28 percent indicated that "rarely" did they experience racial discrimination daily. More importantly, a substantial minority (33 percent) rejected the proposition altogether, declaring that they had *never* been discriminated against. It bears noting that the perception of racial prejudice increases according to the level of education (64 percent for the more educated, 50 percent for the less), while it decreases, more or less, according to skin complexion. As was reported, 69 percent of those polled who self-identified as having a dark complexion indicated that they experience everyday discrimination, as did the 56 percent who self-identified as Métis. Thus, the more educated Black French are, the stronger the perception of racial prejudice, while the lighter their skin color, the less they perceive themselves racially discriminated against. However, one important limitation of the instrument is that it does not control for generational or class differences or for opinions, neither of which neatly correspond to educational levels, and clearly in this context education is not a precise indicator of social class. Contrary to commonly held views, there is an important dissenting minority who does not feel discriminated against in France, and those voices and views warrant greater scholarly attention so that a more complex picture of the Black French population emerges.

On the question of discriminations positives,[23] the most telling evidence from the CSA poll in 2006 emerges in response to the question: "Would you approve of the creation of quotas to give visible minorities easier access to jobs and positions in politics?" While 64 percent supported discriminations positives, a substantial minority (28 percent) disapproved of such an initiative. Moreover, the attitudes toward discriminations positives vary substantially in four critical ways: according to class location, such that the higher the class to which one belongs, the greater the disapproval of discriminations positives; according to educational level, such that the more educated the respondent, the less likely such a person would support discriminations positives; according to generation, such that older generations tend to be less supportive of discriminations positives; and, to a lesser extent, according to phenotype (in particular color), such that the lighter one's skin color, the less supportive such persons tend to be of discriminations positives.

Here again, it should be noted that there is an important dissenting minority against such a race-based social policy of inclusion. Such findings additionally contradict commonly held assumptions about the Black segment of the French population by journalists and, at times, scholars, who tend to represent Black French as being *naturally* inclined to support race-conscious policies. These blind spots need to be better documented and addressed for at least two reasons.[24] First, it would help to draw out internal complexities within Black French identity politics. Second, and more to the point, such documentation can point to some of the fascinating underlying motivations for the self and group distinctions being asserted among Blacks in a context in which the perceptions of them already impact images they project of themselves.

However, a very real divergence in opinion obtains between the French population at large and its Black segment in the CSA survey from 2009, which attempts to measure the public's views about the necessity of collecting ethno-racial statistics and the relevance of such statistics in battling discriminatory practices. Survey findings show that 55 percent of the general public disapproved of this type of data, finding it ineffective in combating discrimination and racism, while 64 percent of the Black population approved of the generation of such statistics. Moreover, the "average French person" indicated that the best way to oppose racial prejudice is to educate the public in order to sensitize them to these issues. The "average Black French person," however, indicated that collecting race data is the most effective way to counter rising discriminatory practices.

Within the Black population, the figures show a non-negligible dissenting minority, that is, 32 percent of those polled expressed opposition to ethno-racial statistics, even as a large majority (64 percent) approved of them. The French state does not count people by "race" or "ethnicity," though proponents of such data think that it is impossible to evaluate the relative well-being of minorities and craft effective solutions to remedy the problems they face without such data. Opponents of these data draw on the logic of the state and its policies that set the tone for the public's understanding of the nation. Thus, those opposed to ethno-racial statistics argue that this move would paradoxically reinforce internal ethnic divisions among citizens. The assumption is that when the state refuses to accept race as a meaningful social variable, it encourages its citizens to think in colorblind terms, which is supposed to yield positive social outcomes. The logic of this argument says that if "race" and "color" are not socially acknowledged, then there are no problems definable in those terms. However, it should not be overlooked that an important debate over "race" data generation is also occurring within the Black population in France. Too often underestimated or silenced, these dissenting voices need to be taken seriously into consideration, as my interview data highlights.[25]

Interviewing the Black French Population

In attempting to render more transparent the range of opinions on the issues under consideration among Black French people, I have also conducted interviews primarily with representative individuals who are associated with what has been identified as a Black elite in France. These data serve to complement the public opinion polls that often fail to capture important complexities underlying and interwoven in the views that they come to represent. Among those whom I interviewed, twenty persons—of thirty interviewees pulled from a larger sample of fifty individuals—are high civil servants, established medical professionals, politicians, lawyers, journalists, middle managers, and businessmen. The other ten interviewees are personnel in the lower social rungs of the public sector (i.e., staff in hospitals, post offices, prisons, and primary education) and in the private sector (i.e., insurance, commerce, security, and ground transportation). Interviewees were primarily born overseas (i.e., Martinique, Guadeloupe, Guiana) with seven having been born in the 1940s, eleven in the 1950s, seven in the 1960s, and five in the 1970s in Paris, but to parents who originated from la France d'Outre-Mer. Those who were not born in the métropole (i.e., twenty-five) went to mainland France to pursue their studies in higher education at the end of the 1950s. After completion of their studies, they settled in mainland France where they pursued their professional careers. About ten years later, five of the thirty worked for a short period of up to five years in the overseas territories, but later returned to mainland France to fully pursue their careers. Most have relatives overseas or have spent holidays there.

Using a snowball approach, I selected interviewees in 2007 and proceeded to conduct formal interviews between June 2007 and May 2008. I also arranged informal meetings and focus groups with some of the interviewees, which allowed me to refine my early findings with respect to shifts in views among my respondents. In most cases, the interviews were conducted in private places, but some took place at the offices of the interviewees out of convenience for them. One important limitation of the study, however, was some of the interviewees themselves. That is, with the notable exception of seven younger interviewees, born in the 1960s and 1970s, it was difficult to elicit responses from my informants about their views on "being Black and French" and, by extension, on other related issues (i.e., racial prejudice, affirmative action policy, racial statistics, and so on). Because they have so fully internalized "Republican principles," such as the (theoretical) "race-neutrality" of the state, they were often disinclined to even address or acknowledge these constructs. To allay their concerns, it was necessary for me to explain repeatedly the scientific purpose of my survey, the relevance of which was not immediately apparent for individuals who illustrate and are the products of the efficiency of France's "colorblind" ideology, as I have written elsewhere.[26] Moreover, to encourage them to speak candidly about their views, I had to reassure them that I would and could guarantee their privacy.

Overall, interview data show strong evidence of the impact of class and education on the perception of racial prejudice among Black French. Further, the generation of the interviewee also played an important role in the significance such individuals placed on the influence of "race" over "class" in their lived experiences, which also appears to reflect the relative importance attributed to these social issues in their life and on their life chances. A retired high civil servant explained it this way: "In our day, we had the unfortunate tendency to explain our setbacks in racial terms instead of social ones, in terms of a 'system' instead of an individual. Of course, there is racial discrimination, which should not exist in a republican form of government such as ours. I do not think that this discrimination constitutes an insurmountable barrier insofar as the integration of a young West Indian or African is concerned, who is really searching more for his or her place in society."

Indeed, an older generation of highly qualified professionals, born in the 1940s and 1950s, believe that they essentially made it on their own, despite whatever racial barriers they may have confronted. To their mind, the social marginalization of many Black youth is less the consequence of racial discrimination and more the outcome of a poor education. These successful professionals—retired or not—tend to stress the behavioral traits of young Blacks as a significant impediment limiting their upward mobility. As a medical practitioner expressed it: "For people of my generation who were educated in the Republican school system of that era, what mattered were the fundamental values of discipline, hard work, and respect for self and others. Today, it is difficult to recognize myself in the behavior of these young people who have lost their sense of purpose—and I am not only speaking about West Indians or African youth—who seem to have no desire to succeed through hard work, and who believe, instead, that everything is owed to them."

A recurring theme in these data is the perception of the waning of values among youth of a younger generation in much of "Black France," a waning of education, hard work, rigor, and personal responsibility, which is a view largely shared by the other interviewees with few exceptions. Emphasis is placed on the need for Blacks of a younger generation to fundamentally change their comportment and how they live so that they resemble French mainstream society.[27] This perspective is well illustrated by a judge of Martinican origin who averred: "These young people claim to be French, but do not want to conform to the principles, customs, or ways of this country; in short, to French culture. When you live in a country that you call your own, you must adopt the existing lifestyle instead of thinking that it's up to the country to adapt to you. It is not the society that has to change but these youth who must evolve in order to find their place within it."

Unsurprisingly, the interviewees (with three exceptions) strongly oppose, in the name of meritocracy, any "race-conscious" remedy to these problems, even affirmative action à la française that additionally takes into account class factors. As one manager put it: "It would be another step-down for the Republic, the defeat of its strongest principle, that of equal rights and of sound competition of which it is the guarantor." Almost unanimously, they denounce what they see as a process of racialization of social relations and reject vehemently any state intervention along ethnic lines. According to a successful businessman, "The racialization of governmental intervention is a form of regression; it's a step backward to that dismal period when people were judged based on their skin color. This is a very bad sign. Nobody wins, and more importantly, it's inefficient."

Moreover, in unambiguous terms, they call for the renewal of the ideals and institutions of the French Republic: "In all respects," a hospital manager asserted, "we must go back to the letter and to the spirit of our Republic. [Otherwise] everyone will take advantage, especially those who consider themselves left out." In other words, most interviewees endorse a type of "bootstraps" rhetoric of "personal responsibility," rejecting any diagnosis of inequalities by "structured exclusion." As one put it bluntly: "Those who really want to make it have to get their act together instead of holding society responsible for their failings. You make something of yourself through your efforts!"

It is important to note that very few interviewees qualified their stances by stressing the importance of other social problems that, in fact, affect life chances, such as poor living conditions and educational inequality. However, blame appears to be largely placed on individuals and their poor choices, behavior, and lack of responsibility. As a nurse explained it: "It is true that most of these young people live in very difficult conditions, so it would be futile to deny that. However, some do make it and manage to hold on, sometimes remarkably. So why should others give up and allow themselves to be distracted?" In many respects, most of the interviewees speak the language of an arrogant version of assimilationism, whose historical and explicit objective is conformity to France, the path to becoming recognized and accepted as "just regular Frenchmen," to quote one interviewee.[28]

Lived Experiences and Diversity of Opinion

In drawing from both polling and interview material on racial prejudice, discriminations positives, and racial data, I have sought to tease out the diverse opinions of Blacks in France in relation to their lived experiences, in particular the perceptions of Blacks as French in relation to how French national identity has been (mis)construed. These narratives and counter-narratives serve to refine and enhance the results from public opinion polls. Obviously, there is a diverse range of views that shift according to situation or context within this population. The limitations of this chapter preclude, however, elaborating upon these complexities in greater detail here.[29] I have opted to focus on the divergent ways in which the elite Black French population expresses how and why they assume (or are made to assume) and/or reject their "blackness" and "Frenchness" to illuminate further a more textured and multilayered representation of this population that often goes unnoticed and undocumented.

On the one hand, the Black French emerge as "French on paper," which signals a certain inauthenticity or a second-tier formation of citizenship that implies foreignness. Although these representations ring quite familiar, it is in that very familiarity where their continued power to appeal resides. As one interviewee sarcastically expressed it: "Legally, we are French like any other, but in practice, we must show evidence of our citizenship everywhere because we are not immediately perceived as French. Welcome to France, the land of liberty, equality, and fraternity!" Here, "race" plays a fundamental role in how one is perceived and self-identifies. As another interviewee nicely put it: "We are foremost Blacks and secondarily French. In this country, it is still hard for many of our fellow citizens to believe that you can be both French and Black. Sometimes, I have the strange feeling that I am asked to choose, that I can't be both." Another major aspect of the politics of "blackness" is the memory of and everyday experiences tied to a traumatic history of racial discrimination. Blackness is tethered to a legacy of slavery, and the vestiges of the colonial past are related to present and persistent patterns of discrimination in employment, residency, and education, among many other examples. Another interviewee captures these points: "It is often said that Blacks do not show much solidarity between one another. But they share a common history of oppressions and experience the same type of discrimination. If someone asked me what unites Blacks in France today, I would say the same experience of discrimination and rejection."

A second understanding of French "blackness" resists imposing an identity that has "race" as the primary or determining referent in the definition of the self. As a prominent surgeon articulates it: "I've been Black my whole life. It is a fact, but I am foremost a man. Therefore, I will never accept being defined by the color of my skin, my complexion, or phenotype. This would be a terrible form of regression, as if I were being asked to give up who I am." Here, achievement prevails over ascription, and such views appear to illustrate the notion of "narratives of the ascent" (to borrow from Henry Louis Gates).[30] That is, although those who subscribe to these views may have come from modest circumstances, they have achieved a certain prominence and socio-economic status or success professionally. As one interviewee put it: "When a client comes in my office, he is looking for the best service possible. And, if he comes in, it's probably because he thinks he'll get it. I don't see why I have to define myself as "Black" when my white colleagues are not approached nor defined in racial terms." Primacy is placed not only on one's professional position but also on one's legal status and citizenship. A retired lawyer echoed these thoughts: "Contrary to many other people, I don't have any problem with the fact that I am a French citizen, and letting that be known. I am first and foremost French because of my education and culture, even if it so happens that I am also Black."

Of course, these ways of inhabiting and not inhabiting "blackness" and "Frenchness" are not mutually exclusive. Obviously, they partially overlap and intertwine, since they are, at times, contradictory in relation to the issues examined in this study (i.e., racial prejudice, affirmative action, racial data), owing in large measure to the ways in which the ideology of universalism operates in the Republican model to foster "Frenchness" through its institutions while masking racial distinctions. For instance, one interviewee (a high civil servant) may be opposed to any "race-conscious" remedies, yet fiercely denounces everyday anti-black racism: "I am aware that racism is on the rise in France, but I totally disagree with 'reverse discrimination' because it would run counter to the interests of its beneficiaries."

Some may refuse any racial ascription and, at the same time, call for more solidarity between Black people, as one middle-aged manager asserted: "Personally, I don't want to be defined by the color of my skin. But, Black people should be more united so that they can defend their views." Further, some see themselves foremost as French citizens rather than Blacks, but approve of affirmative action à la française, which uses proxies for "race," and focuses more on economic rather than racial remedies.[31] As stated by a youth counselor: "If we are citizens like any other, there should be special assistance for those who are having a hard time making it." On the other hand, some emphasized the negative effects of poor living conditions on Blacks but oppose state interventions. A representative retired secondary school teacher observed: "Nobody could contest the hardship experienced by Blacks in the suburbs of our major cities, but I don't think that more welfare will help. On the contrary, they have to take responsibility for their lives in order to improve it." Finally, on the issue of generating racial data in France, many approve but resist race-conscious policies to address the forms of discrimination and racism that these data serve, nonetheless, to document. For instance, a hospital manager explains it this way: "Contrary to most Black people, I am against any form of affirmative action based on 'race,' but I approve collecting statistics based on 'race' because there is no other way to know exactly the condition of Blacks in all aspects of their lives." While these statements may appear contradictory, they are, in fact, not at all. Rather, for all their inconsistencies, they reflect the predicaments of Blacks in France, where the internal complexities are hardly ever discussed or rendered transparent in the paucity of studies and discourse that focus on or target not merely "this" population but "these" populations.

Concluding Observations

What does it mean to be Black and French in the twenty-first century? As my findings show, there is a diversity of opinions among Blacks living in France, which runs counter to conventional perceptions that tend to homogenize these populations and mask critical distinctions when they concern questions of race, identity, and belonging in France. At one end of the spectrum, one finds a certain "nationalist" positioning, where individuals self-assert more as Black than as French. At the other end, one finds those who could be characterized as "integrationist" (or nationalist in reverse), who see themselves foremost as French and secondarily as Black. Yet interestingly, these extremes reflect something more, the same ambivalence of belonging and the same perceived dubiousness pertaining to membership in French society. More to the point, the "nationalists" are definitely more "integrationist" than they would confess, while the "integrationists" are, at the same time, more "nationalists" than they would care to admit.

Accordingly, the views expressed about French national identity, as shown in interviews and public opinion polls, combine elements of "the old France" with features of the "other France," that is, one more visibly plural and always multicultural. On one hand, there are those "integrationists" of an older generation who have internalized an absolutist and ethno-centric model of republican universalism, although they recognize its imperfections. On the other hand, there are the activists of a younger generation who call for a type of multicultural France and who stand to challenge preconceived and timeless definitions of Frenchness, even though they militate foremost for equal opportunity for nonwhite French.[32] Young "integrationists" exist as do older "nationalists," but the point is that far from being contradictory, these opposing poles are related dimensions of the same predicament. More importantly, these groups, whatever their stripe, agree that inclusion in mainstream France goes far beyond equal access to rights, individual or not. It requires tackling issues related to the subjective feeling of membership in society at large. It means that a strategy has to be found not so much to reconcile the "old France" and the "other France" in the nation, but to build "another France" in which plural membership is considered additive not subtractive. In many respects, this is the main challenge France has to take up in order to live up to the political principles that it holds dear.

Notes

This chapter derives from a working paper (i.e., "Black France and the Debate over *discriminations positives"*) presented and discussed at the "Black France—France Noire: The Poetics and Politics of Blackness" conference in Paris, June 6–7, 2008.

1. Throughout its history, France's fascination with its national identity has led to an endless quest to define and clarify itself and mold a national representation of "Frenchness." Perhaps, this peculiarity is related to its deeply rooted rhetoric of "universal principles" that constantly drives public officials to speak out not only for the people of France, but also for humankind. For a remarkable historical study, see F. Braudel, *L'identité française* (Paris: Arthaud, 1986).

2. Over the last six months of 2009, the popularity of President Sarkozy has been steadily on the decline, haven fallen from 41 percent to 34 percent. His prime minister, François Fillon, has faced the same downward trend: his popularity has fallen from 44 percent to 36 percent during the same period.

3. Some political commentators consider regional elections as "midterm elections" of significant importance for the presidential elections in 2012. Most see the electoral process in March 2010 as a national acid test for the French president's politics and policies. At the same time, left-wing parties, especially the Socialist and the Ecologist parties, are under pressure to consolidate their hold over twenty-four out of the twenty-six regions up for grabs. Only two are controlled by right-wing coalitions.

4. Officially, President Sarkozy launched the national discussion on "Frenchness" on November 12, 2009, at La Chapelle en Vercors, a symbolic site of importance to the French resistance during the Nazi occupation. Additionally, in the midst of the national controversy and, at times, violent discussions about this debate, he published an article entitled: "Respectez ceux qui arrivent, respectez ceux qui accueillent," *Le Monde*, December 9, 2009. While it was intended to clarify his position, it only added fuel to an already ignited fire.

5. On the colorblind state in France, see, among many works, D. Schnapper, *La France de l'intégration: sociologie de la nation* (Paris: Gallimard, 1990); Haut Conseil à l'intégration, *Le contrat et l'intégration* (Paris: La Documentation Française, 1998); D. Lapeyronnie, *L'individu et les minorités: la France et la Grande-Bretagne face à leurs immigrés* (Paris: Presses Universitaires de France, 1993); F. Constant, *La citoyenneté* (Paris: Montchrestien, 1998); M. Silverman, *Deconstructing the Nation: Immigration, Racism, and Citizenship in Modern France* (London: Routledge, 1992); A. Favell, *Philosophies of Integration: Immigration and the Idea of Citizenship in France and Britain* (London:

Macmillan, 1998); P. Weil, *La république et sa diversité: immigration, intégration, discriminations* (Paris: Le Seuil, 2005); F. Constant, "Talking Race in Color-blind France: Equality Denied, 'Blackness' Reclaimed," in *Black Europe and the African Diaspora*, ed. D. C. Hine, T. D. Keaton, and S. Small (Urbana: University of Illinois Press, 2009), 145–61.

6. This research is designed to challenge and break down preconceived definitions of the so-called Black minority in France by highlighting the diversity and range of opinions held by people in this population. On the one hand, my attempt is to move from a group-oriented to a problem-oriented sociology of race. On the other hand, I seek to focus on intraracial differentiations rather than restricting attention to interracial relations. Moving from a group-oriented to a problem-oriented sociology of race allows us to focus our attention on the complex work of group-making inscribed in ethnoracial boundaries, in the objectivity of social space and in the subjectivity of mental space. In other words, social groups or groupings are not homogenous; they are always social constructs, forged by power in relation to groups or groupings. In any case, we should not take for granted the existence of these groups as such because it would prevent us from apprehending the dynamic process in which they were fabricated. On these epistemological particular aspects, refer to L. Wacquant, "For an Analytic of Racial Domination," *Political Power and Social Theory* 11 (1997): 221–34.

7. On the rise of racism in France, see Commission Nationale Consultative des Droits de l'Homme, *La lutte contre le racisme et la xénophobie* (Paris: La Documentation Française, 2000); M. Wierviorka, *The Arena of Racism* (London: Sage, 1995); V. de Rudder et al., *L'inégalité raciste: l'universalité républicaine à l'épreuve* (Paris: Presses Universitaires de France, 2000); and more recently, P. Ndiaye, *La condition noire: essai sur une minorité française* (Paris: Calmann-Lévy, 2008), chaps. 4 and 5.

8. Among other references, G. Calvès, *Les discriminations positives* (Paris: Presses Universitaires de France, 2004); M. Doytcheva, *Une discrimination positive à la française: ethnicité et territoire dans les politiques de la ville* (Paris: La Découverte, 2007).

9. For an introduction to the French debate on racial statistics, see the policy brief by D. Sabbagh, "The Collection of Ethnoracial Statistics: New Developments in the French Controversy," 2008, on at http://www.french american.org/cms/files/policybriefs_pdf/Policy%20Brief%20-%20Ethnic% 20Statistics.pdf.

10. Among other references, see S. Peabody and T. Stovall, eds., *The Color of Liberty: Histories of Race in France* (Durham: Duke University Press, 2003).

11. For an illuminating analysis of these two conflicting representations of France, see T. D. Keaton, *Muslim Girls and the Other France: Race, Identity Politics, and Social Exclusion* (Bloomington: Indiana University Press, 2006).

12. As I said above, it seems very important to stress the dissenting voices over "Frenchness/blackness" as they are related to the national identity debate. Moreover, it is necessary to highlight the complexity of views which alternate between universalism and particularism, ascription and achievement, in the definition of the national self. In doing so, my attempt is to show the extent to which the debate over "blackness" among French Blacks echoes the national discussion about national identity in France.

13. "Who is a Black French and what is Black France?" is an uneasy question one must confront from the start. As Stephen Small stated it in his illuminating introduction (Hine, Keaton, and Small, *Black Europe and the African Diaspora*, xxv), "They ["Black Europeans" and "Black Europe"] are, of course, not just questions of legal definition, but of individual and collective definition, of belonging and yearning—even of status and attainment. . . . Blackness is not just, or even, about African ancestry. It is about racialization and the ascription of blackness—which reminds us, once again, you don't have to be Black to be racialized as Black." Accordingly, by "Black France" I refer, of course, to a construct as it came out of public opinion polls and interviews that I conducted in the course of my fieldwork. Far from any reification, it is rather a device used to highlight shifting identity politics and populations in France and should not be taken literally. For further elaboration on problems pertaining to definitions, see my occasional paper, "Les noirs sont-ils solubles dans la république? Notes sur l'invisibilité des minorités visibles en France," (paper presented at the conference "Les Noirs en France: anatomie d'un groupe invisible," École des Hautes Études en Sciences Sociales, Paris, February 19, 2004).

14. Cf. P. Weil, "Pourquoi je refuse de participer au comité de Yasid Sabegh," on the web site of Mediapart (http://www.mediapart.fr).

15. It should be noted that Nora Berra, junior minister for senior citizens, of Algerian descent, walked out of the room and issued a statement of protest to her colleague's statement. Refer to the press coverage online, retrieved January 10, 2010, from http://www.lejdd.fr/Politique/Actualite/Minarets-Ca-chauffe-a-l-UMP-159975, available on the web site of Le JDD: http://www.lejdd.fr.

16. On January 4, 2010, the French minister Eric Besson held a press conference in Paris to present the early findings of the debate on national identity, and a public opinion poll—carried out by TNS/SOFRES—on the views of the general public over this top-down public discussion. Despite his efforts to discard the many criticisms generated by the debate from various sectors of French society, he did not convince any of his detractors that the debate was successful or even pertinent. As I write, its political impact does not seem very positive.

17. Interview retrieved on January 10, 2010, from http://front.liberation

.fr/politiques/0101606585-ce-debat-conforte-des-positions-de-fermeture-et-de
-xenophobie-plus-que-d-ouverture. See also the statement issued by the sig-
natories of those petitions against this office, in particular "Nous exigeons la
suppression du ministère de l'identité nationale et de l'immigration" (We
demand the closing down of the Ministry for National Identity and Immigration), published in the French newspaper *Libération*. Retrieved January
10, 2010 from http://front.liberation.fr/societe/0101606559-nous-exigeons-la
-suppression-du-ministere-de-l-identite-nationale-et-de-l-immigration. Also
on the Libération web site: http://www.liberation.fr.

18. With the notable exception of Jean-Marie Le Pen, president of the
National Front, who stated explicitly in a press conference held at Nice on
November 21, 2009, that "c'est l'immigration qui constitue le danger le plus
grand pour notre identité nationale, en ce qu'il touche la substance même de
la nature ethnique de la France, telle qu'elle existe depuis 1,500 ans!" (It's
immigration that constitutes the greatest danger for our national identity
because it touches the very substance of France's ethnic stock as it has existed
for 1,500 years!) The excerpt is taken from the web site of the National Front.
Retrieved January 5, 2010, from http://www.frontnational.com/?p=2729.

19. Most of the books published on Blacks in France document the trajectory, lived-experiences, indeed condition of its naturalized members, though
much research remains to be done on Black French in the metropolis to draw
out all the complexities of these populations. While not an exhaustive list,
some relatively recent titles include G. Kelman, *Je suis noir et je n'aime pas le
manioc* (Paris: Max Milo, 2004); J.-L. Sagot Duvauroux, *On ne naît pas noir,
on le devient* (Paris: Points, 2004); M. Fall, *Le destin des africains noirs en
France: discrimination, assimilation, repli communautaire* (Paris: L'Harmattan,
2005); F. Durpaire, *France blanche, colère noire* (Paris: Odile Jacob, 2006); R.
Yade, *Noirs de France* (Paris: Calmann-Lévy, 2007); M. Fall, *L'échec de l'intégration des noirs de France* (Paris: Lavoisier, 2007); P. Lozès, *Nous les noirs de
France* (Paris: Stock, 2007); B. Lecherbonnier and P. Lozès, *Les noirs sont-ils
des français à part entière?* (Paris: Larousse, 2009).

20. Racialized, subjugated categories also have their own peculiarities and
distinctions. In Europe, both in theory and in practice, there is a need for
further research and documentation of those represented by such categories,
especially in the French context where "race"—as both a social object and
tool of analysis—has been minimized or dismissed altogether for quite some
time.

21. Unsurprisingly, the self-declared leaders of the "Black population," i.e.,
le Conseil représentatif des associations noires (CRAN), tend to deny this diversity of opinion within the Black population. It would be very interesting to
have a better picture of the 127 associations which are supposed to be the

stakeholders within the CRAN and, as well, a better knowledge of its internal procedures of decision making.

22. Racial prejudice was measured in specific areas (workplace, public transportation, public spaces, neighbourhood, leisure, school or university, family).

23. Here, discriminations positives refers to quotas, although indirect strategies of affirmative action using proxies for "race" have been in play in France since the 1980s. See A. G. Hargreaves, "Half-Measures: Antidiscrimination Policy in France," *French Politics, Culture, and Society* 18, no. 3 (2000): 83–101.

24. Of many studies, refer to L. Wacquant, "For an Analytic of Racial Domination," *Political Power and Social Theory* 11 (1997): 221–34; D. Sabbagh, "L'affirmative action et les aléas de la catégorisation raciale aux États-Unis," *Raisons politiques* 2 (1999): 7–26; E. Bleich, "Antiracism without Races: Politics and Policy in a 'Color-blind' State," *French Politics and Culture and Society* 18, no. 3 (2000): 48–74; P. Simon, "L'enquête expérimentale, mesure de la diversité: test de différentes catégorisations des origines et réaction des enquêtés," proceedings from the conference "La mesure des différences liées à l'origine," Inter Service Migrant–Centre d'Observation et de Recherche sur l'Urbain et ses Mutations (ISM–CORUM), Lyon, retrieved October 22, 2007, from http://www.ined.fr; D. Sabbagh, "Eléments de réflexion sur la mesure de la 'diversité' et des discriminations, 2009," on the web site La vie des idées (http://www.laviedesidees.fr/?lang=fr).

25. These silences about a diversity of views among Black French are equally evident in some of the most recent scholarship in France on this population, such as P. Ndiaye, *La condition noire: essai sur une minorité française* (Paris: Calmann-Lévy, 2008); E. Fassin and F. Fassin, *De la question sociale à la question raciale? Représenter la société française* (Paris: La Découverte, 2007).

26. Among other references, see my *La retraite aux flambeaux: société et politique en Martinique* (Paris: Éditions Caribéennes, 1998), chap. 1; *La Citoyenneté*, chap. 2

27. On this particular conservative way of thinking, it would be instructive to engage further comparative studies with what gets called "Black pathology" in the United States and Britain, for example. Among others, one can refer to the pioneering work of J. W. Wilson, *The Bridge over the Racial Divide: Rising Inequalities and Coalition Politics* (Berkeley: University of California Press, 1999).

28. Keaton, *Muslim Girls and the Other France*, 3.

29. My forthcoming study on the French Black elite will provide a more detailed, in-depth analysis.

30. H. L. Gates, *Thirteen Ways of Looking at a Black Man* (New York: Vintage, 1997), xiv.

31. Calvès, *Les discriminations positives*.

32. E.g., L. Thuram, P. Blanchard, F. Durpaire, R. Diallo, and M. Cheb Sun, *Appel pour une république multiculturelle et postraciale*, retrieved February 5, 2010, from http://www.respectmag.com/acheter-lappel-pour-une-république-multiculturelle-et-postraciale.

Paint It "Black"

How Africans and Afro-Caribbeans
Became "Black" in France

RÉMY BAZENGUISSA-GANGA

To clarify the concept of "Black France," I will approach the French context from the angle of two intersecting realities, what I refer to here as "Little France" and "Imperial France."[1] "Little France" refers to a nation-state located in Europe, that is, to a community of citizens or nationals who share a status and a number of rights and obligations, as well as a certain perception of their identity, which they adapt to a model predicated on an opposition between an inside and outside. That opposition was particularly visible in the "national identity" debate in 2010 launched by the French minister of immigration, Eric Besson, and when the European Union member states were establishing a shared, suprastate citizenship. The term "Imperial France" denotes a slave-owning, colonial power with extraterritorial lands that are both inside and outside national frontiers, or at their confines. "Imperial France" integrates legal and territorial aspects, and, for all kinds of reasons, the linkage between the two blurs the traditional ways of belonging to a nation and the criteria for citizenship. I include "Black France" in "Imperial France" because it refers to a long history of colonization and slavery.

Having clarified this point, it is important to note that I am not concerned with the Afro-Caribbean and African elites.[2] Much has already been written about their interrelations and how, in order to fight racial discrimination, they have claimed collectively and in political terms to be "Blacks," "negroes/nègres," and so on.[3] They have constructed a common identity on the basis of a shared experience of slavery and colonization, indeed, of oppression. At the same time, it is important to examine dynamics and practices in working and middle-class milieus in which these respective positions have mainly taken on two forms. From the 1960s until about the 1980s, the greater possibilities of the two communities cohabiting and meeting in Little France have led them to incarnate, in a more complex manner, a Black identity assigned by whites, even though they do not see themselves as a single "Black community." However, in Little France from the 1990s on, many Africans and Afro-Caribbeans have called themselves "Black" (often preferring the English term instead of French one), or "*renois*," and "*reun*."[4] However, this was not merely a way to understand how they fit in the equation of slavery and colonization, but a way to understand how they were linked to racial events in France, as reconfigured by globalization. Here, the situation of African Americans in the United States, a dominant and omnipotent center of the new world order, represents the ultimate identification reference. To explore these dynamics, this chapter examines how such identity politics operate in the working classes among a complex of socio-economically heterogeneous peoples of African origin.

I must clarify two further points. Very little research on the relations between Africans and Afro-Caribbeans has been carried out in Little France, and I will refer to it in passing. To overcome this limitation, I will occasionally draw from a somewhat unorthodox method for obtaining material: probing my memories and using less frequently cited texts by well-known researchers (i.e., replies to interviews, blogs, and so on). I will also refer to other interviews that I personally conducted that are co-constitutive of my own experiences. This research also takes inspiration from various authors who highlight the heuristic import of an approach that focuses on "plot" as a narrative form indicative of heterogeneous realities, and this study emerges from a broader project in which these issues are situated within historical sociology.[5] For the purposes of this piece, however, my aim is to reconstruct a certain order that allows me to follow the succession of positions taken by working-class Africans and Afro-Caribbeans in order to show how racial meanings are ascribed onto them.

As I have shown previously, two phases mark the presence of Africans in France, with a transition occurring in the 1970s and 1980s.[6] As such, this chapter comprises two related parts: I will begin by identifying the first phase, wherein the differences between working-class Afro-Caribbeans and Africans are clearly expressed. I will then explore the second phase, during which Africans and Afro-Caribbeans became "Black," again, as I maintain, within the context of globalization. A diachronic analysis will allow us to understand and shed light on the process by which this transformation occurred, namely, filiation and generational change.

Africans and Afro-Caribbeans as "Hommes de Couleur" in Little France

The two landmarks in this phase were the First World War and the promulgation of the decree that put an end to economic immigration in 1974. The historical plot that allows us to understand this phase concerns the separation of Africans and Afro-Caribbeans at a time when, in Little France, they shared a negatively designated racial identity as "persons (men or women) of color." In short, this euphemism was a way to speak about racism in color terms without ever actually using the word.

In France, until the 1950s, there were relatively few people from the French Overseas Departments or Africa. The Afro-Caribbean elite sent their children to study in schools and universities in metropolitan France, and the young graduates then returned or stayed on in France as lawyers, doctors, vets, engineers, or teachers. This type of travel was limited because of the cost of the journey.[7] With the Africans, there were merely a few demobilized soldiers (the well-known Senegalese infantrymen from the First World War, who stayed on instead of returning home) along with a small population of general laborers, sailors, and students with state scholarships in Little France.[8]

Whatever their class, (most of) these populations made their way into the working class in the 1960s. To illustrate how this situation has been constituted, I will mainly draw from data specific to the Paris region, a key migration site, to show how this phase was structured around a political, economic, educational, and gendered universe. Indeed, the transcontinental mobility of these populations was configured by the same type of logic, specifically, the strong involvement of the Imperial State in its organization and its domination by the dynamics of strong economic growth in metropolitan France. I will not provide quantitative data about these populations, since these are available in several other works.[9]

African migration to Little France increased following the independence of countries in French West Africa and French Equatorial Africa, and was mainly channeled into two areas: education and labor. The former grew, especially after the Second World War, with the gradual transfer of political power to indigenous people. Since these people needed to acquire the necessary skills through education, many trainees and students received scholarships from Imperial France or from their own countries to pursue their studies in Little France, returning afterward to take up positions in high office. During their stay in France, they lived in student housing and, less frequently, in social housing (French public housing projects and the like).[10] Labor, the other channel, increased between 1963 and 1964, following bilateral agreements on manpower signed between Little France and Mauritania, Mali, and Senegal, and in 1966 between Little France and the Ivory Coast, Cameroon, Upper Volta (now Burkina Faso), and Dahomey (now Republic of Benin). These agreements led to an increase in the flow of a supposedly more docile man power than that from North Africa, with the possibility of controlling it with mandatory work certificates. This migratory net mainly concerned villagers from the Senegal River Valley (the Soninké and Toucouleur ethnic groups from Mali, Senegal, and Mauritania).[11] The result was the arrival in Little France of far more African workers than students, men who envisioned from the outset only a temporary stay in the country. They arrived as bachelors and lived in hostels, but planned to return home as notables who had accrued a certain status from their life and livelihood in France. The majority worked as skilled workers in major private industries, in particular the car industry.

The majority of the Afro-Caribbeans arrived in France between 1961 and 1982 as a result of policies initiated by the Bureau pour le Développement des Migrations Intéressant les Départements d'Outre-Mer (BUMIDOM). This migration contributed to proletarianizing the Afro-Caribbeans. The BUMIDOM, which was jointly administered by the Ministry of Overseas Departments and Territories and the Ministry of Finance, was a state company charged with addressing unemployment and political unrest in the Overseas Departments. Between 1961 and 1968, the BUMIDOM administered the flow of nearly 64 percent of the population from these Overseas Departments in its role as an employment agency for France, which placed Afro-Caribbean workers in private companies and public administrations. Unlike the case of African migration, the professional structure of the Afro-Caribbeans consisted in a large proportion of women in public sector jobs. Because Afro-Caribbeans had French citizenship, they were able to fill a shortfall in the lower-ranking service sector jobs that were disdained by the metropolitan French because of the low salaries. For instance, Afro-Caribbeans worked in the major public hospitals, the post office, the French railways (SNCF), the French airlines (Air France), customs, and the police force. They rented small, usually furnished apartments in old, run-down buildings in the working-class areas of eastern Paris as well as in major suburban agglomerations such as Sarcelles, Créteil, Gonesse, and Bondy.

In this first phase, the transcontinental movement of Africans and Afro-Caribbeans to Little France had a strong political dimension because it was a product of Imperial France. That is, it is possible to retrace its structural characteristics, which were postcolonial and reflected the end of slave ownership. Further, if one takes into account the long period involved, one notes the differing statuses attributed to the descendents of slaves and former colonized peoples in France's peculiar systems of domination in the figures of the *citizen*, the *slave*, and the *native*, the last two having melded in this current period.

In different ways, these statuses comply with the dynamics of Imperial France. Indeed, these migration flows reactivated evocations of systems of domination, the slaves being the ones who, forcefully deported to another continent, lost their "country" and land. As a result, they had to reconstruct themselves as subjects in the plantation system before their descendents acquired citizen status in Imperial France and Little France when slavery was abolished. However, the postcolonial Africans acquired a homeland and a nation, and subsequently became "foreigners" in Little France. In the one case, we are dealing with descendents and in the other with former subjects of the colonial empire who have become foreigners.

This play on status produced a fundamental difference. The majority of Afro-Caribbeans worked for the public sector, while the Africans went to work in private enterprises. Paradoxically, enrolling these subordinate peoples in the economic world of Little France led them to occupy racial positions in a system that ostensibly denied all forms of racism by employing color euphemisms instead. Racism was already inherent in Little France, as seen with the earlier waves of Poles, Portuguese, Italians, and other immigrants inhabiting the working-class world, and the racism that these groups suffered did not refer to a social hierarchy of color differentiation indicating superiority or inferiority. With the arrival in Little France of the Afro-Caribbeans, who, as citizens, were already participating in social universes governed to a great extent by this principle, color-based racism intersected with racism based on nationality. Consequently, having the means to control the socio-economic welfare of African and Afro-Caribbean mobility, Imperial France both disseminated and reconfigured that which was being undone within the citizenship construct in the heart of Little France. That is, while color-based racism was denied, it nonetheless existed for those who came to be identified as "Black" in French society, contributing to the formation of a "Black" identity, both assigned and assumed, in these marginalized groups, whether African or Afro-Caribbean.

While numerous works illustrate how average Afro-Caribbeans perceive Africans and in light of research carried out on the convergent or divergent relationships between the two, I find that Frantz Fanon saliently records how authors in the period from the Second World War until the 1950s describe the relationship between the two groups.[12] In his article on Afro-Caribbeans and Africans, Fanon analyzes the Afro-Caribbean experience in relation to that of Africans as an ordeal in a trajectory that led them from being *noir* (black) to *nègre* (negro): the Afro-Caribbean is "noir" while the African is a "*nègre*."[13] Fanon begins by challenging the idea of Black unity. For him assimilating the two is trying to dissolve difference in color. As he explains it: "By putting all the Negroes together under the term '*peuple noir*' [Black people], we are attempting to remove any possibility of individual expression. We are trying to oblige them to respond to the idea we have about them. . . . When we say 'Black people,' we systematically suppose that all Blacks agree on certain things; that there is an assumption of communion between them. The truth is that that there is nothing that supposes the existence of a Black people. But I believe there is an African people, certainly, and an Afro-Caribbean people."[14] For Fanon therefore, "noir" is an idea that "whites" hold of the "Other." Here, the concept is no longer that of attributing identity but of assigning it. Fanon himself describes his observation as an attribution of identity.

For Fanon, the colonial experience in Africa influenced the creation —or strengthening—of differences between Afro-Caribbeans and Africans. Afro-Caribbeans considered themselves to be "almost" white in their relationship to Africans, because in the colonial scheme of things, and even in Africa proper, they held minor positions. The "almost white" Afro-Caribbeans who recognized themselves as "noir" were positioned and positioned themselves against Africans who were relegated to the status of "negro," or savage, someone outside humanity. According to Fanon, the same difference perceived between the Africans and the Afro-Caribbeans is applied by the inhabitants of Martinique and Guadeloupe, the former considering themselves "noir" and the latter "nègre," and thus closer to Africa. Furthermore, Fanon stated that the Second World War marked a turning point in the relations between Afro-Caribbeans and Africans, the effects of which took fifteen years to spread. At the time, the Afro-Caribbeans began to abandon their noir position and consider themselves nègres and established a kinship with Africans. This change was the result of a disenchantment caused by France's defeat and the pressures imposed by a massive presence in the French West Indies of those deemed "bad whites." These were French sailors who mostly supported the Vichy government: in other words, collaborators. In reaction to this, the Afro-Caribbeans massively sought their roots in Africa and consequently ended up accepting and assuming their "Africanness" while the Africans refused to grant it.

It would be useful to compare this with African representations of Afro-Caribbeans in the same period. Unfortunately, I have found no research of this kind. However, crossing Fanon's analysis of Afro-Caribbeans with the conclusions that I reached based on an analysis of the postslavery system shows that those who lost their homeland adhere more to the assigned identity of "noir." In other words, those who experienced a break with what they consider their motherland (a condition for acquiring citizenship) and the discriminatory designations by whites claim to be "noir" in Black France.

So what is the current state of relations between Africans and Afro-Caribbeans in Little France? Here, I will use data from the Paris region, one of the most cosmopolitan and political in the country, a site that favors cohabitation between the two communities but not necessarily their coming together. In this context, it is important to acknowledge that intermarriage, for instance, has long existed between people from the Ivory Coast and Afro-Caribbeans, with rulers apparently promoting and supporting these unions for political reasons. Aimé Césaire's considerable influence calls to mind another strategy for bringing these communities together. In the 1970s, he devised a cultural policy to promote travel between Martinique and the African continent. This had some repercussions and resulted in several Afro-Caribbeans journeying to Africa as well as Africans to Martinique. On occasion, it led to marriage. However, on the fringes of these movements was a more widespread trend in relations between Africans and Afro-Caribbeans in the working-class milieu of Little France.

I will begin with a test I often carry out and that anyone can try. Simply ask an African or Afro-Caribbean who arrived in France during that period how many friends he or she has in the other population. I have done this many times, and the answer I invariably get is none. To track this parallel cohabitation that never meets, I begin by looking at how each group views the other. The Afro-Caribbeans call Africans "*Africains*," irrespective of their country of origin such that diverse peoples become scripted as a single entity. They also use a shorter name "*caincain*," which is the last syllable of "*African*" repeated twice. However, in Creole, the sound "in" is written "en," making "*caincain*" into "*kenken*," which also means vain and pretentious, a term used to describe an empty-headed show-off.

The Afro-Caribbean relationship to Africans is very ambiguous. In Little France, Afro-Caribbeans, who are French citizens, complain about being mistaken for Africans because of their color. The differences between them depend on those areas in which, to some extent, they feel affinities with Africans and interact. But representations of the "Other" and hierarchies are often generated and established such that the construction of the "African" is marked by ambivalence and duplicity, and the word evokes both attraction and repulsion. There is attraction because "Africa" has a mythical aspect that refers to the place of origin, which is the interpretation that the majority of the elite favor; repulsion because the word also evokes "barbarian." That aspect dominates among average Afro-Caribbeans. For instance, I used to know an Afro-Caribbean who would advise young women not to marry Africans because they were "savages."

Thus a system of representations oscillates between the two interpretations. On the one side, the African is powerful in the field of magic and healing practices, dance and music, a power that results from maintaining ties with nature. As a Malian informant stated, "Afro-Caribbeans come to see our *marabouts*."[15] However, Africans have less legitimacy when it comes to citizenship, from which they are excluded. Thus, Afro-Caribbeans construct the African "Other" as someone more distant by appropriating postslavery history for themselves. The politics of belonging relative to constructs of Frenchness acts as a barrier.

As for Africans, they view Afro-Caribbeans as a single entity and do not differentiate between them. They consider them uneducated people who do not know their history or, worse, deny it. Some Africans, the Congolese for instance, call them *"moi ka double,"* stigmatizing them linguistically, and some contend that every word in Creole begins with one of those words which, they claim, means "I" or "me." This name therefore targets the mother tongue. In fact, *"moi ka double"* has a hidden meaning that refers to a fabled meeting between a Congolese man and an Afro-Caribbean woman: "During the sexual act, the Congolese man quickly reached orgasm and then stopped. The Afro-Caribbean woman asked him, 'You finished already? *Moi ka double,'*" which, translated from Congolese means "You're already done? I want to do that again." The Afro-Caribbean woman thereby signifies her dissatisfaction and desire to repeat the act. This story does not disparage the Congolese man's premature ejaculation, but vilifies the sexual appetite of Afro-Caribbeans. The Malians however, do not use a term with sexual connotations. They use a Mandingo word to describe Afro-Caribbeans, *"djikhammokho,"* which breaks into three smaller words, *dji* (water), *kham* (beyond or over), and *mokho* (water). This translates as "he who lives on the water and is next to water" or "those who come from the other side of the water," the other side understood as referencing the sea and therefore what is taken as their place of origin. To some extent this term may be reversed, since viewed from that perspective, Afro-Caribbeans could call Africans by the same name.

To a considerable degree, all these representations use and exemplify the racist themes used by whites to describe Blacks: barbarism, a relationship to nature, the voracious sexuality and sexual appetite of Black women, and so on. The place held by Afro-Caribbeans and Africans in these identifications always refers to ideologies imposed by whites. That third party is important in all binary oppositions, but here it also acts a mediator in their historic meeting. What matters is how these representations, as modulated by that third party, impacted the interactions between Afro-Caribbeans and Africans and how each relates to their experience of encountering the Other.

Their difference in status complicates the relationship. Afro-Caribbeans have French citizenship whereas Africans are usually foreigners. Consequently, when Afro-Caribbeans arrive in Little France, they anticipate that they will not be subjected to the same police and administrative restrictions as those perceived as outsiders. That advantage confers a certain smugness and disdain with regard to Africans, as though they hold a special place in the representations of foreigners. Their aloofness is a way of playing the social game and confirming their insider status and position. The identity and other administrative controls, whether by the police or the public transport authorities, provide situations that illustrate this point. Africans often deplore the punctilious attitude of Afro-Caribbeans when they act as incarnations of the state. Thus, the Afro-Caribbean complicity with the repressive powers-that-be becomes a strategy of distinction because it is apprehended as the only means, or at least one of the means, at their disposal for not being assimilated with foreigners, particularly those racialized as inferior. However, things become more complicated in this system of denied discrimination and racism. For instance, the prejudicial belief that "all colored people look alike" makes it possible, in certain cases, to carry out illegal activities, such as stop-and-search controls. For example, Africans have been known to borrow each other's ID papers, operating under the notion that if "whites" control their papers, they are presumably unable to distinguish the faces of "blacks." However, Afro-Caribbean controllers are not fooled by this type of situation, which singles them out twice over, as they have to reveal the subterfuge and incriminate the African as a foreigner, while refusing to adopt white prejudice through identifying the differences between Black people. The following case of an identity control carried out by an Afro-Caribbean on an African woman is revealing in this regard, because it shows a number of hidden motivations and preoccupations between the individuals involved that are representative of a broader dynamic.

In 1978, the African women in question had to travel to Belgium. At the time when there were still border controls within the European Union, many Africans were forced to resort to illegal methods to travel or simply "muddle through." This African woman borrowed a French ID card from her sister who had French citizenship. That status made travel conditions far easier and avoided the issue of an entry visa. Once, however, on the train the woman was controlled by an Afro-Caribbean policeman, who said to her, "Madam, these are not your ID papers." She replied, "Hey, brother, can't you let me through?" to which the Afro-Caribbean policeman replied, "No Madam. First, I'm not your brother. Next, you are in serious breach of the law by usurping someone else's identity, and you risk a number of years in prison. Where did you get these papers?" The African woman pretended she had found them, and then changed her mind, admitted to having borrowed them from her sister, and showed her true identity papers. She was subsequently turned back at the frontier. In this case, the Afro-Caribbean not only clearly differentiated the faces of Black people held to be indistinguishable from one another, but also knew about the organizational methods and resourcefulness of the Africans that he disavowed. He refused any tie of kinship. And for her part, the African woman, who would usually challenge such kinship, attempted to activate it in this difficult context. The Afro-Caribbean clearly identified with his role as a civil servant and treated the African as a foreigner. How do these two communities interpret this friction? The Africans view it as a collective reproach by Afro-Caribbeans for having sold their ancestors as slaves. In short, the Afro-Caribbean transfers the burden of slavery to the African, not to the European, and this point of view emphasizes a radical break with Africa.

When I lived in the Paris suburbs in the 1970s and 1980s, some Afro-Caribbeans whom I met daily actually denied their African ancestry. They claimed that their ancestors had always lived in the Islands. In their formulations, the disagreement between sub-Saharan Africans and Afro-Caribbeans appear to be on the "effects" of slavery and the "alleged" responsibility or cowardice of the Africans. This difference of opinion is well illustrated by the following case, which was reported by a friend concerning her mother. Ms. A. entered the subway with her daughter one day while carrying another child on her back. Ms. A. saw a free seat by the window with an Afro-Caribbean woman sitting on the aisle side of the same bench. Ms. A. excused herself and sat down by the window, bumping into the Afro-Caribbean woman as she was sitting down. This woman grumbled and threw her a disdainful look. Ms. A. took this to be nonverbal aggression and asked her, "Why are you looking at me like that for? I wasn't a slave like you, I was never sold." The Afro-Caribbean woman did not reply. My friend pointed out to her mother the impropriety of these rather racist remarks and asked her why she had acted like that. Ms. A. replied that by looking at her in that way, the Afro-Caribbean had shown disdain and viewed her as a "mere savage."

This example shows that the leitmotif in the tensions between Africans and Afro-Caribbeans may be understood as the effect of identification systems based on the dynamics of crossing transcontinental spaces configured by two systems of domination: slavery and colonization. To understand the importance of the colonial system in African constructions, I will return to the results of my "test." That is, although Africans declare themselves far removed from Afro-Caribbeans, they claim to be close to North Africans, calling each other "cousins" in joking relationships. This identification is constructed on an analogy of place and experience. Both populations come from the same continent and suffered the same type of colonial domination configured by the oppositions between citizen and native. Their experience is different from that of the Afro-Caribbeans, who live with the memory of slavery and the break with the motherland. Yet, it is precisely that experience of a break that leads Afro-Caribbeans to claim to be "Black" in Black France, over and above any attribution by "whites," and to acquire the status of citizen. This break corresponds to the effects of deterritorialization practices in Africa and reterritorialization outside of it. People who experienced this distinguished themselves from the "nègres" (i.e., those who stayed behind in the place where deterritorialization began) and therefore could become "noir." In this light, it appears that giving oneself the possibility of "becoming Black" corresponds to achieving the process of deterritorialization and reterritorialization outside the African continent, and this is refracted in the issue of citizenship.

How Africans and Afro-Caribbeans Became "Black" (Again) in "Black France"

The historical enigma we need to unravel here concerns the understanding of why certain working-class Afro-Caribbeans and Africans now claim the very assigned "Black" singularity that they formally refused. There is at present a greater tension between assignation practices and identity claims. This transformation took place in the second phase, which was configured by two events, the promulgation of the immigration decree of 1974 and globalization. The decree put an end to economic immigration and closed the frontiers, while globalization was imposed by a variety of mechanisms in which the issue of mobility dominated.[16] Together, they reconfigured the social order, and societies became entangled in such a complex way and on such a scale as to extend beyond national borders. The rapid increase in flows, real or imaginary, of people, goods, capital, standards, images, and information constitutes the historical specificity of the period. Globalization justifies calling this a singularity, not an identity. The analysis of globalization by Hardt and Negri informs my reasoning, especially their use of "multitude": "The multitude is composed of a set of singularities—and by singularity we mean here a social subject, whose differences cannot be reduced to identity, that is to say, a difference that remains different."[17] In this way, it is possible to affirm that the term "Black" (in English) is one of the transnational singularities related to globalization.

This second phase, like the first one, connects several orders of social reality: political, economic, educational, generational, and so on. From the 1980s, migration changed in form and complied with dynamics related to modes of governance produced by the relative decline of sovereignty based on nation-states in favor of those rooted in polyarchic, nonterritorial, and network systems. These dynamics were also related to the exacerbation of the socio-economic crisis in the Northern countries and its impact on increasing exclusion measures on citizens from the South.[18] The profiles of Afro-Caribbean and African populations changed, either because their descendents began to gain ground in Little France or because of the arrival of new generations through new channels.

All these transformations influenced the living conditions of Afro-Caribbeans and Africans in France who were met by the paradoxical emergence of a xenophobic, if not openly racist, atmosphere. On the one hand, this shift was confirmed by the proliferation of racist attacks and murders and the gain in votes by the far-right National Front after the elections in 1988. Yet on the other, numerous social movements emerged to fight these discriminations and, as a perverse effect, the media neutralized the symbolic charge of the new discourse. The fight against racist discrimination led to the establishment of anti-racism organizations, and slogans such as "Touche pas à mon pote" (hands off my homie) and the slogan "*Black, Blancs, Beurs*" (Black, White, Arab) to evoke the new multicolored identity of Little France. At the same time, the cultural effect on the public by the media industry, which had been reorganized in the meantime, led to a readjustment of racist behavior. The success of stand-up comedians such as Péchin, Coluche, and Leeb, who used this topic in their sketches on television or radio, led to a break with the old order of denied racist discourse. These comedians' sketches challenged the defensive behavior of the victims of racism as they denounced racist attitudes. One of the most striking examples concerned the widespread, everyday use of extracts from Leeb's sketches as jokes between friends of different presumed "races" and, even on occasion, with strangers. One particular sketch was about someone asking a "Black" to take off his sunglasses, and the latter replies, "those aren't sunglasses, they're my nostrils." Using an African accent was also a fashionable way of communicating, and if any African was vexed by this, it was enough to point out that they lacked a sense of humor to defuse and dedramatize the situation.

The two events—the fallout from the decree of 1974 and globalization—settled African movement lastingly in Little France. However, Afro-Caribbean migration was characterized by an increased return to the Islands, especially in the 1980s, which then slowed down in the following decade for various reasons, notably the rise of violence in the DOM, disappointment at not finding the same place they had left several decades earlier, and the high cost of living. Nevertheless, both types of movement gradually gave into logics conforming to modes of governance that extended over and above the order established by the sovereignty of Imperial France.

Indeed, following the economic crisis, Imperial France tried to stem these flows by more flexible methods. To manage African mobility, in addition to restricting labor channels by application of the 1974 decree, Little France also intervened in the educational channel by sparingly granting scholarships to students and trainees for temporary stays, often for a period of a only few months. With Afro-Caribbean mobility, the government closed the BUMIDOM in 1981 and replaced it with the Association Nationale pour l'Insertion et la Promotion des Travailleurs d'Outre-Mer (ANT). This new agency, decentralized into regional delegations, not only handled relocations to metropolitan France, but also returns to the French West Indies. It managed the professional training of Afro-Caribbeans in Little France with short-term stays.

Despite the strategies employed by the rulers of Imperial France to limit migration, the profiles of the African and Afro-Caribbean populations changed. First, the presence of first-phase Africans and Afro-Caribbeans grew by natural reproduction. The decree of 1974 permitted the mobility of wives for the purpose of family reunification, which produced a new channel for them. Both communities used this decree to compose or recompose households where the birthrates were higher than in the average French household.[19] Moreover, in both cases, this mobility was organized in a relatively autonomous way in Imperial France. As French citizens, it was easier for Afro-Caribbeans to circulate between their place of origin and Little France. They continued using the same strategy of family networks to receive them in metropolitan France. Once their situation was stable, they found their own housing for their families. If they failed in France, they returned to the French West Indies.

However, for the Africans, acquiring autonomy was specifically the result of the crisis in the postcolonial state, exacerbated in the 1980s by the Programmes d'Ajustement Structurel (PAS). The PAS promoted the disengagement of the state, the easing of trade restrictions, and the reduction of employees in public service. Consequently, in African cities many people were obliged to resort to the informal sector, often illegally.[20] These crises impacted mobility. New channels— "stowaways" and "asylum seekers"—emerged. In the first case, the flow of city dwellers from central and western Africa, viewed as "adventurers," increased in the 1980s, and these new migrants settled illegally in Little France. Sometimes these flows were organized by informal networks. The proliferation of wars on the African continent since the 1990s supplied the asylum seeker with this channel. This was mainly based on the new transnational civil society that was being established and that imposed standards on states for human rights and quotas of asylum seekers.[21] This channel was both fluid and flexible, in contrast to the rigid structure of the traditional state apparatus and new imposed solidarity networks and more labile modes of action. These newcomers to France, the stowaways and asylum seekers, constructed their identity in the same way as the generations who had arrived in the first phase. They organized themselves mainly by frequenting their fellow citizens. They did not fully engage with Africans of other nationalities and still less with Afro-Caribbeans.

Thus, one finds the descendents of Africans and Afro-Caribbeans on one side and the second phase migrants from Africa and the

French West Indies on the other. Relationships within and between these groups were no easy matter. In a situation of rampant and more blatant racism, Afro-Caribbeans and Africans in Little France continued to avoid and even ignore each other, despite the greater opportunities for them to meet. For those who did, the ties they established were not necessarily based on equating colonization and slavery, but followed the already marked tensions of the first phase. Only a handful of descendents actively worked to build relations between Afro-Caribbeans and Africans, but in a particular way; they distinguished themselves from those who arrived in the second phase, from their own country, and joined up with those born in Little France.

On the one hand, those young people born in Little France looked down on and envied the recent arrivals. They were a source of fascination and evoked nostalgia for a golden age associated with cultural purity. The descendents of Africans treated them as "*blédards*," whereas descendents of Afro-Caribbeans called them "*locaux*" (locals).[22] Of the two, the blédard is negative as far as authenticity goes. In the eyes of the young people born in Little France, the problem with the blédards was their excess of "authenticity" whereas the locaux were short of it. The latter are more highly valued because locals are characterized as cultural hybrids with a long-standing social intimacy between Blacks and whites. Moreover, the locaux's social universe is comparable to the experience of "Blacks" socialized in France. In both cases, they are born on French territory and have French citizenship, but that citizenship is systematically challenged in media and political discourse as well as in daily events. In cases of open racism, the Afro-Caribbeans are subject to twofold exclusion, both as French citizens and as segments of underprivileged classes. They no longer have the advantage of a few subordinate public sector jobs.

While distinguishing between blédards and locaux, they also declare themselves to be "black" (using the English word), "*renois*," or "*reuns*." As mentioned earlier, "Black" (in English) was already used in social movements with the slogan "Blacks, Blancs, Beurs" to evoke a Rainbow France. But, in fact, young people born in Little France have conferred another meaning on the word. In the working-class milieu, "Black" refers to a universe of meanings, where it coexists with other words and whose interrelation clarifies its significance. All the other terms are from Verlan, a slang that has its roots in the suburbs. This uses accents and the deconstruction of standard French words for

certain excluded populations, for instance *noich* (Chinese) and *beurs*
(Arabs), to achieve social visibility. However, at the level of national
representation, the term "Black" is the one used in social movements
to depict this racial singularity. Personally, I prefer to translate "Black"
as "renois" or "reuns" rather than as "noir," for the latter refers to
another social reality, that is, not to a social movement but rather to
daily life.

How do people both understand and experience this "Black" singularity? For a better analysis of the shared construction process of
renoi, I will use the "ideal type" method. I will associate different
specific situations to reveal what they have in common, starting with
an extract from the life story of an African woman who recounted one
of the various types of relationships between Afro-Caribbeans and
Africans. As this informant conveyed: "Now, I know more Afro-
Caribbeans than I used to because I work in the public sector and
there are lots of them there. I can't say that I am very close to them
because I only mix with those Afro-Caribbeans who dream of going to
Africa, not the others, the ones who hate Africa. I have friends in
mixed African and Afro-Caribbean couples. I know several Afro-
Caribbean women who have married Gabonese men. They told me
that there are quite a few mixed Afro-Caribbean and Gabonese or
Ivory Coast marriages." As this interview excerpt shows, intergroup
marriage does occur, and the social ties that seal singularity are often
based on gender relations (e.g., marriage) or the search by Afro-
Caribbeans for their African "roots."

To complicate the approach to this cohabitation, it seems more
heuristic to concentrate in a general way on Africans and Afro-
Caribbeans born in Little France because some of them actively attempt to forge this link. They live in a situation of job precariousness
and unemployment and consequently do not have the same advan-
tages as their parents had.[23] Most live with their parents until the age
of twenty-five or more, or settle close by, and view their French citizenship in a complex way. They consider themselves to be both
"French" and "foreigners."[24] As French citizens, they feel like strangers
in the *bled*, for despite being French they are made to feel foreign in
Little France. So Afro-Caribbeans are now in the same situation as
Africans. The similarity of their situation comes from activating the
difference between citizenship and nationality. The former refers to
recognized political rights while the latter simply marks the belonging

to a homogenous entity in terms of people and race. This national belonging then becomes one of the conditions for having one's rights recognized, and while citizenship protected Afro-Caribbeans during the first phase of migration, it no longer operates the same way, particularly for their children, who now find themselves, to some extent, with the same status or position as the descendents of Africans whom they may have denigrated.[25]

This hazy area is one of the many effects that globalization has had on citizenship, where friction arises from the fact that the dominant national sovereignties are no longer in command.[26] In our case, this invites the question of how the citizenship of descendents of postslavery societies interacts with that of descendents of postcolonial societies, since the configurations were different. Clearly, there is a problem here and with the tensions over the acquisition of citizenship, as incarnated by the Afro-Caribbeans (French people begetting French people) and the Africans (foreigners begetting French people). Descendents of African parents access French citizenship by *jus soli*, and their citizenship is therefore now also based on their loss of homeland. That is why they express the feeling of being considered foreigners, excluded from national unity but nevertheless part of it. Globalization leveled out the political status of African and Afro-Caribbean descendents. Citizenship does not provide the same prospects for Africans as for Afro-Caribbeans. But it is nevertheless based on the loss of homeland (or country). Afro-Caribbeans are born in a territory belonging to Imperial France while Africans are born in Little France. In Little France, these tensions are a component of difference in all cases of French citizenship, which, in the era of globalization, is not merely based on a restrictive concept of nationhood. The status of the descendents of postslavery and postcolonial societies contributes directly to consolidating a new French reality that surpasses the framework of nationalism. We must therefore consider the experience of these descendents not only in their mode of exclusion but also in their differing modes of inclusion, that is, not against a line of national separation between citizens and foreigners, but as internal hierarchies that are common to "globalized" peoples.

These young people flaunt their renoi singularity in certain Parisian locations such as the metro stations and adjoining districts of Châtelet–Les Halles, Château d'Eau, Château-Rouge, and the markets of Clignancourt, as well as the Rue de la République and Saint-Denis, Sarcelles, and other suburban places that have come to be defined by these populations. They construct their virtual worlds on the web and visit personal pages (on sites such as skyblogs, myspace, hi5). In fact, the Internet plays an important part in forming networks, which often reach back to their place of origin and give rise to a feeling of belonging to that space, suggesting that ties to a homeland are far from broken.

A good way to understand this process is by analyzing the musical tastes of these young people. As Paul Gilroy has shown, music helps to create and consolidate a transnational singularity through cultural and political meaning.[27] These experiences occur in particular spaces, namely, the Afro–West Indian clubs, as opposed to specifically African or specifically Afro-Caribbean ones, which specialize in musical selections that seek to reproduce the "back home" atmosphere within Little France and are frequented by the first-phase generations and the blédards. Young people born in France do not as a rule frequent these clubs, preferring instead the Afro–West Indian clubs. The blending of both terms aims to mix the two social universes in their musical selection and clientele (between ages eighteen and twenty-five), since these clubs are both African and Afro-Caribbean, in different proportions depending on the evening. However, the organizational side usually falls only to the Afro-Caribbeans. The preferred music is dancehall Jamaican and zouk. Some clubs play equal proportions of American hip hop and dancehall while others clearly prefer dancehall over hip hop. These clubs have made popular the Afro–West Indian hybrid genres, such as zouk-rnb, n'dombolo, and coupé-décalé to an Afro-Caribbean beat. The "African" session mixes n'dombolo and coupé-décalé. Carnival type music, such as soca or vidé, is also played. Clothing fashions resemble those worn in North American hip hop clubs, but with the addition of a few Rasta motifs.

In these clubs, one finds a renoi construction that manifests itself as a ritual orchestrated by DJs that can be seen in the "nationalities roll call" sessions:

> As the room filled up, the DJ turned up the volume of the music and the spotlights began to flash strategically. People knew the evening was about to begin and excitement rose when the DJ activated sounds of sirens and triggers associated with dancehall. Over an avalanche of sirens, sounds of triggers, and gunshots, with flashing spotlights, the dancehall session began and people rose together to get onto the dance

floor. It was mainly *local* dancehall being played, the current hits, and then Jamaican dancehall. DJ Mike One, the "star" of the Starter club, caught the mood when he started a first short nationalities roll call: "Good evening Starter! / Are you there? / I don't hear you / an pa ka tann zòt [I don't hear you] / Make some noiiiiiiiise! (This was spoken in the carnival soca rhythm.) People began to chant "pooouh!" to the music as they do during carnival. Then Mike One continued: "Good evening Madinina [Martinique]! / Are you there? Then he called "darling" Haiti, Cap Verde, La Réunion, Guyana [French Guiana], Gwadada [Guadeloupe], Africa. And the young people who belonged to each of those "countries" raised their arms and shouted.[28]

A first analysis of the construction of the renoi singularity based on musical tastes shows that the music of Afro-Caribbeans, as organizers, dominates and supplants that of Africans. The nationalities roll call indicates that the renois, born in France or living there, are more concerned with their relationships to their "country," their bled, and mark their distance in relation to France. Among other things, it makes independent nations of the French Overseas Departments, similar to African nations. In elaborating this history, these young people refer to the original creation of these territories, since Madinina is the old name for Martinique, although they do not use the old name for Guadeloupe, which is Karukera. In constructing their renoi singularity, they make choices and re-create an authentic history. This ceremony also disseminates national sentiment, even among the Afro-Caribbeans who are growing closer to the Africans. We should mention that the nationality roll call never includes France, since it is implied, and, on another level, dominance need not call to itself when it is internalized.

On the other hand, it is significant that the various African countries are often grouped together under the single name "Africa," whereas the DOM receives individual treatment. This may be explained by the smaller number of Africans, although the use of this term does suggest that young people are staging the same Africa–West Indies relationship as their parents. Note, however, the special treatment reserved for the "Cap Verde," which has a similar population history as the French West Indies since the island only came into existence through slavery. However, this specificity does not prevent the whole African continent from being viewed as a single entity. This special treatment also shows that over and above the actual territory, the term "Africa" (the English word used in French, rather than "*Afrique*") can also refer to an imagined community. The formal reference to Jamaica and the Rastafarian borrowings strengthen the ties to this mythical Africa by raising the issue of roots.

The renoi identity is built from the meeting between the Afro-Caribbeans and the French and also feeds itself by highlighting the differences with other "racial" groups, as is seen in the musical tastes. The relationship with "whites" can be very tense in the Afro–West Indian clubs as well, as the following illustrates:

> The crowd at the Intense & DSF anniversary celebration was difficult to control because of its size [four to five thousand people)]. The roots singers Tiwony and Fefe Typical stopped their show and started talking in the hope of easing tensions. Tiwony and Fefe (dancehall roots) decided to stop the song that was playing (pull up) because they saw that a fight had started. They made a speech, explaining that this was an adult party and that this immature behavior had to cease. . . . They said we must "stop this violence against Blacks," "stop thinking in terms of Blacks, whites, Chinese," "it's the system that's dividing us, we're all brothers." They finished by chanting "I Sellasiai, Jah Rastafarai" (the religious phrase at the heart of the Rastafari religion), which all the audience took up in chorus. There were several messages in their speech: . . . a demand for racial harmony (we are all brothers, the "system" is dividing us). At the time I didn't understand why that second message was important. I learned later on the zouker.com chat room that there had been a "white hunt" in the club, with attacks specifically targeting whites. (Hot Méga Night Kréol, Tenth Anniversary of Intense & DSF, April 30, 2005)[29]

These young renois also distinguish themselves from the beurs. French rap has no place in these renois clubs, or in any other party context. Opinions are divided about whether French rap is associated with Arabs. Even though there are several "Black" rappers, they are perceived as being "Arabized," and therefore not really "Black" anymore. Many other factors come into play, such as French rap's association with the negative image of the suburbs and North African youth. However, the emergence of hybrid styles that blend French spoken rap with more danceable rhythms, such as zouk or African music, have brought French rap into these clubs, albeit only in this hybrid form, such as with the hit "Un Gaou à Oran" by 113.[30] These hybrids often include snippets of rap and R&B sung in French, and they appear to have made it commercially by being played in clubs.

These cases show that the construction of a shared singularity between young Afro-Caribbeans and Africans is more related to the dynamics of discrimination proper to Little France, which are amplified by the effects of globalization (blogs, Internet, and the like). These practices refer not only to an equation of slavery and colonization, but also to the situation of Afro-Americans who take on a third-party role and symbolize yet another reality in this context. This is revealed to a great extent in tastes in music and clothes. By asserting themselves as Black, renoi, or reun, these young people activate and intensify contacts with figures with whom they have only a virtual relationship (through television, Internet, specialized magazines, and so on) rather than a face-to-face one. The renois thus refer to the experience of the civil rights movement in the United States, to affirmative action, the sporting world, show business, fashion, and, sometimes, "anti-black racism," racism in the parlance of everyday, non-analytic discourse.

Paint It Black: The Diaspora Experience and Becoming Black

My historical sociological approach to the diaspora experience has enabled me to show that working-class Afro-Caribbeans and Africans built their reciprocal ties differently, in two phases. In the first, totally controlled by Imperial France and marked by the denial of color racism in Little France, Afro-Caribbeans and Africans fought against the "person of color" identity attribution by highlighting the differences between them. To some extent, these claims dissolved the object of discrimination. In the second phase, one configured by globalization that fed off the decline of Imperial France's sovereignty, some Afro-Caribbeans and Africans have actively constructed ties between the two communities and, in so doing, have laid claims to identity discourses, such as Black, renoi, and reun. In this way, they are fighting the discriminatory assignations of Little France at a time when racist discourses have become more openly explicit. An analysis of the two successive phases clarifies the social dynamics behind this shift. Several singularity construction methods are in competition, but I have mainly focused on those of descendents of Africans and Afro-Caribbeans who actively carry this out.

The matrix was formed during the first phase through the experience of Afro-Caribbeans from postslavery societies. Their experience fed a tension between citizenship and nationality. At the very time when racism was denied, this tension led people to openly proclaim themselves to be "Black." The Afro-Caribbean experience was in two parts, the real or imaginary loss of a homeland or "nation" and the acquisition of citizenship in Imperial France well after the abolition of slavery. In the first phase, the activation of this citizenship reinforced their difference with Africans, whom they portrayed as strangers. At the same time, in the racist attributions by "whites" in Little France, the Afro-Caribbeans found that they themselves were excluded from this nation and identified with the Africans as "men of color." This situation drove them back into the positions of second-class citizens.

In the second phase, descendants of Africans from postcolonial societies had the same experience of the loss of country or origin and the acquisition of citizenship. The dissemination of this method ensured the "Black" transformation of Africans in Little France. A comparison of the two experiences shows that the descendants have recomposed the distinction between nationality and citizenship. Thus, most members of that generation of Africans and Afro-Caribbeans who constructed the "Black" singularity have descendant status. Filiation for them establishes the "true" political dimension, the one that has the capacity to confer the right to have rights.

In focusing on the issue of filiation, one sees that in "Black France" it produced differences in the laws of the French Republic. The existence of people whose parents were born in the former colonies, or in the empire incarnated by the DOM, challenged the frontiers of political domination and nationality. They were born in the middle of the border that traced the difference between the native population (the "true" nation) and the foreigners. They are therefore perceived as a living threat to the clarity of social and political categories that organize the entire French hierarchy. From the point of view of citizenship, even a discriminatory one, filiation equates the social conditions for the existence of Afro-Caribbeans and Africans in Little France by evoking multinationality.

Their ancestry is always raised in political discourse aimed at Africans and Afro-Caribbeans and the country's underclass. Whatever their origins, these descendents absorb those themes and react as though they were foreign. Since this discourse excludes them from the nation, the principle of filiation, taken from their perspective, is related to the issue of mobility. In the second phase, this linkage becomes and represents a social problem in Little France, since those children are viewed as the incarnation of one of the threats to the security of the French Republic. Their mixed filiation (since their parents may have been strangers in Imperial France) must therefore be understood as being at the intersection of the two crises, immigration and citizenship, which feed off each other, result in racism, and become a feature of everyday life in Little France. The children who were born or grew up in Little France are more aware of institutionalized racism, especially with the increase in identity checks, which makes the children of immigrants potential delinquents and having the "wrong" color a crime. The filiation order sheds light on some of the deepest and most disturbing undercurrents in French society and allows us to glimpse certain long-standing but hidden ideological issues that belong to a concept of Imperial France.

Notes

1. These ideas are also discussed in J. Genova, *Colonial Ambivalence, Cultural Authenticity, and the Limitations of Mimicry in French-Ruled West Africa, 1941–1946* (New York: Peter Lang, 2004); G. Wilder, *The French Imperial State: Negritude, and Colonial Humanism between the Two Wars* (Chicago: University of Chicago Press, 2005). Also, my views have been enriched by discussion with the scholar, Achille Mbembe, which was published in "Mobilités africanes, racisme français," *Vacarme* 43 (2008): 83–86.

2. I do not intend to enter into the debate on the "African" signifier in terms of whom it does and does not designate, as others have already done. I use the term "African" solely for sub-Saharan Africans and, more specifically, francophone Africans from Senegal, Mali, Cameroon, Ivory Coast, and the like, whose countries were former French colonies, as well as to Africans from the Democratic Republic of the Congo and Nigeria who arrived massively in Little France after the 1980s. By Afro-Caribbean, I mean the populations from the French Overseas Departments (*Départements d'Outre-Mer* [DOM]), namely the French West Indies (Martinique and Guadeloupe), Guiana, and Réunion Island.

3. Among the authors who have discussed this are P. Blanchard, E. Deroo,

and G. Manceron, *Paris noir* (Paris: Hazan, 2001); P. Dewitte, *Les mouvements nègres en France, 1919–1939* (Paris: L'Harmattan, 1985); M. Fabre, *La rive noire: de Harlem à la Seine* (Paris: Lieu Commun, 1985); P. Ndiaye, *La condition noire: essai sur une minorité française* (Paris: Calmann-Lévy, 2009); D. Thomas, *Black France: Colonialism, Immigration, and Transnational Culture* (Bloomington: Indiana University Press, 2006).

4. These names come from the *Verlan* slang used by young people in the suburbs, *renois* being slang for *noir* (Black) and *reun* an abbreviated form.

5. On the use of "plots," I have mainly drawn from A. Abbot, *Time Matters: On Theory and Method* (Chicago: University of Chicago Press, 2001); P. Ricoeur, *Temps et récit*, 3 vols. (Paris: Le Seuil, 1983); and P. Veyne, *Comment on écrit l'histoire* (Paris: Le Seuil, 1978). For P. Veyne, e.g., plotting is what qualifies an event as being historic: "Facts only exist in and by plots where they acquire the relative importance imposed on them by the human logic in the drama" (70). The plot approach enables me to freely dissect the historic order of events, even as the plot itself is a "very human and very unscientific mix of material causes, effects and coincidences" (46). In more concrete terms, I will develop a phase-based approach that I began to establish in previous research. By phase-based, I mean an "intelligible" spatio-temporal order that can be reconstructed in the framework of a general plot, that is, one with a duration (a beginning, a middle, and an end), but one that must not drift into excess, lest comprehension be compromised. Several levels of social reality intervene in the plot, which may also be seen in people, objects, and practices.

6. It seems obvious to me that including Afro-Caribbeans in no way perturbs the phases in this genealogy. See R. Bazenguissa-Ganga, "Au-delà de l'Atlantique noir, les Afrique des banlieues 'mondialisées,'" in *Autour de l' "Atlantique noir": une polyphonie de perspectives*, ed. C. Agudelo, C. Boidin, and L. Sansone (Paris: IHEAL, 2009), 133–53.

7. C.-V. Marie, "Les antillais en France: une nouvelle donne," *Hommes et migrations* 1237 (2002): 26.

8. F. Manchuelle summarizes information concerning the presence of Africans in the early twentieth century in *Les diasporas des travailleurs soninké, 1848–1960: migrants volontaires* (Paris: Karthala, 2004).

9. A. Anselin, *L'émigration antillaise en France: du bantoustan au ghetto* (Paris: Anthropos, 1979), and *L'émigration antillaise en France: la troisième île* (Paris: Karthala, 1990). For a more general understanding of the Caribbean situation see H. Domenach, "L'évolution au XXᵉ siècle du système démographique et migratoire caribéen," *Hommes et migrations* 1237 (2002): 13; C. Félicité, *La traite silencieuse: les émigrés des DOM* (Paris: idoc, 1975), 28; S. Condon and P. E. Ogden, "Afro-Carribean Migrants in France: Employment,

State Policy and the Migration Process," *Transactions of the Institute of British Geographers* 16, no. 4 (1991): 445.

10. G. Boudimbou, *Habitat et modes de vie des immigrés africains en France* (Paris: L'Harmattan, 1991); M. Eliou, *La formation de la conscience nationale en République Populaire du Congo* (Paris: Anthropos, 1977); A. Gueye, *Les intellectuels africains en France* (Paris: L'Harmattan, 2001); F. Guimont, *Les étudiants africains en France, 1950–1965* (Paris: L'Harmattan, 1997); M. Sot, *Étudiants africains en France, 1950–2001* (Paris: Karthala, 2002).

11. J. Barou, *Travailleurs africains en France: rôle des cultures d'origine* (Grenoble: POF-PUG, 1978); C. Daum, *Les associations de maliens en France: migration, développement et citoyenneté* (Paris: Karthala, 1998); Manchuelle, *Les diasporas des travailleurs Soninké*; C. Quiminal, *Gens d'ici, gens d'ailleurs* (Paris: Bourgois, 1991); M. Timera, *Les soninké en France: d'une histoire à l'autre* (Paris: Karthala, 1996).

12. Claude McKay was interested in this issue well before Fanon (*Banjo* was published in 1929) as was René Maran (*Batouala* was published in 1926) as may be seen from their various newspaper and magazine articles at the time. We must also take into account Aimé Césaire's attitude to Négritude, as criticized by R. Confiant in *Aimé Césaire: une traversée paradoxale du siècle* (Paris: Stock, 1993), and A. Césaire's reply in *Nègre je suis, nègre je resterai: Aimé Césaire: entretiens avec Françoise Vergès* (Paris: Albin Michel, 2005), as well as the work by Michel Fabre, *La rive noire: les écrivains noirs américains à Paris, 1830–1995* (Marseille: André Dimanche, 1999), which introduced another group, the African Americans, who were to have a considerable influence on the interpretation of racial issues in France.

13. F. Fanon, "Afro-Caribbeans and Africans," *Esprit* (February 1955): 261–69.

14. Ibid., 261–62.

15. Which confirms Liliane Kuczynski in her work on *marabouts* in Paris as well as her more recent surveys of Africans in the French West Indies. See L. Kuczynski, *Les marabouts africains à Paris* (Paris: CNRS, 2003).

16. Regarding globalization, I refer, among others, to the following works: A. Appadurai, *Après le colonialisme: les conséquences culturelles de la globalisation* (Paris: Payot, 2001); S. Lash and J. Urry, *The End of Organized Capitalism* (Madison: University of Wisconsin Press, 1987); J. Urry, *Sociologie des mobilités: une nouvelle frontière pour la sociologie?* (Paris: Armand Colin, 2005); S. Lash and J. Urry, *Economies of Signs and Space* (Thousand Oaks, Calif.: Sage, 1999).

17. M. Hardt and A. Négri, *Multitude: guerre et démocratie à l'âge de l'empire* (Paris: La Découverte, 2004), 126. If, as Stuart Hall has remarked, we are all hybrids, that does nothing to stop difference. It is the matter of this difference in hybridity that holds us back and we want to think of as singularity.

See S. Hall, *Identités et cultures: politiques des cultural studies* (Paris: Amsterdam, 2007).

18. For this perspective, see among others, Z. Bauman, *Le coût humain de la mondialisation* (Paris: Hachette-Pluriel, 1999); M. Duffield, *Global Governance and the New Wars: The Merging of Development and Security* (Paris: Zed, 2001); H. M. Enzensberger, *La grande migration*, followed by *Vues sur la guerre civile* (Paris: Gallimard, 1995); D. Dal Lago and S. Mezzadra, "Les frontières impensées de l'Europe: Cette constitution est-elle une troisième voie pour l'Europe?" *Lignes*, February, 2004, 67–80.

19. M. Claude-Valentin, "Les populations des DOM-TOM, nées et originaires, résidant en France métropolitaine," *Rapport INSEE*, 1990.

20. See J. Barou, *Europe, terre d'immigration: flux migratoires et intégration* (Grenoble: PUG, 2006); *La planète des migrants: circulations migratoires et constitution de diasporas à l'aube du XIXe siècle* (Grenoble: PUG, 2007); J. MacGaffey and R. Bazenguissa-Ganga, *Congo-Paris: Transnational Traders on the Margins of the Law* (Bloomington: Indiana University Press, 2000); C. Poiret, *Familles africaines en France* (Paris: L'Harmattan, 1997); C. Quiminal and M. Timera, "Les mutations de l'immigration ouest-africaine," *Hommes et Migrations* 1239 (2002).

21. Composed of NGOs, UNHCR, human rights organizations, and so on.

22. A term from the Arab word *bled*, which means "village" but is used by young people today to mean country of origin. A *blédard* is therefore "one who comes from the *bled*."

23. See T. Sauvadet, *Le capital guerrier: concurrence et solidarité entre jeunes de cité* (Paris: A. Colin, 2006); L. Steil, "Phaser, parler et 'faire croquer': la cohésion sociale dans un milieu des jeunes danseurs noirs" (master's dissertation, EPHE).

24. See P. Dewitte, "Des citoyens à part entière ou entièrement à part?," *Hommes et Migrations* 1237 (2002).

25. See É. Balibar and I. Wallerstein, *Race, Nation, Class: Ambiguous Identities* (London: Verso, 1991).

26. For the discussion on the effects of globalization on citizenship and nationality, I referred to (among others) J. Butler and G. C. Spivak, *L'état global* (Paris: Payot and Rivages, 2007); M.-C. Caloz-Tschpp, *Les sans-état dans la philosophie d'Hannah Arendt: les humains superflus, le droit d'avoir des droits et la citoyenneté* (Paris: Payot Lausanne, 2000).

27. P. Gilroy, *Atlantique noir, modernité et double conscience* (Paris: Kargo, 2003).

28. This example derives from a moment in "Le Starter" club as described in Steil, *Phaser, parler et "faire croquer*," 127–28.

29. Ibid., 125–26.

30. "First Gaoua" was a hit single by Magic System, a group from the Ivory

Coast, that popularized a musical and dance style in France known as the coupé décalé. "113," a French rap group inspired by the success of "Magic System," comprised three individuals of Algerian, Malian, and Guadeloupian origins that served to evoke a type of multicolor and multicultural "French" hybridity. This hybridity transforms, at the same time, the nature of the rap and the African music.

The "Question of Blackness" and the Memory of Slavery

Invisibility and Forgetting as Voluntary Fire and Some Pyromaniac Firefighters

MICHEL GIRAUD

The mastery of memory . . . is the apanage of all those avid for glory.—PAUL RICOEUR

This chapter, devoted to the social and intellectual debates on the memory of slavery in the French West Indies and the West Indian "diaspora" in "metropolitan" France, will use—and even abuse–quotation marks. In so doing, it draws mainly from a famous speech by the Jamaican academic Stuart Hall on notions of identity and ethnicity, from the high-profile speech in Philadelphia by Barack Obama, and from the celebrated study *Peau noire, masques blancs* by Frantz Fanon from Martinique. All these quotes are used on purpose. We do so not, of course, to shelter our reflections under the umbrella of reference to such illustrious predecessors or contemporaries, but to emphasize that the intelligentsia, Francophone thinkers included, of the "Black world," as it is named—quite uncertainly—did not wait for the current deployment of neo-racialism in France to obsess about the condition of "Negroes."[1] Furthermore, the peoples (and a number of writers) from the French West Indies began to think about and to heal the trauma of the slavery of "Negroes" in the Americas long before they began regularly to be charged with forgetting the slave past, starting in the late 1990s.[2] The abundance of quotations in our text, whose deliberate character we recognize, equally testifies to the fact that there are still "Black" intellectuals who resist the use of such neo-racialism.

Above all, it highlights that the illustrious predecessors whom we have mentioned, we believe, address the plight of "Blacks" with much more accuracy than many of their successors today, sometimes by resolutely displaying strong political positions closely tied to the words—if not the recent acts—of the new American president.

How Can One Be Black in France Today?

The Stakes and the Context of a New "French Dilemma"

The mobilization in France around a "Black" identity and the debates it generates, both within what is not universally acknowledged to be a "Black community" and in what lies outside of it, have become so omnipresent that the mainstream media can no longer ignore it, even if they tend to diminish its significance in order to relegate the discussion to issues of secondary importance, such as whether to recruit Black anchors on television or to increase awareness of high-profile individuals of African, Caribbean, or Guyanese descent.

This mobilization and these discussions derive in part, especially among West Indians or in relation to them, from a strong engagement with the memory of the slavery of "Negroes" and from the controversies that have given rise to the idea of a "duty to remember" this servitude. It is as if the slave trade and the enslavement of Africans in the New World have become the paradigm of all subordination to which the "Blacks" of France are still subjected. As a matter of fact, since racism was the keystone of the slave system, "Black" populations originating from this system are almost naturally inclined to perceive the many instances of racist discrimination they are still fighting against—nearly two centuries after the "final" abolition of slavery—as a prolongation of servitude. It is precisely the sense of this continuity that explains why, within the context of the valuing of their "racial" membership to which their experience of discrimination leads them, many West Indians attach a key importance to bringing back the memory of their enslaved ancestors. To the extent that, in our opinion, this regards West Indian populations, the analysis of the "race" question and of the memory of slavery must systematically be associated with each other, as is the case in this chapter. In this chapter, this association will receive final confirmation from the emphasis repeatedly put on the fact that it is—in relation to the debates tackling these two questions—the same argumentative scheme that, behind the mask of denouncing colonial alienation, is used against all those who, anxious to promote "true" French citizenship, do not want to be tricked into the "color trap" or the sacredness of the memory of slavery, an argumentative scheme based, in both cases, upon the same socio-political strategies, endorsed by the same nationalist elite aching for recognition.

Indeed, the public excitement about race (notably by the media), which is completely new in France, will be brought up as a great national question: "the question of blackness." It has become legitimate to wonder—as the magazine *Alizés* does in the title of its first issue in 2008[3]—"Why do we talk so much [in France today] about Blacks?"[4] While some continue to say that there is little racism against "Blacks" in the national media coverage of French current events, in the beginning of a book recently published on these topics, the author persists in speaking of "the invisibility of Black populations" in France.[5] With this excitement, it seems to us that it is the constitution of an effective group, the "Blacks of France" (what Anglophone anthropologists would call a "corporate group") that is the real issue of the mobilization in question. Constitution is meant in the true sense of the word, that is, as an invention, since that group—similar to any other group of people—does not actually exist until it is invented by a discourse that enunciates what it is supposed to be and announces what has happened, according to the mechanism of self-fulfilling prophecy.[6]

The advent of the group the "Blacks of France," which is happening before our eyes, apparently has found a "favorable context" in the historical dynamics of the last four decades. This corresponds roughly to a long phase of economic and social crisis in major industrial societies, during which racial exclusion has emerged as an important subject of social concern.[7] This is not because these exclusions have become more intense or more overt than in the past, but because, condemned by a certain change in attitudes, they gradually began to be heavily criticized by those who experienced them and also to be deemed unacceptable by a growing segment of public opinion. Accordingly, these exclusions have become the subject of a particularly lively public debate, and there has been a renewed "racialization" of social relations in these societies, because—one must never forget—racism is always assumed in "racialization."[8]

We do not have the space here to dissect in detail the complexity of this new process of "racialization" and how it is now developing in French society. However, it is probably beneficial to give at least a brief overview of the social and intellectual context that allowed its existence by showing pell-mell some of its key elements. There has been a profound transformation in proletarian employment, which now includes numerous workers "of color," the net loss of influence of increasingly more bureaucratized "working-class" political organizations (especially in areas where large numbers of "indigenous" and "immigrant" workers live together), and a certain sclerosis of socialist doctrines (especially Marxian). The universalist intellectual stance of these organizations and doctrines has long been the main obstacle to the growth of racism. In addition, there has been a growing recourse by the mass media to traditionally colonialist perspectives in the analysis of contemporary social phenomena.

The Trap of "Racial" Categories

The tendency—which is called "racialization"—to make of certain inequalities of condition racial oppositions and thus to view social struggles as racial clashes has prompted a number of "racialized" people to respond to the racism that they face by embracing as an emblem the particular identity that was initially imposed as a stigma. This embrace or enthusiasm is a kind of leap into the unknown that creates a vicious circle, because in taking and thus reinforcing the logic of racial profiling, these reactions can only strengthen and expand the harm they seek to eradicate. Thus, as stated by the West Indian writer Claude Ribbe in response to the survey by the magazine *Alizés*, those who consider themselves "Blacks" "are only applying, to themselves and to others, the racist criteria imposed by the colonizer." The sociologist Alain Anselin of Martinique echoes these sentiments in his writing, showing that by buttressing their identity with the racial data from the old colonial order, they become "the managers of their own slavery," to use the words of the Haitian writer Maximilien Laroche.[9] Racism, because it is a negation of the universality of humanity, can, in fact, only be truly fought in the name of universalist principles and through mobilizations that transcend all "communities" and all specific identities.

The existence of instances of discrimination known as racist, and therefore the social efficacy of "racial" categorizations (as undeniable

as they are), constitutes misleading evidence by concealing or disguis-
ing (in the guise of "racial" characterizations posed as natural) the
social aspect of the stakes, interests, strategies, and mechanisms behind these instances of discrimination and categorization. In doing so,
this evidence validates, in order to legitimize, the improper (because
artificial in a strict sense) separation which is imposed on a group—
for example, in France, the "Blacks"—in relation to the social body to
which it definitely belongs (whether it be the proletariat, with which it
objectively shares many interests, or even that of all French). It thus
serves to support the division and the weakening of the social bodies
concerned. So, just talking about "Blacks," regardless of the intentions
of the statement, must attribute to the internalization of this separation; and with the formidable strength of "without even thinking
about it," there is a social relevance in itself to the "racial" characterization fallaciously motivating this separation. In truth, this characterization is relevant in all social processes of domination and exploitation
that have constructed it throughout history and are still reconstructing it today. By accepting such a simple racial characterization, even if
it is to better fight it, one ends up doing that which is the most
disastrous: it is the most effective way to conceal or disguise the
processes that determine it. Albert Camus was right to say, "to mis-
name things is to increase the evil in the world!"

We must therefore keep clear of the reversal which leads one to
mistake the effect for the cause, colorism for domination. It tends to
suggest that groups of a certain "race"—for example, people of West
Indian or Guyanese descent residing in metropolitan France—are
sociological minorities because of the "visibility" of their phenotypes.
But surely these groups are in the place reserved for them, in the
society where they live, by colonial history and the context of current
social subordination. That explains why the groups are particularly
"seen" and discriminated against. Thus, Stuart Hall is ten, a hundred,
a thousand times right in arguing, about "Blacks" of England, that
"their histories are in the past, inscribed in their skins. But it is not
because of their skins that they are Black in their heads."[10]

It is therefore reasonable to put the notions of "race" and "racial"
categories in quotations because one cannot develop a nonracist conceptualization of "race" without beginning by deconstructing the concept and its categories. Therefore, as C. Ribbe is eminently justified in
arguing: "The 'Black question' only exists for racist thinkers who di-

vide humanity according to purely fantasmatic criteria. The only reality is Negrophobia. . . . Racism doesn't begin when one affirms the preeminence of one 'race' over another. It begins from the moment that one accepts that the notion of 'race,' which is a term appropriate to the husbandry of rabbits or chickens in the poultry-yard, should be applied to the human species."[11] The questioning of the use of "racial" categories in scientific analysis cannot in any way—contrary to the bad faith arguments of the neo-racialists[12]—be reduced to colorblindness, a desire to make the visible invisible, or a refusal to talk about these categories or to deconstruct the methods of construction, and even less so can it be reduced to a wavering in recognizing the force of racism and hence the absolute necessity to fight it. In truth, contrary to what is often criticized, it is supported and carried by the demand to discuss the categories in question as accurately as possible, that is, to refuse to reify them and to articulate—not just juxtapose!—in detailed analysis the various social parameters (class, "race" or "ethnocultural identity," gender, and so on) at issue. The purpose of the debate is not reduced to either talking or not talking about "race," as the neo-racialist would like to propose. Instead, the debate is about our collective responsibility to know how to speak correctly about "race." And from this point of view, it seems a poor evasion of responsibility to pretend to hide behind social actors to justify the simplistic use of these words and categories of analysis in science on the grounds that one must always "take into account and respect the real logic of social movements," as Fassin said in an interview, as if taking this logic of social agents into account implied ipso facto the need to consider it as a valid account of these social movements, as if the only salvation for social science was to align itself with the voices of social actors. What is this strange social science that—heedless of the founding principle of our disciplines, the need to break with all *doxa*—would require producers to be nothing more than the voices of those they observe?

Therefore, on the one hand, there is ultimately no analytical legitimacy in prescriptively denouncing, through objectivist blindness, the concept of race merely because it is the product of ideological production. On the other hand, scientific analysis has an intrinsic duty to unveil the mechanisms of this production and its validation and thereby to challenge the allegedly inevitable character of "race" as something natural and thus intangible. This challenge opens the discussion of the racial problem. Scientific analysis does not deny individuals the right to recognize themselves in particular communities, especially "racial," by saying loudly that they belong to them, but instead seeks to highlight the dangers that the will to found a political organization based on such membership entails for the achievement of any emancipatory project.

Multiple and Labile Affiliations, Necessary Alliances

By stressing, along with other researchers, that "race" is in fact an ideological construct that disguises the social reality it addresses, it is not so much a question of throwing overboard, because of this distortion, the various historical experiences of those people who some call or who call themselves "Black." This would be an intellectually unjustified and politically inconsequential position. It is rather about "holding both ends of the chain," as Stuart Hall has asked of us many times: that is, "attempting to valorize and defeat the marginalization of the variety of Black subjects and to really begin to recover the lost histories of a variety of Black experiences, while at the same time recognizing the end of any essential Black subject."[13] One must therefore guard against reducing such experiences, and the social dynamics that underlie them, to essentialist conceptions of identity which would reify them by using them to constitute a "Black history" or, even worse, a "Black tradition." Instead, one must consider them as an expression of creativity which—although rooted in part in the dead weight of the past—is not confined by the respect of any orthodoxy of identity or a "duty of memory," but instead proclaims a freedom and a multiplicity of identification. These identifications that are ultimately motivated by the social and political issues of various situations, notably by struggles, deeply involve the populations in question while at the same time going well beyond them, in addition to being variable and instable.

Therefore, any politics which advocates the social promotion of "Black" populations in European or American societies must take into account—if it does not wish to fail—the fluidity and complexity of the dynamics that characterize these populations. It must be a policy built in the manner of those Hall has advocated frequently: "a politics which . . . is able to address people through the multiple identities which they have, . . . [which understands] that those identities do not remain the same, [that] they are frequently contradictory, that they cross-cut one another, that they tend to locate us differently at different moments."[14] Therefore, there is no "identity house arrest" that is worth it, whether in the master's house or in the slave cabin. The freedom of the collective and individual choice of identification must alone be conquered and then preserved, ensuring to the greatest number of people possible the physical, symbolic, and intellectual conditions to exercise that freedom.

In this context, the absolute priority of the politics in question arises directly in opposition to the aims of the venture it wishes to combat. The ideology and the racist practices facing "Black" peoples have a primary goal, as we have said, of separating these populations from the social bodies with which they share in large part—sometimes consciously—the conditions of existence and of therefore breaking the solidarities that could unite these bodies, a sort of "divide and conquer." Therefore, nothing is more necessary to anti-racism than to challenge this venture of separation and division by forming cross-community alliances. This is the heart of the whole discussion that we have outlined about whether or not there exists a group of Blacks of France, and specifically of our critique of neo-racialism and of identity politics that it supports.

Barack Obama, in the case of the United States, has emphasized this importance on numerous occasions, most notably in his great speech delivered in Philadelphia,[15] cautioning his listeners against the danger of identity-based withdrawal and glorification, as he pointed to an image of anger that "prevents the African-American community from forging the alliances it needs to bring about real change," stressing that if his position "means continuing to insist on a full measure of justice in every aspect of American life . . . it also means binding our particular grievances—for better health care, and better schools, and better jobs—to the larger aspirations of all Americans." He prophesied that there is

> a choice in this country. We can accept a politics that breeds division, and conflict, and cynicism. . . . We can do that. But if we do, I can tell you that in the next election, we'll be talking about some other distraction. And then another one. And then another one. And nothing will change. That is one option. Or, at this moment, in this election, we can come together and say, "Not this time." This time we want to talk about the crumbling schools that are stealing the future of Black children and

white children and Asian children and Hispanic children and Native American children. . . . This time we want to talk about the shuttered mills that once provided a decent life for men and women of every race. . . . This time we want to talk about the fact that the real problem is not that someone who doesn't look like you might take your job; it's that the corporation you work for will ship it overseas for nothing more than a profit. This time we want to talk about the men and women of every color and creed who serve together, and fight together, and bleed together under the same proud flag. We want to talk about how to bring them home, from a war that never should've been authorized and never should've been waged."

An Elitist Strategy

Among the factors of the new process of "racialization," now at work in French society, two interest us in particular: the political interests of many activists from associations or movements based on "visible minorities," and the academic interests that some researchers studying the situation of these "minorities" invest strategically in the field of what is called "ethnicity." This investment demonstrates that the determination of opinions and individual actions by "racial" representations, which remains strong today in French society, is not the exclusive property of those who engage in anti-black racism, but is also among those trying to protect themselves from it. And after much disillusionment with the possibility of seeing it defeated by the mere invocation of the "republican" ideal of equality for all citizens irrespective of their origin and color, larger and larger groups of individuals, assigned with condescension or hostility the inferior status of "Black," are no longer willing to submit to it. Therefore, to combat the racism they face, they make the color that has been hurled at them as an insult into an emblem of pride around which they mobilize in affirming and claiming a particular identity. Black is beautiful!

The political and intellectual elites of that "community" have played and still play a central role in this transformation of a racial stigma into a positive emblem. Therefore, they bear a heavy responsibility for the essentialization of identity most often accompanying Black politics. Indeed, it is incumbent upon them to shape the information and produce the arguments in support of this politics, and they have usually performed and still perform this task by making—for the purposes of propaganda—out of a complex history of struggles illuminated by light but also suffused with shadows and strewn with contradictions, a glorious heritage, unambiguous and binding, with values defined in an elementary way. The cultural forms derived from this simplistic history end up creating a tradition all the more rigid in that it excludes many contributions that it does not wish to recognize. Therefore, it is not the ambiguity of the actual historical experience and the versatility of cultural dynamics that are put forward, but the correctness of an improbable mission that is invented, causing one to lose sight of the fact that the "race" constituted by these experiences and by these dynamics is a socio-historical construction, not a natural one.

In truth, the new "racialization" of society has reconfigured the idea of "race" in such a way that the color black, finally recognized as symbolic capital, has come to challenge the dominant position of the color white, which has remained unchallenged until recently. This reconfiguration supports—in connection with the aspirations of power that some sectors of the elite "Black world" and the members of the elite "white world" who try to join them—a strategy in which racialism is a means of social upward mobility, despite the frequent denials of those who use it. It is beyond the scope of this chapter to detail this strategy and its relevance. Rather our goal is to criticize one of the major intellectual processes on which it rests: a deep mystification of the past and, consecutively, a recurring deformation of historical data. This process seriously distorts these debates, as legitimate as they are, in the concerned populations on issues of identity or, more recently, of "collective memory," leading as a consequence into an impasse those political practices which deceptively use their own history.

The Forgetting of Slavery: A Phony Fiction

In this part of the text, we will use the critical insights of the first part to examine the specific case of the memory of slavery in the French West Indies and in the West Indian "diaspora" in "metropolitan" France. At least since the flurry of initiatives that arose in 1998 to commemorate the sesquicentennial of the abolition of the institution of slavery in the French colonies, the public debate on this matter and, especially, on the current consequences of this past servitude has been rising in the French departments of the Americas and in Caribbean-Guyanese immigration in metropolitan France. However, the scholarly analysis and political discourse on the slavery of the people transferred from Africa to the New World continue, for the most part, to stress and often stigmatize the existence of a huge repression of the slave past among West Indian peoples. We remain puzzled by this contradiction, which evokes the now-famous dilemma of "not enough" and "too much memory" highlighted by Paul Ricoeur.[16] We can clearly see the interest that some might have in using a mediocre strategy for personal advancement to appear as the first pioneers in an already-plowed field and as the breakers of a taboo, the importance of which they have, in truth, deliberately exaggerated. However, by not noticing the complexities of memory and by persisting in asserting that a general forgetting of slavery exists in the French West Indies, one runs the risk of shutting a large number of people inside the implausible belief that an uncontrollable epidemic of amnesia has mysteriously befallen the West Indian population! Why such low self-esteem, all the more strange in that it comes from those who are champions of West Indian pride?

From a Caricature of Discourse to . . .

In truth, the argument for a generalized forgetting of slavery in the French West Indies is a caricature, or even a fable, produced by political or cultural actors interested in—for reasons we will touch upon later—making West Indians feel guilty for the choices they made in 1946 to transform their countries into departments of the French Republic. It is a caricature and a fable that a rigorous examination of historical data or a brief socio-anthropological study of present events would challenge, and in reality already has challenged, definitively. And, simple common sense suggests that it does not seem very likely that after only a few years or even decades or, at most, a century and a half that the memory of a condition as horrible as that experienced by the slaves on American plantations would have been erased from the memory of those groups. This is especially true since the abolition of the legal institution of slavery was not enough to guarantee these groups living conditions much more decent than those of slaves. Furthermore, racism, the keystone of the slave system, has long persisted in all its force. All of these reasons have been quite sufficient in reminding these individuals what they, or their recent ancestors, including those who just wanted to forget, were not so long ago.

It is also worth noting, along with this discussion of a supposed forgetting, that it is incredible that at a time when the discourse on forgetting has proliferated in the West Indian countries and their Hexagonal diaspora, there has not been until recently any survey- or interview-based fieldwork among the general population about the current memory of slavery in these countries, and consequently, there have been no accurate representations of this memory.[17] Therefore, in the absence of investigations of this type, the only works that have been at our disposal have been influenced, or at least pressured, by the dominant ideological discourses of the moment, discourses that their authors were very happy to be able to justify—in a circular motion of mutual validation—through "independent" academic analyses, which in fact their own words in part helped to create.

Thus, a caricature—leading to a fable—is there. The argument in question is based entirely on an abusive extrapolation: since the abolition of slavery portions of metropolitan elites and colonial ruling classes wanted (obviously) to make former slaves and their descendants forget as quickly as possible the horror of the servile condition, to suggest—without any data to support this induction—that the "new freemen" had themselves desired this, as if, in the fairly common fantasy of the omnipotence of dominant groups, there was no reason to consider that the subordinated could do anything but submit to the dictates of their oppressors!

In an attempt to account for such an improbable submission, the most elaborate arguments for a general forgetting of slavery in the French West Indies claim to find the source of the explanation in what they consider to be a massive will to forget caused by the irrepressible desire for citizenship, which seized those who came from slavery and which has long been held and is still held by many of their descendants. They thus imagine a phony fiction, a type of "barter"[18] in which "forgetting the past" was exchanged for being granted French "citizenship," an exchange implicitly made between the "new freemen" and their former masters, backed by the state which remained colonial. This argument, however, is doomed to fail because the idea upon which it rests is absurd. Indeed, former slaves had already achieved the formal citizenship they wanted the moment their opponents found themselves in a position to offer them the "barter" in question, and more importantly, this victory was a direct result of their constant refusal of slavery, the very thing they were asked to forget. It is not clear, therefore, why and by what rationale former slaves and their descendants would have consented to an amnesia that would have made them renounce what ultimately ensured the success of the struggle against slavery and thereby definitively lose the sense of success and jubilation it provides them!

. . . the Truth of the Facts

In fact, all caricatures and all fictions aside, the available indices of the memory of slavery in the French West Indies are very far from confirming the bias of a widespread forgetting of slavery in these countries. To the secondary evidence of written and oral literatures (see note 1), we can add primary evidence. We will present the most important types of such evidence—those Laurent Dubois and those we were able to collect in Guadeloupe and Martinique with the use of a questionnaire, combined with in-depth interviews of a sample of just over two hundred people of both genders, all ages, and all social statuses—and briefly to analyze the lessons that they provide, to which we will now turn.

The main and most important of these lessons is that there is no common amnesia that prevails in the French Antilles about the slave past, but on the contrary, people in general expressed a vivid memory of that past, and expressed it in essentially the same way in both West Indian islands, in most cases with modesty but also with suppressed pain. Both tortured and torturous, this memory would appear conflictual.

Moreover, contrary to popular belief, it is only on rare occasions that respondents have hinted in their attitudes and in their words shame at having to discuss the history of slavery, including cases—albeit uncommon—when this evocation took on a personal dimension, nourished by the concrete intimacy of distant family memories. During the interviews we had with these people, they were more likely to articulate both a silent determination that nothing comparable to the past slavery of Negroes should crush men today and a genuine concern that such a possibility could arise again.

It even happens—and this is not exceptional—that some of them make the exaggerated claim that slavery persists to this day in Guadeloupe or Martinique, and not just in a metaphorical sense. As a twenty-seven-year old woman from Martinique said, "Slavery was only abolished on paper, because the slaves were uneducated and did the will of their masters who did not accept their liberation. For a long time afterward, they were still considered slaves, and sometimes they still are today."

There is no doubt that this sense of a current continuation of slavery among many respondents is based on the importance they continue to give to a sustained opposition of race and class between the vast majority of West Indian people and the heirs of the great white Creole planters and their metropolitan successors. Thus a seventy-five-year-old retired farmer from Martinique said, "Slavery continues by other means here. In Martinique there has always been a gulf between the Békés [descendants of slave-owning whites] and the Blacks. We are not equals." A forty-six-year-old mason from Martinique noted that the subject of slavery inevitably arises when it comes to the Békés and their wealth: "Inevitably, when speaking of the Békés, one ends up talking about slavery." He thought this even before there were commemorations of the abolition of slavery because, "look[ing] at our lives, you see how difficult things are for us. This is our life, we can see the way we live, everything depends on them. So necessarily we talk about it." He spoke of how he and his friends recall the difficulties of life: "We come back time and time again to this point, we consider that these things are connected, that is why I tell you that for me slavery is not finished, this is something we constantly talk about. We are still under the yoke, we have not escaped. The power of the Békés proves that this continues—we didn't make this up, we are living it. You can't invent something that is a living reality, you live it. You see it everyday. The Békés still have control, so you are still a slave, you are still dependent. One protests, one says, 'me, I'm not a slave, I'm free.' But, when you really think about it, you say to yourself, 'but, myself, I can't, even if I want to work hard, I can't do it. And you wonder why them and not me.'" Several people we interviewed considered racism a reality synonymous with that of slavery. A woman from Martinique who answered our questionnaire felt that the discrimination that Blacks face in France shows how "slavery never ended." A young girl from Rivière Pilote (Martinique) argued that "slavery still exists because whites remain superior to Blacks."

This idea of permanent servitude is also based on the equivalence that all the interviewees established between persistent colonial domination and slavery. Thus, they argued that, in many ways, the subordination and exclusion that characterized slavery is not over, because they are consubstantial with the colonial situation. A thirty-year-old unemployed Guadeloupean woman argued that if "we are still slaves" it is because Guadeloupe "is still a French colony." The aforementioned retired farmer from Martinique clarified his conviction that slavery is still valid in his country by stating that this impression is based on the fact that there will be "always the same French lack of respect vis-à-vis West Indians, in particular, for all those Martinicans who went to war in '14 to '18 or '39 or '45, without counting those who enlisted in the 'dissidence.' There is no reciprocity in relations between Martinique and France."[19] He added that he was "shocked to hear M. Sarkozy say that France will not eternally apologize. That's insulting."

While most people who responded to our survey do not, for the most part, believe that slavery continues to exist de facto in their country, their responses demonstrate that the servile past remains a central reference for the vast majority of them. The mason from Martinique said nothing else when he told us that for him the history of slavery constantly illuminates the way he perceives his situation, and that "inevitably" in the discussions that he has with his friends, slavery "marks" him because "one does not escape just because one has made a detour. In other words, one is not tied by the hands or the feet, but in the head. . . . One has to work in order to eat. Before we were forced. Slavery isn't really over, we remain under its domination." Beyond individual situations, the reference to slavery serves to strongly encode and decode the great moments of political and social history of the West Indies, including when those events are separated from the abolition of slavery by nearly a century, as in the following case. In Guadeloupe, a woman near eighty vividly guarded in her memory the "Sorin Period" (like others interviewed in Martinique did so for the "Robert Period").[20] She remembers how people experienced the harshness of that time, citing constantly the possibility of a restoration of slavery: "My dad said, 'we'll go back to slavery,' yes my dad said that." She also rememebed how at school they made her and other students work in the fields under the supervision of their teachers. They were made to grow radishes and salads without being allowed to eat what they grew. This made many parents angry, probably in part because it reminded them of the time of slavery. Slavery was and remains to this day the paradigm in the French West Indies of all situations of oppression and racism.

More generally, the memory of slavery is, for many of the individuals interviewed, a main key to the understanding and interpretation of many experiences they live now and of the imagination of many scenarios concerning their future where their current status either gives them some satisfaction in the progress made since the abolition of slavery or, conversely, gives them the feeling that these developments remain very inadequate. As a thirty-seven-year-old driver from Guadeloupe indicated to us, "every people has a specific reference for its suffering." In the French West Indies, this reference is slavery.

And thus, our surveys, in discussions of various aspects of daily life in the French West Indies, have yielded numerous examples of situations that evoke the slave past, whether in labor relations or other exchanges (especially with Békés or metropolitan Whites). Such evocations, which are not necessarily consistently thought through nor reflectively used as conscious representations of the past, are often presented as inevitable in discussions with friends or family members. For example, several people we interviewed told us they regularly use or have used the expression, which is widespread in the West Indies, "I am not your slave" to respond to someone asking them to do something they do not or did not want to do.

The slave past is decidedly present in the psyche of many West Indians, to whom it is an inescapable referent of memory: a characteristic of memory but, above all, an agent of comparison between different historical and social contexts, a prism through which present experience is read, a compass within which this experience lies in the continuity of history, and a plan to better enter the future. Thus, the interviews we have collected suggest (as do studies of oral and written Caribbean literature to which we have already alluded) that there is, in the French West Indies, a sort of "cultural grammar" and "common code" where the memory of slavery allows those who possess such a code of thinking, as a hint and as innuendo, to conceptualize their existence. To a point, we could with complete legitimacy defend the hypothesis that the situation concerning this memory does not come from amnesia but from a sort of hypermnesia, an abnormally strong remembrance of the past. Therefore, the fable of a widespread forgetting of slavery in the French West Indies would be laughable except for the eminent services it renders (if only by judging from the fair hearing from which it benefits) for questionable strategies of dubious political methods or personal career advancement. But who is still fooled by these strategies? Certainly not the mason from Martinique, who said that if the media and elites did not always talk about slavery, it would still exist in "the hearts of the people, where one speaks of it," and that "it is not always the elites who have historical knowledge." He protests against the elitist contempt that the argument for a generalized forgetting of slavery in the last analysis levies against the people.

A Certain Silence about the Past of Slavery: Amnesia or Refusal?

A paradox nonetheless remains, that of the silence that adults have long imposed and still impose on the history of slavery within Caribbean families, according to the cliché which flourishes in Guadeloupe and Martinique. How does one explain this silence if the memory of slavery is as perennial as the data from our survey seem to confirm?

First of all, it must be said that not all or even a large majority of people who completed our survey confirmed the veracity of this cliché. A significant number of them shared with us that much of their knowledge and memories of slavery and, in particular, of the struggles against it had come from their families, from mothers, fathers, or, more commonly, from grandparents or great uncles. This transmission would often occur during traditional celebrations, where many stories were told and exchanged in the home or among neighbors, a tradition that is now disappearing. Sometimes the resulting stories, as they have been reported in the interviews, involve "important ancestors" of families or places where the celebrations in question were supposed to have taken place. They are then supplied with many details, marked with a great accuracy of facts, geography, and dates, and in the case of Guadeloupe, a remarkable historical exactitude, if we are to believe the excellent expertise of our colleague Laurent Dubois.

It is useful to take into account the psychological necessity for any individual to protect himself from the devastating aftereffects of injuries suffered, directly or indirectly, collectively or individually, in order to be able to continue as quietly as possible down his road and build his future by advancing toward the light. Who is entitled to completely avoid this necessity, which involves not so much an annihilation through forgetting that horrible past as keeping oneself—as much as possible—at a considerable distance from the bite of poisonous memories?[21]

Finally, and most importantly, one should remember that "silencing the past" is not necessarily a sign of indifference to the harm that was brought.[22] One should also see that behind the undeniable reluctance of many West Indians to talk about the history of slavery to their children or, to a lesser extent, to their grandchildren (as evidenced by the remarks of a significant number of the people we interviewed) often lurk reasons—a far cry from amnesia—other than the resignation of historical responsibility for which they have been reproached. More specifically, it is important to understand that this reluctance rarely derives from a negative process of avoidance, but that it is, in most cases, motivated by a positive desire to build a better collective future, primarily for younger generations.

To understand this, one must begin by hearing what these people have to say about themselves, to hear, for example, that "our" mason from Martinique explained that if his parents "did not like" to talk about slavery to their children, it was chiefly because they "simply wanted to free us from that. They avoided speaking about it in order to help their children *aller de l'avant*." "De l'avant," a key phrase that says more in its brevity than long speeches do, shows that the modality of time which governs thinking about slavery in the hearts of Caribbean peoples represents the future more than the past.[23] As Stuart Hall writes, "Identity is not in the past to be found, but in the future to be constructed."[24] This approach leads the present and the future far beyond the past and, indeed, promotes less the forgetting of slavery than its final transcendence.

In the same vein, a young civil servant from Guadeloupe who currently lives in the West Indies but who has spent most of his life in metropolitan France also worries that too much emphasis on the slave past could hinder people's abilities to improve their present lives. He fears that "in talking too often about slavery and in repeating 'no more,' people stagnate, they don't move forward." Even if he admits that "you can't make the future without the past . . . [and that] we can't forget our past," it is to add that "you can't stay stuck in the past."

It is also the orientation toward improving present lives which explains that when parents evoke the slave past and its tragedies with their children, when they agree to such a reminiscence, it is often to sensitize their offspring to the profound difference that already exists between their present and this past, to highlight changes since the days of slavery, and sometimes to express the desire for a future that, above all, takes shape in stark contrast with servitude. This is not surprising since, as we have said, the history of slavery is, for West Indians, a major common reference for understanding their present and imagining their future. A young schoolgirl from Martinique, speaking about her family and especially her grandmother, told us they are willing to inform their children and grandchildren of the past realities of slavery so that they can "share the experiences" of their ancestors in order to "understand how things were in the past" and, as an irrefutable conclusion, admit that "you shouldn't complain too much about conditions today."

In these circumstances it does not seem to us that one can negatively view as a simple "repression" of the slave past the desire to escape the history of slavery, to build a future beyond the inheritance of it, a desire that those we interviewed sometimes expressed strongly. Rather, it should be seen, in a positive sense, as the refusal to remain in continuity with the past, the will to see the past definitely abolished or marginalized, everything that could, more or less, resemble the past. In that way, such a refusal rejoins, without knowing it, a whole intellectual tradition, one of many philosophies of freedom that turn their backs on the simplistic determinism according to which individuals in the present and the future are defined by what they and their ancestors were in the past. That is, as heavy as the burden of the past is on our shoulders, as restraining as the conditions of existence are that we have inherited, they do not determine us as genes do: automatically. Because we always have to return to them—if only by agreeing to conform to or, rather, to fight them—we constantly deconstruct and reconstruct them. We instead prefer to follow philosophies that argue, in the vein of Jean-Paul Sartre's formulation, that what matters is not what they made of us but what we do and will do with what they made of us.

The refusal at issue is also reflected in the cry of that great intellectual Frantz Fanon, calling on his "brothers," with ample justification, to "refuse to imprison ourselves in the substantialized Tower of the Past," repeating both iteratively and vehemently like a psalmody: "I am not a prisoner of History. I don't look there to find the meaning of my life. In my world, I am constantly creating myself. . . . I have no right to anchor myself. . . . I have no right to let myself get stuck by the determinations of the past. . . . One must not try strictly to determine the human condition, because our destiny is to be released. The density of History determines none of my acts. I am my own foundation. . . . And it is in going beyond the historical context, crucially, that I begin the cycle of my liberty. . . . I am not the slave of the Slavery which dehumanized my fathers. . . . I do not have the right, me, man of color, to call down upon the white man a sense of guilt about my race's past. . . . Neither do I have the right nor the duty to demand reparation for my domestic ancestors. There is no Black man's mission; there is no white man's burden."[25]

Incidentally, this whole approach which gives priority to what needs to happen rather than what has already happened, and which asks to transcend past time rather than to commemorate it, destroys the ability to lay claim to a "duty of memory" because it prohibits making the past sacred by giving it a value in and of itself, and because the supreme good is the achievement of a just social order, which is always undertaken in the present for a completion that can only be in the future. If there is a need to remember the past—and, undoubtedly, such a need actually exists—it is therefore primarily for a higher purpose that has to do with the present and the future of society: the reign and the dream of justice.[26] In other words, the working of memory finds justification in the cares of the present and the designs for the future and not in the weight of the past.[27] Therefore, when it is undertaken, "memory is dethroned . . . to profit not forgetfulness, of course, but certain principles."[28]

In fact, the necessity of this work lies precisely in the necessity of not repeating the crimes and mistakes of the past. As Tzvetan Todorov aptly remarks: "Appeals to memory have themselves no legitimacy without specifying toward what ends one plans to use them. . . . We should keep the memory of the past alive: not to demand reparation for offense, but to be alerted to new, perhaps analogous, situations."[29] And that is why faithfulness to the past can only be negative, prompting the cry "never again, neither in this nor another form!" Therefore, every individual and every social group must ensure that its necessary reappropriation of the past, which still affects but does not imprison it and which must be effected in the political context of the present, does not transform itself into an obsession with the past which would close off the future, which is always invention, not repetition. Memory

—which is taken from the past—is not an "objective" heritage that positively prescribes contemporary action, but is rather the current expression of what we have called a negative fidelity to a past experience, one that creates a spirit of generosity and openness to others. This means, according to the words of Barack Obama in his Philadelphia speech, "embracing the burdens of our past without becoming its victims."

The Misinterpretation of History and the Political Instrumentalization of Memory

It is thus the ideal of justice which has given rise in Guadeloupe and Martinique to a strong rejection of slavery and, especially today, of everything that could in some way recall it, a rejection so powerful that it goes sometimes—we have just seen—so far as to wrap itself in silence. The ideal in question carries, in the French political tradition (but not only in that one: far from it!), the name of Republic and, as an emblem, the motto "Liberty, Equality, Fraternity," which is inscribed on the facade of some public buildings. That is the reason why we have described elsewhere as a "citizen's rejection"—which we could have called "Republican"—the rejection inspired by this ideal.[30]

This refusal has a long history, going back precisely to the struggle against slavery, a struggle which, from its conception, was placed in the political perspective of what is today called human rights. It has thus sanctioned, in the words of the historian Florence Gauthier, "citizens' revolutions" rather than struggles for the establishment of improbable—and at the time, probably unthinkable—national sovereignty. Focused, in advance, on the ideal of citizenship rather than the desire for the nation, it somehow transformed those who led it into the "slaves of the Republic."[31]

The refusal in question was for a long time maintained and is still maintained among the peoples of the four "old colonies" of France (Guadeloupe, Guiana, Martinique, and Réunion) in its original inspiration, that of an integration of citizens into the French Republic. It is, in fact, in these countries the same dynamic that led to the abolition of slavery in 1848 and then to the transformation of these colonies into departments of the Republic by the Law of March 19, 1946: a search for emancipation in the process that was mistakenly called "assimilation" in France. It was an unfortunate name, because in truth the

challenge of the law called departmentalization was "to use departmentalization not to turn the West Indian into a Frenchman, not to
prolong colonization under a new form, but to destroy it. In other
words, departmentalization was intended to be a 'ruse of Reason.' "[32]
At least for the popular forces, which were headed by local federations
of the Communist Party, this law was somehow imposed on a colonial
authority reluctant to enact it.

Since the implementation of departmentalization, nationalist movements of these four countries have been, in an increasingly predictable
manner, in extreme disagreement with popular aspirations to integrate
citizens into the French Republic, the main historic (and now the most
maligned) expression of which was the claim for the political "assimilation" of the old colonies to France. They saw in this aspiration a
sickly will toward mimetism, a neurotic impulse to lose oneself in
another body, in the body of the Other, that of the *Mère-trop-pôle*,
according to the famous expression of an Antillanist psychoanalyst.[33]

In truth, however, the West Indian peoples have hardly agreed to
buy political assimilation into France at the cost of denying their own
personalities. Aimé Césaire, who handled the "departmentalization"
of the "old colonies" since he was the draftsman of the law which
introduced their new status, continued ceaselessly until his death to
trumpet the Négritude of the peoples of these countries, without ever
seeing the shadow of a contradiction, in what still appears to some as a
paradox. The fact is that, far from excluding the assertion of a specific
identity, the demand for equality necessarily implies this affirmation
so long as that identity is devalued and that devaluation is the principle of existing inequality. Rendering the identity of a people or group
inferior leaves no other possibility for achieving the equality that they
claim other than recognizing the dignity of this flouted identity. Thus,
in seeking to become citizens of France, the peoples of the "old colonies" did not intend, in their great majority, to blend into French
identity—assuming such an identity exists!—but to suppress colonial
injustice by giving themselves the means of benefiting, on an equal
footing with the other French, from the rights that citizenship is
intended to guarantee.

Moreover, the initial choice of integration into citizenship, as vague
as this representation was in the minds of many who pursued it, was
not paradoxical, because in the last analysis the peoples of the "old
colonies" had no choice in beginning to work toward their emancipa-

tion other than to conquer social and political equality within the French nation, that is, to finally rid it of its colonial trappings. And to make this work, culturally speaking, to master the dominant codes of this group, it was necessary to turn against the colonizer, the "miraculous arms" of which Aimé Césaire spoke first. In effect, since their "identity" was not, or was no longer, rooted in a native hinterland said to exist before colonization, but instead was formed entirely in the crucible of the slave plantations under pressure from the colonial relationship, which was founder of all things, they could no longer claim a radical cultural difference in relation to the colonizer. In conceptualizing and fighting for their liberation, they did not have— unlike the victims of most other colonial situations, who were colonized in the land and the culture of their ancestors—the resource of associating their ideals of emancipation with a project, even illusory, of returning to a tradition and a precolonial order that one only needed to exhume from the historical layers covering them. Therefore, under the colonial regime, the claim of equality emerged in the French Antilles to the detriment of a claim of independence.

The divorce of nationalist elites from the popular aspiration to integrate citizens in the French Republic has led these elites, over the past ten years or so, to undertake, concerning the issue of slavery, a double rereading done in a spirit of radical critique, to the point that the historian Edouard de Lépine from Martinique has characterized it as "tropical neo-revisionism."[34] This rereading occurs at the moment —probably considered opportune by those who carry it out—when the deficiencies and repeated disappointments of "departmentalization" (regardless of its undoubted successes) and the succession of promises that the Republic failed or was unwilling to make good on have given rise in the public opinion of the West Indies to a great doubt about the possibility of one day achieving effective citizenship, which was until recently still overwhelmingly demanded.[35]

The rereading in question is concerned, first of all, with an interpretation suitable to the historical dynamics of Caribbean antislavery movements. Above all, for the supporters of a nationalist or at least an indigenous reading, the purpose is to "purge," as far as possible, from the history of these movements influences from the ideals of the French revolutions of 1789 and 1848. The goal is to challenge radically the analysis that, in this history, focuses on the universalist, "citizen" dimension of the dynamics in question, and to open the way for the

idea that these movements are, on the contrary, the first manifestations of national struggle in the Caribbean.[36] It would however be an
error of time and place to make of these movements examples of
Enlightenment thought, the first manifestations of national liberation
struggles that will develop later (and elsewhere) in the post-Romantic
century of decolonization. The outraged accusation of the retraction
of "the national question" is indeed only a bad case inspired by an
optical illusion that the historian of ancient Greece Moses Finley
called "the teleological error," that is, when one, in "criticizing one's
ancestors for not having done that which they could not then do [e.g.,
national revolutions], refuses to integrate into the development of
History that which they did do [e.g., the establishment of the Re-
public], in the limits of the possible."[37]

Moreover, we must remember that the antislavery revolutions in the
West Indies are not the epiphenomena of the French and the American revolutions simply because of their undoubted influence. Because, as certain as it is that the antislavery struggles drank in part
from the source of the principles of other revolutions, they did not
stop there, and in fact went much further; it is through turning these
principles against the power which gave birth to them, thus giving
them a new significance, that they secured for themselves and for
others a certain sustainability. There was never a servile imitation but
rather a meeting of convergent yet autonomous dynamics, a meeting
which was surely no accident but the necessity of which reflects the
dialectics of mutual fertilization, without which the Revolution of
1789 would not have begun to realize its promise of universality in
action, though this realization has remained incomplete.[38]

Finally, the rereading evoked concerns, above all, about the relationship of French West Indians with the memory of slavery. Regarding
this relationship, this rereading is entirely dedicated to accrediting the
idea according to which there exists in these countries a huge forgetting and a thick silence about slavery that is ultimately only an additional mark of the old colonial alienation. Again, it sanctions an optical illusion, which is in the same vein and in the same breath as that
which we spotted earlier. Recently, it considered the forgetting of the
"national question" a kind of national betrayal, where there could be
nothing more than an appetite for the Republic. Now it takes as a
desire for blindness, as a perverse repression, that which indeed constitutes the exercise of a memory, but a memory conceptualized in

terms that are now considered "politically incorrect" by the nationalist (or more broadly, nativist) ideology, which currently stands in the forefront of the West Indian intellectual scene. Thus, its "wish," the mission it accomplishes, is to "throw back into the ocean" everything that comes to express or reinforce the desire for a "real" French citizenship, which this ideology abhors and sees as the ultimate form of colonial alienation.

Clearly, contemporary political issues, rather than a sudden desire to seek in all things regarding historical truth, have led in the French Caribbean to the "discovery" of a supposedly widespread denial of slavery. Nationalist and nativist elites developed as a part of this issue a political tactic that more or less aimed to make large sectors of the Caribbean peoples pay the price of national treason, which they allegedly committed against their countries for turning them into French departments. This is a tactic which consists, to paraphrase an image taken from the writer Daniel Maximin of Guadeloupe, "of injecting the epidemic [of guilt for the pretended forgetting of slavery] in order to offer the vaccine [of the nationalist position]," which the vast majority of Caribbean opinion continues to resist.[39] Édouard de Lépine demonstrates the mechanism of such tactics well, with a certain brutality but also, in the very passionate context of the debates we have outlined, with an undeniable intellectual courage, when he writes: "Ultimately, to call things by their proper name, our champions of the duty of memory couldn't care less about slavery. What bothers them is not that the people have lost the memory of slavery, but their inability to convince them of the only solution which seems to them appropriate to the colonial problem, that of national independence."[40] Clearly, once again, with the political instrumentation of memory, debates about the past are nothing more than times when the present tortures itself, in anticipation of the future to come.

Conclusion

To examine the two main themes that we followed in this text—that of the "question of blackness" and of the memory of slavery—one can only be struck (in the analyses devoted to them) by their general parallelism and by the specific parallels of their different sections. Such parallels include inventories or diagnostics marked by errors similar in nature to those that we called in our text "fables" and likewise to what Jean-Paul Sartre called "the good faith of the bad faith": on the one hand, the reproach of a desire for invisibility and colorblindness to the color of another; on the other hand, the accusation of the widespread forgetting of slavery and a guilty silence with respect to this past; with, as a bonus on both sides, the same suspicion of active colonial alienation. In both cases there are nonetheless other issues at work: in one the desire simply to be a human being, in the other a citizen's refusal of the unacceptable, both of which are, after all, very reasonable.

The proposed solutions go hand in hand with the similarly outdated ruts of voluntarism and have the same weakness, baptizing these difficulties by helping to reinforce rather than resolve them: here, the retreat into or enthusiasm for identity, called—for the sake of the cause—ethnic pride, which always calls forth opposing reactions of group pride; there, the guilt-inducing indoctrination of the "duty of memory," which, instead of facilitating understanding, restrains it. Finally, the same political impasse arises from the same inadequate solutions and leads to similar divisions and deleterious fragmentations that base social life on a uniform competition of history's victims demanding compensation (competition of phenotypes and cultural heritages as well as memories), where only solidarities across community boundaries would have a salutary effect.

Such a parallel has something about it so perfect that it could be judged mysterious. For our part, we do not believe there is any mystery but rather the path of a single social logic, which the sociologist Pierre Bourdieu referred to as "struggles for classification" (as we have in this text preferred to call "elite strategies"): struggles or strategies in which and for which groups of individuals—suitably equipped with different kinds of capital (economic and financial, cultural and intellectual, or even "racial")—are particularly apt to capture as their only benefit the mobilization of identity or memory that they have often helped trigger, but in which others, more often, form the bulk of the infantry.

We have arrived at an age where we finally get tired of observing that all the liberation movements—when they were not crushed before beginning to bear fruit—only very imperfectly attained their desired objectives. However, probably naively, we remain convinced that in our position the only contribution that we can modestly make to prevent or at least seriously impede this fate is to tear apart, to tear apart again, always to tear apart the mechanisms and the false pretenses of the fraud that we have mentioned, wherever we can study them. We are not sure of succeeding, but as "there is no need to succeed in order to persist," we will continue to do so.

Notes

1. We call "neo-racialist" a whole group of fairly young researchers who have denounced in recent years what they see as a trend in French social sciences toward systematic blindness to the question of "race" (in the wider sense of the term). In addition to this shared effort of criticism—which, though partly justified, is excessive insofar as it brushes aside the many French social scientists who dealt with this question long before it became commonplace to do so—they agree on the vague intuition (which they use as a basis for their denunciation) that social sciences should finally turn, in order to name and indeed study "racial" phenomena, to the discourse or representations which social agents, especially those who encounter different forms of racism, hold or form in relation to these phenomena. But to what purpose? So scientific analyses may take into account such discourse and representations, which is reasonable, or they may take them as valid accounts of those phenomena, which is debatable? That is the question! A question which, in our opinion, those researchers elected to not answer clearly in their work; hence our criticisms leveled at them—which we will expound on in this chapter.

The ensemble into which we group a number of colleagues, for the sole purpose of stressing the emergence of a new trend in French social sciences, and whom we call "neo-racialist" with the self-conscious intention of causing controversy, is far from homogeneous: these colleagues may diverge greatly on this or that particular analysis, and they would probably reject the adjective we use to designate them. A good idea of what this "movement" represents can be formed by consulting the book edited by Didier and Eric Fassin, *De la question sociale à la question raciale: représenter la société française* (Paris: La Découverte, 2007). However, it is worth mentioning here that, in our mind, not all contributors to this book qualify as "neo-racialist" (by a long way), and some of the colleagues whom we consider as such are not featured among the authors of this book. In the end, it will be up to the reader, therefore, to pass his own judgment.

2. Thus the literary works of major writers such as Aimé Césaire and Edouard Glissant were fully formed—just before the Second World War for

the former, and shortly after the war for the latter—in the fundamental matrix of the memory of slavery. And it could easily be shown that large parts of the oral literature of the French West Indies, including folktales, constituting what might be called the "popular wisdom" of these countries, found much of their intelligibility in the complex syntax of a memory of slavery. See M. Giraud and J.-L. Jamard, "Travail et servitude dans l'imaginaire antillais," *L'Homme* 96, no. 35 (October–December 1985): 77–96.

3. *Alizés*, January/March 2008, 1. *Alizés* is a Christian-based magazine published in Paris by the Association Pour l'Expression et la Formation des Antillais et Guyanais. It is fifty-seven years old.

4. And this, after the magazine put forth in April–June 2005 "Le devoir de mémoire en débat" in a dossier with an unambiguous title: "Un passé toujours présent."

5. P. Ndiaye, *La condition noire: essai sur une minorité française* (Paris: Calmann-Lévy, 2008), 17. The same people, or others, argue that it is equally the history of slavery and sometimes go so far as to argue for a widespread forgetting of slavery (e.g., see M. Cottias, " 'L'oubli du passé' contre la 'citoyenneté': troc et ressentiment à la Martinique (1848–1946)," in *Cinquante ans de départementalisation outré-mer, 1946–1996*, ed. F. Constant and J. Daniel (Paris: L'Harmattan, 1997), 293–313.

6. It is certain that initially objective characteristics already foreshadow its shape, but they make up only an idealized sketch of a potentiality that awaits the hour of its act, the abstract schema of a group that exists only "on paper" as Pierre Bourdieu said. An actualization will happen only if the discourses that call it into being are in line with a favorable historical context and if the actors are socially recognized as legitimate to keep them. Meanwhile, the individuals to whom these speeches are directed will be able to internalize the principles of division and categories of perception of the social world that the speeches in question convey, principles and categories through which these individuals are now capable of understanding the reality and behaving according to this understanding. Finally the group in question may perhaps be revealed to itself and to others.

7. The situation that we analyze here from the sole point of view of the "racial" issue goes far beyond this single dimension and the analysis that we make is equally valid for the "ethnic" issue, these two issues not being very distinguishable in the common opinion.

8. In the case of French society, the title of the aforementioned book published under the direction of Didier and E. Fassin, *De la question sociale à la question raciale: représenter la société française* (Paris: La Découverte, 2007) alludes to this movement.

9. A. Anselin, *L'émigration antillaise en France: la troisième île* (Paris: Karthala, 1990), 141.

10. S. Hall, "Old and New Identities, Old and new Ethicities," in *Culture, Globalization and the World-System Contemporary Conditions for the Representation of Identity*, ed. Anthony D. King (London: Macmillan, 1991), 53.

11. "Entretien avec Claude Ribbe," *Alizés,* January–March 2008, no. 1, "Pourquoi on parle tant des noirs?," 10.

12. On what seem to be the errors of neo-racialists in this regard, we refer to the short but very revealing interview that the sociologist Eric Fassin granted the journalist Laetitia Van Eeckhout, which is published under the title "Pourquoi et comment notre vision du monde se 'racialise,'" in *Le Monde*, March 4–5, 2007. One should also, at this point, see the introduction and first chapter of Pap Ndiaye that we have already quoted.

13. Hall, "Old and New Identities, Old and new Ethicities," 57.

14. Ibid., 59.

15. Politico web site (http://www.politico.com), May 27, 2008.

16. P. Ricoeur, "Vulnérabilité de la mémoire," in *Patrimoines et passions identitaires: actes des entretiens du patrimoine 1997*, ed. Jacques Le Goff (Paris: Arthème Fayard, 1998).

17. After we strongly denounced this deficiency, in a symposium held in Guadeloupe in 2001 by Erik Bleich, Laurent Dubois, Stéphane Dufoix, Mickaella Perina, and Patrick Weil on the theme "L'héritage de l'esclavage et de l'émancipation en Europe et en Amérique"—see Michel Giraud, "Les enjeux presents de la mémoire de l'esclavage," in *L'esclavage, la colonsation, et après . . .*, ed. Patrick Weil and Stéphane Dufoix (Paris: Presses Universiatires de France, 2005)—we undertook with our colleague and friend Dubois an investigation on this subject, whose initial results have been the subject of a report: see L. Dubois and M. Giraud, *La mémoire de l'esclavage en Guadeloupe et en Martinique: les faits, les discours et les enjeux* (Report submitted to the Ministère d'Outre-Mer on the memory of slavery in the French Antilles, 2008).

18. We take one of the key terms used by the main producer of this fiction in the very title of his article already cited, see Cottias, " 'L'oubli du passé' contre la 'citoyenneté.' " The explicit loan of the idea of "barter" that the member of Parliament elected from Guiana, Christiane Taubira, made in the text of this historian in the report of the law declaring slavery and the slave trade as "crimes contre l'humanité" presented in 2001 before the French National Assembly is a perfect illustration of what we said above. It is the existence of a circular movement of mutual validation between the rhetoric of politicians and the analysis of researchers.

19. The movement of young West Indians who left their island illegally to join the Forces Françaises Libres of General de Gaulle.

20. Sorin was the governor of Guadeloupe under the Vichy regime during the Second World War, a regime that in the West Indies has been character-

ized as a very authoritarian administration, not devoid of racist attitudes toward people "of color." At the same time, the administration of Governor Robert in Martinique was the exact counterpart of that of Sorin in Guadeloupe. During his governorship, the Békés, or white Creoles, the heirs of the slave plantocracy, gave free rein to their old discriminatory tendencies.

21. The philosopher Tzvetan Todorov subtly describes the specific actions of such distancing when he writes: "the subject . . . does not try to give them [traumatic memories] a dominant place—but rather to repress them into a peripheral position where they are inoffensive; to domesticated and, in a word, to defuse them. To the extent that they were repressed, these memories remained active (they hindered the subject from living): now that they have been recovered, they can be, not forgotten, but put aside." T. Todorov, *Les abus de la mémoire* (Paris: Arléa, 1998), 23.

22. We of course borrow this expression from the work of M.-R. Trouillot, *Silencing the Past: Power and the Production of History* (Boston: Beacon, 1995).

23. Translator's note: *aller de l'avant* means to transcend, to go beyond.

24. Stuart Hall, "Negotiating Caribbean Identities," *New Left Review*, January–February 1995, 12.

25. Frantz Fanon, *Peau noire, masques blancs* (Paris: Le Seuil, 1952), 204–6.

26. See, on this point, the essential structure of the philosopher P. Ricoeur, *La mémoire, l'histoire, l'oubli* (Paris: Le Seuil, 2000): nothing can replace this study.

27. "The recovery of the past is indispensable; that does not mean that the past should rule the present; it is the present, on the contrary, that uses the past as it will. . . . That group that does not succeed in wresting itself away from the haunting commemoration of the past, all the more difficult to forget the sadder it is, or those within the group who incite it to live it, deserves less sympathy [than the individual in mourning]: this time, the past serves to repress the present, and this kind of repression is no less dangerous than the other [the repression of the past]." Todorov, *Les abus de la mémoire*, 24, 33.

28. Ibid., 19.

29. Ibid., 52.

30. F. Gauthier, "Et du citoyen!," *Chemins Critiques* 3, no. 302 (January 1997): 190–205. See also Giraud, "Les enjeux presents de la mémoire de l'esclavage," 537–46. In that contribution, we have quoted, in a more developed manner than we do here, some elements of analysis, including historical, which are discussed in this section of our present text.

31. We refer here to the title of the excellent work of L. Dubois, *Les esclaves de la république: l'histoire oubliée de la première émancipation, 1789–1794* (Paris: Calmann-Lévy, 1998).

32. Roland Suvélor, "Éléments historiques pour une approche sociocul-

turelle," in "Antilles," special issue, *Les Temps Modernes* 441–42 (April–May 1983): 2174–2208. On the limits of this "ruse," see Giraud, "Sur l'assimilation: les paradoxes d'un objet brouillé," in *Entre assimilation et émancipation: l'outre-mer français dans l'impasse*, ed. Thierry Michalon (Rennes: Les Perséides, 2006), 89–101.

33. "Mère-trop-pôle" is forged after "Métropole" (mainland) and can be divided into three words: mère (mother), trop (too much), and pôle (pole, center).

34. Édouard De Lépine, "À propos du 22 mai 1848: contre le néo-révisionnisme tropical," in *Les abolitions de l'esclavage: de L .F. Sonthonax à Victor Schoelcher, 1793–94, 1848*, ed. Marcel Dorigny (Vincennes: Presses Universitaires de Vincennes–Unesco, 1995), 355–58.

35. The very important protest movement that took place over several weeks in the French West Indies early in the year 2009 is, despite the multiplicity of meanings—not all congruent in relation to each other—that we can attribute to it, certainly exemplary of such developments.

36. This also seems to be debated in the Haitian historiography, if we are to believe the criticism by Carlo Célius against the "Ontologie de la Révolution haïtienne" according to which Michel-Rolph Trouillot presented this revolution "as an ensemble which developed closed in upon itself. . . . in a complete impermeability to all 'outside' influences." Carlo Célius, "Le modèle social haïtien: hypothèses, arguments et méthode," *Pouvoirs dans la Caraïbe*, 1998: 116, and as a reality " 'unthinkable' in the categories of western Enlightenment philosophy." See Trouillot, *Silencing the Past*, 82.

37. Suvélor, "Éléments historiques pour une approche socioculturelle," 2194.

38. The work of Laurent Dubois has brilliantly exposed this dialectic through what he says is, giving a nod to Paul Gilroy's *Black Atlantic*, the "transatlantic" process: "while metropolitan France and the Caribbean were transformed in concert, . . . the ideas and symbols born of the French Revolution were reformulated in the Caribbean, where the sense of citizenship and membership in the national community took unforeseen directions," but also—and this is the main original point of this work—which in turn produced the French Revolution "as an historical event fashioned in depth by the process that marked the Caribbean during the years of the Revolution," Dubois, *Les esclaves de la république*, 8–9).

39. Daniel Maximin, "J'habite un paradis raté . . ." in *Tropiques métis*, catalogue of the exhibit of the same name held at the Musée National des Arts et Traditions Populaires (Paris: Réunion des Musées Nationaux, 1998), 27.

40. De Lépine, "À propos du 22 mai 1848," 175–76.

PART III

Black Paris—Black France

The New Negro in Paris

Booker T. Washington, the New Negro, and the Paris Exposition of 1900

MARCUS BRUCE

In January 1900, the U. S. Congress passed, and President William McKinley signed, a special appropriation bill awarding $15,000 to Thomas Calloway, an official in the War department and a protégé of Booker T. Washington, for the organization, assemblage, and installation of an American Negro Exhibit to be sent to the Paris Exposition of 1900.[1] The first exhibit of its kind sponsored by the United States on foreign soil, the American Negro Exhibit was designed to show the social and economic progress of American Negroes since Emancipation. Housed on the right bank of the Seine in a building devoted to exhibits of "social economy, hygiene, and public assistance," the American Negro Exhibit greeted visitors both at the entrance to the building and in a small corner of the first-floor section that displayed American social and economic progress. Swinging panels containing five hundred photographs were hung from the walls of the exhibit and offered a stunning visual presentation of the history, progress, and present conditions of the American Negro since Emancipation. Most notable here were the photographs showing the buildings, grounds, and student bodies of Hampton Normal and Industrial Institute, Tuskegee, Fisk, Atlanta University, Howard University, and other Black educational institutions. Bookcases below the panel displayed 200 volumes written by African American authors, a bibliography of over 1,400 titles by African Americans documented by the Library of Congress, a volume recording the 350 patents issued to Black inventors, and a compilation of newspapers. The American Negro Exhibition, as a whole, received a total of fifteen awards: a Grand Prize for its overall presentation, gold medals for Thomas Calloway and W. E. B. Du Bois for their work, respectively, as the special agent and compiler of the exhibit, a gold medal for Tuskegee University, and a silver medal for Booker T. Washington's monograph on the education of the Negro.[2]

The American Negro Exhibit was a widely discussed and celebrated event during its heyday, yet it is virtually forgotten today. With the exception of a few fine scholarly discussions of the photographs included in the exhibit, scholars have found little of significance in the exhibit, its historical impact, or the issues and problems it addressed.[3] This is a far cry from the importance and standing W. E. B. Du Bois gave to the exhibit and the moment of its emergence. In a review entitled "The American Negro in Paris," Du Bois described the contents of the exhibit in detail and declared it "an honest, straightforward exhibit of a small nation of people, picturing their life and development without apology or gloss, and above all made by themselves."[4] Over fifty years later, Du Bois returned to the event again, continuing to ruminate on its meaning, giving it even greater weight. "In 1900," Du Bois wrote in his final autobiography, "came a significant occurrence which not until lately have I set in its proper place in my life."[5]

For Du Bois, the American Negro Exhibit was the occasion for discovering just how complex the problem of the color-line actually was. It represented more than the achievements of African Americans; it also represented "a problem" with a complex set of challenges for African Americans. Thus, the declaration for which Du Bois has become famous, and which accompanied the American Negro Exhibit at its debut in Paris, becomes not only prescient of the century of race relations that lay ahead but also marks the emergence of new ways to understand the art and politics of representing African Americans at the turn of the century: "The problem of the twentieth century is the problem of the color-line."[6]

In the chapter that follows, I want to propose three ways in which the American Negro Exhibit might be viewed as an instance of "the problem" confronting Du Bois at the turn of the century, a realization that took Du Bois a lifetime to understand. First, the American Negro Exhibit can be viewed as contested ground, as a "ritual of representation," where African Americans struggled with each other over how to define themselves and their achievements. Booker T. Washington, a figure visibly absent from Du Bois's subsequent accounts of the event, is but one of a number of African Americans whose contributions to the exhibit have been forgotten.[7] Second, the American Negro Exhibit can also serve as an archive, documenting the material achievements of African Americans, their efforts at self-definition, and the emergence of a new self-awareness at the dawn of a new century. Posterity may have given Du Bois the final word, yet a review of the archive reveals a striking diversity of views regarding the exhibit, its meaning, and its significance. Third, the American Negro Exhibit represents an important *lieu de memoire* (a site of memory) in the history of African Americans in Paris, a moment when they entered what Du Bois called "the Kingdom of Culture" and began defining themselves and their culture.[8] Paris would be both the context in which African Americans represented themselves to a larger world and the occasion for wrestling with the art and politics of representation.

The American Negro Exhibit as Contested Representations

Burton Benedict has rightly called the world's fairs "rituals of representation" where the exhibits were often little more than occasions for participating nations to construct their vision of the world and their place within it.[9] While the American Negro Exhibit was certainly "made by" the African Americans who gathered and organized its content, it was also "contested ground" where African Americans, the U. S. government, and the French commissioners of the exposition struggled to define African Americans, African American culture, and their place in the world. An instance of the politics of representing African Americans through an exhibit is illustrated in the struggle between Du Bois and Washington to take credit for the success of the American Negro Exhibit.

Though W. E. B. Du Bois is often identified as the creator and primary sponsor of the exhibit, Booker T. Washington, president of the Tuskegee Normal and Industrial Institute, played a major role in the conception, placement, and final success of the exhibit. More than the relatively unknown scholar Du Bois, Washington represented for many educators, politicians, white Southerners, and African Americans "a new type" of Negro—or what has come to be known as the New Negro. An inveterate exposition participant, sponsor, and exhibitor, Washington viewed the American Negro Exhibit to the Paris Exposition of 1900 as one more opportunity to broadcast and publicize the work of Tuskegee and confirm his status as the preeminent African American leader in the nation. What he did not anticipate was the manner in which the American Negro Exhibit would serve as a contested site marking the emergence of the New Negro and plant the seeds of dissension that would undermine his leadership. Long before the debate between Washington and Du Bois, the Niagara Movement, or the NAACP, the American Negro Exhibit would serve as the occasion for defining and debating how to represent African Americans.

Washington had risen to national prominence with his famous Atlanta Exposition speech of 1895 in which he advised African Americans to seek economic rather than social or political opportunities. This speech, later derisively referred to as the "Atlanta Compromise" by Du Bois, Washington's most articulate and vociferous critic, would —after it initial reception—anger Black leaders who favored a more aggressive campaign for social and political rights and equality.[10] Yet Washington had witnessed and benefited from the impact that a single speech at an exposition could make and viewed an exhibit of Negro achievement as a new opportunity, at the dawn of the twentieth century, to announce the emergence of what is often referred to as the New Negro. In fact, one reporter, following the success of Washington's speech, posed a question as the title of his article: "Is He [Washington] a New Negro?"[11] Washington's presence and work announced the arrival of a self-reliant, industrious, determined, and visionary freedman, one less a ward of the state than a co-worker. More importantly, Washington's speech and the accompanying Negro Building at the Atlanta Cotton States Exposition of 1895 were "evidence of an awakening of the race. It seems to me, however," wrote the journalist of the *Chicago Inter Ocean*, "that it would be more appropriate to speak of the awakening of the white race to the real merit of the earnest effort the work accomplished, and the possibilities of the colored people."[12]

Washington's role in gaining African Americans a place at the Paris Exposition of 1900 was unprecedented. He would use every contact and resource available to him—and his resources were considerable— to assure himself, Tuskegee, and African Americans an exhibit. As early as 1898, Washington was contacted by the National Educational Association Advisory Board and asked to be a part of a U. S. commission appointed by the president of the United States to select American exhibits to represent the nation at the Paris Exposition of 1900.[13]

Washington's Atlanta speech had not only won him wide praise in Northern and Southern newspapers but also brought him to the attention of educators and even the president of the United States. One can only speculate whether Washington and President McKinley discussed a possible American Negro exhibit during McKinley's visit to the Tuskegee campus in December 1898. What is certain is that Washington actively petitioned President McKinley for his support.[14]

In the summer of 1899, Washington made his first trip to England and France, arriving in Paris with letters of introduction provided by Francis J. Garrison, the son of the famous American abolitionist William Lloyd Garrison.[15] Among those letters was one introducing Washington to a Frenchman named Auguste Laugel, a scientist, journalist for the *Nation*, professor at the École Polytechnique, abolitionist, and author of a book on the American Civil War supporting the cause of abolitionism. Laugel was also married to an American woman, Elisabeth Bates Chapman, the daughter of one of Boston's most famous abolitionists and feminists, Maria Weston Chapman.[16] Thus within days of his arrival in Paris, Washington met with a Frenchman whose sympathies were aligned with those of American abolitionists and who was also a commissioner for the Paris Exposition of 1900. More important, Laugel introduced Washington into the salon of French and American abolitionists in Paris.

Washington continued his campaign for a special Negro exhibit from Europe by submitting a series of articles to a number of African American newspapers—the *New York Age*, the *Colored American*, and the *Indianapolis Freeman*—and making references to the Paris Exposition of 1900 and another event planned for the same summer: the first Pan-African Conference to be held in London.[17] He encouraged "as many of our people as can possibly do so . . . to attend this conference. In my opinion," Washington wrote, "it is going to be one of the most effective and far reaching gatherings that has ever been held in connection with the development of the race."[18] Yet one additional piece of evidence demonstrating Washington's crucial role in securing governmental and financial support for a Negro exhibit is his letter to the president of the United States, William McKinley, making an appeal for "a separate educational exhibit representing the progress of the Negro race at the Paris Exposition," and recommending a specific person, Thomas J. Calloway, a supporter of Washington's, an official in the U. S. government, and an African American, to take charge of organizing the special exhibit.[19] He also informed the president that Howard J. Rogers, representing Ferdinand W. Peck, assistant commissioner general of the U. S. commission to the Paris Exposition and who was in charge of the educational and sociological exhibits of Americans, had already agreed to a separate Negro exhibit.

This brief historical review of Washington's role in the creation of the American Negro Exhibit reveals the extent to which Du Bois all but erased evidence of Washington's significant contribution, barely concealing the ideological conflict that would shape their interactions and the course of African American culture following the Paris Exposition of 1900. Yet further investigation of historical documents, especially those pertaining to the collection, construction, organization, and installation of the American Negro Exhibit, reveals that Du Bois and Washington were but two participants in an event that for a brief time absorbed the attention of African Americans.

The American Negro Exhibit as Archive

Looking beyond the conflict between Du Bois and Washington, the American Negro Exhibit can serve as an archive of an enduring challenge and problem: the art and politics of representing African Americans. This was certainly the case with Du Bois, who on a number of occasions, puzzled in his writings over the meaning of the exhibit and the specific period in his life.[20] More important, Du Bois, Washington, Calloway, and a host of other individuals and organizations created an archive of an emergent moment in African American culture when African Americans began to define themselves in a variety of new ways. The American Negro Exhibit forms a substantial archive of a moment otherwise lost to us, an awakening and new awareness of just how complex the problem of the color-line was. It is the archive of the thoughts, feelings, and responses of a group of Americans to the problem of race at the turn of the century.

The principal figure who helped to put the plan for a special exhibit into motion and, unwittingly, created an archive was Washington's protégé, Thomas Calloway, former president of Alcorn Institute in Mississippi and an administrator in the war department in Washington.[21] In a letter dated October 4, 1899, Calloway solicited Washington's support for a Negro exhibit to the Paris Exposition. Calloway reasoned that "to the Paris Exposition thousands upon thousands of Europeans and Americans will go and a well selected and prepared exhibit, representing the Negro's development in his churches, his schools, his homes, his farms, his stores, his professions and pursuits in general will attract attention as did the exhibits at Atlanta and Nashville Expositions, and do a great and lasting good in convincing thinking people of the possibilities of the Negro."[22] Capitalizing on Calloway's eagerness to organize such an exhibit, Washington solicited President McKinley for assistance.

Once Calloway's appointment was confirmed, he quickly set about gathering material for the exhibit and hired his old Fisk University classmate, W. E. B. Du Bois, to provide a detailed sociological study of African Americans in Georgia. Setting up a main office in the Washington area, Calloway corresponded with prominent African American leaders throughout the country, wrote articles for Black newspapers soliciting exhibition material, and traveled extensively with a photographer in tow to Southern states to make a photographic record of the progress of African Americans. He commissioned Daniel P. Murray, a Black bibliophile and librarian with the Library of Congress, to collect every known work published by African Americans. He designated Andrew Franklin Hilyer, an author, inventor, civil rights leader, and the future president of the Union League in the Washington area, to gather data for a directory of Negro businesspeople that would form a fairly unique exhibit of its own entitled "Collective Exhibit of Negroes in Merchandise, Factories, and Allied Occupations."[23] He invited Frances Benjamin Johnston, an Anglo-American woman who served as the "unofficial White House photographer during the administrations of Cleveland, Harrison, McKinley, Roosevelt, and Taft," to include her recent photographs of the Hampton Normal and Industrial Institute in Virginia.[24] And finally, Calloway identified his own reporter and journalist, Morris Lewis, a special correspondent for the *Colored American*, to document the exposition and regularly send back richly detailed descriptions and accounts of the doings, peregrinations, and activities of African Americans at the exposition.

With the announcement of Calloway's appointment, a host of prominent Negro organizations, social clubs, colleges and universities, churches, and newspapers all expressed their support of the American Negro Exhibit in one form or another. The newly formed American Negro Academy made three of its founding members—Du Bois, Calloway, and Murray—its official delegates to the Paris Exposition.[25] Black institutions of higher learning such as Atlanta University in Georgia, Fisk University in Nashville, Tuskegee Normal and Industrials Institute in Alabama, Howard University in Washington, and Wilberforce University in Ohio sent material evidence of the educational advances made by African Americans since Reconstruction as evidence of their intellectual ability.[26]

Over the course of the six months that elapsed between the official announcement that Calloway was a special agent of the American Negro Exhibit and the opening of the Paris Exposition of 1900, Black newspapers and magazines kept up a steady chatter about the upcoming event. In this respect, they were not unlike their white counterparts who viewed the exposition as good copy and a chance to increase their circulation. The *New York Evening Telegram*, a predominantly white newspaper, turned the upcoming exposition into a contest, offering five all-expenses-paid tickets for six weeks to the Paris Exposition and a tour of Europe to the teacher whose students sent in the greatest number of votes.[27] J. Imogene Howard, a Black educator, was one of the fortunate winners of the contest and is further evidence that the interest in the Paris Exposition and the American Negro Exhibit was fairly widespread among African Americans.

The *Colored American*, a Washington newspaper, one of at least ten Black newspapers that followed the progress of the assemblage of the exhibit, offered Calloway an opportunity to explain why the American Negro Exhibit represented an important moment in the progress of African Americans.[28] His comments are revealing because they show how profoundly the contents of the American Negro Exhibit had been shaped to conform to the social and political philosophy of Washington. First, Calloway argued, the current European invasion into Africa (as represented by the Fashoda Incident and the Boer War) would only bring European and African peoples into closer proximity. America, especially as exemplified in the achievements, could furnish Europe with such "evidences" of the Negro's value as a laborer, a producer, and a citizen that the statecraft of the Old World will be wiser in the shaping of its African policies.[29] Second, the progress and development of ten million former slaves in thirty-five years would silence criticism of America's presence in the Philippines, Cuba, and other nations where there were dark-skinned people. In other words, the American Negro Exhibit was tantamount to a justification for

American imperialism and speaks volumes about the accommoda-
tionist and assimilationist rhetoric at the heart of the exhibit. The
exhibit, Calloway reasoned, could be used as a rationale for American
foreign policy. Finally, the exhibit would provide an opportunity and
occasion for American Negroes to show in one place their rich and
varied "value to the body politic."

Though the American Negro Exhibit contained material drawn
from a variety of sources and awakened a wide appeal among disparate members of the African American community, Washington, Calloway, and eventually Du Bois attempted to control its message and
impose their own conceptions of African American culture. Yet the
American Negro Exhibit when viewed as an archive resists the gaze
that would view African Americans and African American culture
from one perspective. Despite its message of progress, the exhibit
complicated rather than conformed to the viewers' preconceived
ideas about African Americans by showing both the diversity of African Americans and the variety of ways in which they represented
themselves.

A full-page photograph of the exhibit published on November 3,
1900, in the *Colored American* wonderfully illustrates the manner in
which the exhibit itself, like the people it was said to represent, resisted a single definition.[30] The exhibit, tucked away in one small
corner of a room, in its Parisian setting in the Palace of Social Economy, is shown with Calloway seated before the entire display holding
an open book. In cabinets on the floor, the books written by African
American authors are arranged. Above the books, Du Bois's sociological charts comparing the progress of African Americans with the nations of the world boldly declare their achievements. One level above
that, swinging panels with nearly five hundred photographs of African
Americans held a breathtaking display of their diversity. Still higher
are placed the enlarged portraits of three African American leaders:
U. S. senator Blanche Bruce; the president of Tuskegee, Booker T.
Washington; and the registrar of the U. S. Treasury, J. W. Lyons. Yet if
these representations of African American culture were not enough,
the photographs unwittingly record at least three terms—"Colored
American," "Negro," and "Nègres d'Amérique"—each with its own
complex and nuanced history, used to reference African Americans
and, in doing so, invites a deeper reflection on the problem of the
color-line.

The American Negro Exhibit as *Lieu de Mémoire*

Finally, the American Negro Exhibit can be viewed as a *lieu de mémoire* that is often overlooked in scholarly examinations of the emergence of the "New Negro." While the exhibit was surely evidence of a new awakening among African Americans, those African Americans attending the Paris Exposition were also a visible manifestation of the "New Negro."[31]

During the summer of 1900, a group of African Americans gathered in Paris to celebrate the arrival, installation, and success of the American Negro Exhibit. Their celebration took the form of a banquet held in the plush rooms of the United States Pavilion, a special building erected by the U. S. commissioners on the left bank of the Seine for French and American visitors to the Paris Exposition. A domed structure that resembled the Capitol building in Washington, the pavilion boasted four floors of spacious and luxuriously decorated rooms displaying the artwork of major American painters and sculptors of the day. Many of the rooms bore the names of individual states and some, such as the room in which the African American visitors dined, bore portraits of President William McKinley. On lower floors, a restaurant, post office, and sitting rooms were available to American visitors seeking a quiet and pleasant place that reminded them of home.

The twenty-five African Americans attending the early August banquet gathered in the spacious room that held the portrait of President McKinley, the individual whose initial generosity had made possible the special American Negro exhibit. At one long table spread with a feast before them, the guests spent a lively evening eating, drinking, and marveling at the wonders of Paris, the exposition, and the American Negro Exhibit. According to one newspaper account, the rare privilege that had been accorded this special group of African American citizens in Paris was not without irony. Just four years after *Plessy v. Ferguson*, the United States Supreme Court decision that institutionalized the "separate but equal" doctrine, thereby legalizing the segregation of Black and white American citizens, a small group of African American citizens were extended an honor denied to them in the United States. Those attending the dinner delighted in the chance to meet with each other "under the hospitable roof of the United States building in a foreign land and under the stars and stripes" as well, and noted that in Paris "equal rights reigned supreme." "Too bad," wrote a reporter for the *Colored American* on August 11, 1900, "that we have to go abroad to get what is promised at home."[32]

Those African Americans assembled to mark the significant occasion beneath the towering dome of the American Pavilion on the left bank of the Seine were evidence of a group of Americans yet unknown to their fellow countrymen and women. They were an august and accomplished assemblage of people by any standards and represented a cross section of African Americans from eight different states. Their presence at the dinner most certainly stirred Du Bois and confirmed in him the belief that only the "talented tenth," an elite group of educated, visionary, and sophisticated African Americans, would lead the race and Americans to greater economic, political, social, and cultural freedom.[33] Among those present were painters, sculptors, actresses, musicians, religious leaders, diplomats, businessmen and -women, journalists, educators, doctors, and U. S. government officials, some of whom were living in Paris, others who had traveled great distances to witness the reception of the Negro Exhibit. Among them were the minister Adam Clayton Powell Sr.; the educator and author Anna Julia Cooper; the sculptor Meta Vaux Warrick; the journalist Morris Lewis; the successful Atlanta businessman Alonzo Herndon and his wife, Adrienne Herndon, a professor at Atlanta University; a member of the U. S. Guard, C. B. Smith; and the award-winning chef of the American Corn Kitchen at the Paris Exposition of 1900, the famous "Aunt Agnes," Mrs. Agnes Moody.

Thomas Calloway served as the master of ceremonies for the evening and spoke for all gathered when he expressed both pride and pleasure "that Afro-Americans had been able to meet together and exchange the hand of fellowship in a foreign land." George Jackson, the U. S. consul to La Rochelle, France, also welcomed his fellow African Americans and viewed the gathering as a positive sign that the "reversals met with by the Afro-Americans in the United States were only receding tides in the great wave of progress of the Negro people." Anna Julia Cooper, a Washington schoolteacher, author of *A Voice from the South*, and a Black feminist who would later return to France to earn a doctorate from the Sorbonne, remarked sarcastically that while her passport served as a pledge by the U. S. government to protect her abroad, the same government could not, or at least would not, protect her in North Carolina or Louisiana—a veiled reference to *Plessy v. Ferguson*.

Ms. J. Imogene Howard was also introduced, and she thanked the African American people for sending her to Paris. A contestant in a state-wide competition sponsored by the *New York Evening Telegram*, Howard was one of five successful contestants, and the only African American woman, chosen by student votes (more than 350,000) sent to the newspaper to win a six-week, all-expenses-paid trip to the Paris Exposition and a tour of Europe. Black students, churches, and organizations as far way as Washington and Georgia had sent in their votes to ensure that Ms. Howard, a public school teacher with an advanced degree in education from the University of the City of New York, won. Howard would later remark that among all of the exhibits at the exposition none had "caused men of the greatest intellect and widest research to pause and reflect upon, to turn away from their former ideas of the degeneration of a people and awaken to higher conceptions of their intellectual and industrial and aesthetic progress" than the exhibit of the American Negro in the building devoted to social economy and congresses.[34]

A thirty-two-year-old W. E. B. Du Bois was present that evening. He stood and prophesized that two events, the Pan-African Conference, held just one week before in London, and the evening's dinner, would go down in history and were steps in the right direction and a step forward in the progress of the our race. "I now ask you," he spoke with his voice rising to those gathered before him, "to join me and drink to the Colored race."[35] Years later Meta Vaux Warrick, a young African American sculptor studying in Paris at the time, would recall sitting next to Du Bois and watching as everyone in the room turned to watch and listen as he eloquently spoke of and toasted the future of the race.

For those African Americans fortunate enough to attend the banquet in Paris, the evening would become a cherished and life-changing memory. The festive evening and their activities throughout the summer would be chronicled in African American newspapers. Yet from the vantage point of Paris, those gathered, and the readers who followed their stories, would come to see themselves differently. They represented visible proof of something new. They had entered what Du Bois would call "the kingdom of culture" and had won recognition. The success of the exhibit gave them renewed hope and pride in the achievements and prospects of African Americans. And their stories, though still untold, reveal the rich variety and complexity of African American culture at the turn of the century. Through their lives, works, and ruminations, they form a complex portrait and, in many respects, their story is the story of the American Negro Exhibit.

Notes

1. D. L. Lewis and D. Willis, eds., *A Small Nation of People: W. E. B. Du Bois and African American Portraits of Progress* (New York: Amistad, 2003), 29.

2. W. E. B. Du Bois, "The American Negro at Paris," *American Monthly Review of Reviews* 22 (November 1900): 575–77.

3. S. M. Smith, *Photography on the Color Line: W. E. B. Du Bois, Race and Visual Culture* (Durham: Duke University Press, 2004).

4. W. E. B. Du Bois, "The American Negro at Paris," *American Monthly Review of Reviews* 22 (November 1900): 577.

5. W. E. B. Du Bois, *The Autobiography of W. E. B. Du Bois: A Soliloquy on Viewing My Life from the Last Decade of Its First Century* (New York: International, 1968), 220.

6. W. E. B. Du Bois, *The Souls of Black Folk* (New York: Oxford University Press, 2007), 3.

7. Du Bois, *The Autobiography of W. E. B. Du Bois*, 220–22.

8. Du Bois, *The Souls of Black Folk*, 9.

9. B. Benedict, "Rituals of Representations: Ethnic Stereotypes and Colonized People at World's Fairs," in *Fair Representations: World's Fairs and the Modern World*, ed. R. Rydell and N. Gwinn (Amsterdam: Vu University Press, 1994), 55.

10. Du Bois, *The Souls of Black Folk*, 34.

11. Washington, "Is He a New Negro?" (September 28, 1895), in *The Booker T. Washington Papers*, vol. 4, ed. L. Harlan (Urbana: University of Illinois Press, 1975), 34.

12. Ibid., 4:35.

13. Ibid., 4:525.

14. Ibid., 5:244.

15. Ibid., 5:81–82.

16. Ibid., 5:131–32.

17. Ibid., 5:154–57.

18. Ibid., 5:156.

19. Ibid., 5:244.

20. Du Bois, *The Autobiography of W. E. B. Du Bois*, 220–22.

21. Harlan, ed., *The Booker T. Washington Papers*, 3:415–16.

22. Ibid., 5:226–27.

23. T. Calloway, "The Negro Exhibit," in *Report of the Commissioner-General for the United States to the International Universal Exposition, Paris, 1900*, U.S. Senate Document no. 232 56th Cong., 2d Session (Washington: U.S. Government Printing Office, 1901), 463–67.

24. Smith, *Photography on the Color Line*, 171.

25. A. Moss, *The American Negro Academy: Voice of the Talented Tenth* (Baton Rouge: Louisiana State University Press, 1981).

26. Calloway, "The Negro Exhibit," 463–67.

27. I. Howard, "The American Negro Exhibit," *Colored American*, September 1, 1900, 13.

28. T. Calloway, "Negro Exhibit at Paris," *Colored American*, December 16,1899, 1.

29. "Negro Exhibit," *Houston Daily Post*, December 31, 1899, 5.

30. T. Calloway, "The American Negro Exhibit at the Paris Exposition," *Colored American*, November 3, 1900, 1–9.

31. H. L. Gates and G. A. Jarrett, *The New Negro: Readings on Race, Representation, and African American Culture, 1892–1938* (Princeton: Princeton University Press, 2007).

32. "Shreds and Patches," *Colored American*, August 18, 1900, 11.

33. H. L. Gates and C. West, *The Future of the Race* (New York: Alfred A. Knopf, 1996), 133–58.

34. J. I. Howard, "The American Negro Exhibit," *Colored American*, September 1, 1900, 13.

35. "Paris Banquet: Afro-Americans Give A Reunion at Exposition," *Appeal*, August 25, 1900.

The Militant Black Men
of Marseille and Paris, 1927–1937

JENNIFER BOITTIN

> Si Paris est la plus belle, Marseille est la plus jolie.
> —Massilia Sound System

Moussu T (also known as Tatou) is one of the founding members of the reggae or trobamuffin-style music group Massilia Sound System. He was inspired by Claude McKay's novel *Banjo* (1932)—set largely on and around the docks of Marseille during the 1930s—when he started a parallel band, Moussu T e lei Jovents, featuring the Brazilian percussionist Jam Da Silva.[1] McKay's text inspired in Moussu T a desire to honor through this new band and its transnational membership the extent to which Marseille had long been an extraordinary melting pot of cultures and in particular music that, to his mind, owed much to the Black musicians who haunted the port, much like the character Banjo and his friends during the interwar years.[2] In addition, Moussu T read *Banjo* as a text demonstrating that Marseille's history was as, or even more, richly multicultural than that of Paris—a positive trait that allowed him to reinforce a loyalty to the city that both Massilia Sound System and Moussu T e lei Jovents reveal in their lyrics.[3]

The intensity of regional pride on the part of inhabitants of cities and regions other than the capital Paris and its surrounding area, the Île-de-France, has long inspired scholars to decentralize their study of France's history.[4] Within the urban context of that decentralization, focusing on the marginality of one neighborhood versus another or of one city versus another encourages scholars to tease out distinctions and trends within urban and national histories. According to the historian Nancy L. Green, who uses words that gain particular meaning when applied to cities profoundly shaped by their waterways, "comparative history is one of the best approaches to navigating when stuck between deep waters and turbulent waves, methodologically and metaphorically speaking."[5] However, for the most part, scholars of the rich and expanding field of African and Black diaspora studies that relate to France have tended either to speak about the Black experience in general terms that move beyond the geographic specificity of the places Black migrants lived and worked after they arrived in France, or to focus on precise geographic regions—often Paris or its surroundings—in isolation, and thus without any sustained contrast between regions.[6] These are valuable approaches, but scholars such as Brent Hayes Edwards, Paul Gilroy, and Michelle Stephens, who have anchored their projects in several geographic locations, have also in the process shown to what extent transnational and colonial studies can benefit from combining a comparative approach with a sense of place.[7]

As our readings of the experiences of African and African Caribbean men and women in France continue to expand, one question that has yet to be fully explored is how the places they carved out for themselves when they set out to determine their autonomy within the French Empire, a space that includes its métropole, were determined by the cities in which they lived.[8] This chapter provides one example of how comparative studies can expand our understanding of such experiences. It contrasts two urban spaces, Paris and Marseille, and thereby situates the transnational, which shapes diasporic studies in precise localities. More specifically, this approach illuminates some of the ways that Black communities defined themselves, as well as the ways the networks linking these communities within France were established and maintained.[9] Since more is currently known about the experience of the African and Black diaspora in Paris, this chapter draws heavily upon Marseille for specific examples, while leaning upon Paris as a sustained counterpoint.[10]

The main sources for this endeavor are monthly police reports focusing upon the activities of one anti-imperialist association that had branches both in Paris and in Marseille—the Ligue de Défense de la Race Nègre (LDRN).[11] Focusing on just one organization invites reflection upon whether and how its members, and those it purported to represent, were impacted in their militancy and experiences by their place of domicile within France. Furthermore, the LDRN reached out to working-class men, who were defined by their mobility and about whom we still have much to learn, especially in contrast to what we know of more highly educated migrants. Thus examining such an organization has the added benefit of accentuating the variety of Black experiences in France. Indeed, to reflect on how actively Black migrants shaped their urban lives, and in this way to situate their voices both in and out of police reports, the sources considered here also include creative work and militant newspapers written by members of the LDRN and those who crossed paths with them.

The LDRN was one of several anti-imperial associations set up by Black Caribbeans and Africans during the 1920s and 1930s to unite men of the African and Black diaspora in their anti-French sentiment. They were set up in deliberate contrast to organizations such as the Union Intercoloniale (founded in 1921), which, while originally gathering colonial migrants from all French colonies, soon came to be dominated by its North African contingent, to the disappointment and frustration of its Vietnamese and Black members.[12] After their failure to make the Union Intercoloniale defend their interests, Africans and Antilleans were set apart from other colonial migrants because almost every association they established thereafter was predicated upon one unifying factor: race.[13] The Ligue Universelle de Défense de la Race Noire (founded in 1924, not to be confused with the LDRN), the Comité de Défense de la Race Nègre (1926–27), the LDRN (1927–32), and the Union des Travailleurs Nègres (founded in 1932) all had the word noir or nègre in their titles.[14] In other words, the experiences of diaspora, conjoined with colonialism, united these migrants, rather than merely their colony or region of origin.

These organizations followed one another during the interwar years, and both leaders and members were dependably present throughout the interwar period. Still, individuals from within the Black communities did not always find it easy to cohabit—especially politically—with others. The meetings of all of these groups were marred by divisiveness. In particular, members disagreed over how to deal with colonialism. For some, the answer was nationalism, anti-Frenchness, and ultimately a complete overthrow of French rule overseas. For others, it was a complex negotiation with France that they hoped would result in the nation fully applying basic rights that could be traced back to the Revolution of 1789, including access for all colonial subjects to French citizenship and suffrage. Others turned to worldwide movements such as communism and Garveyism as an answer to the problem of French colonialism. Not surprisingly, many members borrowed parts of these positions, added their own experiences, and combined them into individual politics. Certainly, the confusion that resulted from the question of how to respond to French colonialism was reflected in the rapid turnover of anti-imperial organizations.

The LDRN emerged from the ashes of the Comité de Défense de la Race Nègre, which had splintered over the questions of whether or not the organization should present itself as anti-French, whether or not its members wanted to have any association with the French Communist Party (PCF), and whether intellectuals and workers should coexist in one organization. The communist-leaning members as well as the intransigently anti-imperialist members of the Comité de Défense de la Race Nègre joined the newly formed LDRN, which was under a leader named Tiémoko Garan Kouyaté.

The LDRN was influenced in part by the changes in structure and policies that took place in the PCF between 1924 and 1929, which led communists to increasingly emphasize pitting class against class and evicting those with multiple allegiances (such as Free Masons or members of the Ligue des Droits de l'Homme), even if they were fervent anti-imperialists.[15] During this phase, the PCF was engaged in trying to gain and maintain control over anti-imperial organizations. After the Union Intercoloniale, with its communist influences, lost the trust of its Black contingent, the PCF had to work through communist members of African and Black Caribbean organizations such as the LDRN. Kouyaté was one such individual, a communist who traveled several times to Moscow and was a very hands-on leader within France. Born in Segu in the French Soudan (modern-day Mali), Kouyaté studied at the École William Ponty on the Île de Gorée in Senegal before teaching in the Ivory Coast from 1921 to 1923.[16] He made his way to Paris via Aix-en-Provence, where he was briefly a student at the École Normale. After moving to Paris, he actively engaged in organizing not only the headquarters of the LDRN in Paris—where he lived—but also in creating and then sustaining active branches of the LDRN in ports across France, and more specifically in Marseille, Bordeaux, and Le Havre.

His trips across France, and the people he met during his forays outside the Île-de-France, led police informants in all these regions to turn in reports that provide some interesting insights into the politics and lives of African and Black Caribbean men in France. These reports were collated into monthly summaries. Informants were both recruited and put into place locally because colonial communities were rightly suspicious of outsiders coming in with too many questions. As a result, informants were often deeply embedded in local communities and were by necessity politically active themselves, and therefore their reports reflected nuances in Black men's experiences across France.[17] Thus, the monthly summary of revolutionary activity was divided not only by community (i.e., Vietnamese versus North African versus Black), but also by city.

Like those all over France, diasporic circles in Paris, where the LDRN originated, were dominated numerically by men; perhaps 2 percent of all Africans in the métropole (including North Africans) were estimated to be women.[18] The numbers of African and Caribbean migrants remain notoriously difficult to determine, and estimates have ranged from the hundreds to the tens of thousands. In 1926 French authorities calculated the presence of 2,680 West Africans, Equatorial Africans, and Malagasies throughout the métropole. In 1932, the official number had dropped to 1,453, although it seems probable that they should have increased since more and more sailors had made their way to France (albeit often illegally) by then.[19] These numbers can thus be considered rather low. The historian Philippe Dewitte, adding to them estimates for all those who were present without papers, has suggested that 3,000 to 5,000 Africans and Malagasies could be found throughout France in the interwar years, a third of them living in the Paris region. Dewitte adds that the police occasionally announced estimates of African and Caribbean students and workers (who were French citizens and thus not counted in police reports) in the Seine department alone at 10,000.[20]

In Paris, the members of the LDRN were extremely diverse in their professions, which included factory worker, window washer, dishwasher, accountant, writer, lawyer, nurse, student, and professor, among others.[21] They ranged from the working class, including the service class, to the intellectual. Anti-imperialist leaders, who edited and contributed articles to newspapers about metropolitan members of the Black diaspora, often seemed to lead parallel lives as workers and intellectuals. These migrants' living situations—they could be found in almost every arrondissement of Paris, as well as throughout the Paris suburbs—certainly reflect the diversity of professions but also help to explain the importance of establishing networks through which to maintain a sense of community within the Île-de-France.[22]

Parisian anti-imperialists formed the LDRN on April 17, 1927.[23] They invited all Black individuals without any distinction of nationality to join, and also welcomed the white wives of members. Soon after its creation, the LDRN printed the first issue of its newspaper, La Race Nègre. The Senegalese Lamine Senghor, one of the first anti-imperialist leaders, initially headed the organization. But a prolonged struggle with tuberculosis, which had been aggravated by the fact that his lungs were weakened from inhaling gas during the First World War, led to his death in March 1927 and placed Kouyaté firmly in charge. Before his death, Senghor wrote an editorial in the first issue of La Race Nègre in which he explained that the LDRN was a militant group that rejected the sensational exoticism often imposed upon Blacks in France. "To those who would like to turn us into a troop of dancers of the 'Charleston' and other exotic dances, as some white politician or other presides and gazes benevolently on, to all those: the sons of Africa, truly worthy representatives of the nègre race, gave a magnificent slap across the face."[24] Its ultimate goal was "the defense of the rights, the interests, and the very prestige of the race."

Before his death, Senghor had worked hard to create sections of the Comité de Défense de la Race Nègre in Marseille (250 members); Bordeaux (150 members); Le Havre (300 members); and in Paris (200 members).[25] Kouyaté worked just as arduously to transfer the allegiance of Black men from ports around France to the newly formed LDRN. His travels grant us considerable insight into how diasporic communities around France understood their relationship to one another, and to the French state, as a result of their particular urban surroundings.

Contact between the Blacks of Marseille and the LDRN in Paris was initiated by Pierre M'Baye, from the Casamance region in Senegal, who owned a bar at 42 Quai du Port, on the waterfront in Marseille. His story strongly resembles that of a café owner mentioned by Claude McKay in both his memoir A Long Way from Home (1937) and his novel Banjo. In the former McKay describes the Vieux Port of Marseille as full of excitement: " 'men's fights and prostitutes' brawls,' sailors robbed, civilian and police shooting. One Senegalese had a big café on the quay and all the Negroes ganged there with their friends and girls. The Senegalese was a remarkable type, quiet, level-headed, shrewd."[26] McKay's unnamed café owner knew Senghor, and in *Banjo* McKay added, about a character who appears to have been patterned on this same café owner, that he had copies of "*La Race Nègre*" on him. This was a journal for the '*Défense de la race Nègre*' published in Paris by a group of West Africans. The journal was displayed for sale in the café."[27] And indeed, in 1929 M'Baye wrote to Kouyaté, asking for a hundred copies of the newspaper published by LDRN, *La Race Nègre*.[28]

A few months later, Kouyaté sent a telegram to M'Baye announcing his arrival in Marseille. There he hoped to encounter the city's several hundred (on the low end of the estimate) African men, who mostly lived in and congregated around the Vieux Port.[29] Soon after disembarking from the train, Kouyaté created a Bouches-du-Rhône section of the LDRN. The title referred to the name of the department in which Marseille is located, just as the Paris section was officially known as the Seine section of the LDRN. Initially Kouyaté gleefully reported that the Africans and Afro-Caribbeans of Marseille were extremely receptive to anti-imperialist rhetoric, and that he could not understand why Senghor had always complained about their reluctance. Soon, however, Kouyaté was forced to admit that the Marseillais had minds of their own, and that their concerns were not always those of Parisian anti-imperialists.

The most apparent difference between the populations in Paris and Marseille was that while the Parisians represented an extremely eclectic and mostly employed (although not always very permanently so) batch of individuals, the Marseillais were forced into a more transient status by the nature of the work available to them in the city in which they lived. Moreover, unlike the Parisians who were spread throughout the city, the Marseillais were pressed into contact by their concentration in one part of the city, the Vieux Port.[30] In Marseille, Africans and Afro-Caribbeans depended above all upon the sea for their livelihood. They were sailors, dockers, packers, or fishermen, or more rarely, like M'Baye, owned cafés or bars near the port (which still depended upon colonial sailors for their existence).[31] McKay summed up the situation in Marseille in *A Long Way from Home* when he noted that "the Negroes had hard industrial problems to face in Marseilles. On the boats they were employed as stokers only, and they were not employed on the boats making the 'good' runs: that is, the short runs, which the white seamen preferred. Also as dockers they were discriminated against and given the hardest and most unpleasant jobs, such as loading and unloading coal and sulphur."[32]

McKay's description reflected the precariousness of these workers' situation, something imposed in part by a city known for the "Marseille system," a system that resisted legislation and legalization and fed instead upon migrants' and other workers' insecurity.[33] The Africans and African Caribbeans did not only worry about not receiving equal pay for equal work and being treated well while out at sea. They also worried about high unemployment rates and about their lack of legal status when in France. After Kouyaté visited several ships including the ss *Bernardin de St-Pierre*, the *Général Voyron*, and the *Providence* in September 1930, he urged Black sailors to keep a log documenting their conditions at sea, and to go on strike if necessary to demand better living conditions on board.[34] In exchange for more information about the situation of Africans and African Caribbeans in Marseille, Kouyaté wrote regularly about their lives in *La Race Nègre*, and transmitted their complaints to the Inscription Maritime (the port authority).[35] For example, in September 1930 one article explained that the nègres of Marseille were "poorly paid, poorly fed, poorly housed," and that their miserable conditions were aggravated by their lack of work.[36]

However, most of the articles in *La Race Nègre* and in the newspaper that replaced it, *Le Cri des Nègres*, focused on unemployment rather than on the work conditions. Most writers acknowledged that the unemployment was a symptom of a more widespread crisis in France after the Great Depression traversed the Atlantic, but the early phases of economic depression were portrayed as more acute for Black workers, who were subjected, in the words of an article published in 1931, to "a harrowing life on credit at hotels and restaurants for the lucky ones. But how many of them don't eat very often and don't know where to sleep at night?"[37] The anonymous authors of one article emphasized that the solution was not to move to Paris, tempting as this solution apparently was to some, but to remain in the ports and join ongoing strikes. "The nègre, Indo-Chinese, Malagasy, Arab, Somali, and Djibouti seamen who make up the most exploited strata of this proletariat will be at the forefront of the combat," declared Kouyaté in one of his articles.[38] In a lyrical turn of phrase, Siragnouma added that by 1932, as a result of crippling unemployment, colonial sailors were sleeping on the wharves or in tunnels, like troglodytes: "we no longer hear the diabolical rhythms of the music of the player pianos in the port's bars."[39]

With the music fading out, the question of what the LDRN could do to protect Africans in Marseille gained urgency, in particular with respect to those who did not hold French citizenship (in other words, all those who were not born in the Four Communes of Senegal). Most seamen working on ships were not legally domiciled in France. As a result, they did not have access to pensions and unions could not easily protect them. Moreover once they were declared unemployed, these men were required to return home, which hardly fixed the problem: "if colonials return home, they will not find work; they'll die of hunger and misery."[40] Not surprisingly, a number of the unemployed refused to leave Marseille and found themselves facing first jail and then expulsion when they were picked up by the police without papers. Two characters in McKay's *Banjo*, Lonesome Blue and Ginger, are regularly caught in raids after losing their status. Lonesome usually ends up in jail, while Ginger sweet-talks his way back onto the streets.

Most Africans in Marseille faced expulsion from France because they did not technically reside in the métropole. In contrast, the majority of Black anti-imperialists in Paris appear to have been, comparatively speaking, legal residents. Not surprisingly, those in Paris brought up concerns other than expulsion or unemployment. In fact, they rarely brought up the question of their own work during meetings in Paris, and focused instead upon worldwide injustices that plagued Black diasporic populations. Topics during meetings of the LDRN in 1931 and early 1932 included the organization of a counter-exposition to the massive Colonial Exposition of 1931 and the decision to try to defend the eight African American boys condemned to death in Scottsboro.[41] The general goals to which LDRN members adhered in 1931 included the defense of nègre workers' rights; the organization of workers, peasants, and all those in the educational system; the unification of the anti-imperialist struggle; and opposition to prejudices based upon race and barriers imposed by color.[42] Many of these questions were posed in passionate terms but nonetheless lacked the urgency of the questions about work and food driving militants in Marseille.

Moreover, in Paris LDRN members often spoke for others when it came to specific abuses, rather than for themselves. For example, when an eighteen-year-old was found wandering around Paris wearing little more than an item of clothing described as a sort of loincloth, the LDRN intervened.[43] They discovered that a white French doctor had brought the young man from Senegal to Paris as a servant. Allegedly kept without clothes to prevent him from running away, and considered by his masters to be their property (in other words, a slave), the young man was taken under the protective wing of the LDRN. Still, other than occasional complaints about police brutality, LDRN members rarely brought up personal problems or situations and instead focused overwhelmingly on broader issues.

Another difference between Marseille and Paris was the self-perception in these communities about what constituted unifying identity traits. Whereas Parisian Blacks demarcated themselves with racial terminology, and in particular whether they proudly considered themselves to belong under the traditionally negative term "nègre" or preferred the more neutral denomination of "noir," those in Marseille often described themselves by referring to their peoples of origin. Kouyaté quickly learned that while he had the support of Malagasies in his effort to unite the Blacks of Marseille, many groups stemming from French West Africa were either indifferent or openly resistant to his Parisian influence.[44] These included the Soninkés (known as Sarakolés by the French), who were the dominant West African people in France, but also the Bambaras (Bamana in English) and Toucouleurs (a subgroup of the Peuls known as Tukolor among Anglophone, colonial historians).[45] In Paris, those who preferred "noir" and those who preferred "nègre" were frequently at odds. In contrast, there were few specific references to local affiliations within West Africa in Parisian circles, while in Marseille different peoples viewed one another with suspicion.

The subtlety of affiliation and self-perception was further complicated by the fact that within circles in both cities, Africans and Caribbeans were also suspicious of one another. McKay wove this theme through *Banjo* with several passages that reflect upon how in Marseille "the Martiniquans and Guadeloupans, regarding themselves as constituting the dark flower of all Marianne's Blacks," could be set apart from the "Senegalese"—which was often used as a ubiquitous term for all West Africans—"who are the savages."[46] In Paris, the tension was articulated repeatedly, with some Africans accusing African Caribbeans of collaborating with the French state, and others expressing the sentiment that the "Antillean question" was insidious and should be largely downplayed because it had the power to completely divide the metropolitan community.[47]

This difference in self-identification between a focus on precise, local, African affiliations in Marseille and monikers of race in Paris, like the question of which issues most concerned the Marseillais, can be attributed in part to the comparatively short-lived nature of the passage of many Africans and African Caribbeans through Marseille. They were more likely to return home regularly on board the ships which employed them, while Parisians could rarely afford to travel overseas. The nature of their presence in France also meant that the Marseillais were more likely to speak to one another in their mother tongues. During one of his first visits to Marseille in 1930, Kouyaté spoke to his audience both in French and in Bambara. After him Maudy N'Diagne spoke in Soninké, Demba Diallo in Toucouleur, and an unidentified Arab in Arabic.[48] In opposition, meetings in Paris were dominated by the French language and rarely did police reports mention the use of other languages, although they did note their use in passing and knowledge of several languages was an essential skill for informants in both Paris and in Marseille. Occasionally articles published in the anti-imperialist newspapers in Paris were not written in French, a linguistic choice which had the advantage, among other things, of making any sort of censorship or control over the articles' contents (including by the PCF) more difficult.[49]

Still, in Marseille the migrant community was more explicitly defined by contrasting languages and ethnic origins that guided individuals in their choice of social destinations, companions, and domiciles, and also in their suspicion of outsiders. Kouyaté noted early on that his organizing in Marseille might be limited by two factors: the "distinctions among races that exist in Marseille and the opposition to him from supporters of M'Diagne, who has declared himself the adversary of communist machinations."[50] Such divisions reflect a pattern in the history of immigration to cities in France, and other countries for that matter, where migrants regularly used networks that allowed them to locate the protection, support, and companionship of other immigrants from the same region of origin or who shared the same language.[51] In Marseille, the Soninké dominated the overall community in part because as a group they considered sailing prestigious. As a result, the historian François Manchuelle explains, during the interwar years, as more and more French sailing companies recruited colonial sailors without paying much attention to registration papers, which were either questionable or nonexistent, the Soninké were ascendant among these undocumented sailors, many of whom arrived in Marseille as stowaways.[52] Although Wolof sailors in Marseille created an Amicale des Originaires de l'AOF in the mid-1920s that in some ways functioned as a sailors' union, and also sought to oppose the arrival of these undocumented Soninké, by 1930 the Soninké had emerged as the force with which Kouyaté and the rest of the Black population in Marseille had to reckon.

All these differences between the social networks and living conditions of Marseille and Paris migrant communities explain in part why the Bouches-du-Rhône section of the LDRN Kouyaté attemped to create metamorphosed quickly into a nègre union.[53] In a reflection of how differently Black communities in Paris and Marseille approached racial questions, the statutes of this union, known as the Syndicat Nègre de Marseille (SNM), stated that each "ethnicity" in Marseille would elect a representative to be a member of the central bureau. The reason given for this particular statute was "to resolve the ethnic issues of our section in a spirit of fraternal understanding."[54] To create the SNM, Kouyaté first had to convince Parisian anti-imperialists that their struggle with French imperialism would not be sublimated to the goals of this new association, which focused on workers. He argued that the LDRN simply would temporarily reorient its goals toward "goals of professional defense, those of a political order thus being merely moved to the background."[55] In making this adjustment, Kouyaté appeared to recognize that ethnicity and unemployment were not the only concerns in Marseille.

Another contentious point, but in this case one which the Paris and Marseille communities shared, was the rancor that plagued relationships between workers and intellectuals. Kouyaté noted during his initial trip to Marseille that three quarters of the migrants there did not appear to believe in his anti-imperialist ideas. He believed that Marseille's reluctance to create an LDRN section was a result of the "absence of intellectual elements" within Marseille.[56] Yet he also stipulated that if Black intellectuals (who in Marseille might include individuals such as M'Baye) wanted any chance of successfully promoting their political ideologies, they needed to "rely on the mass of their compatriots who are manual workers."[57] Similar problems plagued the Seine section of the LDRN, leading, for example, in 1929 the communist member Stéphane Rosso to complain that in France students received an education that alienated them from workers and guided them toward administrative positions that naturally set them apart.[58] Kouyaté's flexibility in creating the SNM alongside the LDRN was thus a result in part of his inability to bridge the gap between worker and intellectual in any other fashion than by founding a different sort of organization, which might better cater to the "desiderata of the noirs of Marseille."[59]

His success in gratifying these desires turned out to be limited. Not only did he find himself largely unable to maintain both organizations, which led to the quick slip of the Bouches-du-Rhône LDRN and its more eclectic group of members from his grasp, but furthermore, West African sailors and workers remained just as reticent to join the SNM. One Soninké man explained in July 1930 that the abstention of the noirs could be explained by how little they had to gain from their membership in the SNM.[60] Malagasies, from the French colonial island off the eastern coast of Africa, appeared initially more willing to join. However, soon after the Soninké's complaint was registered, a Malagasy Muslim added, during another meeting, that the SNM had promised them raises but that even after everyone had paid their membership dues nothing had changed.[61]

Kouyaté thus soon found himself having to change tactics yet again and started trying to convince SNM members that they should ultimately sign up for membership in the Syndicat Unitaire des Marins, an organization that was affiliated with the Confédération Générale de Travail Unitaire, and through it to the Communist Party. Ultimately, Kouyaté's organizing in Marseille, much like his organizing in Paris up through his expulsion from the Communist Party in late 1933, appears at first glance to have been guided by communism as much as it was by anti-imperialism. Members of the SNM appeared more comfortable with this communist affiliation than did Parisian members of the LDRN. When in 1930 François Coty—a perfumer and editor of the extreme right-wing newspaper L'Ami du Peuple—targeted the LDRN in a series of articles that bitterly attacked communism more generally, members of the Seine section of the LDRN complained that his defamation of the association, including statements that the LDRN "was being towed along by the PCF and was receiving money from Moscow," was completely inappropriate. LDRN members demanded that the leaders of the organization, who were at the time largely communist themselves, publicly reject Coty's assertion of communist affiliation (although they were indeed receiving money from Moscow; something to which many members managed to remain oblivious).[62] Kouyaté himself was quite aware of this problem, and under pressure from Parisian LDRN members protested as part of his response to Coty: "to hear him talk, the communists are the ones fostering among the nègres the idea of an African homeland [patrie], and national independence."[63]

The willingness of communist anti-imperialist leaders in Paris to bow to the wishes of their members and refute accusations of communism shows just how contentious this political designation could be within Black circles. Indeed, even among Africans or African Caribbeans who embraced aspects of communism, the problem in both cities ultimately was whether European communists took the Black cause seriously—whether the root of the problems guiding the cause was an inability to find work, lack of protection in the workplace, violence on the streets of French cities, or how to completely reject imperialism. Thus SNM members in Marseille, when asked to join the more general organization of the Syndicat Unitaire des Marins, were reluctant. Abdoulaye, for example, explained in April 1930 that an autonomous syndicat nègre would be better able to attract Africans than a mixed union.[64] This reluctance was understandable considering that some of the problems facing Black seamen stemmed from the fact that West Africans were included in a quota imposed by French unions and designed to protect Frenchmen's own interests. The quota stated that foreigners (including West Africans) could only make up 25 percent of the workforce on metropolitan ships.[65]

Even if some militants in Marseille preferred to keep their organizations separate from French ones, the consistent presence of European men in their midst appeared to further differentiate the Marseille groups from the Parisian ones. Perhaps because the headquarters for many meetings of the SNM, the Club International des Marins, was a public space for sailors affiliated with the Confédération Générale de Travail Unitaire, who were of many "races" and origins, Europeans were consistently present at Marseille meetings in larger numbers than at a typical meeting of the LDRN in Paris. The LDRN in Paris specifically limited membership to Black men or their wives (who could be white) and thereby excluded white men, who were almost never present. At a typical meeting of the Seine section of the LDRN in July 1930, twenty or so noirs were present, but no Europeans.[66] In Marseille, early meetings of the LDRN included, for example, twenty-four Africans, twenty-one Europeans (including four women), and two Arabs. Another example includes twenty-five Senegalese, three Arabs, one Indochinese, and seventeen Europeans, who were present by virtue of being members of the Club International des Marins.[67] While fewer Europeans were present after the SNM had been around for a few months, they still turned up regularly at meetings and repeatedly invited Africans to join French unions. Nonetheless, unlike in Paris, women—European or other—were not mentioned as being active within the militant circles of either the LDRN or the SNM in Marseille. In Paris, Black women were not often present and white women were only admitted to meetings through the bond of marriage. Nonetheless, women were not only consistently but also actively present.[68] In Marseille, the sort of long-term relationships that might have induced women to turn up at meetings may have been made rare by the fact that many workers depended on the sea for their livelihood and thus were out at sea or in other ports for long periods of time.

Just as the constant pressure by Kouyaté and French communist leaders to join French unions had the potential to weaken the networks and communities being built by all-Black organizations, so did the lack of strong leadership from within Marseille. Although early on men such as M'Baye appeared deeply motivated to organize Africans and African Caribbeans, it soon became clear that no one leader along the lines of Kouyaté or, before him, Lamine Senghor, was ready to come forth in Marseille. Yet the suspicion reserved for outsiders included Africans from Paris, even if they shared a language or people of origin with the Marseillais, so that Kouyaté and Senghor could not truly replace the strength of a Marseillais leader. For example, when Kouyaté first presented his project to create a branch of the LDRN in Marseille, a man named Sékou, from Saint-Louis (the Senegalese home of many of the Wolof sailors already organized), stood and "declared that the nègres of Marseille had no need to join an association that doubtless had as its only goal their exploitation," thereby explicitly uniting his fellow travelers under the term "Marseille."[69] Shortly thereafter Kouyaté was taken aside at a meeting and warned by Bernard Sagna, originally from Casamance, that he should be more careful when dealing with the Blacks of Marseille, who were being alienated by Kouyaté's intimations that those reluctant to join him were colluding with the French administration.[70]

Kouyaté was certainly met with distrust by some Africans and African Caribbeans of Marseille, but no clear alternative leader presented himself, even among those who seemed to believe in Kouyaté's ideals. The Marseillais were concerned that joining either the LDRN or the SNM could cause them to be fired. The first president of the Bouches-du-Rhône section of the LDRN, Alfred from the Côte d'Ivoire, resigned his office after only one month, convinced that he would lose his job as a chauffeur with the Compagnie Fabre if they learned that he was a member of the LDRN.[71] Furthermore, most were only prepared to lead the SNM if they were paid. The demand appeared outrageous to Kouyaté, perhaps because he was used to Paris militants, who appeared disinterested because they did not ask for payment.[72] However, the request fell into the logic of a population for which work was a constant obsession and which defined the SNM as a union that required paid organizers, not simply a political organization. A second problem was that those who might have been the most passionate leaders were blocked from having their names listed as heads of the SNM. Only French citizens could be listed for the legal purpose of registering this organization with the French authorities. Thus, although initially the bureau of the SNM was supposed to include representatives from each ethnic group, the official bureau included only individuals from the old colonies and in particular Guadeloupe, Saint-Louis in Senegal, and Saint-Pierre in La Réunion.[73] This device was recognized as such by all involved, but the bizarre disconnect between appearance and reality was nonetheless confusing even to members.

Finally, there can be no question that Marseille militants were even more harassed by the police than those of Paris. While Africans and African Caribbeans in Paris were trailed by the police, stopped on the street, arrested, had their homes searched, or were subjected to spying that wore on their nerves, the Marseillais were more likely to be caught up in stings and jailed for long periods of time. Stéphane Rosso, an Antillean who adhered to the PCF during the entire interwar period, is one example of an individual subjected to an insidious practice of arrest in Paris. He was attempting to enter the Colonial Exposition of Vincennes on August 1, 1931, when he was "preventatively arrested" by Paris police who held him until noon of the following day. This marked at least the third time that he had been arrested without being charged with anything, in a series of gestures considered by LDRN members to accurately illustrate France's repressive police regime.[74]

In contrast, both Lamine Senghor and Kouyaté were not only arrested but also condemned and imprisoned in Marseille—something that rarely happened to anti-imperialist leaders in Paris. When Kouyaté was caught in a raffle by the police, also on August 1, 1931—which as the anniversary of the outbreak of the First World War was being used by the PCF to organize pacifist protests in Marseille—M'Baye was present. M'Baye's actions caught the eye of whoever was spying upon him that day. He was down on the streets, mixed in with the passersby, but "sufficiently on the sidelines so as not to be swept up, if it came to that, in the swirl of protestors."[75] In contrast, Kouyaté was encouraging followers to make their way to La Cannebière, on the waterfront. He was arrested for resisting the police and sentenced to forty-five days in prison. M'Baye's reluctance to get caught, in contrast to Kouyaté's fearless attitude, suggests that among other factors the Parisian was not as aware as his Marseille counterpart of just how easily Black men in Marseille, and for that matter almost anyone in the Vieux Port area, could find themselves in jail. Such penalties ensured that all those who were not protected by French citizenship and did not have a regularized status, or those who simply did not want to have any brushes with the law, would stay away from positions of power in Marseille.

The oppressive police presence in Marseille is experienced by several characters in *Banjo* as well. Early in the novel the tone is set with this description: "they were more likely to be stopped, questioned, searched, and taken to the police station. Sometimes they were only locked up for a night and let out the next morning. Some of them complained of being beaten by the police."[76] One of the characters in the novel, a writer named Ray, had heard several times from Senegalese sailors that the French police sought them out in particular. After witnessing the police harassing and arresting everyone around the port, however, Ray at first concludes that while "the French police had unlimited power of interference with the individual," the neighborhood around the port—known in the novel as the Ditch—was so seedy that violence was a natural part of life both for the police and for everyone else.[77] However, after Ray leaves this neighborhood for a more chic part of Marseille, he is simply walking along the street alone one evening when two policemen in quick succession stop him and then question, beat, and finally arrest him. When Ray registers a complaint (he has his papers on him at the time) and asks whether he had been treated in this manner because he was Black, the inspector skirts the question by stating "that the policemen had made a mistake, owing to the fact that all the Negroes in Marseilles were criminals."[78] The Vieux Port thus appears as a somewhat exceptional space in which everyone is subjected to daily violence, in opposition to other parts of Marseille where race could be a determining factor in the police's perceptions of a passerby. In many ways, such incidents were daily occurrences both in Paris and Marseille, but the longer prison terms imposed upon Senghor and Kouyaté, and the threat and at times enforcement of deportation in the Mediterranean city, reflected a level of state-enforced repression that was rarely mentioned by anti-imperialists in Paris, although they complained early and often at the least sign of police intervention.

In part, as a result, Black men who wandered the streets of Marseille, and in particular those of the Vieux Port, shaped their politics as a reflection of the constraints imposed, and opportunities provided, by this particular city. Their interactions with French authorities, access to work, and self-identification within the diaspora through language, ethnicity, or region of origin, as well as their perceptions of the rights they wished they had, were all influenced by their presence in Marseille. The disorganization that travel and unemployment threatened to impose upon a community shaped by proximity to the Mediterranean was countered by a strong social bond within the Vieux Port, described by McKay as "a great bond of black and brown humanity" that lent him "the strength and distinction of a group and the assurance of belonging to it."[79] As a result they could not function as merely an outpost of the LDRN in Paris, hard as Kouyaté might try, but instead needed concrete local organizations, manned by individuals they could trust and who could look out for their complaints related to work. The Parisians were perceived as distant and more settled off in the capital. McKay's character Ray sums up how negatively Parisians could be viewed when he characterized them, and it was not a compliment, as "society folk."[80]

In fact, Parisians also needed to be creative when looking for work and could find themselves subjected to violence that reinforced the need for the political organization of the Black community. Violence took many forms for the Black communities of interwar France, from the physical to the more insidious but nonetheless destructive disturbance of interactions, beliefs, self-perceptions, and contacts by individuals and groups external to these communities. The police and police spies were a constant underlying threat. Those very informants were also subjected to a different sort of violence as they were torn between service to the French administration and their affiliation with, and often belief in the ideals of, militant communities. The PCF's pressures to present a united front based on class further threatened these communities, even while presenting them with new opportunities for connections that moved beyond the diaspora. Finally, although not as colorful or as concentrated as the violence in the Vieux Port of Marseille that inspired creative works such as those of McKay, occasionally men in Paris also experienced corporeal violence. For example, one spy noted that during a meeting in 1925 of la Fraternité Africaine, an organization that grouped those originating from French West Africa, "two white men forced an entry and picked a quarrel with the noirs for no reason. One of these, named Tounkara, was knifed.... While Tounkara was being brought to the hospital, other Black men pursued the two aggressors who were finally apprehended by two policemen."[81] In this case, one of the assailants was a criminal known to the police, but this was neither the first nor the last time that Black Parisians were exposed to such hostility. Thus, as divisive as issues such as work, class, people or region of origin, and city of domicile within France might have been for the groups of Paris and Marseille, each of these issues also helped to create, reinforce, and define these respective communities, as well as to shape both the need for networks throughout France, and the manner in which these networks were initiated and sustained.

Ultimately, Parisian Blacks organized anti-imperialism from within the capital because they entered into a centralized system that they perceived as characteristic of the French state. In a sense, the Marseillais followed suit when they became defiant in their attitudes toward the LDRN and the SNM's Parisian center, like many French provincials when faced with Paris. Their reactions reveal that our visions of Black France, past and likely also present, have much to gain from careful considerations of how regions inspired and sculpted the communities and lives of Black men and women. Both comparative and geographically specific approaches to the study of Black France can only further augment our growing field of inquiry. Here, this methodology has illuminated how during the 1920s and 1930s Black anti-imperialists who on the surface appeared constricted by a narrowly defined politics and class in fact constructed incredibly nuanced societies. Diasporic communities were united and created networks demarcated by migrants' struggles against imperialism, by their origins in the African diaspora, and by their attempts to defend both philosophical and bread-and-butter rights. Yet the militant men of Marseille, and those of Paris, also shaped their relationships to one another because they entered into the logic of regional identities that decades later were still motivating the Marseille band Massilia Sound System to jibe "Marseille est la plus jolie."

Notes

1. P. Sweeney, "A Troubadour for Today," *Independent*, September 1, 2006. Note that the group is credited with starting a new form of reggae, "trobamuffin," which combines the word "troubadour" with the musical style ragamuffin.

2. McKay was so inspirational to Moussu T that upon the release in 2007 of Massilia Sound System's latest album the original group quipped during one interview that if the band were a book, it would be *Banjo*. Interview du Massilia Sound System, October 2007, on the web site ConcertandCo.com (http://www.concertandco.com/interview/massilia-sound-system/interview-1-19403.htm, retrieved 24 April 2008).

3. Massilia was the name given to Marseille first by Greeks and then by Romans, and the group's title is thus a throwback to a time before northern France's imposition of a language, Languedoïl (or Languedoui), and a government upon France's south.

4. C. Ford, *Creating the Nation in Provincial France: Religion and Political Identity in Brittany* (Princeton: Princeton University Press, 1993); S. Gerson, *The Pride of Place: Local Memories and Political Culture in Nineteenth-Century France* (Ithaca: Cornell University Press, 2003); S. L. Harp, *Learning to Be Loyal: Primary Schooling as Nation Building in Alsace and Lorraine, 1850–1940* (DeKalb: Northern Illinois University Press, 1998); J. M. Merriman, *The Margins of City Life: Explorations on the French Urban Frontier, 1815–1851* (New York: Oxford University Press, 1991); P. Sahlins, *Boundaries: The Mak-*

ing of France and Spain in the Pyrenees (Berkeley: University of California Press, 1989); T. Stovall, "From Red Belt to Black Belt: Race, Class, and Urban Marginality in Twentieth-Century Paris," in *The Color of Liberty: Histories of Race in France*, ed. S. Peabody and T. Stovall (Durham: Duke University Press, 2003).

5. On the uses and limits of comparative history, see N. L. Green, "Repenser les migrations," in *Le noeud gordien*, ed. L. Bély, C. Gauvard, and J-F Sirinelli (Paris: Presses Universitaires de France, 2002), 21. All translations are the author's own.

6. For examples of the former, see B. A. Berliner, *Ambivalent Desire: The Exotic Black Other in Jazz-Age France* (Amherst: University of Massachusetts Press, 2002); P. Dewitte, *Les mouvements nègres en France, 1919–1939* (Paris: L'Harmattan, 1985); L. Kesteloot, "Les écrivains noirs de langue française: naissance d'une littérature" (doctoral diss., Université Libre de Bruxelles, Institut de Sociologie, 1963); C. L. Miller, *Nationalists and Nomads: Essays on Francophone African Literature and Culture* (Chicago: University of Chicago Press, 1998); T. D. Sharpley-Whiting, *Negritude Women* (Minneapolis: University of Minnesota Press, 2002); J. Spiegler, "Aspects of Nationalist Thought among French-Speaking West Africans, 1921–1939" (D.Phil. thesis, Oxford University, 1968); M. Steins, "Les antécédents et la genèse de la négritude senghorienne" (Université de Paris III–Sorbonne Nouvelle, 1980); D. Thomas, *Black France: Colonialism, Immigration, and Transnationalism* (Bloomington: Indiana University Press, 2007); G. Wilder, *The French Imperial Nation-State: Negritude and Colonial Humanism between the Two World Wars* (Chicago: University of Chicago Press, 2005). For examples of the latter, see, among others, J. Blake, *Le Tumulte Noir: Modernist Art and Popular Entertainment in Jazz-Age Paris, 1900–1930* (University Park: Pennsylvania State University Press, 1999); P. Blanchard, E. Deroo, and G. Manceron, *Le Paris noir* (Paris: Hazan, 2001); A. Conklin, "Who Speaks for Africa? The René Maran-Blaise Diagne Trial in 1920s Paris," in Peabody and Stovall, *The Color of Liberty*; M. Fabre, *La rive noire: les écrivains noirs américains à Paris, 1830–1995* (Marseille: A. Dimanche, 1999); Y. S. Simpson Fletcher, "Unsettling Settlers: Colonial Migrants and Racialised Sexuality in Interwar Marseilles," in *Gender, Sexuality and Colonial Modernities*, ed. A. Burton (New York: Routledge, 1999); B. Jules-Rosette, *Black Paris: The African Writers' Landscape* (Urbana: University of Illinois Press, 1998); T. E. Stovall, *Paris Noir: African Americans in the City of Light* (New York: Houghton Mifflin, 1996).

7. B. H. E. Edwards, *The Practice of Diaspora: Literature, Translation, and the Rise of Black Internationalism* (Cambridge: Harvard University Press, 2003); P. Gilroy, *The Black Atlantic: Modernity and Double Consciousness* (Cambridge: Harvard University Press, 1993); M. A. Stephens, *Black Empire:*

The Masculine Global Imaginary of Caribbean Intellectuals in the United States, 1914–1962 (Durham: Duke University Press, 2005). Another excellent example from colonial studies is E. T. Thomas Jennings, *Vichy in the Tropics: Pétain's National Revolution in Madagascar, Guadeloupe, and Indochina, 1940–1944* (Stanford: Stanford University Press, 2001).

8. Mary Dewhurst Lewis has noted this problem within immigration studies more generally, and offers a valuable example of how to do a comparative history of migrants. See M. D. Lewis, *The Boundaries of the Republic: Migrant Rights and the Limits of Universalism in France, 1918–1940* (Stanford: Stanford University Press, 2007).

9. On networks and African communities in France, see the implicit and explicit discussions in C. Daum, *Les associations de maliens en France: migrations, développement et citoyenneté* (Paris: Karthala, 1997); F. Manchuelle, *Willing Migrants: Soninke Labor Diasporas, 1848–1960* (Athens: Ohio University Press, 1997); C. Quiminal, *Gens d'ici, gens d'ailleurs: migrations Soninké et transformations villageoises* (Paris: Christian Bourgois, 1991); S. Randrianja, *Société et luttes anticoloniales à Madagascar* (Paris: Karthala, 2001).

10. In addition to the many works listed above, see also dissertations by G. B. Glaes, "The Mirage of Fortune: West African Immigration to Paris and the Development of a Post-colonial Immigrant Community, 1960–1981" (Ph.D. dissertation, University of Wisconsin, 2007); E. F. Manchuelle, "Background to Black African Emigration to France: The Labor Migrations of the Soninke, 1848–1987" (Ph.D. dissertation, University of California, Santa Barbara, 1987).

11. On policing and surveillance of immigrants and foreigners during the Third Republic, see among many others J.-M.Berlière, "A Republican Political Police? Political Policing in France under the Third Republic, 1875–1940," in *The Policing of Politics in the Twentieth Century: Historical Perspectives*, ed. M. Mazower (New York: Berghahn, 1997); M.-C. Blanc-Chaléard, C. Denys, and R. Morieux, *Police et migrants: France, 1667–1939* (Rennes: Presses Universitaires de Rennes, 2001); J.-C. Bonnet, *Les pouvoirs publics français et l'immigration dans l'entre-deux-guerres* (Lyon: Centre d'Histoire Économique et Sociale de la Région Lyonnaise, 1976); M. D. Lewis, "The Strangeness of Foreigners: Policing Migration and Nation in Interwar Marseille," in *Race in France: Interdisciplinary Perspectives on the Politics of Difference*, ed. H. Chapman and L. Frader (New York: Berghahn, 2004); C. Ourgaut, *La surveillance des étrangers en France: thèse pour le doctorat présentée et soutenue publiquement en Décembre 1937 par Ch. Ourgaut, Université de Toulouse, Faculté de Droit* (Toulouse: Imprimerie du Sud-Ouest, 1937); R. Rey, *La police des étrangers en France: thèse pour le doctorat présentée et soutenue le 15 mai 1937 à 14 heures par René Rey, Université de Paris, Faculté de Droit* (Paris: Presses Modernes, 1937); C. Rosenberg, *Policing Paris: The Origins of Modern Immigration Control between the Wars* (Ithaca: Cornell University Press, 2006).

12. C. Liauzu, *Aux origines des tiers-mondismes: colonisés et anticolonialistes en France, 1919–1939* (Paris: L'Harmattan, 1982).

13. J. A. Boittin, "Black in France: The Language and Politics of Race in the Late Third Republic," *French Politics, Culture, and Society* 27, no. 2 (2009): 22–46.

14. For more on the problem of translating these terms, see Edwards, *The Practice of Diaspora.*

15. Liauzu, *Aux origines des tiers-mondismes*; J. Moneta, *La politique du Parti Communiste Français dans la question coloniale, 1920–1963* (Paris: F. Maspero, 1971). On communism and a different colonial community, see also D. Hemery, "Du patriotisme au marxisme: l'immigration vietnamienne en France de 1926 à 1930," *Mouvement Social* 90 (1975).

16. Dewitte, *Les mouvements nègres en France*, 34–35; Edwards, *The Practice of Diaspora*, 250.

17. On spies in colonial milieus, see P. Morlat, *La répression coloniale au Vietnam, 1908–1940* (Paris: L'Harmattan, 1990); E. J. Peters, "Resistance, Rivalries, and Restaurants: Vietnamese Workers in Interwar France," *Journal of Vietnamese Studies* 2, no. 3 (2007); Wilder, *The French Imperial Nation-State.*

18. G. Mauco, *Les étrangers en France: leur rôle dans l'activité économique* (Paris: Armand Colin, 1932), 175. On similar statistics for immigrant communities in Marseille, see M.-F. Attard-Maraninchi and E. Temime, *Migrance: histoire des migrations à Marseille*, vol. 3, *Le cosmopolitisme de l'entre-deux-guerres, 1919–1945* (Aix-en-Provence: Edisud, 1990), 27.

19. See the introductory notes to the CAOM's SLOTFOM archives and CAOM, 1SLOTFOM/4.

20. Dewitte, *Les mouvements nègres en France*, 25, 26, and 40; P. Dewitte, "Le Paris noir de l'entre-deux-guerres," in *Le Paris des étrangers depuis un siècle*, ed. A. Kaspi and A. Marès (Paris: Imprimerie Nationale, 1989), 157–69.

21. J. A. Boittin, *Soleil Noir: Race, Gender and Colonialism in Interwar Paris* (New Haven: Yale University Press, 2005), 307. For more on workers and Paris during the Third Republic, including their relationship to the PCF, see J.-P. Brunet, *Saint-Denis la ville rouge: socialisme et communisme en banlieue ouvrière, 1890–1939* (Paris: Hachette, 1980); A. Fourcaut, *Bobigny, banlieue rouge* (Paris: Editions Ouvrières/Presses de la Fondation Nationale des Sciences Politiques, 1986).

22. On defining communities in Paris, see D. Garrioch, "Neighbourhood and Community in Paris, 1740–1790," in *Cambridge Studies in Early Modern History*, ed. J. H. Elliott, O. Hufton, and H. G. Koenigsberger (Cambridge: Cambridge University Press, 1986), 2–5.

23. AN, F/7/13166, PROM, 30 April 1927.

24. L. Senghor, "Debout les Nègres," *Race Nègre* 1, no. 1 (June 1927).

25. CAOM, 3SLOTFOM/37, Agent Désiré, 16 October 1926.

26. C. McKay, *A Long Way from Home* (London: Pluto, 1985), 278.

27. C. McKay, *Banjo* (London: X Press, 2000), 62.

28. PROM, May 1929: 14. On links between spaces such as cafés and bars and both formal and informal working class politics, see W. S. Haine, *World of the Paris Cafe: Sociability among the French Working Class, 1789–1914* (Baltimore: Johns Hopkins University Press, 1996).

29. By 1942, when African sailors were grounded in Marseille after ties were cut off between France and Africa, Attard-Maraninchi and Temime state that the 400 Somalis and minimum of 1,000 Soudanese, Senegalese, and Soninkés who were blocked in Marseille represented 3 to 4 times the previous numbers of Africans living in Marseille. Thus during the early 1930s, numbers on the low end would have been of approximately 350 to 450 Africans, not taking into account all the transient sailors, unemployed, unregistered, and so forth. Attard-Maraninchi and Temime, *Le cosmopolitisme de l'entre-deux-guerres*, 151.

30. On movement, relocation, and migrant populations in Marseille, see Attard-Maraninchi and Temime, *Le cosmopolitisme de l'entre-deux-guerres*, 151.

31. AN, F/7/13167, PROM, March 1930: 6.

32. McKay, *A Long Way from Home*, 279.

33. Lewis, *The Boundaries of the Republic*, 85.

34. AN, F/7/13167, PROM, September 1930: 7.

35. Ibid., 10.

36. "Les ouvriers nègres de Marseille," *Race Nègre* 4, no. 2 (September 1930).

37. "Pour la défense des salaires, contre le chômage: navigateurs nègres faites triompher vos revendications," *Cri des Nègres* 1, no. 2 (September 1931).

38. T. Kouyaté, "La grève nationale des marins," *Cri des Nègres* 1 (November–December 1931): 4–5.

39. Siragnouma, "Avec les marins coloniaux dans les ports," *Cri des Nègres* 2 (January–February 1932): 6–7.

40. AN, F/7/13168, PROM, December 1931: 10.

41. Ibid., 8; AN, F/7/13168, PROM, January 1932: 6.

42. AN, F/7/13168, PROM, January 1931: 7.

43. "Une intervention en faveur d'un compatriote maltraité," *Race Nègre* 4, no. 2 (September 1930).

44. AN, F/7/13167, PROM, March 1930: 7.

45. Manchuelle, *Willing Migrants*.

46. McKay, *Banjo*, 37.

47. CAOM, 3SLOTFOM/73, Agent Paul, 11 November 1932.

48. AN, F/7/13167, PROM, January 1930: 9.

49. See, e.g., an article written partly in Malagasy: "Madagascar: Une plate apologie de la colonisation," *Cri des Nègres* 2, no. 2 (September 1933); and an article written in Douala: "Miango ma rwed'a muaned'a kamerun Rudolph Douala Manga Bell, o 8 august 1914, o njom'a bwambo ba minyangaru ma Douala," *Cri des Nègres* 2, no. 3 (November–December 1933).

50. AN, F/7/13167, PROM, February 1930: 6.

51. For a few examples of work on networks and the maintenance of communities, in addition to Manchuelle, see A. Corbin, "Les paysans de Paris: histoire des limousins du bâtiment au XIXᵉ siècle," *Ethnologie Française* 10 (1980); C. Tilly and K. Brown, "On Uprooting, Kinship, and the Auspices of Migration," *International Journal of Comparative Sociology* 8 (1967); O. White, "Networking: Freemasons and the Colonial State in French West Africa, 1895–1914," *French History* 19, no. 1 (2005); J.-L. Amselle, ed., *Les migrations africaines: réseaux et processus migratoires* (Paris: François Maspero, 1976); J. Barou, *Travailleurs africains en France: rôle des cultures d'origine* (Grenoble: Presses Universitaires de Grenoble, 1978); L. Chevalier, *La formation de la population parisienne au XIXᵉ siècle* (Paris: Presses Universitaires de France, 1950); P. Milza, ed., *Les italiens en France de 1914 à 1940* (Rome: École Française de Rome, 1986); J. Ponty, *Polonais méconnus: histoire des travailleurs immigrés en France dans l'entre-deux-guerres* (Paris: Publications de la Sorbonne, 1990); B. Stora, "Les algériens dans le Paris de l'entre-deux-guerres," in Kaspi and Marès, *Le Paris des étrangers depuis un siècle*.

52. Manchuelle also mentions in a footnote that the LDRN failed in Marseille in part because it followed the Wolof lead regarding the deportation of undocumented sailors, and also because Kouyaté personally was against the principle of African emigration to Europe. Manchuelle, *Willing Migrants*, 197, 305n188.

53. Yaël Simpson Fletcher informs us that during the years 1920 and 1921 West African and Malagasy seamen had already organized one such union. Y. S. Fletcher, "'Capital of the Colonies': Real and Imagined Boundaries between Metropole and Empire in 1920s Marseilles," In *Imperial Cities: Landscape, Display and Identity*, ed. F. Driver and D. Gilbert (Manchester: Manchester University Press, 1999), 144.

54. "La vie de nos sections," *Race Nègre*, February–March 1930.

55. AN, F/7/13167, PROM, January 1930: 13–14.

56. Ibid., 8.

57. Ibid., 14.

58. AN, F/7/13167, PROM, March 1929: 25.

59. AN, F/7/13167, PROM, March 1930: 4.

60. AN, F/7/13167, PROM, September 1930: 8.

61. Ibid., 9.

62. AN, F/7/13167, PROM, February 1930: 9.

63. T. G. Kouyaté, "François Coty, directeur de 'l'Ami du Peuple' a calom-
nié," *Race Nègre*, February–March 1930.

64. AN, F/7/13167, PROM, April 1930: 11.

65. Bernard-Duquenet, "Les débuts du syndicalisme au Sénégal au temps
du Front Populaire," *Mouvement Social* 101, no. 43 (1977). For more on how
unions were established in West Africa, see Y. Person, "Le Front Populaire au
Sénégal," *Mouvement Social*, May 1936–October 1938. 107. On black dockers'
experiences in Marseille and elsewhere, see UMR TELEMME Research group:
France, ed., *Dockers de la Méditerranée à la Mer du Nord: des quais et des
hommes dans l'histoire: colloque international, 11 au 13 mars 1999, Cité du Livre,
Aix en Provence, Musée d'Histoire de Marseille* (Aix-en-Provence: Edisud,
1999); S. Ousmane, *Le docker noir* (Paris: Présence Africaine, 1973).

66. AN, F/7/13167, PROM, July 1930: 5.

67. AN, F/7/13167, PROM, January 1930: 9 and 12.

68. On women and black migrant communities, see in particular J. A.
Boittin, "Black and White: Gender, Race Relations and the Nardal Sisters in
Interwar Paris," *French Colonial History* 6 (2005); Fletcher, "Unsettling Set-
tlers"; Sharpley-Whiting, *Negritude Women*.

69. AN, F/7/13167, PROM, January 1930: 7.

70. Ibid.

71. AN, F/7/13167, PROM, February 1930: 8.

72. AN, F/7/13167, PROM, March 1930: 8.

73. Ibid.

74. "Alerte! camarades nègres la répression s'accentue," *Cri des Nègres* 1, no.
2 (September 1931).

75. AN, F/7/13168, PROM, September 1931: 8.

76. McKay, *Banjo*, 19.

77. Ibid., 227.

78. Ibid., 229.

79. McKay, *Long Way*, 277.

80. This particular statement may well have been aimed primarily at African American writers from the Harlem Renaissance who were living in Paris,
but reflects a pattern of Paris versus Marseille discussions in both *Banjo* and
A Long Way from Home. McKay, *Banjo*, 99.

81. CAOM, 3SLTOFOM/34, "La Fraternité Africaine," Agent Désiré, April 7,
1925.

Reflections on the Future of Black France

Josephine Baker's Vision of a Global Village

BENNETTA JULES-ROSETTE

> If my village
> Could serve one day
> As a witness
> And a symbol of love
> If all people from here and there . . .
> Had one heart
> All villages
> Then would be happy.
> —"Dans mon village,"
> a song performed by Josephine Baker,
> composed by Henri Lemarchand
> and Francis Lopez, 1953

Preamble

It is critical to explore the diverse voices that have contributed to the ideologies and self-writing of Black France and the African diaspora. At the turbulent time of the colonial struggles of the 1950s, the Franco-American performer Josephine Baker began to build her multicultural Rainbow Tribe, consisting of twelve adopted children of different ethnicities and nationalities. Baker's plan to establish an ideal family in southwestern France surfaced in the wake of her experiences of racism and surveillance while performing in the United States and in the shadow of Négritude's domination as a key identity discourse in France. Baker brought her own versions of Négritude and multiculturalism to the public. In 1947, she purchased a medieval château in the hills of the Dordogne in southwestern France. She had rented the château during the war years and, in the 1950s, it became the base of operation for her Rainbow project. As the charismatic leader of a utopian family movement, Baker attempted to transcend the racial and cultural barriers that she had previously encountered. Her adopted children became the honorary acolytes of her movement and the symbols of her multicultural dream. This utopian vision served as the inspiration for her global village.

Much political and personal history surrounded Baker's projects and choices. The image of a colorblind France of liberty and equality had intrigued African American artists and expatriates who settled in France between the 1920s and the 1950s. Ignoring the plight of the Senegalese soldiers and the rising North African and Antillian populations migrating to France during the interwar years, African Americans sought new freedom in a society that was not, in their terms, overtly segregated.[1] In the Paris that Baker encountered in 1925, the rosy possibilities seemed endless, but her experiences in Germany, Austria, and Hungary immediately before the Second World War had opened her eyes to bleaker alternatives. Baker's Rainbow Tribe was a manifestation of the dream of equality. Behind this dream lurked a variety of tensions ranging from colonial exoticism to nationalism and xenophobia.

Alternative Visions of Community

One might ask whether the concept of the Rainbow Tribe and its dream stood in a positive or an antithetical relationship to official France. Although the tribe incarnated the French values of equality and fraternity, the family clearly represented an unconventional alternative lifestyle that challenged accepted social norms. The family's ideal was based on "the spiritualization of politics" described by Karl Mannheim and a politics of representation used as the foundation of all utopian communities.[2] Exile and isolation are often distinguishing features of utopian communities. Some utopian religious communities, such as the Shakers, also use adoption as the primary mode of recruitment. In liberal democracies when utopian challenges occur, the groups may co-exist peacefully with outside institutions until a point of legal and socio-economic infraction or a publicly acknowl-edged weakness is found. In the case of the Rainbow Tribe, these weaknesses were epitomized by the departure of the group's co-founder (Baker's fourth husband, Jo Bouillon), the vulnerability of the children, and the financial fragility of the enterprise. By the late 1960s, Josephine Baker's charisma as a performer, a mother, and a group leader was not sufficient to offset these obstacles. Nevertheless, the ideal of world unity lives on in the legacy of her universalistic discourse and the revival of Château des Milandes as a site of tourism and pilgrimage.

The moral and ethical objectives of the Rainbow project involved the creation of a perfect community with appreciation for all forms of diversity. Similar propositions have a long history among utopian and communal movements. Isolation of the community to avoid contami-nation from outsiders' beliefs and practices is also a common feature of utopian communities. Baker's experiment is no exception in this regard, as seen by her reluctance to allow the Rainbow children to attend schools outside of her domain. Baker wished to shield her community from negative external influences and, at the same time, to receive praise and public acclaim for her accomplishments. It was her hope that once the utopian multicultural community came to fruition, it would function as a model for other communities, states, and na-tions. This imagined community would become a global reality.

Numerous antecedents and contemporary parallels come to mind when Baker's domain is viewed as a utopian community. The biogra-pher Stephen Papich compares Les Milandes to New Harmony, a utopian community established in upstate New York in the 1820s.[3] But the conditions of that experiment differed from Baker's both in finan-cial support and in the political tolerance for pioneer communities during that era in the United States. Utopian visions often emerge when older social forms become outmoded. Seventeenth-century Pu-ritans in England and the colonies hoped that their perfect commu-nity of saints would replace what they perceived as the corrupt social order of the monarchy.[4] From the utopian communes following the French Revolution to late-twentieth-century religious utopianism, charismatic leaders have encouraged their followers to dream of idyl-lic lives that transcend the struggles and temptations of the outside world. In recent times, some of these dreams (such as Jim Jones's controversial People's Temple and Agricultural Project) have ended in tragedy, while others (such as Michael Jackson's Neverland) remain suspended creations of childlike fantasies. Unlike these cultlike closed utopias, Baker was attempting to create a model multicultural community for the future. The theodicy of this utopia entailed the return to a world in perfect harmony with nature and the creation of a social universe in which all prejudice and conflict would be absent.

The Primal Family and French Patriarchy

The French family was historically based on a patriarchal model. James Corbett explains: "Under absolute monarchy, it mirrored the organization of the state—the pater familias ruled over his household just as the king ruled over his subjects. The Napoleonic code consecrated fatherhood—the famous *puissance paternelle*, tempered by the revolutionary idea of equity husbands were supposed to be endowed with."[5]

Josephine Baker's upbringing in East St. Louis had little in common with this conventional patriarchal model. Eddie Carson, Josephine's putative father, disappeared before her birth and made no visible contribution to the family. Josephine was brought up under her mother's strict hand, with her half-siblings Richard, Margaret, and Willie Mae Martin. Richard remembered these years vividly. Carrie McDonald, Josephine's mother, had been an amateur dancer, but worked as a laundress to support her family during Baker's youth. The children were also forced to work. Reared in a culture of austere poverty in what has come to be interpreted as a stereotypical Black matrifocal family, Josephine's fragmented family life contrasted starkly with the Napoleonic patriarchal ideal characterized by male authoritarian protection and financial stability.

Baker's early years as a performer were based on appropriating and manipulating racialized gender stereotypes in her *danse sauvage* and glamour images. As she entered middle age, Baker deployed, and was perhaps forced into using, the family as the symbolic locus for building her new image and dreams of multiculturalism. As both the primal figure Fatou in her savage dance of 1925 and the flashy fashion icon of the 1930s, Baker had existed in a world without children, although the seeds of the self-sacrificing Madonna image were foreshadowed as early as 1931 in the novella *Mon sang dans tes veines*, written by Baker's manager and partner Giuseppe (Pepito) Abatino and Félix de la Camara.[6] All of Baker's films involved unrequited love resulting from crossing racial barriers without children, and, to a certain extent, her life followed a similar pattern. The Rainbow Tribe became an ideologically charged vehicle for confronting these social obstacles while simultaneously rewriting her life and attempting to change the world. The cultural historian Jan Relf argues that women's utopias often involve a "retreat into fantastic pastoral enclosures, or walled spaces in which they guard and protect a cluster of values perceived as characteristically feminine."[7] The Rainbow experiment displayed some of these characteristics, with Baker as the ultimate mother figure who dominated the children, her natal family, and a utopian community within the enclosure of Les Milandes.

Elements of the Rainbow project exhibited continuity with the root paradigm of the primitive image. The master narrative of return to an idyllic paradise—a lush garden of Eden—might be applied to the Rainbow Tribe's living on the vast and isolated property and experimental farm at Les Milandes. On June 3, 1947, Baker's birthday, Josephine and Jo (Joseph Jean Étienne) Bouillon married at the Château des Milandes in a civil ceremony presided over by André Lahillonne, prefect of Dordogne, immediately followed by a religious ceremony in the château's Gothic chapel and a festive reception. Bouillon stated that in marrying Josephine, he was also marrying her dream. In this idyllic landscape, Baker hoped that the prejudices and social obstacles of the outside world would vanish, to be substituted by a life of harmony, cooperation, and bliss. The famous photograph, now a popular postcard, of Baker and Bouillon with eight of their Rainbow children in front of a Christmas tree at Les Milandes, circa 1956, reflects this harmonious ideal.

In 1948, after Josephine's brief tour in the United States with Jo Bouillon, Carrie joined her daughter at Les Milandes along with Josephine's half-sister Margaret and her husband Elmo. After some persuasion from Josephine, Carrie left her husband in the United States to follow her daughter. Everyone was put to work on a strict schedule. Carrie helped with the household duties and later the children. Margaret worked on the farm and, for a short time, ran a bakery where she sold American-style pastries. Elmo was in charge of the paddleboats on the Dordogne River abutting Les Milandes. Baker also hired governesses, gardeners, farm hands, and a postal clerk, all of whom she supervised closely. Josephine's half-brother Richard joined the group in 1952. Leaving behind a trucking business and a family in St. Louis, he became a chauffeur at Les Milandes and later ran a gas station that Josephine had purchased for him near the estate. More extended relatives (nieces and nephews) later joined the group for a brief period. Yet, the Rainbow Tribe was not a natural family. It was what the sociologist Erving Goffman describes as a fabrication intended to convey a specific impression and message to the public.[8]

Josephine began the Rainbow family project when she was well into her forties, informally adopting the children at the rate of two a year between 1954 and 1956. Formal adoption proceedings were conducted for eight of the children as a unit at the administrative prefecture of Sarlat, in Dordogne, on June 21, 1957, making the commemoration of their joint adoption just three weeks after Baker's own birthday. The eight children formally adopted in 1957 were Akio (of Korean origin from Japan); Luis (from Colombia); Janot (from Japan); Jean-Claude (from France); Moïse (French of Jewish background); Brahim (now called Brian B. Baker, Berber from Algeria); Marianne (French from Algeria); and Jari, or Jarry (from Finland).

Subsequently, four more children were added to the family: Mara (from Venezuela); Koffi (from Côte d'Ivoire); Noël (from France); and Stellina (Moroccan, born in France). All children received the surname, Bouillon-Baker.[9] Baker herself signed the documents as Josephine Bouillon. The group represented nationalities from four continents, and they were of diverse cultural and religious backgrounds of which none of them was fully aware. Baker's desire to have children of her own as part of the legend is confirmed by Jo Bouillon, who claimed that she miscarried during the early years of their marriage, an assertion that appears to have been embellished, since she had a hysterectomy in Morocco during the war. Phyllis Rose points out: "To have had that many children so close in age, had they been biologically hers, she would have had to bear three sets of twins in three years."[10]

Initially, there were to have been four male children of different ethnicities and nationalities, but Josephine's plan expanded to include eight more children, two of them girls, Marianne and Stellina.[11] The pattern of patriarchy was overturned by Baker's domineering matriarchal control of her mostly male brood in their sheltered medieval castle. The primal family was matriarchal, matrifocal, experimental, iconoclastic, and legendary. Josephine was the boss. Just as she had with her primal exotic image, Baker used existing family stereotypes to break the rules and challenge bourgeois norms and expectations about domestic life and education. She created a composite community based on the ideals of ethnic and cultural blending in a simulated touristic space. The acquisition of each child was surrounded by a nested narrative that paralleled Josephine's own life story. There was a sense in which the Rainbow Tribe reflected Baker's performative persona by representing the multiple national and cultural identities that she assumed on stage, within films, and in song. The children's public stories subtly wove together to reduplicate Baker's foundling myth in a new narrative program, and they cleverly excluded some of the financial and interpersonal negotiations surrounding the adoptions. The Rainbow family was converted into a spectacle in which Josephine, her family, and the children were the stars on stage for tourists and politicians who visited the château.

Life with the Rainbow Tribe

In interviews with the press, Josephine repeatedly stated that the Rainbow Tribe "represented" for her the ideal of universal brotherhood. Her use of the unique term "representation" in connection with the family is interesting. It points to the complex and contradictory symbolic status of the Rainbow Tribe as a narrative fabrication. Families are the locus of tradition, heritage, and a sense of belonging. Baker consciously built an international family as a representation in which she wished to instill this sense of belonging symbolically and even mythologically. Yet, modern families are also situated in territories, nations, and neighborhoods. Les Milandes would become not only the home but also the territory of Baker's family in the utopian world that she wished to construct beyond the French nation-state.

Les Milandes was an island that magnified Josephine's escape from her two loves, the United States and France. The territory had its own rules, regulations, and sense of order. It was the *village du monde, le domaine*, and the international capital of brotherhood. This world of brotherhood was, nevertheless, located in the Dordogne in France and was therefore subjected to the governance and norms of the state and the region. The children would be prepared to be citizens of the world. They were also French, went to local schools on and off, and interacted with their neighbors. The multicultural dream left open the question of socialization and the interface between the ideals of brotherhood and the realities of social life in a remote rural community in southwestern France. The world village at Les Milandes evolved into a utopia with a unique structure. As with other utopian communities, its success would depend on its internal harmony and its relationship to the external forces of territory and state.[12]

Aspects of colonial discourse evident in Baker's primal image were also at play in the conceptualization of Les Milandes as an autonomous territory. It was a neo-feudal fiefdom ruled by Baker, a property in the French Département de Dordogne, and a family home. Although the plan did not entirely work for a variety of practical reasons, the award-winning experimental farm at Les Milandes was intended to feed both the tribe and part of the surrounding community and make Les Milandes self-sufficient year-round. For several years, the farm did feed the family and provided enough produce for the hotel restaurant at Charteuse, which is indicated by surviving menus. Vegetables, poultry, dairy products, and bread were all produced locally. Josephine had finally become the real Queen of the Colonies. In her military uniform, she would represent the domain as its head of state. As a colony, Les Milandes would ultimately return to the control of the state when the debts were recalled and Baker's multicultural vision was challenged. The taxes owed to the French state were symbolic of Les Milandes's political, economic, and cultural dependency.

Given the territorial and ideological organization of Les Milandes, it was inevitable that the conflicted and split identity of the colonial subject would be reflected in the socialization of the Rainbow children. In everyday life, issues of identity conflict emerged as disciplinary problems and internal family disputes. The onus was placed on Baker for being inconsistent in her child-rearing practices, frequently absent on tour, and, in the end, overwhelmed by the organizational and financial responsibilities of her vast global project. Jean-Claude Baker (Rouzaud), Josephine's protégé, quotes her confidante Marie Spiers as remarking, "everything was overdone, the punishment was overdone, the love was overdone, the makeup was overdone."[13] Others comment on the inconsistent disciplining of the children and Josephine's practice as *Maman Cadeau*, showering the children with lavish gifts on holidays and upon returning from each of her tours.[14] A larger issue concerns the objectives of these practices and how they shaped the children's lives in the composite community. The contradictory child-rearing practices were not simply a by-product of Baker's personality and whims. They were rooted in a deep-seated ideological conflict between the family as a utopian composite community suspended in space and time—a "representation" in Baker's own terms—and the larger social world in which the experiment existed. Although they felt distant from the outside world, the children were trained to be tolerant of racial and cultural differences, and their strong bonds to each other were evident and genuine.

As already emphasized, each child was surrounded by a myth of adoption that mirrored Baker's own Cinderella story. During a tour of Japan in 1954, Josephine visited an orphanage where she found Akio (which means autumn, in honor of the season of his discovery at the orphanage), whose mother was Korean and whose unknown father was believed to be an American serviceman. At the same orphanage, she found another child of similar parentage, Teruya, and made plans to adopt him, renaming him Janot.[15] Both of these children were cast-offs in their society—marginalized in Japan as Korean war orphans. Their Asian background fulfilled the first step in Baker's quest for an international composite community.

A year later, while on tour in Colombia, Baker searched for another child. She made arrangements with a family near Bogotá to adopt one of their many children, Gustavio Valencia, and changed his name to Luis. She also wanted to adopt a Native American child from either South America or the United States and ultimately found Mara in Venezuela. While on tour in Scandinavia in 1955, she visited an orphanage in Helsinki, where she discovered a two-year old, Jari (or Jarry), and brought him to Les Milandes. Her project was now gaining more momentum and publicity. People would send her press clippings and leads about abandoned children and would even help her to locate them.

In an orphanage in Paris, she found Jean-Claude, who was French. While on tour in the Middle East, she looked for a Jewish son in Israel, but was turned down because of strict Israeli government regulations on international adoptions. Returning to France, she located Moïse in an orphanage in Paris to fulfill this part of her dream. Moïse was the sixth child to be brought to Les Milandes, and Josephine had now exceeded the limit set in her original plan with Jo Bouillon. An interview with one of the children's nurses, Juliette Pallas Jâton, revealed Baker's scrupulous organization of every minute of the children's activities from dawn to dusk with the assistance of her aides and her family.[16] Nevertheless, Jo Bouillon became increasingly concerned about the efficiency of running a large estate with so many children. Family photographs and his own statements demonstrate that he was a caring father, very close to the children, and he served as their major parental figure during Josephine's long absences on tour. His family was also involved in the purchase and touristic renovation of Les Milandes, which was beginning to take on the allure of a resort and mini-state.

When she was on tour in North Africa in 1956, Baker found two children who were refugees from the Algerian war, allegedly hidden under a bush after a skirmish. She brought Brahim (Brian), of Berber descent, and Marianne, a French colonial, back from North Africa, filling out her tribe with displaced war victims. The following year, while in Africa, she adopted Koffi, an orphaned child from an Ivoirian hospital. Although it was three years before he became president of the country, Félix Houphouët-Boigny is said to have facilitated the transaction, acted as the child's godfather, and also helped out later with a donation to the Rainbow Tribe.[17] On June 21, 1957, with the formal adoption of the first eight children at the Tribunal of Sarlat, Les Milandes regularized its relationship to the state, making the Rainbow children not only citizens of the world, but also French, with two French parents. During this period, the couple's conflicts escalated, and Jo Bouillon moved out of the château into a small cottage on the grounds and eventually left for Paris and Buenos Aires.

In 1959, after adopting Mara from Venezuela, Josephine impulsively responded to news from Paris that an abandoned child had been found in a trash dump. It was near Christmas time when she rushed to claim him at a Parisian hospital, naming him Noël because of the season. Three years later, she received distressing news about a Moroccan baby born to an indigent mother in Paris. Baker took in Stellina in 1962 even though her resources were quickly dwindling. Stellina completed the Rainbow Tribe and, by this time, Les Milandes was already in serious financial difficulty.

Because of her philosophy of universalism, Josephine decided to give the children an education in their cultures of origin. Moïse had Hebrew lessons. Brian learned about Islam. Akio and Janot were instructed in Buddhism and Shintoism and eventually given an opportunity to visit Japan. The children had tutors in French, their languages of origin, and basic subjects. For a time, they attended local schools and were later sent to boarding schools. Josephine's educational philosophy was visionary and far ahead of her time. Had she been exposed to contemporary approaches to multiculturalism, she could certainly have instructed the children more explicitly about what she conceived to be the family's mission. Nevertheless, they all came to understand her version of the battle against racism. They considered her ideals to be rooted in the experiences of exclusion and prejudice that she had endured while growing up in the United States. Josephine was pleased when she saw evidence of tolerance, bonding, and solidarity among the children as they joined forces in the face of outsiders who remained both curious about and occasionally hostile toward them.

Nonetheless, the children lacked a full grasp of Josephine's daily decisions and strategies, viewing her courses of action as arbitrary and capricious. When Moïse was given Hebrew lessons, he schemed to run away from the tutor, and, fearing ridicule and exclusion by his classmates, he refused to wear a yarmulke to school.[18] Stephen Papich described an incident that he witnessed at Les Milandes:[19]

> Little Moïse had three times run away from his Hebrew lessons; each time he was found alone, playing about the pool. The Israeli tutor wanted to discipline him but felt that a confrontation involving himself, Moïse, and Josephine would be good.
>
> When the child saw his mother in bed, he began crying and ran to her. She put him under the covers with her.
>
> "Now, what is the matter here, Monsieur? Tell me all about this."
>
> The tutor, I felt, told his story very well. It was really only a matter of a little discipline.
>
> "But, sir," she responded, "you obviously don't understand children. Don't you see, there is something down by the pool that is more important to him than his Hebrew lesson. So you must go to the pool with him and discover what that is. Then, as his tutor, you will see that that desire is fulfilled first, then the Hebrew lesson will come easily for him."

Without further notice, the tutor resigned and left Les Milandes the next day. Josephine then sent Moïse to a Jewish couple of Polish descent, André and Jacqueline Barasche, who resided nearby. Moïse also resisted their instruction, and Josephine's plan for the transmission of cultural traditions was thwarted.

Josephine sent Akio and Janot to Japan for a year to learn Japanese and explore the possibility of continuing their education in Tokyo. This plan also backfired, as the two had difficulty adjusting to the Japanese language and culture and became homesick for French food and the comforts of life in the château.

Papich states, "The children of Josephine Baker were the most pampered, looked after, educated, played with, and cared for children of any in the entire world."[20] Relatives and governesses found them difficult to control and discipline when they were young. Margaret Wallace, Josephine's sister, considered her child-care duties in Josephine's absence to be very trying. Marie Spiers, Josephine's close friend and supporter from Paris (and the wife of her pianist and conductor, Pierre Spiers), was equally frustrated when she had the children on her hands. Although the strict dormitory-like structure of Les Milandes resembled a boarding school, the pedagogical philosophy was diffuse, and there was no central source of authority apart from Josephine's charismatic leadership and Jo Bouillon's displays of ludic paternal warmth. As the couple's relationship began to deteriorate, the family ideal disintegrated as well. The children found tutors and schools to be too limiting and, as they grew up, they resented Josephine's master plans for their lives and careers.

Living a utopian dream in the fishbowl of Les Milandes was challenging. According to Baker's biographers, the children were occasionally vociferous in expressing their complaints about Josephine's absences and the constraints of their unusual upbringing.[21] But each child had his or her own multifaceted experience that was both positive and negative. For them, the struggle to the hilltop was long and hard, and the path of multicultural redemption as role models for a new era was not one that they had freely chosen. As with the offspring of other celebrities, the Rainbow children were caught in a maelstrom of grandiose dreams and incessant, confusing publicity. Hammond and O'Connor quote Brian as explaining: "The main problem was that for the best part of our school days, we had all the disadvantages . . . we were orphans *and* then we were children of a broken home. Over and above that, coming from different origins, we had nothing to compare our lives with."[22]

Resource mobilization for Les Milandes as a family home, a social movement, and an enterprise was ad hoc and inconsistent. In May 1957, while Josephine and Jo Bouillon were completing the final adoption papers for eight of the Rainbow children, Josephine contacted Maître Bardon-Damarzid, her lawyer in Dordogne, to initiate divorce proceedings against Jo Bouillon.[23] While the finances of the château and Josephine's obsession with adoption were the underlying issues motivating the rupture, the couple's interpersonal conflicts had also escalated. Jo's family fortune had been invested in the château, and his brother Gabriel had even signed the purchase papers in proxy on behalf of the couple during their absence on tour. His sister Maryse occasionally helped out with the children. Bouillon argued that Les Milandes should be more efficiently managed, and that he should play a greater role in the control of the business, agricultural, and domestic affairs of the enterprise. Contrary to popular accounts of the story in documentary films, docudramas, and some of the press coverage of the day, it was Josephine, rather than Jo, who formally initiated the divorce proceedings and refused to reconcile. She sued Bouillon in the Tribunal of Sarlat for alienation of affection and refusal to perform his marital duties, although she ultimately never divorced him.

A prevailing narrative surrounding Bouillon, which has become part of his mythical persona, portrays him as the anchor of reason and stability in Baker's life at Les Milandes, in keeping with the Pygmalion and rescue motifs. Bouillon, however, like Baker, was a bon vivant as well as a loving parent. Bouillon continued to work throughout the Second World War, but subsequently wished to avoid the stigma of having worked during the German occupation. Both Lynn Haney and Ean Wood comment on Bouillon's allegedly creative financial dealings in balancing the budgets of the tourist hotel and the farm.[24] Nevertheless, Bouillon was a mainstay of the utopian family, a musical partner, and a tremendous source of support for Baker and Les Milandes in spite of the couple's disagreements. A preliminary divorce hearing with a possibility of reconciliation was set in Sarlat for July 5, 1957. At this time, the newspaper L'Aurore claimed to have received a personal letter sent by Bouillon from La Charteuse des Milandes hoping for total reconciliation and blaming the rupture on Josephine's "nervous depression" and "extreme fatigue."[25]

Bouillon continued to be present at Les Milandes on and off for the next two years and took charge of the funeral arrangements for Josephine's mother, Carrie McDonald, who died at Les Milandes on January 12, 1959, while Baker was away. He left Les Milandes in 1960. The official divorce was never actually finalized. Many people tried to come to the moral and financial assistance of Les Milandes after Bouillon's departure, but to no avail. Although Baker was able to hold onto the château for another decade, its days of prosperity and glory had passed, and Baker's original utopian dream was rapidly fading away.

Photographs and Collective Memory

The Christmas photograph of Baker and Bouillon with eight of the Rainbow children from 1956 represents a moment of harmony and celebration. Seated beneath an ornately decorated Christmas tree, Josephine holds Brian, and Jo clutches Marianne, with the six other children between them. Dressed in matching white outfits, the children appear angelic. The tribe of cherubs was nearly complete and ready to face the public. Although this photograph is part of a family album, it is also well crafted as a publicity tool. Posed photographs and studio shots unite the public and private images of a family. In the case of the Rainbow Tribe, the public images also accentuated the myth and message of blissful interracial harmony.

Most of the publicly available photographs of the Rainbow Tribe are from 1956 and 1957, when Jo Bouillon was present and the family was still unified. Group photographs were also used as publicity shots well into the 1960s, after Bouillon's departure. In these later photographs, Josephine is often pictured on tour with the children. Taken collectively, the photographs fall into three categories: group poses of the entire tribe, candid shots of the children at play among themselves, and action shots of a parent, relative, or nurse with one or more of the children. While group poses such as the Christmas postcard and a publicity shot from 1959 in front of the château reflect the ideal family, the candid shots are intended to show that the children had a normal upbringing full of spontaneous moments of love, happiness, and good humor. These photographs reproduce the family by iconizing moments of togetherness as familial narratives.

One group photograph from the Departmental Archives of Dordogne, Collection Diaz, shows eleven of the children (Stellina is absent) posed in front of the château wall, circa 1962, with the caption

"All eleven children reunited in happiness!"[26] Akio is seated in the middle of the front row with Jari to his right and Jean-Claude to his left. Luis and Janot are standing behind Jari, and Janot has his arm around Jari's shoulder. Moïse is kneeling in profile next to Jean-Claude with his face turned away from the camera. Noël is in the middle of the second row, with Marianne to his right and Brian to his left. Koffi stands to the far right on the end, and Mara to the left, framing the second row like two matching ebony bookends. The older boys in the front row are all in suits, which are similar but not identical, with shiny leather shoes and string bowties. The suits have a uniformlike quality. Brian, in the second row, also sports a suit and tie, and Marianne wears a fancy dress. Koffi and Mara wear matching checkered jumpsuits, and Noël has on a white tunic top with a large collar. The children pose for this photograph with varying degrees of interest, but they all look as though they cannot wait to have the session end. The formality and near uniformity of the clothing suggests that the family is on display. On special occasions, Josephine insisted on this type of uniform dress and even encouraged her mother Carrie and her sister Margaret to dress in matching white outfits and aprons. Unlike the Christmas shot, however, the parents are absent in the picture of the happy children (Bouillon having left by this time), and the occasion is ambiguous. The message projected by this photograph is one of staged solidarity. It also resembles the type of photograph made for school yearbooks and class reunions.

In one series of photographs with Josephine in the garden of the château circa 1960, the children are crying and scowling. Earlier candid shots show Jo Bouillon playing with the children and Josephine changing diapers, feeding the children, and putting them to bed with Carrie rocking them to sleep. Personal photographs from Juliette Pallas Jâton's collection depict the governesses, Margaret, and Carrie dressed in white with white aprons as they escort the children out of the château. The photographs also present images of the children in a wider society as they play out their roles as representatives of multiculturalism. On the whole, the photographs convey an ideological message that emphasizes the family's unity in the context of its larger social mission. Marianne Hirsch states that "the family photograph . . . can reduce the strains of family life by sustaining an imaginary cohesion, even as it exacerbates them by creating images that real families cannot uphold."[27] Photographs of the Rainbow Tribe also reflect the dual processes of family cohesion and rupture transferred into the public sphere of media representation. Examining these tensions through photography provides insight into the challenges and contradictions surrounding the Rainbow Tribe's goals.

Universal Brotherhood

Today, Baker's adoptions have a great deal of resonance in the light of the adoptions resulting from global disasters. International celebrities adopt children as part of global relief plans and as a strategy for drawing attention to humanitarian causes. Baker's Rainbow project may also be interpreted both in terms of contemporary French political developments and in the context of rising global movements for civil rights and minority pride. At the conclusion of his discussion of Richard Wright in *The Black Atlantic*, Paul Gilroy asks, "What would it mean to read Wright intertextually with Genet, Beauvoir, Sartre, and the other Parisians with whom he was in dialogue?"[28] Baker also needs to be "read" intertextually with respect to recent developments in multiculturalism and as well as the French intellectual and ideological environment that she adopted, with its concepts of universalism, and utopian visions of liberty, equality, and fraternity. With the transformation of the French educational system, the debates on secularization (e.g., the Islamic veil controversy), and the rise of the new groups promoting immigrant rights and minority media representation in France, Baker's utopian dream still remains controversial.[29] Although Baker's activism in the United States and worldwide during the 1950s placed her under FBI surveillance and restricted her movements for nearly a decade, her utopian community is arguably a separate and successful development.

The rainbow concept of universal brotherhood treats the ideal of "fraternity" literally. It also closely follows Sartre's dialectic of Négritude, in which white supremacy is the thesis, Négritude (as an affirmation of blackness and a riposte) is the antithesis, and a society without races is the synthesis.[30] In their various versions of Négritude, Césaire, Senghor, Damas, and their colleagues emphasized the antithetical moment in the dialectic as an essentialist affirmation of cultural pride, providing a basis for Black participation in universal civilization. Although it was performative rather than literary and philosophical, Baker's primal image shared much in common with Négritude's essentialism, and the Rainbow Tribe paralleled Sartre's society without races. Sartre viewed Négritude's ultimate goal as self-destructive because of the erasure of the antithetical moment of racial affirmation in favor of a universal ideal. Sartre argued that Négritude is like a "woman who is born to die and who senses her death even in the most rewarding moments of her life."[31] Baker also believed that racial antagonism was destined to disappear. In a interview in 1970 with John Vincour of the *International Herald Tribune*, Baker supported her view of interracial marriage and stated, "Mixing blood is marvelous. It makes strong and intelligent men. It takes away tired spirits."[32]

Born of racism, poverty, alienation, and neglect, like Baker herself, the orphaned Rainbow children would learn to transcend their suffering in a new, harmonious environment. As seen through the photographic documentation of their lives, the children were exposed to an environment in which social and racial boundaries were removed, leaving only the inflection of cultural traditions transmitted to them through tutors. Baker's plan for maintaining this utopian ideal as the children grew older, however, was not fully articulated, and they experienced frustration as role models for an ideal community that could be described to them only in vague and general terms. They were no longer disadvantaged children, nor were they adults reclaiming civil rights and equal job opportunities. Instead, they were members of the *village du monde* being groomed as citizens of the world. In a nine-page letter to Stephen Papich, excerpted here, Baker outlined her goals for the world village:[33]

I wanted the Milandes to be known and respected as a world village.

Destiny wanted me to find this little hamlet which is, without a doubt, a little earthly paradise for those in search of peace for their soul.

I didn't look for it specially.

I found it naturally, and I held on to it fiercely, for it is my resting place.

It is here that my children can pursue their brotherly education in peace, without being influenced by bad spirits, for this is very important for the ideal which they represent.

It must not be thought that I am trying to make little gods of them, but only normal beings—just, honest toward themselves and toward others, guided by purity and the conscience of sensible men.

I know that we are ahead of our time.

That is why there has been so much confusion about me and about others who think as we do.

Beyond the Rainbow Tribe, Baker hoped to create a Universal College of Brotherhood at Les Milandes where students of all backgrounds would devote their attention to problems of racial discrimination, human rights issues, and the religions and cultures of the world. Education would be based on new experimental methods that would take into account the diverse backgrounds of all of the students. Blueprints for the college campus reflected an open environment with circular pods for classrooms. Josephine wrote numerous letters and proposals concerning her college and had several offers to help support it, including one from President Tito of Yugoslavia to take her family there after she left Les Milandes, but the plans never materialized. Although the demise of Les Milandes was, in large part, material, the confrontation between a utopian dream and the practices of the surrounding society came into play as a crucial determinant of the end of the experiment. Ultimately, the uneasy relationship of this composite community to the surrounding countryside and the French state made the dream impossible to sustain at Les Milandes.

A Dream Deferred

During her last years at Les Milandes with the Rainbow Tribe, the press covered Baker's every move. She wanted the media there to witness her situation down to the last hunger strike in 1969, on the steps of her château when she was cloaked in her nightgown of misery. Journalists found her to be good copy. Debates escalated in newspapers and on television about whether the family deserved help from the state, whether the children were to be privileged or pitied, and whether they constituted a true family. On Monday, June 4, 1964, immediately following the ten o'clock news, Brigitte Bardot launched a televised appeal for support for Josephine and the Rainbow Tribe as a result of the threat of the château's sale. While some people responded sympathetically, there was a tremendous negative backlash. In an article entitled "Television to the Aid of the Orphans of Luxury," the journalist Raymond de Becker wrote, "Not everyone is Josephine Baker or Brigitte Bardot. This is a sham [*le comble de l'imposture*]."[34] De Becker also argued that television, which was an arm of the French state (before privatization), should under no circumstances be used to support private interests. Articles debating the pros and cons of the problem appeared in *Le Monde, Le Figaro, France-Soir,* and *Paris-Jour* during the summer of 1964. Some journalists, like Jacqueline Cartier, were favorable toward Baker, noting the plight of her children, the promises of support, and the successes of her various comeback concerts across Europe, while others were more cynical about the fundraising efforts. Bardot's campaign also resulted in a committee of celebrities to aid Baker, consisting of, among others, the author François Mauriac, the actor Jean-Paul Belmondo, and the theater producer Bruno Coquatrix.[35]

As the situation deteriorated, the children were even sought out for interviews. At the time of the final sale of Les Milandes, Akio gave an interview to the journalist Jacqueline Cartier, which was frequently quoted and described the creditors: "I had the impression of seeing ferocious beasts. But the important thing is that we are all together, and we can pursue our ideal elsewhere."[36] Cartier's article placed Akio's quotation under the title and adopted a sympathetic attitude toward the situation. One of the most poignant short pieces was an interview with Baker published in the *International Herald Tribune* on September 30, 1968. The article concluded with Backer lamenting, "I have nowhere to go and I do not know who is going to look after us."[37] Josephine was transformed from an independent matriarch into a dependent child looking for support from the state and private investors.

It is symbolically interesting that Princess Grace came to the rescue, not only on personal grounds, but also because Monaco, as an isolated principality, in many ways represented a benevolent monarchical utopia, such as the one in Baker's dream of the Cinderella narrative.[38] Josephine and her Rainbow children were housed in Roquebrune-Cap-Martin on the French side of the Monaco border under the care of the state of Monaco and the Red Cross, for which Baker performed fundraising benefits. Josephine and, later, Jo Bouillon were interred into the same plot in Monaco. The state of Monaco, through Princess

Grace, had miraculously intervened to restore the fragile balance between ideology and utopia, and the dream of the multicultural world village was, once again, deferred. As we reflect on this dream, years after Baker's death, its relevance and its lack of resolution become even more poignant.

Notes

This chapter is based on data collected and assembled for my book-length study of Josephine Baker's life, art, and politics entitled *Josephine Baker in Art and Life: The Icon and the Image* (Urbana: University of Illinois Press, 2007), 184–210. The copyright of 2007 for this book is held by Bennetta Jules-Rosette. The quoted materials on the Rainbow Tribe in this chapter are used with the permission of the University of Illinois Press.

1. M. Fabre, *From Harlem to Paris: Black Writers in France* (Urbana: University of Illinois Press, 1991), 50–54.

2. K. Mannheim, *Ideology and Utopia: An Introduction to the Sociology of Knowledge* (New York: Harcourt Brace Jovanovich, 1936), 212.

3. Stephen Papich argues that Baker's communitarian ideal should be interpreted in a broad comparative perspective. S. Papich, *Remembering Josephine* (Indianapolis: Bobbs-Merrill, 1976), 145–50.

4. See P. Miller, *Errand into the Wilderness* (Cambridge: Harvard University Press, 1964), 217–20; M. Walzer, *The Revolution of the Saints: A Study in the Origins of Radical Politics* (New York: Atheneum, 1968), 191–92.

5. J. Corbett, *Through French Windows: An Introduction to France in the Nineties* (Ann Arbor: University of Michigan Press, 1994), 82.

6. F. de la Camara and P. Abatino, with the collaboration of Josephine Baker, *Mon sang tes veines* (Paris: Isis, 1931).

7. J. Relf, "Utopia and the Good Breast," in *Utopia and the Millennium*, ed. K. Kumar and S. Bann (London: Reaktion, 1993), 107–28.

8. E. Goffman, *Frame Analysis: An Essay on the Organization of Experience* (New York: Harper and Row, 1974), 86.

9. Jean-Claude Bonnal reproduces a summary of the adoption proceedings at the Tribunal of Sarlat in 1957. Four of the children were not included in the original document: Mara, Koffi, Noël, and Stellina. J.-C. Bonnal, *Joséphine Baker et le village des enfants du monde en Périgord* (Le Bugue: PLB, 1992), 55.

10. P. Rose, *Jazz Cleopatra: Josephine Baker in Her Time* (New York: Vintage, 1989), 233.

11. Baker's biographers note how quickly plans for the expansion of the

Rainbow Tribe changed when Josephine started her quest. Papich, *Remembering Josephine*, 149; L. Haney, *Naked at the Feast* (New York: Dodd, Mead, 1981), 269–70; Rose, *Jazz Cleopatra*, 231–38.

12. William Kephart and William Zellner examine religious movements in which the parental metaphor is used as the basis for establishing a utopian community. The movement of Father Divine (George Baker), founded in New York in 1915, is one such case. In these movements, adults, rather than children, generally constitute the primary family group and believe that their movement will change the world. W. M. Kephart and W. Zellner, *Extraordinary Groups* (New York: St. Martin's, 1989), 198–239.

13. J.-C. Baker and C. Chase, *Josephine: The Hungry Heart* (New York: Random House, 1993), 384.

14. Haney, *Naked at the Feast*, 274–75.

15. J. Baker and J. Bouillon, *Josephine* (New York: Paragon House, 1977), 195.

16. Juliette Pallas Jâton, interview with Bennetta Jules-Rosette, Paris, October 6, 2004.

17. Baker and Chase, *Josephine*, 340.

18. Haney, *Naked at the Feast*, 270

19. Papich, *Remembering Josephine*, 151–52.

20. Ibid., 151.

21. Ibid., 156–57; Haney, *Naked at the Feast*, 273–74.

22. B. Hammond and P. O'Connor, *Josephine Baker* (London: Jonathan Cape, n.d.), 203.

23. Bonnal, *Joséphine Baker et le village*, 133.

24. Haney, *Naked at the Feast*, 278–79; E. Wood, *The Josephine Baker Story* (London: Sanctuary, 2000), 351.

25. "Jo Bouillon: 'Je ne veux pas divorcer.'" *L'Aurore*, July 3, 1957.

26. Bonnal, *Joséphine Baker et le village*, 56

27. M. Hirsch, *Family Frames: Photography, Narrative, and Postmemory* (Cambridge: Harvard University Press, 1997), 7.

28. P. Gilroy, *The Black Atlantic: Modernity and Double Consciousness* (Cambridge: Harvard University Press, 1993), 186.

29. Both the Sans Papiers movement and the Collectif Égalité promoting minorities in the media reflect aspects of Baker's multicultural vision. B. Jules-Rosette, "Identity Discourses and Diasporic Eesthetics in Black Paris: Community Formation and the Translation of Culture," *Diaspora* 9, no. 1 (2000): 39–58.

30. J.-P.Sartre, "Orphée noir," in *Anthologie de la nouvelle poésie nègre et malgache de langue française*, ed. L. Senghor (Paris: Presses Universitaires de France, 1948), ix–xliv.

31. Ibid., xliii.

32. J. Vincour, "At 64, Josephine Baker Looks at Black Power," *International Herald Tribune*, August 31, 1970.

33. Papich, *Remembering Josephine*, 155. On September 18, 1964, Stephen Papich received a nine-page letter in French from Josephine entitled "The Ideal of Brotherhood in Les Milandes as Seen by Josephine Baker." Papich had the letter translated and excerpted a large portion of it in his biography of Baker in 1976. The letter is a short treatise describing Baker's rationale for her experiment in universal brotherhood and discusses the Rainbow Tribe in idealistic terms. In the letter, Josephine poignantly states: "Equality, my ideal, my children are my reason for living."

34. R. de Becker, "La télévision au secours des orphelins de luxe," *Arts*, June 10, 1964.

35. E. Bonini, *La véritable Joséphine Baker* (Paris: Pygmalion, 2000), 260; "Pour sauver Joséphine Baker Bardot payera ce soir de sa personne," *Le Figaro*, June 4, 1964.

36. J. Cartier, "L'un des enfants de Joséphine Baker: 'Si nous quittons les Milandes, nous poursuivrons notre idéal ailleurs,'" *France-Soir*, May 17, 1968.

37. "Another Eviction Story for Josephine Baker," *International Herald Tribune*, September 30, 1968.

38. Baker and Bouillon, *Josephine*, 270. Josephine Baker found the atmosphere in Monaco to be supportive, and she was able to continue her Rainbow experiment there within limits and to watch her children mature into early adulthood.

Site-ing Black Paris

Discourses and the Making of Identities

ARLETTE FRUND

> I met Africa in Paris through Africans.
> —AIMÉ CÉSAIRE

> We are consumers, not decision makers.
> —DOGAD DOGOUI

The appearance of a "Black France" on the national stage can be traced back to the World Cup Soccer Championship in 1998 and the phrase that was coined to describe the French team: "*Black, Blanc, Beur.*" The use of the English term rather than the French "noir" is emblematic of language and politics that deny recognition to minority populations in France. Though it is possible to envision other rationales for the choice of a foreign racial expression, such as the influence of American culture on European youth and its impact on popular media, this particular act of sampling actually functions as both ellipsis and metaphor. It articulates a break in the discourse that exemplifies both avoidance and replacement: by refusing to acknowledge its authorship, the message performs on an additional level and translates what French society finds inappropriate to name. Whatever the terminology employed to define the presence of Blacks in France, "Black France" or "France Noire," those labels behave as an oxymoron in a Republic whose ideals of equality and universalism encompass a fundamental belief in the French nation as a unique entity and in "Frenchness" as a common denominator for achieving citizenship.

While consecrating a national event, the phrase from 1998 itself became an event which opened up a critical space from which forms of "repetition, transformation, and reactivation" could be expressed and recorded.[1] Furthermore, France's official efforts at preserving an indivisible nation-state have been contradicted by local, national, and international events and conceptual mutations. The desire for homogeneity has been questioned by the postcolonial reconfigurations of international relationships after the Second World War, by a greater involvement in a politically influential and culturally plural European Union, by the new geopolitical rules agreed upon after September 11, 2001, and by the challenges of a global world order. However, the main challenge to France's ideal of the equality of man is the resurgence of the legacy of its colonial history and imperial domination in the twenty-first century. Though President Sarkozy opposes repentance and emphasizes pride in France's past, that history and memory have surfaced, not "only at the service of nostalgia or melancholia," but also, at times, to disrupt the political, economic, and social life of the country.[2] Riots in the Hexagon and economic and cultural claims in the French Overseas Departments (DOM) and French Overseas Territories (TOM) have confirmed the impact of the colonial past on the present and the existence of "novel forms of colonial rule."[3] In light of the events in recent years, it seems difficult to contest the realization of a "Black France" even though law and power still prohibit the generation of ethno-racial data about minority groups.

Though disputed, the concept of "Black France" has become a reality. The creation of the Conseil Représentatif des Associations Noires (le CRAN), the institution of a day to commemorate the slave trade, slavery, and their abolitions, as well as the creation of lobby groups committed to a better representation of Blacks at all levels of society are a few examples of recent national changes. Besides its obvious and problematic "racial" designation, the phrase "Black France" encompasses people from sub-Saharan Africa, the Caribbean, and Asia who live in France or in the DOM or TOM, and who were once colonized by France. The historical connection goes mainly unnoticed though, and more so since the focus on ethnic identity has been replaced in official discourses by a growing awareness of economic migrant flows since the proliferation of theories of globalization and the new logics of transnationalism. The challenge comes from recognizing historically constructed minority identities and identifying recent occurrences of immigration and displacement. The events of Ceuta and Melilla in 2005 and the legal issues of undocumented people in France have complicated the understanding and view of "Black France."[4] It appears as though claims of authenticity or cultural nationalism find themselves in a paradoxical and complex position shaped by "a transnationality that suggests the intersection of "multiple spatiotemporal (dis)orders."[5] Furthermore, state politics of identification and administrative categorization have created selective beliefs that emphasize some events and mask others.

Those visions get contested when they disagree with personal and communal histories, with the expression of "affective strains," and with the possibilities of interpretation.[6] To engage with the archeology of knowledge that is produced at the intersection of those conflicted forces, I will concentrate my analysis on "Black Paris" or "Paris Noir," a seemingly bounded central location that embodies an assemblage of conceptual mappings and overlapping dynamics. For instance, there is the "Paris Noir" of African American writers and artists; the Parisian landscape of African and Antillean students, authors, and politicians; the Paris "Black" and diasporic sites in the northern and eastern districts; and the *banlieues* which "play in the dark," to use an expression by Toni Morrison, since no racial qualifier is needed to designate them.[7] It is possible to find guidebooks on "Black Paris" and routes are designed to discover its literary, historical, and cultural landmarks. The "Black Paris," however, on which I am focusing emphasizes the practices of everyday life (which Michel de Certeau discusses), and is framed by a Foucauldian analysis of the spatial mechanisms of power and its vertical forms of domination.[8]

Perception and Knowledge

The year 2005 was a major landmark in sighting "Black France." Firstly, the Parliament passed the infamous article 4 of the law on February 23, 2005, demanding a reform of educational programs to recognize "the positive role of the French presence in the excolonies, particularly in North Africa." There was then the postponement of a commemoration to celebrate the abolition of slavery in the French colonies following the Taubira Law of May 21, 2001, which established slavery and slave trade as crimes against humanity. During the summer, immigrant shelters burnt down, killing men, women, and children, and in the fall, the uprisings in the banlieues destabilized the concept of the mythic

French identity based on the idea of equality, fraternity, and liberty, as well as the idea of the Republic being one and indivisible. This series of events shed light on the unrecognizability of "the Other" within French society and marked a critical stage for the interrogation of norms governing recognition that would generate discussions on race and questions of national identity in France.[9]

During and after the riots, which started after two African teenagers were accidentally electrocuted in a power plant in a suburb outside Paris where they took refuge after being chased by the police, the debate moved on to the cultural field and to racial profiling. The media targeted young men and teenagers from different ethnic backgrounds and Congress launched an attack against ethnically mixed rap groups and artists who have articulated a critique of the state policing system and of the cultural politics of social marginalization and racialization of the banlieues.[10] Indeed, young people living in those areas face racial and social discriminations based on their skin color or identities, and there has also been a stigmatization of the Black and Beur populations, which characterizes them as immigrant, meaning non-French, even though most of them are born in France of parents coming from the French ex-colonies.[11]

The racialized representation of these young people as "a menace to society" and the mistaken assumption that rap was responsible for fueling urban violence triggered an unexpected turn of events. They lifted the veil and made visible the hidden face of the French Republic: its minority groups. The appearance of the "Other" on the national scene shook the nation's foundations and raised questions about the place of former colonial subjects on French soil in the historic context of France's colonial past and involvement in the slave trade. France, which has long believed in the ideology of assimilation or integration, has silenced color and other ethnic differences from its language. The concept of homogeneity and a common French identity died when young people in the banlieues were ostracized for violently expressing their desire to be French and fully integrated in the Republic instead of being given just a place to inhabit. The revelation of France's multicultural and multiethnic diversity called for a critical and reflexive (re)examination of identity nationally and transnationally, the reach of which extended to Europe, Africa, and the Americas within the broader framework of the "Black Atlantic."

In the aftermath of those events, French Blacks came together and established the CRAN, and Aimé Césaire refused to welcome and meet with Sarkozy during his visit to Martinique.[12] These events contributed to defining a new racial dynamic that called into question the pursuit of a present torn between multiculturalism and abstract universalism as well as between indifference and recognition, and that addressed issues of race and of minority subjects' positioning for power and status. The emergence on the national scene of a deferred history and a divided geography provided an opportunity to evaluate the Black presence in France and to articulate new approaches to discussing the experiences of its Black populations and figuring ways to represent the attitudes and performances that make up the "infinite variation of diversity" on French soil.[13]

Since then, there has been a multiplication of movements, projects, and acts that seek to sensitize the public to multiple Black identities and Black spatial configurations. Many events that took place between 2006 and 2008 reflect the dilemmas and questions that pervade French opinion and policies, including the inauguration of the Musée du Quai Branly in 2006, the creation of the Cité Nationale de l'Histoire de l'Immigration in the Palais de la Porte Dorée in 2007, the first commemoration of slavery and its abolitions in 2006, the future opening of the International Center of the Memory of Slavery and its Abolitions, the Fiftieth Anniversary of the First International Congress of Black Writers and Artists at the Sorbonne in 2006, the protests and demonstrations of undocumented workers in Paris, and the passing of Aimé Césaire in 2008.

Persons and Things

The site-ing of "Black Paris" involves paradox and perplexity.[14] At the beginning of the twentieth century, W. E. B. Du Bois examined the ways people are brought into contact and into relations: action and communication occur through the "physical proximity of homes"; economic, political, social, intellectual, and religious interactions; and the communal formation of public opinion, through which he called for "new exemplification" of "the contact of diverse races of men."[15] His observations and statements were made in conjunction with the famous assertion that "the problem of the twentieth century is the problem of the color line" and with his questioning of the "Negro

Problem." The scholar Mireille Rosello argues for "performative encounters" between subjects who belong to different cultural groups.[16] According to her, "no first encounter can ever take place when history, language, religion, and culture exert such pressures upon the protagonists... that their desire to speak or be silent is trapped by preexisting, prewritten dialogues and scenarios." That is why she calls for the "creation of new subject-positions," for the invention of a new language to shape new relationships and types of engagement: "a performative encounter must invent both the words for the thing and the thing through the words." Even though scripts have preceded them, encounters and performative encounters are possible in Paris. The continual fluidity of population movements along economic and cultural lines cannot hide other forms of separation such as housing. Whether their reality is contingent upon race or class, whether they are called ghettos or low-income areas, some neighborhoods in the northeast of Paris stand out for their important Black population. It seems as though the city administration enforces a policy of diversity for its low- and medium-income lodgings in many districts of the capital. Because of what they are, the *flâneur* of Walter Benjamin[17] and the *marcheur* of de Certeau[18] are in a position to perceive the political and economic architecture of the place and glimpse at the patterns of relations that govern contact and encounters between dominant and minority groups. They may even engage with such geography by confounding its borders and pursuing connections between the sites of governance and intimate sites of knowledge. The present exploration of such relationships in Paris focuses on the raison d'être of two recent institutionalized sites of art and history, the Musée du Quai Branly and the Cité Nationale de l'Histoire de l'Immigration, as well as on the horizontal model of communication exemplified by the Aimé Césaire exposition in the political center of the city.

In an interview with *Magazine Littéraire* in 1969, Césaire declared, "I met Africa in Paris through Africans, but my geography is before and foremost human." By emphasizing the human dimension of the encounter, the poet from Martinique argues against a process of turning people into objects: "No human contact, but relations of domination and submission. . . . My turn to state an equation: colonization = 'thingification.'"[19] In the postcolonial era of "Black Paris," to give an account of oneself and of the Other presupposes that individuals and

groups embrace a comprehensive knowledge and sensibility of historical forces and dynamics of rule.

Michel de Certeau, in the first volume of *The Practice of Everyday
Life*, defines models of action that carry changes both strongly affective and effective and that are central to any production of knowledge.[20] In accordance with his theory, the visible sites of "Black Paris"
are first revealed by the act of walking, which de Certeau considers as
a tactic with three enunciative functions: it permits a spatial appropriation, a realization of places, and a production of relationships between differentiated positions. This practice enables the wanderer to
form an intuitive and temporal vision of the forces at stake and to
envision disseminated structures of resistance to a universalizing approach to the representation of society. But that action, whether calculated or circumstantiated, belongs to the sphere of the individual,
the common or anonymous hero according to de Certeau's identification. The privatized consciousness it entails can be effective enough,
though, to subvert the order of things by interrogating the dominant
ideological discourse and deconstructing the structures of power. Yet
the question of its cognition and propagation remains problematic
when confined by circumstances and geography or bereft of any
proper political grounding.

In that sense, there are sites of "Black Paris" that exist in the realm of
the visual experience whether they are the anonymous scene of the
streets or the popular modes of cultures. Their performances take
place randomly and generate ideas or conceptions which can either
isolate individuals or arrange them into groups. Whatever the procedures at work, the steps toward the laying out of Black spaces trace
facts which, to tell a truth and reveal meanings, need to be exposed
and explored in the elaboration of archives, the making of documentation, the writings of texts, and the creation of a common memory and
history.

That work has been done and is still being done for the African
American presence in France and its broader contours of interaction
with Caribbeans and Africans by many scholars and by the late Michel
Fabre. In the article he wrote in *History and Memory in African American Culture*, Michel Fabre illustrates how prominent Black people
became *lieux de mémoire* (sites of memory) in France because of their
talent and economic success but also because of official recognition

and international popularity.[21] One noteworthy example of the creation of such a landmark was Josephine Baker, who, on the one hand,
embodied American contributions to dance aesthetics, while on the
other hand symbolized the complex co-existence of colonial and modern France and its intricate arrangement in the construction of a
national identity.[22] There are plenty of Black French, such as Alexandre Dumas (another figure mentioned by Michel Fabre), who
could have been selected by French institutions as cultural race models to legitimize racial equality through achievements and activism,
but Dumas's racial heritage was a part of his identity that was not
identified or discussed.

Such an event though seemed to take place when Aimé Césaire
passed away. His death was given national coverage and honors, and
his life and deeds were celebrated in various arenas of French society.
What he asserted in 1956 at the Sorbonne and what the Fiftieth Anniversary of the First International Congress of Black Writers and Artists
remembered in 2006 was much less significant compared with the establishment of a memorial site in front of the Assemblée Nationale in
Paris. In the heart of Paris, amid the politics, wealth, and tourism,
across from the Concorde, the institution exposed on its front wrought-
iron gate three portraits of Césaire at different moments in his life. The
montage was meant to honor the French congressman who represented Martinique from 1945 to 1993 at the legislative chamber. The
photographs are accompanied by quotations from *Cahier d'un retour
au pays natal* (1939) and Césaire's address to the House in 1982 concerning the passing of a law establishing the official commemoration
of the abolition of slavery in France. The pictorial narration of Aimé
Césaire's life and works constructs him as a French statesman and as
the poet and philosopher of Négritude; it does not represent him as a
critic of France and its colonial past. The selected quotations emphasize a never-ending secular fight for liberty, equality, and fraternity,
Césaire's role as the spokesman for those who have been silenced, and
a universal call for the preservation and conquest of human rights.
Because the former palace where this celebration takes place was con-
fiscated by revolutionaries in 1789, Césaire's legacy is appropriated and
nationalized by the French government in an attempt to inscribe it
within the principles of the Republic. The only excerpt that hints at
Césaire's racial identity and France's racial history stands on the right
of his portrait made late in life: "no race has the monopoly of beauty,

intelligence, and strength." The message is subdued in accordance with the task of regulating socially and politically acceptable images of French colonials to educate the public. Césaire's rehabilitation in that ruling place seeks to tell a successful story devoid of hardship and prejudice. The beautiful photograph of the aging Césaire testifies, though, of the painful experience of the struggle for freedom but may have seemed harmless to state representatives.

The display of photographs offered passersby a personal and privileged—though unexpected—moment of encounter with a distinguished personality. The installation in that formalized setting may have signaled a victory over place and time or, on the contrary, an attempt to circumscribe a site of tribute and memory. Whatever the implications of that operation, there is a reclamation of public space and a redefinition of relations through the fleeting looks of city dwellers in movement and the outward gaze of Césaire. Though immobilized, it momentarily engages the attention and the sensibilities of pedestrians and commuters. Furthermore, when vision is able to differentiate, it seizes and recognizes elements of written material, such as the word "race," which stands out, and mirrors the "liberty, equality, and fraternity" of the French Republic's motto. At that crowded intersection there is the possibility of a performative encounter, which transforms the memory of the historical building and the experience and perception of its location in accordance to the ever-particular feeling and remembrance of each individual. The three images of Césaire at different stages in his life participate in the elaboration of a common history and memory by confronting and challenging the collective imagination of what determines French history and geography. But the placement of these images in an open and busy transit zone raises questions about the space and the content of the narration: its writing requires ascertaining the relations of power at work in the telling and knowing of the here and now of the exposition and also the choice of a visionary mode of transforming that projects onto readable material to the advantage of the individual appraisal and collective knowledge. Can Michel Foucault's notion of utopias and heterotopias apply,[23] or the concept of "non-lieux" as explicated by Marc Augé,[24] or the "elegiac art" coined by Susan Sontag?[25] It is important to determine if there is a willingness to "change the joke and slip the yoke," as Ralph Ellison says,[26] that is, either to accept that the image is created to usurp one's own identity or to contextualize

(facing pages) 1–4: Aimé Césaire's triptych in front of the Assemblée Nationale in Paris. *Photo by Arlette Frund, June 2008.*

« Se rappeler que le combat, le séculaire combat pour la liberté, l'égalité et la fraternité, n'est jamais entièrement gagné, et que c'est tous les jours qu'il vaut la peine d'être livré.»

Discours à l'Assemblée nationale, 1945.

« Ma bouche sera la bouche des malheurs qui n'ont point de bouche, ma voix, la liberté de celles qui s'affaissent au cachot du désespoir.»

Cahier d'un retour au pays natal, 1956.

Hommage à **Aimé Césaire** député de la Martinique de 1945 à 1993.

« mais l'œuvre de l'homme vient seulement de commencer et il reste à l'homme à conquérir toute interdiction immobilisée aux coins de sa ferveur

Cahier d'un retour au pays natal, 1956.

et aucune race ne possède le monopole de la beauté, de l'intelligence, de la force »

Cahier d'un retour au pays natal, 1956.

"the motives behind the mask" to create a new field of studies where the motives would be "as numerous as the ambiguities a mask conceals."[27] On the one hand, the horizontal framework and its transitory existence suggest the possibility of a locus of dialogue and resistance where hope and desire are expressed and the reality of both the Other and the self experienced. On the other hand, the protocol of the installation calls into question the use of its substance and of the subject.

Following Michel de Certeau's approach to the understanding of "practices of everyday life," the next examples of the site-ing/sighting of "Black Paris" deal with his concept of strategies, which he defines as a manipulation of relations of force based on the edification of a proper place, circumscribed enough to ensure mastery. This totalizing system and type of discourse distinguishes the place by its own power and will. When the Musée du Quai Branly was opened to the public in 2006, a debate was ignited on the appropriateness of its appellation and its mission. As the scholar Barbara Johnson states: "a museum is a display of objects out of context: one could not return everything to its rightful place without destroying the very idea of a museum. On the other hand, taking something from another place and displaying it as testimony to the power of one's own nation is an imperialist gesture par excellence."[28] The Branly building was designed to preserve and protect artifacts and works of art produced by ancient civilizations and cultures, which were previously part of the collections of the Musée de l'Homme and the Musée National des Arts d'Afrique et d'Océanie in Paris.

It also organized exhibits in relation to the museum's geographical areas of concern, and one of them, "Diaspora, Exposition Sensorielle," was an example of an aesthetic and sensory experience aimed at channeling life in the interface between the animate and the inanimate.[29] Directed by the filmmaker Claire Denis, it was conceived as a "formal essay" (to quote Stéphane Martin, the president of the museum) about the African Diaspora, composed of performance pieces by musicians, choreographers, clothes designers, and graphic artists (Mathilde Monnier, Jean-Pierre Bekolo, Mahamat-Saleh Haroun, Agnès Godard, John Galliano, Yousry Nasrallah, and the DJ Jeff Mills), whose purpose was to evoke in a sensory and poetic way the experiences of exile and migration. It was juxtaposed to a showcase of art depicting royalty from Benin in which each object was placed under glass and offered for the edification, curiosity, or interest of the visitors. On the one hand, the spectator is asked to walk from one installation to another through the dark passages between them with the recurring voice of Lilian Thuram, a former French soccer player and now an activist, as the articulation and unifying thread. On the other hand, the visitor is faced with a ritualized and aesthetic exposition where the objects are removed and reduced to ancient art forms or immemorial appearances representative of other places and other times.

Whereas the Benin exhibit legitimizes a natural order, "Diaspora" stages the realm of the "sensible" by emphasizing relationships between heterogeneous forces.[30] Though the different performances exist on their own, their assemblage and the trajectories, which are paced by the people visiting, define a common space where variations of sensory and bodily perceptions find expression. From the photomontage of frozen silhouettes in movement, to an African woman in space, to passing shadows in historical slave ports, to a video installation of people in search of their own in flooded villages in Egypt, to young French-speaking Africans living in New York, the experience of "Diaspora" is multiple for the person in exile and for the spectator. For the latter, it is "less the discovery of the essence of human activity than a recomposition of the landscape of the visible,"[31] a recomposition which underlines the relationship between "doing, making, being, seeing, and saying."[32] The two exhibits focus on opposite configurations of Africans; their combination, though, seems to reconcile them or at least contextualize present and future. The suspension of the African identification from the title "Diaspora" seems to indicate a movement toward a contingent situation where spacing and placing is not the basis for naming, where identity or racial categories are not the fabric of lives. Individuals are recognized through specific *types of sensibilities* in an attempt to rethink the human as a universal value in a postracial world or to conform to immediate and practical ends established by the institution.[33]

The second strategic museum setting in Paris useful for site-ing/ sighting "Black Paris" is the Cité Nationale de l'Histoire de l'Immigration, inaugurated in fall 2007 at the site of the Palais de la Porte Dorée, formally called, until 1935, Musée Permanent des Colonies, then Musée de la France d'Outre-Mer, and from 1960, the Musée National des Arts d'Afrique et d'Océanie. It is interesting to note the different appellations of the museum and to remember the controversies surrounding its new identity: the institutional renaming was intended to mark the historical passage from colonialism to the middle ground of French overseas territories and departments and finally to postcolonialism and its aesthetic displacement on art. The place still encloses the relics of an earlier time, such as the office of the French representative in charge of colonies, and an impressive room adorned with murals and statues of a mythic African past. By preserving the memory of a glorious life, that out-of-time space, full of memorabilia, confers on that presumably new structure the air of a monument and lieu de mémoire. So far, the exhibits have offered new ways of looking at the waves of European, African, American, and Asian immigrations. Using video installations, testimonies, displays of objects, and cultural icons of unrootedness and exile, such as suitcases, mattresses, and wallpapers, exhibits document and tell stories of successful integration into French society. The overall project exemplifies a semantic revision of French history and a turn toward a new reading of the presence of Black people in France. But the attempt to redefine national and cultural identities is conflicted when negotiated in a building whose architecture is perverted by the colonial past of the Republic. The competing visions at work in the museum reflect the distinct positions and ideologies at play in the contested territory of the articulation of the discourse on "Black France." Étienne Balibar argued, as early as the 1980s, that the word "immigration" is the cipher for race thinking and has become a paradigm in France.[34] The shift in naming or renaming the Black population demonstrates clear evidence of hesitation even though the French political language of race has been revised to accommodate the novel rules of globalization that favor migratory displacements and movements of population. Toni Morrison captured that development when she entitled her performance at the Louvre the "foreigner's home."[35] By identifying migrants and strangers, the new terminology seeks to supply an explanation for the presence of minorities away from the constitutional and political discourse on citizenship.

Conclusion

These sites of study partake of a production of installations and thoughts institutionalized by the last two French administrations in response to political actions related to France's responsibilities to slavery in its past. They are not representative of all the locations of Black presence, but they explore the possible meanings for the present and the future of this country, which cannot ignore anymore the ethnic diversity of its population. The sites of "Black Paris" engage with racial and postracial approaches as they co-exist in the French landscape. Michel Fabre claimed that Paris "has become a vast monument that new generations of Black visitors come to sample."[36] Though his comment is more concerned with the African American presence in Paris, it emphasized a shift from an intimate and living experience to a public and memorial one. Monuments are not to be dismissed since they keep memory alive and confer immortality, and the three sites of "Black Paris" highlighted in this chapter call into question the political interests at stake. Though they are not intended as monuments, they are marked by the desire to enforce an idea or an ideal at the expense of a more dynamic relation of mutability and movements of peoples and cultures.

Notes

1. I quote here Michel Foucault's analysis of the occurrence of the statement/event: "[the statement] emerges in its historical irruption; what we try to examine is the incision that it makes, . . . However banal it may be, however unimportant its consequences may appear to be, however quickly it may be forgotten after its appearance, however little heard or however badly deciphered we may suppose it to be, a statement is always an event that neither the language nor the meaning can quite exhaust. It is certainly a strange event: . . . it opens up to itself a residual existence in the field of a memory, or in the materiality of manuscripts, books, or any other form of recording; secondly, because, like every event, it is unique, yet subject to repetition, transformation, and reactivation." M. Foucault, *The Archeology of Knowledge* (New York: Pantheon, 1972), 28.

2. P. Gilroy, *Postcolonial Melancholia* (New York: Columbia University Press, 2004), 2.

3. Ibid., 3.

4. In the fall of 2005, hundreds of sub-Saharan Africans tried to reach the Spanish enclaves of Ceuta and Melilla on the Northern Moroccan coast, the only territory of the European Union in Africa. Spain responded by sending troops to the frontier and deported some of the new arrivals back to Mo-

rocco. Rabat flew some of the migrants back to Senegal and Mali, and abandoned others in the desert. By highlighting sub-Saharan illegal migrants, those events racialized the question of immigration and citizenship in France.

5. "The national is no longer the site of homogeneous time and territorialized space but is increasingly inflected by a transnationality that suggests the intersection of "multiple spatiotemporal (dis)orders." S. Sassen, "Spatialities and Temporalities of the Global: Elements for a Theorization," *Public Culture* 12, no. 1 (2000): 221.

6. "Affective strains" is an expression used by Ann Laura Stoler in *Along the Archival Grain: Epistemic Anxieties and Colonial Common Sense* (Princeton: Princeton University Press, 2009), 39.

7. Interestingly enough, the term "Black" is more favored than "noir" in the French context.

8. Among the many places Foucault analyzes spatial mechanisms of power, see *Discipline and Punish* (New York: Pantheon, 1978).

9. "If and when, in an effort to confer or to receive a recognition that fails repeatedly, I call into question the normative horizon within which recognition takes place, then this questioning is part of the desire for recognition." J. Butler, "An Account of Oneself," in *Judith Butler in Conversation: Analyzing the Texts and Talk of Everyday Life*, ed. B. Davies (New York: Routledge, 2008), 31.

10. After the riots, the debate moved on to the cultural field and to racial profiling. On November 23, the conservative lawmaker François Grosdidier (from Moselle) issued a petition claiming that rap music helped fuel the suburban riots and asking the justice minister to press charges against seven French rappers and groups for inciting anti-white racism and hatred of France through their lyrics. (He said that "the message of violence of those rappers when heard by young people who lack a sense of belonging and culture can legitimize violent behavior, and even provoke terrorist acts.") The petition backed by 153 members of Parliament and 49 senators targeted the following groups: 113, Smala, Ministère Amer, Lunatic, and the rappers Fabe, Salif, and Monsieur R. First, the Justice Department had to determine if prosecution was possible given that most of the groups were no longer acting. But an investigation and sanctions were called for against Monsieur R., Lunatic, and Smala because their albums were still available online.

11. On those points, see, e.g., É. Balibar, *Droit de cité* (Paris: Presses Universitaires de France, 2002); T. Stovall and G. Van Den Abbeele, eds., *French Civilization and Its Discontents: Nationalism, Colonialism, Race* (Lanham, Md.: Lexington, 2003); M. Diawara, *We Won't Budge* (New York: Basic Civitas, 2008).

12. Aimé Césaire refused to meet with the interior minister for two rea-

sons: (1) he did not agree with the use of foul language by Sarkozy, (2) he did not want to be associated with the February 2005 Law—also referred to as the shameful law—recognizing "the positive role of the French presence in the ex-colonies."

13. E. Glissant, *La cohée du Lamentin* (Paris: Gallimard, 2005).

14. I am indebted to Barbara Johnson for the title. B. Johnson, *Persons and Things* (Cambridge: Harvard University Press, 2008).

15. W. E. B. Du Bois, *The Souls of Black Folks*, ed. Brent Hayes Edwards (New York: Oxford University Press, 2007), 111–12.

16. M. Rosello, *France and the Maghreb: Performative Encounters* (Gainesville: University Press of Florida, 2005), 1.

17. U. Marx, G. Schwarz, M. Schwarz, and E. Wizisla, eds., *Walter Benjamin's Archive: Images, Texts, Signs* (London: Verso, 2007).

18. M. De Certeau, *L'invention du quotidien*, vol. 1, *Arts de faire* (Paris: Gallimard, 1990), 139–64.

19. A. Césaire, *Discourse on Colonialism* (New York: Monthly Review Press, 1972), 21.

20. De Certeau, *L'invention du quotidien*, 1.

21. M. Fabre, "International Beacons: Alexandre Dumas père, Henry O. Tanner, and Joséphine Baker as Examples of Recognition," in *History and Memory in African American Culture*, ed. G. Fabre and R. O'Meally (New York: Oxford University Press, 1994).

22. In *Playing in the Dark*, Toni Morrison demonstrated that "a real or fabricated Africanist presence was crucial to [writers'] sense of Americanness." Similarly, it can be argued that this presence is instrumental in shaping a sense of Frenchness. For instance, the film *Princess Tam-Tam* shows that a Black woman played by Baker and a "nègre" (a derogatory French term for Blacks but also for ghostwriters) are influential in constructing the dominant story. For critical views on this issue, see B. Jules-Rosette, *Joséphine Baker in Art and Life: The Icon and the Image* (Urbana: University of Illinois Press, 2007); T. Sharpley-Whiting, *Black Venus: Sexualized Savages, Primal Fears, and Primitive Narratives in French* (Durham: Duke University Press, 1999).

23. "But among all these sites, I am interested in certain ones that have the curious property of being in relation with all the other sites, but in such a way as to suspect, neutralize, or invent the set of relations that they happen to designate, mirror, or reflect. These spaces, as it were, which are linked with all the others, which contradict, however, all the other sites, are of two main types." M. Foucault, "Des espaces autres," in *Dits et écrits*, vol. 4 (Paris: Gallimard, 1994), 752–62.

24. "The "non-lieu" is the opposite of utopia: it exists and does not contain any organic society." M. Augé, *Non-lieux: introduction à une anthropologie de la surmodernité* (Paris: Le Seuil, 1992).

25. "Photography is an elegiac art, a twilight art. Most subjects photographed are, just by virtue of being photographed, touched with pathos. . . . All photographs are memento mori." S. Sontag, *On Photography* (New York: Picador, 2001).

26. R. Ellison, "Change the Joke and Slip the Yoke," in *Shadow and Act* (New York: Vintage, 1995), 45.

27. Ibid., 55.

28. Johnson, *Persons and Things*, 110.

29. Available on the web site of the museum (http://www.quaibranly.fr).

30. I refer here to the concept of the distribution of the sensible in the politics of aesthetics as formulated by Jacques Rancière. The distribution of the "sensible" is concerned "with aesthetic acts as configurations of experience that create new modes of sense perception and induce novel forms of political subjectivity." *The Politics of Aesthetics: The Distribution of the Sensible* (New York: Continuum, 2004).

31. Ibid., 45.

32. Ibid.

33. I refer to the notion of the "human" as exemplified by Judith Butler in a conference at Reid Hall in Paris on March 2008, "Humanité, inhumanité, déshumanisation: pour qui valent les 'droits humains'?"

34. É. Balibar, "Uprisings in the Banlieues," *Lignes* 21 (2006): 50–101.

35. *Toni Morrison: invitée au Louvre: étranger chez soi* (Paris: Christian Bourgois, 2006), 13–26.

36. M. Fabre, *From Harlem to Paris: Black American Writers in France, 1840–1980* (Urbana: University of Illinois Press, 1993), 338.

Coda: Black Identity in France in a European Perspective

ALLISON BLAKELY

We need only consider the first Pan-African Congress convening in European capitals at the beginning of the twentieth century to recall that the deliberate search for Black identity and equality in Western societies has a long history there, with Paris as one of the main sites. The African Association founded in London by Henry Sylvester Williams from Trinidad and the British involvement in the Pan-African Conference represent a parallel to the French Négritude movement's drawing inspiration from the American Harlem Renaissance in the period between the World Wars. In Germany, Africans put together a self-help organization called the Afrikanischen Hilfsverein in Hamburg as early as 1920, which was led by the Cameroonian Peter Makembe. In the Netherlands, a similar initiative during the same period can be seen most clearly in the figure of Anton de Kom from Suriname.[1] Yet it is only at the beginning of the twenty-first century that this dilemma concerning Black identity has reached such intensity in Europe that the broader public can no longer ignore it. The reason for this of course is that, even after ending their colonial empires, these former colonial powers find themselves with growing non-European populations due to a degree of continuing dependence of these peoples of different cultures and colors; and at the same time they find themselves under pressure to live up to the democratic principles operative in Europe, in contrast to their patently authoritarian and racist former colonial societies. Many of the same themes treated here regarding France apply as well to other European societies, especially to other former major colonial powers.

In addition to viewing the question of Black identity in the European perspective, the present chapter at the same time represents a Black American perspective that seeks to learn whether in the face of an unprecedented level of conspicuous Black populations in Europe a blanket "Black" identity may be emerging, comparable to that imposed on those of Black African descent in the United States. I should also begin with a note concerning my definition of "Black," which is inherently ambiguous, because the related concepts have always been ambiguous and arbitrary. Keeping in mind that this definition was originally imposed on peoples of Black African descent by others, I am not here proposing a new definition, only offering observations on how the most prevalent and conventional one may be becoming operative in Europe. With respect to France and other countries that discourage the formal stipulation of racial or ethnic categories by law or tradition, I am simply counting those who within those societies routinely suffer personal indignities and adverse discrimination because of their skin color or known Black African ancestry, regardless of census categories.

The French Discourse

In France, what is at present transpiring is more a passionate discussion of French identity than of Black identity per se; but due to the lingering legacies of the slave trade, slavery, colonialism, and racism, all the local commentators I have found have discovered that it is inescapably also a discussion of Black identity.[2] The current upsurge of publications on Blacks in France within the past few years is in itself an indication of the growing societal interest in related themes. Now there is a much larger audience than existed in the era of the Négritude movement of the early twentieth century, whose message fell largely on deaf ears in France. In those decades, there were only around 5,000 Blacks in France proper; now I make what I consider a conservative estimate of around 3 million Blacks out of around 65 million total population.[3] A similar new demographic has brought about involuntary reflection on the colonial past in all the former colonial societies, producing gestures of atonement and related public education initiatives, and bringing to light Black contributions to European history.

In France, examples of such actions include the recovery of such figures as General Thomas Alexandre Dumas and the brilliant musician and swordsman the Chevalier Saint-George, both of whom served in the army under Napoleon during the French Revolution, and recent financial compensation to Senegalese soldiers for earlier discriminatory treatment during their sacrifices in defense of France. Nevertheless, respect for a French Republican tradition that rejects the acknowledgment of ethnic categories based on color prevented until now open discussion of what is being called "*la question noire.*"

In her related study, Myriam Cottias notes, in regard to the Republican tradition, that while at the beginning of the Third Republic the justification for colonization was a Christianizing and civilizing mission, it changed at the end of the century to a claim of following a natural law requiring freedom of the individual, and of liberating Blacks from African slavery and the trade conducted by the Muslims. She says the legacy of this old cultural and racial hierarchy continues to poison the present.[4] Actual discussion of ethnic categories in France has been even more taboo because of French pride in not having the notorious "Negro problem" of the United States. As recently as 2005, when the French media was covering Hurricane Katrina, a tone of self-righteousness could be heard in criticism of America's neglect of the poor and powerless. Yet, later that year some of those same voices were in psychological denial concerning the possible root causes of the violent outbursts in Paris's *banlieue*. And it was of course this explosive social unrest, in which the participants included a significant proportion of Blacks, that finally made this public discussion unavoidable.

My findings suggest that it is precisely this type of collective blindness and deafness in the prevalent French attitudes on such matters that gnaws most painfully on the sensibilities of Blacks experiencing the French reality. The subject is still not taken sufficiently seriously, even by the academic establishment; and in fact only a handful of the many works now available are written by academic specialists. The tenor of the discussion in France is like that of all the countries that had significant colonies resulting in current populations with a claim to full citizenship and national identity—in the case of France actually being told officially that they are French. This is different, for example, from countries where Blacks have come into the European sphere mainly for work or education, although many of the issues are the same because the European societies are democracies promising equal opportunity and treatment for all. Like my own approach to this subject, the French commentary I have read itself considers this question in a very comparative perspective, casting an eye on and drawing examples from not only the United Kingdom and the Netherlands but also the United States in its discourse.

There is a broad spectrum of attitudes in France toward being Black, and it continues to be widely considered impolite and inappropriate to talk about race at all. Onana echoes this sentiment with irony in the title of his book *Sois nègre et tais toi!* Now that the silence is broken, it is clear that there is an inadequate vocabulary to discuss it. President Nicolas Sarkozy's resort to new terms such as "thugocracy" is but one example; and among Blacks what has become equally clear is the diversity of perspectives.[5] In general, regarding the attitude toward Blackness, my sense is that the majority experiencing color prejudice in French society would wish to simply be considered French and treated like all other citizens and residents. However, some do wish to be respected as both Black and French; and still others long to make France into an actual colorblind society, in place of the pretense of the one they feel they are now experiencing. An example of a scholarly study expressing this same hope is the historian François Durpaire's *White France, Black Anger*.

A sampling of the arguments on various sides of the issues suggests that this is a polemic that is just beginning. Rama Yade recognizes that she is neither allowed to feel French, nor African, nor Antillean, finding society constantly pointing a finger at her skin color. In her own words, "Le Black est une énigme. Il ne se sent pas français, encore moins africain ou antillais. Il est d'abord noir. Non pas par volonté de se mémarquer. Mais parce qu'il ne peut faire autrement que d'assumer une couleur que la société montre sans cesse du doigt." (The Black man is an enigma. He does not feel French, even less African or Antillean. He is first black. Not because of his own willingness to mark himself as such. But because he cannot do otherwise but to accept a color to which society constantly points a finger.)[6] Patrick Lozès expresses in his book that there is cause for having pride in being Black, even if it is an imposed identity, and holds that it is crucial to organize socially and politically accordingly. Christiane Taubira agrees; she recalls crying at the age of seven upon seeing pictures of the Nazi concentration camp victims, but feels deprived of having seen in school images about the slave trade or slavery, or of ever shedding a tear about that, or of having been allowed to feel pride over the forbearance of the enslaved, their uprisings against their masters, and the success of the various maroon communities. She is among the most militant voices and is dedicated to exposing what she and like-minded others consider the Republican myth of integration and equality, and to uniting Africans and Antilleans. Toward that end, after the riots in the suburbs in 2005, she collaborated with Lozès and others to found the Conseil Représentatif des Associations Noires (CRAN). They seek to unite a multitude of French organizations of Black people in a federation that will enlist political parties, unions, and other bodies in a concerted fight against racial discrimination, highlighting such issues as racial profiling and the so-called glass ceiling in professional ranks. Their most notable actual achievement to date is bringing about the first national statistical survey on Blacks in France, which was conducted in January 2007; there had not been an official census in which Blacks were counted as a category since 1807. Conducted by the marketing research firm TNS / SOFRES, the CRAN's survey included not only an estimate of the total Black population, but also data on its perceptions of discrimination. One finding especially notable for the present discussion is that fewer than 4 percent of the 13,559 interviewed self-identified as Black.[7]

With sharply contrasting views concerning the appropriate response, the author Claude Ribbe is a particularly strident opponent of the CRAN initiative and dreams of a day when there is no such designation as Black. Ribbe's stance also highlights the other main division shaping the discourse in France, that between the Antilleans / Départements d'Outre-Mer (France Overseas Departments [DOM]) and the main body of Africans who fall more into the category of immigrants or the children of immigrants. This divide exists not only because of variations in culture and color, but also because of a difference in legacies from the Atlantic slave trade and colonialism. Ribbe says the CRAN is merely symbolic of the wishful thinking of those who believe there should be a Black community, which, according to him, does not exist. The assertion that there is a Black community is inherently controversial because of the prevalent sentiment among the broader public that this violates the popularly accepted image of the Republic in which such societal categories are rejected. Repeating an argument often heard in other Western societies in recent discussions about racism, some assert that even to speak of a Black community is racist in itself. Others fear cooperation with the CRAN may weaken dedication to Antillean traditions or may cause a loss of autonomy for the Collectif DOM, the main organization already in existence before the launching of the CRAN. Critics of the notion of a Black community often employ the term "communitarianism" in reference to those proposing a Black community, viewing it as an allusion to an essentialized American formation and concept of Black community. Many French claim this is inapplicable to France because their Black population is not directly descended from Black slaves in France. Thus, the concepts of diaspora and minorities are also considered harmful.[8]

Gaston Kelman is another who sees no reason to have to feel proud to be Black. He says this pressure is not on other groups and in any case that it is just a borrowing from the United States, for example, with the slogan popularized by the rhythm-and-blues artist James Brown, "Say it loud, I'm Black and I'm Proud." However, Kelman is nonetheless incensed by the superficiality of racial labels experienced daily in France, violating his assumed right to be received as an individual, as "a French adult, not a Black baby." He states his belief that citizenship is determined by three things: heredity, birth, or choice of lifestyle, not by where one is from, but what one becomes. Thus, by personal choice he is Bourguignon, not because he was born there, but because he took on that identity. He is stymied by finding that only white Antilleans born in the Antilles are considered French. He also denies the claim by some that ghettoization in France is only economic.

Kelman makes a plea for the integration of Black migrants into French society, and expresses envy for the respect Blacks have been accorded in the United States, which is evidenced by high posts in several public spheres. These and similar developments in the United Kingdom, such as Lady Valerie Amos heading the House of Lords for several years, lead him to view France as lagging far behind, leaving the vaunted slogan "liberté, égalité, fraternité" ringing very hollow amid what he experiences as the social and psychological isolation of Blacks in France. As an illustration, he recounts how he was dismayed when his four-year-old daughter asked him after returning from preschool one day whether she was Black—and then adamantly rejecting his affirmative answer, insisting that she was light brown! It was mainly his dealing with her identity sojourn that inspired his writing *Je suis noir mais je n'aime pas le manioc*. He believes Black children in

France naturally start out identifying themselves as white and French; then, after beginning to have perceptions of difference forced upon them, they try to be mainstream by mimicking African American fashions. But nothing works to improve their assimilation chances— they are not even being accepted as European, let alone French.[9]

Jean-Baptiste Onana for this very reason insists that it is imperative that all Blacks unite to confront the common challenge of racism. He concludes that at present there is no common voice that can be heard and notes as well that although the Antilleans seem to consider themselves superior to the Africans, in reality the only advantage they have is citizenship, which brings easier access to the job market, but usually in lower posts. He thinks it is competition for low jobs that divides them from Africans, and even drives some Antilleans to vote Lepinist (i.e., for the far-right party of Jean-Marie Le Pen). He also concludes that despite their great diversity, it is just as meaningful to speak of Blacks in France as it is to speak of Jews collectively or the Black communities in the United States and United Kingdom, and that in France they must unite because otherwise there will be no one to plead their cause.[10]

Pap Ndiaye prefers the concept of minority to that of community in considering the plight of Blacks in France and the remedies needed. His surmise that what they share is a "condition" shaped by a shared experience of adverse treatment, which led him to join the Black Associations movement in France, first as a member of the Cercle d'action pour la promotion de la diversité en France (CAPDIV), and later becoming one of the founding members of the CRAN, whose objectives include encouraging university scholars like himself and other professionals to help organize Blacks in France. While acknowledging the potential pitfalls of use of ethnic categorization, Ndiaye finds it indispensable to even be able to discuss vital social issues, and especially to measure important indirect forms of discrimination.[11] Geraldine Faes and Stephen Smith in Noir et français, their substantial investigative study based on intensive interviewing in the Black community about where Black France is headed, view the organizations framed around the DOM (mainly Antilleans) and the CRAN (mainly Africans), which wish to unify all Black interest organizations, as opposing poles that could move either way in relation to each other, and perhaps combine forces pragmatically in spite of their sharp differences.[12]

Concerning the question of whether the future holds an overarching, imposed "Black" identity for Blacks in France, one Afro-French scholar who believes so is Abdoulaye Gueye, who chose to pursue a career as a professor of sociology abroad after completing his doctorate in France. In an article from 2006, "The Colony Strikes Back: African Protest Movements in Postcolonial France," he argues that "mobilizations of the 2000s are more appropriately viewed as 'black' instead of 'African.'" He sees what he terms the reemergence of a "pan-nègre" dynamic in which Africans and Afro-Caribbeans in France sense a common Black destiny, a destiny that can only become the full membership in French society they desire if they force a redefinition of its socio-political organization.[13]

In European Perspective

The discourse in France echoes similar ones in all the European societies with a significant Black population. Important differences in the respective histories make for very different details in the discussions; but the question of Black identity is a common thread precisely because of the pervasive persistence of social exclusion, poverty, and racism, and the physical and psychological consequences of these.

The United Kingdom, perhaps as a consequence of having had the most vast colonial empire and having that reflected in its current population (1.8 million out of 63 million) is the most advanced European society in terms of acknowledging multiculturalism. The crux of the identity question haunting Blacks in France is relatively moot in England since it has recently become generally accepted that one does not have to be white to be British. At the same time, those taking pride in the French Republican tradition may take some satisfaction that this has aided passage of legislation condemning the slave trade as a crime, while government leaders in the United Kingdom persist in the view that they find nothing for which to apologize. On the question of race relations, it seems very quiet, at least on the surface, in, for example, London, one of the cities witnessing major race-related disturbances, particularly in the 1980s. Now Africans and West Indians are rather silent, leaving the articulation of the new multiculturalism, at least in published works, mainly to Indians, with the one exception of the commemoration in 2008 of the ending of the slave trade.

Brixton, the main site of violent protests in London in the 1980s, which helped to advance improvements in race relations in England, seems at ease, taking the persistence of racism simply as a given. It should also be noted that the concentration of Blacks and the social dynamic has changed over the interim years. For instance, now many who work in Brixton cannot afford to live there, because like many Londoners in general, they must commute from many miles away. This makes it difficult to generalize about life in Brixton as some sort of community apart. Furthermore, like France, the United Kingdom has wealthy ethnic communities in addition to the neighborhoods of the estates or the banlieues.

By the 1990s, Black culture seemed to be accepted in the mainstream of British life. But in the final analysis, this seeming public acceptance is not an end to racism. The data of a study from 2007 finding Blacks six times more likely to be stopped by the police seems ironically an improvement over data collected in 1979 that showed a ratio of fifteen times more arrests for "suspicious behavior." However, the recent lower ratio still does not bode well, since some credit this practice as the underlying cause of the violent outbursts of the 1980s.[14] One noticeable recent shift in attitudes toward Blacks in the broader British society is an apparent preference for West Indians over Asians, which began in the 1990s with such incidents as Salman Rushdie's *The Satanic Verses* and was later reinforced by the attacks in Manhattan on September 11, 2001.[15] My research also suggests that there is a phenomenon of what might be described as the "conspicuous acceptance" of high-profile Black celebrities and elites all across Europe, and the United States as well, who are distinguished from the mass of the Black populations, yet similarly discriminated against, leaving them frustrated.

Spain, with a Black population of around 228,000 out of 46 million, while a onetime colonial power with subject Black populations, experienced a pattern of postcolonial immigration different from the others because she had lost nearly all of her colonial holdings in the nineteenth century, and migrants from Black Africa began arriving in significant numbers only in the 1980s, mainly from West and Central Africa.[16] In the 1990s, they formed over 100 nationalistic and cultural support associations, though none were politically oriented. However, it was also in that decade that a more vocal and public Black-consciousness movement against racial discrimination and police brutality emerged, inspired by the African American experience and rap music and borrowing liberally from the ideas of such figures as Marcus Garvey and Malcolm X, as well as Nelson Mandela and others from African liberation struggles. A particularly inspirational leader was the Haitian-born physician Alphonse Arcelin (1936–2009), who became a Spanish citizen and waged vigorous public critiques of racism. There was even a small network of groups established on the model of the Black Panther Party, led by an activist journalist Abuy Nfubea, but it was committed to nonviolence in tactics.

The dramatic outbreak of violence in France in late 2005 drew special attention among Black activists in Spain. A concrete sign of continued growth of an organized movement and public awareness of Black issues in Spain is a recent, related, international scholarly conference in Cadiz in 2011; the Second Spanish Pan-Africanist Conference held in 2009 attracted more than 200 delegates, representing groups from a number of Spanish cities.[17] There has never existed in Spain any precept comparable to the popular mythology in France, which alleges that full adoption of the dominant culture makes one an equal member; so it is not surprising that the main sentiment in the Black consciousness movement in Spain is simply the desire to organize to advance the cause of equal rights and acceptance.

Portugal is another country that makes for an interesting comparison with France (over 100,000 out of 10.5 million). The Black population there has come mainly from the former African colonies of Angola, Mozambique, and Guinea Bissau, which were finally relinquished only in the mid-1970s after years of liberation struggles. Cape Verde was the home of the second-largest contingent that moved to Portugal. In Portugal too, initiatives have had to be taken against racism, especially after a riot in 1995 in Lisbon where dozens of skinheads rampaged one neighborhood and murdered a young citizen from Angola.[18] Among the Cape Verdean community (the largest of the Black communities), perspectives on race and color vary according to class. The Cape Verdean elite, though remaining aloof from the masses in the *bairros*, nevertheless uses the presence of the masses as leverage to advance their own interests and to claim a right to be placed in related leadership roles by the Portuguese government. It appears that if allowed, the elite would probably have long ago abandoned the poorer majority, but prejudice prevents them from achieving that degree of separation in the eyes of the dominant society.

Even as the Cape Verdean elites frequently experience blatant racism in their careers, their striving for "Portugueseness" is undeterred; some prefer to ascribe such bias to class and background rather than race. The elites also side with the mainstream population in blaming the new wave of immigrants for crime and so on, and for embarrassing them by association. This type of attitude regarding the new arrivals of the same ethnic groups has its counterparts in France, England, and the Netherlands. For the most part, Cape Verdean immigrants from the 1960s on live in the bairros and are never referred to as Portuguese by the mainstream, only Cape Verdean, Black, or African, including the second generation born in Portugal. By contrast, the second generation of elites shows no interest at all in gaining or preserving a Cape Verdean identity.[19]

The respective African communities in Portugal have organized numerous neighborhood and nationwide associations, most of which tend to center on specific African cultures, although some neighborhood associations combine African groups of various origins. There is also religious division, since those from Guinea are heavily Muslim. The question of identity among the Mozambicans is also compounded by the fact that there is an Indian element, in addition to the cleavage between those who chose to retain their "Portuguese" identity after Mozambique became independent in 1975 and those who chose to become citizens of Mozambique. However, all the Black populations confront a common experience of racially motivated social and economic exclusion. Thus far, efforts at launching a national, unifying organization, such as the CRAN initiative in France, have failed.

In the Netherlands (with around 500,000 Blacks in a population of around 16.8 million), as has been mentioned, assertive Black consciousness dates in the Antillean colonies from the early twentieth century. Of the various Black peoples now in the Netherlands, some came directly from Africa and some from Africa indirectly by way of Suriname, the Antilles, and Cape Verde. They largely self-identify in terms of their specific origins, such as Surinamers (including Bush Negroes), Antilleans, Somalians, Cape Verdeans, Ghanaians, South Africans, Ethiopians/Eritreans, Congolese/Zaireans, Nigerians, Angolans, Sudanese, Liberians, or Kenyans. Nevertheless, as in the other countries already discussed, they find themselves viewed by their host society as sharing a common Black identity. In this regard, from the late twentieth century there have been developments comparable to those in the other countries discussed.

Philomena Essed's description of "everyday" racism in her *Alledaagse racisme* is similar to what is described with vivid examples in Patrick Lozès's *Nous les noirs de France*. Though published in the 1980s, it still provides a good summary of the present experience of being Black in the Netherlands.[20] Meanwhile, the question of how to relate to the slavery and colonial past has been rarely discussed. This is an especially thorny issue in a country so famous for tolerance and democratic principles. There has existed an unspoken admonition to remain silent about what in the recent public revival of historical memory is admitted to be the skeleton in the national closet. The Dutch variant on the recent greater acceptance of Blacks, mentioned earlier in connection with France and England, favors the Black Surinamers (the largest segment of the Black population). This rather sudden, comparatively warmer embrace by Dutch society comes in the wake of turmoil with Muslims, just as with Blacks in France and West Indian Blacks in England. Is it because Blacks have always been more passive? Are they more respected, or just considered harmless and less threatening because of having been shaped by Western religion and language? These questions necessitate further exploration in all of the societies under discussion.

Germany today is still at a less advanced stage in defining "Blackness" than the other major powers due to smaller numbers (around 270,000 out of around 82 million) and the lack of a concentration of a Black population; but there too the past decade has witnessed a growing body of literature on the subject. An anthology entitled *Farbe bekennen*, published in 1992, was the first to highlight organizing efforts against discrimination in Germany and to engage the issue of Black identity.[21] There, as in the United Kingdom, the movement has allied those of Asian as well as African descent, and in Germany, it also draws the support of those opposing discrimination based on sexual orientation and gender as well.

As for the rest of Europe, the engagement with the question of Black identity is much different in societies where Africans have come mainly for education or work, therefore laying no historical claim for European identity and seeking only equal treatment as citizens or residents; but even in such cases, they are still unable to escape the European perception of them as Black. Russia, where I estimate a Black population of only around 40,000 out of 143 million, provides a glaring example of extreme Black awareness of a negative sort and ill treatment by the dominant society. For example, human rights organizations have documented hundreds of apparently racially motivated murders of Blacks and Asians over the past several years.[22] Nearby Norway, with a population approaching 30,000 Blacks, was rocked in 2001 by the unusual occurrence of a racially motivated murder of a mixed-parentage teenager by members of Norway's small neo-Nazi community.[23] In Eastern Europe in general, because of the level of skinhead and ultra-nationalist activity, it is dangerous, especially for Black males, even to go out in public alone, particularly on Adolf Hitler's birthday. In no other countries are racism and xenophobia so rampant. Although numbering altogether only around 4,000, the Black population in the Czech Republic, Slovakia, Hungary, and Bulgaria is also experiencing imposition of a Black identity and a sufficient level of violence to warrant organized efforts to mobilize the public against racism.[24]

If we look westward, the country with the largest Black population yet to be mentioned is Italy, with a figure now approaching 243,000. The largest African groups are the Senegalese, at around 53,000, and the Nigerians, who are upward of 20,000, both of which are also beginning to experience an involuntary Black identity. This occurs even though Italy, as a major gateway into Europe, is a country where public attitudes have at least *appeared* more tolerant of cultural differences in the past for a nation seemingly determined to learn from the negative lessons shown by the British, French, and German examples. Yet, predictable racial problems are manifest there. What is more ominous in the conservative government of Prime Minister Silvio Berlusconi is the anti-immigrant legislation that has been promoted under the rubric "Security Decree," which would forbid mixed marriage and official recognition of parentage to children born to women lacking residency permits.[25] Neighboring Switzerland, a very popular destination for asylum seekers, hosts around 65,000 Black Africans, and although earlier widely considered to be above racial problems, now has a White Power movement developing and a counter-initiative of a federal commission against racism that has promoted anti-discrimination legislation.

The one remaining country with a small but significant Black population is Ireland. The total immigrant population of Ireland from all origins grew from around 4,000 in 1997 to 40,000 in 2001. According to the reports of the United Nations High Commissioner for Refugees, most immigrants to Ireland come from Nigeria, Romania, Congo,

Libya, and Algeria. Unfortunately, racial incidents in Belfast alone have begun to be counted in the hundreds, which lays potential groundwork for the development of a group Black identity there. There are also very positive signs of cultural adjustment in Ireland as well, including the election of Rotimi Adbari from Benin as the mayor of Portlaoise, the first such achievement in Ireland.[26]

Community Formation

Meanwhile, seemingly quite independently of all the hot debates, there are silently emerging signs of Black community formation. And some leaders in the burgeoning Black communities in Europe are looking to the North American Black experience for organizational models. For instance, borrowing from the African American celebration, there are Black History Month celebrations in over a dozen European countries, including the United Kingdom, Germany, the Czech Republic, the Netherlands, and France. An annual African festival called the Panafest in Vienna aims at intercultural understanding. Black communities in several of the countries have staged Black beauty contests and fashion shows. African shops, hair salons, restaurants, and nightclubs abound not only in London and Paris, but also Ireland, the Netherlands, Russia, and Denmark. A small section of Parnell Street in central Dublin has been dubbed "Little Africa." Published guides (with yellow pages) to all sorts of Black establishments can be found in Paris and Amsterdam. Churches with Black majorities are springing up within all of the sizable Black communities. The conscious formulation of concepts of Black identity is in progress both in academic circles and among Black professionals in the community. Most of the organizational efforts in Europe surrounding the identity question reject a narrow focus on blackness and emphasize alliance with others suffering from ethnic or racial discrimination and educating the general public about the plight of immigrants. The Internet now hosts countless web sites of community associations and other organizations all over Europe addressing these matters.

   With regard to the reactions of the European majorities to this quest for identity, it is important to keep in mind that a corollary to the search for Black identity is the self-conscious reflection by Europeans about their own identity, which was also the case when they first imposed a Black identity on Africans centuries ago. Indeed, the current European confrontation with the sudden swell in non-Western immigrant population has in some countries brought about the most thorough introspection since the Europeans encountered the non-West in the age of exploration. Further complicating all of these issues are underlying demographic patterns showing declining birthrates among traditional Europeans. Continued economic needs for immigrant labor will likely heighten tensions as the proportion of newcomers rises. Despite the great diversity in the views on Black identity all across Europe, a strong, common thread is the prejudicial perception and treatment of Blacks regardless of Black peoples' own attitudes toward blackness. As in the case of France, it is too early to tell how these matters will be resolved.[27]

Notes

1. See D. Dabydeen, J. Gilmore, and C. Jones, eds., *The Oxford Companion to Black British History* (Oxford: Oxford University Press, 2007), 531; P. Martin and C. Alonzo, eds., *Zwischen Charleston und Stechschritt: Schwarze im Nationalsozialismus* (Hamburg: Dolling und Galitz, 2004), 59; A. de Kom, *Wij slaven uit Suriname* (Amsterdam: Contact, 1934).

2. See, e.g., P. Ndiaye, *La condition noire: essai sur une minorité française* (Paris: Calmann-Lévy 2008); M. Cottias, *La question noire: histoire d'une construction coloniale* (Paris: Bayard, 2007) [a professor of history at EHESS]; R. Yade, *Noirs de France* (Paris: Calmann-Lévy, 2007) [born in Senegal, currently state secretary for human rights under the Ministry of Foreign Affairs, and a member of Sarkozy's UMP]; P. Lozès, *Nous, les noirs de France* (Paris: Danger Public, 2007) [the author, a pharmacist, born in Bénin, is first president of CRAN, the most prominent Black consciousness organization]; J.-B. Onana, *Sois nègre et tais-toi!* (Nantes: Éditions du Temps, 2007) [the author studied law and is a university instructor in urban planning]; C. Taubira, *Rendez-vous avec la république* (Paris: La Découverte, 2007) [the author is a member of the National Assembly representing Guyane, her birthplace, a member of the PRG, was a presidential candidate in 2002, and is the author of the law declaring French participation in slavery a crime against humanity]; F. Durpaire, *France blanche, colère noire* (Paris: Odile Jacob, 2006) [a professor of North American history at the University of Paris]; G. Kelman, *Je suis noir et je n'aime pas le manioc* (Paris: Max Milo, 2004) [the author, born in Cameroon, is a writer and a private consultant on socio-

cultural issues]; C. Ribbe, *Les nègres de la république* (Monaco: Alphée, 2001) [born in Paris of Caribbean parents, the author is a historical writer serving a three-year term on the Commission on the Rights of Man]; G. Faes and S. Smith, *Noir et français* (Paris: Panama, 2006) [the authors are journalists and historical writers].

3. Estimates of Black populations in Europe are inherently imprecise. This is partly due to variant official categorization of Black identity that parallels the subjective identity issues treated in this chapter and partly due to the deliberate rejection of such categories in many countries. The question of numbers is of course further compounded by a pervasive presence of un-counted illegal immigrants, and also by the fact that the Black population is in flux and, in most cases, growing. The estimates presented here reflect my own assessment based primarily on official census statistics, taking into account estimates by nongovernmental organizations as well. For France, the findings of reputable scholars and journalists consistently advance estimates ranging from 3 million to 5 million. By this standard, I am using a conservative esti-mate. See Michéle Lamor and Éloi Laurent, "Identity: France Shows its True Colors," *International Herald Tribune*, 6 June 2006; John Tagliabue, "Taunts on Race Can Boomerang," *New York Times*, 21 September 2005. That such uncertainty on Black population estimates for Europe has always been the case can be seen from historical accounts of the Black population in the United Kingdom, the country with the second largest population of Black African descent. For example, see Norma Myers, *Reconstructing the Black Past: Blacks in Britain 1780–1830* (London: Frank Cass, 1996); Folarin O. Shyllon, *Black Slaves in Britain* (London: Institute for Race Relations and Ox-ford University Press, 1974). An example of how I have estimated the black population in countries rejecting such categories in their census data is my approach to Germany, where starting with the figures provided in the *Statis-tisches Bundesamt Deutschland*, I subtract from the total for all of Africa the numbers indicated there for specific African countries above the Sahara. It should be noted that France and the Netherlands share the characteristic of in-cluding territories in the Americas with the Black population that I am count-ing. The following is a representative sample of sources I have employed to arrive at estimates of current Black population across Europe. All of Europe: http://www.oecd.org/home/0,2987,en_2649_201185_1_1_1_1_1,00.html (Organisation for Economic Co-operation and Development); http://www .migrationinformation.org/GlobalData/countrydata/data.cfm (Migration Policy Institute). France: http://www.ined.fr/fr/pop_chiffres/france/im migres_etrangers/pays_naissance_1999 (Institute national d'études démo-graphiques); http://www.insee.fr/en (National Institute of Statistics and Economic Studies). United Kingdom: http://www.statistics.gov.uk. The Netherlands: http://www.cbs.nl/nl-NL/menu/home/default.htm (Cen-

traal Bureau voor de Statistiek). Spain: http://www.ine.es/jaxi/tabla.do (Instituto Nacional de Estadistica). Italy: http://demo.istat.it/str2006 (Instituto Nazionale di Statistica). Germany: http://www.destatis.de/basis/e/bevoe/bevoetab10.htm (Statistisches Bundesamt Deutschland). Belgium: http://www.statbel.fgov.be (Statistics Belgium). Czech Republic: http://www.czso.cz/csu/2008edicniplan.nsf/engkapitola/1414-08-2008-0900 (Foreigners in the Czech Republic). Finland: http://www.stat.fi/til/ vrm_en .html (Foreigners in Finland). Ireland: http://www.cso.ie (Central Statistical Office). Portugal: http://www.ine.pt (Instituto Nacional de Estatistica). Switzerland: http://www.swissinfo.org/eng/swissinfo.html?siteSect=108 & sid=6293285&cKey=1133861757000 (SwissInfo).

4. Cottias, *La question noire*, 14.

5. M. Moore, "Sarkozy Says Riots Were 'Thugocracy,' Not a Social Crisis," *Washington Post*, November 30, 2007.

6. Yade, *Noirs de France*, 73.

7. See web site of le CRAN (http://lecran.org); and Lozès, *Nous, les noirs de France*. See also S. Sachs, "In Officially Colorblind France, Blacks Have a Dream—and Now a Lobby," *Christian Science Monitor*, January 12, 2007; and Taubira, *Rendez-vous avec la république*, 70–71, 115.

8. Ribbe, *Les nègres de la république*, 34, 142.

9. Kelman, *Je suis noir et je n'aime pas le manioc*, 32, 65, 71, 73, 132, 154.

10. Onana, *Sois nègre et tais-toi!* 51, 150, 174.

11. Ndiaye, *La condition noire: essai sur une minorité française*, 25, 278, 371–79.

12. Faes and Smith, *Noir et français*, 399.

13. A. Gueye, "The Colony Strikes Back: African Protest Movements in Postcolonial France," *Comparative Studies of South Asia, Africa and the Middle East* 26, no. 2 (2006): 227, 242.

14. J. Taylor, "Police Do Stop More Blacks," *Metro*, October 31, 2007; L. Lucassen, *The Immigrant Threat: The Integration of Old and New Migrants in Western Europe since 1850* (Urbana: University of Illinois Press, 2005), 129.

15. A. Kundnani, *The End of Tolerance: Racism in 21st-Century Britain* (London: Pluto, 2007), 181. For further insight into the context of this discussion in the United Kingdom, see T. Modood, *Multicultural Politics: Racism, Ethnicity, and Muslims in Britain* (Minneapolis: University of Minnesota Press, 2005).

16. Spain is a society where it is especially difficult to arrive at a figure for the Black population. Not only is it among countries that resist employing statistics that would indicate race or color; the problem is further compounded by the fact that tens of thousands of Blacks in Spain from Ibero-American countries such as Colombia and Cuba are even more difficult to capture from census data than are those from Black Africa. Antumi Toasijé, director of the Centro de Estudios Panafricanos in Madrid, estimates that

the true population figure of those of Black African descent is between 700,000 and 1.6 million, allowing for variation in definitions. He derived this from assessing official government records and those of nongovernmental migrant organizations. Pending more precise documentation of this from his continuing research, I am here (as elsewhere in this chapter) using a conservative figure hewing closely to my own research from available official data. See Antumi Toasijé, "La Memoria y el reconocimiento de la comunidad Africana y Africano-Descendiente negra en Espana; El Papel de la vanguardia Panafricanista," *Nómada Revista Critica de Ciencias Sociales y Juridicas* 28 (2010), 4.

17. See http://www.anglistik.uni-muenster.de/imperia/md/content/en glischesseminar/es2009/newsandannouncements/pre-programa_web_1_ .pdf and http://panafricano.atspace.org/ENG/2CPE.eng.htm.

18. Della Piana, "Choose Your World: Race in Portugal and the New Europe," *Color Lines Magazine* 2, no. 4 (winter 1999–2000).

19. L. Batalha, *The Cape Verdean Diaspora in Portugal: Colonial Subjects in a Postcolonial World* (Lanham, Md.: Lexington, 2004), 10, 26, 84, 114, 117, 131. Batalha thinks that the second generation of black Cape Verdeans is doing itself a disservice by giving priority to race and color over class in understanding its place in society.

20. For a comprehensive overview of the various groups of Blacks in the Netherlands, see A. Blakely, "African Diaspora in the Netherlands," in *Encyclopedia of Diasporas: Immigrant and Refugee Cultures around the World*, vol. 2 (New York: Kluwer Academic/Plenum, 2004), 593–602.

21. *Farbe bekennen: Afro-deutsche Frauen auf den Spuren ihrer Geschichte* (Frankfurt am Main: Fischer Taschenbuch, 1992). See also T. Campt, *Other Germans: Black Germans and the Politics of Race, Gender, and Memory in the Third Reich* (Ann Arbor: University of Michigan Press, 2004).

22. See, e.g., the annual report. While currently the main aspirations of Blacks in Russia center on societal tolerance and humane treatment, there have historically been some who have considered themselves Russian. This can be seen in recent memoirs from two generations of one Afro-Russian family: L. Golden-Khanga, *My Long Journey Home* (Chicago: Third World, 2002); and Y. Khanga and S. Jacoby, *Soul to Soul: The Story of a Black Russian American Family, 1865–1992* (New York: W. W. Norton, 1992).

23. L. Bevanger, "Norway Coming to Terms with Racism," on the BBC News web site (http://www.bbc.co.uk). This paper was presented before the terrorist attacks in Norway by the identified suspect Anders Behring Breivik in 2011.

24. J. Halkova, "Fighting Borrowed Prejudices about Africa," Radio Prague Archives, November 12, 2004; M. Reynolds, "African Expats Long for Safe Streets," *Slovak Spectator*, June 26, 2000; *The Skinhead International: A World-*

wide Survey of Neo-Nazi Skinheads (New York: Anti-Defamation League, 1995); "Higher Deficit Feared . . . Libya Quagmire . . . The Art of Hospitality," *Sofia Echo* 35 (September 2005): 2–8.

25. W. Horsley, "The New Italians," on the BBC News web site (http://www.bbc.co.uk); A. Camilleri, A. Tabucchi, D. Maraini, D. Fo, F. Rame, M. Ovadia, M. Scaparro, and F. Amelio, "Against the Reintroduction of Race Laws in Europe: To European Democratic Public Opinion and the Press That Keeps It Informed," *MicroMega*, June 29, 2009.

26. J. Milly, "Ireland Tackles Refugee Influx," on the BBC News web site (http://www.bbc.co.uk).

27. For thoughtful reflections on the broader parameters of this question, see T. Holt, *The Problem of Race in the 21st Century* (Cambridge: Harvard University Press, 2000).

About the Contributors

Editors

TRICA DANIELLE KEATON is an associate professor of African diaspora studies in African American and Diaspora Studies at Vanderbilt University. Her publications include *Muslim Girls and the Other France: Race, Identity Politics, and Social Exclusion* (2006), *Black Europe and the African Diaspora* (edited with Darlene Clark Hine and Stephen Small; 2009) and "The Politics of Race-blindness: (Anti)blackness and Category Blindness in Contemporary France" (in the *Du Bois Review: Social Science Research on Race*, 2010). Her current project examines race and racism in contemporary France.

T. DENEAN SHARPLEY-WHITING is the Gertrude Conaway Vanderbilt Distinguished Professor of African American and Diaspora Studies and French and the author or editor of eleven books, including *Beyond Negritude* (2009), *The Speech* (2009), and the *Norton Anthology of Theory and Criticism* (2010).

TYLER STOVALL is a professor of French history at the University of California, Berkeley. His books include *The Rise of the Paris Red Belt* (1990), *Paris Noir: African Americans in the City of Light* (1996), and *The Color of Liberty: Histories of Race in France* (edited with Sue Peabody; 2003).

Foreword

CHRISTIANE TAUBIRA is a deputy from Guiana and member of the Foreign Affairs Committee in the French National Assembly. She lent her name to the the Taubira Law of May 21, 2001, which recognizes the Atlantic slave trade and slavery as crimes against humanity. Among her numerous publications are *L'Esclavage racontée à ma fille* (2002), *Rendez-vous avec la République* (2007), and *Égalité pour les exclus: le politique face à l'histoire et à la mémoire coloniales* (2009). In 2002 she became the first Black woman in history to run for the presidency of France.

Authors

RÉMY BAZENGUISSA-GANGA is a professeur at the Université de Lille 1, France, and chercheur associé at CEAf-EHESS. His research focuses on displaced refugees from Africa. His many publications include *Les voies du politique au Congo: essai de sociologie historique* and *Congo-Paris: Transnational Traders on the Margins of the Law* (with Janet MacGaffey; 2000).

ALLISON BLAKELY is a professor of European and comparative history at Boston University and the author of *Blacks in the Dutch World: The Evolution of Racial Imagery in a Modern Society* (1994) and *Russia and the Negro: Blacks in Russian History and Thought* (1986; winner of an American Book Award in 1988). A past president of the Phi Beta Kappa Society, he was appointed by President Obama to the National Humanities Council in 2010.

JENNIFER ANNE BOITTIN is an associate professor of French, francophone studies, and history at Pennsylvania State University. She is the author of *Colonial Metropolis: The Urban Grounds of Anti-Imperialism and Feminism in Interwar Paris* (2010).

MARCUS BRUCE is a professor of religious studies and chair of the Religious Studies Department at Bates College in Lewiston, Maine. His research focuses on race and African Americans in France. He is the author of *Henry Ossawa Tanner: A Spiritual Biography* and is currently writing a book entitled *The Ambassadors: W. E. B. Du Bois, The American Negro Exhibit and the Paris Exposition of 1900*.

FRED CONSTANT is a professor of political science, governance, and public policies, and Ambassadeur, délégué à la cooperation régionale pour la zone Antilles-Guiana, at the French Ministry for Foreign Affairs. His numerous publications include "Le débat sur l'identité nationale au miroir des Outre-mer," *Regards sur l'actualité* 361 (May 2010): 82–93; "Talking Race in a Color-blind France: Equality Denied, 'Blackness' Reclaimed," in *Black Europe and the African Diaspora*, ed. Darlene Clark Hine, Trica Keaton, Stephen Small (Urbana: University of Illinois Press, 2009), 267–91.

MAMADOU DIOUF is the Leitner Family Professor of African Studies and History, Middle East, South Asian, and African Studies and History Departments and the director of the Institute of African Studies at Columbia University. He is the author and editor of numerous books and articles, including *Rhythms of the Afro-Atlantic: Rituals and Remembrances* (edited with Ifeoma

Nwankwo; 2010) and *New Perspectives on Islam in Senegal: Conversion, Migration, Wealth, Power, and Femininity* (edited with M. Leitchman; 2009).

ARLETTE FRUND is an associate professor of American literature at the Université François-Rabelais in Tours, France. She specializes in African American literature and culture. She is the author of *Phillis Wheatley et Olaudah Equiano: Figures pionnières de la diaspora atlantique* (2006).

MICHEL GIRAUD is a researcher in sociology at the Centre National de la Recherche Scientifique, affiliated with the Centre de Recherche sur les Pouvoirs Locaux dans la Caraïbe at the Université des Antilles-Guyane (Martinique campus). He works on the politics and strategies of identification—in terms of race, culture, and nation—in Antillean populations in the Antilles as well as in the metropolitan space. His recent publications include "Colonial Racism, Ethnicity, and Citizenship: The Lessons of the Migration Experiences of French-Speaking Caribbean Populations," in *Caribbean Migration to Western Europe and the United States: Essays on Incorporation, Identity, and Citizenship*, ed. Margarita Cervantes-Rodríguez, Ramón Grosfoguel, and Eric Mielants (2009), and "La promesse d'une aurore," *Les Temps Modernes*, "Antilles," (January–April 2011), 662–63.

BENNETTA JULES-ROSETTE is a professor of sociology and director of the African and African-American Studies Research Center at the University of California, San Diego. Her work addresses contemporary African art and literature, semiotic studies of Black Paris, religious discourse, and new technologies in Africa. She has conducted research in France, Congo (DRC), Zambia, Kenya, Côte d'Ivoire, and Senegal, and has also published eight books and over one hundred articles. Her most recent work, *Josephine Baker in Art and Life: The Icon and the Image* (2007), was published by University of Illinois Press.

JAKE LAMAR was born in 1961 and grew up in the Bronx, New York. He is the author of the memoir *Bourgeois Blues* and five novels, including *The Last Integrationist* and *Rendezvous Eighteenth*. He has lived in Paris since 1993.

PATRICK LOZÈS is an equality activist, founder and former president of the Conseil Représentatif des Associations Noires (CRAN), candidate for the French presidency in 2012, author, community organizer, and pharmacist. His publications include *Nous, les Noirs de France* (2007) and *Are Blacks Fully-Fledged French Citizens* (with Bernard Lecherbonnier; 2009).

ALAIN MABANCKOU is a Franco-Congolese author and professor of French and Francophone studies at University of California, Los Angeles. His novels include *Bleu Blanc Rouge* (1998), *L'enterrement de ma mère* (2000), *Et Dieu seul sait comment je dors* (2001), *Les Petits-Fils nègres de Vercingétorix* (2002), *African psycho* (2003), *Verre Cassé* (2005), *Mémoires de Porc-épic* (2006), *Black Bazar* (2009), and *Demain j'aurai vingt-ans* (2010). He has also published an essay on James Baldwin, "Lettre à Jimmy" (2007). He was awarded the Prix Renaudot in 2006.

ELISABETH MUDIMBE-BOYI is a professor of French and comparative literature at Stanford University and the author of numerous articles and books on Francophone literature. Among her books are *Jacques-Stephen Alexis: une écriture poétique, un engagement politique* (1992) and *Essais sur les cultures en contact: Afrique, Amériques, Europe* (2006).

DOMINIC THOMAS is the former chair of the departments of French and Francophone studies and Italian and a professor of comparative literature at the University of California, Los Angeles. He is the author of *Nation-Building, Propaganda and Literature in Francophone Africa* (2002) and *Black France: Colonialism, Immigration and Transnationalism* (2007). He edits the series "Global African Voices" at Indiana University Press.

GARY WILDER is an associate professor in the Ph.D. program in anthropology and director of the Center for Globalization and Social Change at the Graduate Center, City University of New York. He is the author of *The French Imperial Nation-State: Negritude and Colonial Humanism between the Two World Wars* (Chicago: University of Chicago Press, 2005).

Index

Library of Congress Cataloging-in-Publication Data

Black France / France noire : the history and politics of blackness /
Trica Danielle Keaton, T. Denean Sharpley-Whiting and Tyler Stovall, eds.
p. cm.
Includes bibliographical references and index.
ISBN 978-0-8223-5247-1 (cloth : alk. paper)
ISBN 978-0-8223-5262-4 (pbk. : alk. paper)
1. Blacks—France. 2. France—Race relations.
I. Keaton, Trica Danielle. II. Sharpley-Whiting, T. Denean.
III. Stovall, Tyler Edward.
DC34.5.B55B53 2012
305.896′044—dc23
2011041905